# KEY FACTS IN
# SOVIET HISTORY

# KEY FACTS IN SOVIET HISTORY

## Volume I
## 1917 to 22 June 1941

## Stephen de Mowbray

PINTER PUBLISHERS, LONDON
*in association with John Spiers*

© Stephen de Mowbray 1990

First published in Great Britain in 1990 by
Pinter Publishers Limited
*in association with John Spiers*
25 Floral Street, London WC2E 9DS

**British Library Cataloguing in Publication Data**

A CIP catalogue record for this book is available from
the British Library

ISBN 0–86187–013–1

First published 1990

Phototypeset by Input Typesetting Ltd, London
Printed and bound in Great Britain by
Biddles Ltd, Guildford and King's Lynn

To
Patricia

# CONTENTS

List of Maps                                        viii
List of Terms and Abbreviations                      ix

Introduction                                          1
1917                                                  7
1918                                                 41
1919                                                 86
1920                                                109
1921                                                130
1922                                                148
1923                                                160
1924                                                170
1925                                                182
1926                                                192
1927                                                202
1928                                                215
1929                                                225
1930                                                242
1931                                                253
1932                                                262
1933                                                269
1934                                                279
1935                                                288
1936                                                295
1937                                                307
1938                                                320
1939                                                328
1940                                                345
1941                                                355

List of Sources                                     361
Index                                               376

# LIST OF MAPS

1.  The Civil War in European Russia 1918–19.                83
2.  N.E. Russia, Siberia, Transcaspia and Central Asia.      84
3.  The Kuban and the Caucasas.                              85

# TERMS AND ABBREVIATIONS

| | |
|---|---|
| *Agitprop* | Agitation and propaganda department of the Central Committee. |
| *Amtorg* | Soviet trading organisation in the USA. |
| ARA | American Relief Administration. |
| *Arcos* | All-Russian Co-operative Society, Soviet trading organisation in London. |
| *Arcos America* | A branch of *Arcos*, London. |
| *artel* | Type of collective farm in which peasants retain a private plot of land and some livestock and implements. |
| ASSR | Autonomous Soviet Socialist Republic. |
| AUCCTU | All-Union Central Council of Trade Unions. |
| AUCP(B) | All-Union Communist Party (Bolsheviks). |
| *Basmachi* | Muslim freedom fighters in Central Asia. |
| *Bezbozhnik* | (*Godless*), anti-religious newspaper. |
| Borotbists | Ukrainian nationalist Left SRs. |
| CGTU | *Confédération Générale du Travail Unitaire*, French affiliate of Profintern. |
| Cheka | See VCHEKA. |
| *Chervonets*/(pl. *chervontsy*) | Unit of gold-backed currency introduced in 1922. |
| *Clarté* | International pro-Soviet literary group founded by Henri Barbusse in 1919. |
| Comintern | Communist International, central apparatus of international communism. |
| *Dobrokhim* | Society for Chemical Defence. |
| Duma | Lower house of pre-revolutionary Parliament. |
| DVR | Far Eastern Republic. |
| *Dynamo* | Sporting organisation founded by the state security service. |
| 'fellow-travellers' | Bourgeois writers generally sympathetic to the revolution. |
| Flagman | Revolutionary equivalent of Admiral. |
| FOSP | Federation of Organisations of Soviet Writers. |
| *Glavelektro* | Chief Administration of the Electrical Industry. |
| *Glavlit* | Chief Administration for Literary and Publishing Affairs (censorship organisation). |

| | |
|---|---|
| *Glavrepertkom* | Chief Administration for Control of Repertoire. |
| *Glavsevmorputi* | Chief Administration of the Northern Sea Route. |
| GOELRO | State Commission for the Electrification of Russia. |
| Gosbank | Soviet State Bank. |
| *Gosizdat* | State Publishing House of the RSFSR. |
| Gosplan | State General Planning Committee. |
| GPU | State Political Administration (state security and intelligence organisation). |
| GSE | Great Soviet Encyclopedia. |
| GUGB | Chief Administration of State Security. |
| GULag | Chief Administration of Camps. |
| *Hetman* | Chieftain or leader in Ukraine. In Russian, *ataman*. |
| IFTU | International Federation of Trade Unions based in Amsterdam. |
| IKKI | Executive Committee of the Comintern. |
| ILO | International Labour Organisation. |
| INO | Foreign Department of the Cheka. |
| *Istpart* | Commission on the History of the October Revolution and the RKP(B). |
| *Iuzhamtorg* | Soviet trading organisation in Buenos Aires. |
| Kadet | A member of the liberal Constitutional Democratic Party. |
| *khozraschet* | System of profit-and-loss accounting. |
| *kolkhoz* | Collective farm. |
| *Komseveroput'* | Committee on the North Sea Route. |
| Komsomol | All-Union Leninist Communist League of Youth. |
| *Komuch* | Committee of Members of the Constituent Assembly (Samara government). |
| KP(B)U | Communist Party of the Ukraine (Bolsheviks). |
| *krai* | Region. |
| Krestintern | Revolutionary Peasants' International. |
| KRO | Counter-espionage department of the Cheka. |
| kulak | Rich peasant. |
| *Litbel* | Lithuanian-Byelorussian SSR. |
| Mezhraiontsy | Members of Trotsky's previously independent group who joined the bolshevik party with him in 1917. |
| *Mezhsovprof* | International Council of Trade and Industrial Unions. |
| *mir* | Traditional agricultural commune. |
| MOPR | International Organisation for Aid to Revolutionaries (International Red Aid). |
| MOS | Multinational General Trade Union Federation, Czechoslovak affiliate of Profintern. |
| *Moscow News* | Weekly publication of the Union of Societies for Friendship and Cultural Relations with Foreign Countries and *Novosti*. |
| MRP | International Workers' Aid Society. |
| MTS | Machine Tractor Station. |

| | |
|---|---|
| *Na Postu* | (*On Guard*) – VAPP journal. |
| *Narkomprod* | People's Commissariat of Supply. |
| NCO | Non-commissioned officer. |
| NEP | New Economic Policy. |
| NKGB | People's Commissariat of State Security. |
| NKVD | People's Commissariat for Internal Affairs. |
| *Novaia Zhizn'* | Maxim Gorky's independent but menshevik–inclined newspaper. |
| NSZRiS | People's Union for the Defence of Motherland and Freedom. |
| *oblast* | Local government region or area, a basic administrative territorial unit in the USSR. |
| ODVF | Society of Friends of the Red Air Fleet. |
| OGPU | United State Political Administration (state security and intelligence organisation). |
| Okhrana | Tsarist secret police apparatus. |
| *okrug* | Local government area or department. |
| OO | Special department of Cheka. |
| Orgburo | Organisational bureau of the communist party. |
| ORPO | Central Committee's Department of Leading Party Organs. |
| OSO | Society for the Promotion of Defence. |
| *Osoaviakhim* | Society for Assistance to the Defence Industry, Aviation and Chemical Defence. |
| PBO | Petrograd Fighting Organisation. |
| Politburo | Political bureau of the communist party. |
| *politruk* | Assistant political commissar. |
| *polpred* | Head of a Soviet diplomatic mission. |
| Profintern | Red International of Labour Unions. |
| *Proletkul't* | Proletarian Cultural and Educational Organisation. |
| PUR | Political Administration of the Red Army. |
| *Rabkrin* | People's Commissariat of Workers' and Peasants' Inspection. |
| *Rabpros* | Union of Workers in Education and Socialist Culture. |
| *Rada* | Term for a collective organ of power in Ukrainian and other Slavic languages. |
| *raion* | Local government district. |
| RAPM | Proletarian Musicians' Association. |
| RAPP | Russian Association of Proletarian Writers. |
| *Revvoensovet* | Revolutionary Military Council of the Republic. |
| RIIA | Royal Institute of International Affairs. |
| RKP(B) | All-Russian Communist Party (Bolsheviks). |
| *Rosta* | Russian Telegraphic Agency. |
| *Rote Hilfe* | International Red Aid (see MOPR). |
| ROVS | Russian Armed Services Union. |
| RSDLP(B) | All-Russian Social Democratic Labour Party (Bolsheviks). |

| | |
|---|---|
| RSFSR | Russian Soviet Federated Socialist Republic. |
| *seim (sejm)* | Elected assembly in Ukraine, Poland, Transcaucasia. |
| *skhod* | Meeting of heads of households in a *mir*. |
| *Smena Vekh* | (*Change of Landmarks* or *Signposts*) – a collection of essays published by a Russian *émigré* group in Prague. |
| *Smersh* | Nickname for Soviet military counter-intelligence in the Second World War. |
| SOD | Council of Men in Public Life. |
| *Sotsialisticheskii Vestnik* | Menshevik publication based in Paris. |
| Soviet | Council. |
| *sovkhoz* | State farm. |
| *Sovnarkom* | Council of People's Commissars. |
| *Spartak* | Trade union sporting organisation founded by the producers' co-operatives. |
| Sportintern | Red Sport International. |
| SR | Socialist Revolutionary. |
| SSR | Soviet Socialist Republic. |
| STO | Council of Labour and Defence. |
| *subbotniki* | Voluntary working holidays. |
| SVR | Union for the Regeneration of Russia. |
| SVU | Union for the Liberation of the Ukraine. |
| SZRis | Union for the Defence of the Motherland and Freedom. |
| *Trudoviki* | Labour group in Duma. |
| *Truppenamt* | Post-Versailles equivalent of German general staff. |
| TsDKA | Sporting organisation founded by the Red Army, later TsSKA. |
| *Tsektran* | Joint Central Transport Committee. |
| *Tsentrokomdesertir* | Organisation dealing with desertion from the armed forces. |
| *Tsentrosoiuz* | All-Russian Central Union of Consumers' Co-operatives. |
| *Uchraspred* | Records and assignments section of the Central Committee. |
| USSR | Union of Soviet Socialist Republics. |
| VAPP | All-Russian Association of Proletarian Writers. |
| VCHEKA | All-Russian Extraordinary Commission for Combating Counter-revolution and Sabotage. |
| *Vesenkha* | See VSNKh. |
| VKPG | All-Russian Committee for Famine Relief. |
| VKP(B) | All-Union Communist Party (Bolsehviks). |
| *Vneshtorg* | People's Commissariat of Foreign Trade. |
| VOAPP | All-Union Organisation of Associations of Proletarian Writers. |
| *Vsevobuch* | Central Board of Military Training. |
| VSNKh | Supreme Council of National Economy. |

| | |
|---|---|
| VTsIK | All-Russian (All-Union) Central Executive Committee. |
| VUS | All-Russian Teachers' Union. |
| VVS | Supreme War Council. |
| WSI | Workers' Sport International. |
| *Znamia Truda* | Left SR journal. |

# INTRODUCTION

The idea of gathering together in one book the salient facts of Soviet history arranged in chronological order originated with John Spiers, the Chairman of John Spiers Publishing Ltd. I am grateful to him for asking me to compile the book. I am even more grateful for the latitude he has given me over the length of the work and the time needed for its completion.

A chronology is not an outline history. It is a collection of items dealing with events, meetings, speeches, resolutions, decisions, decrees, treaties, changes of policy and miscellaneous facts to which dates can be attached. By dispensing with narrative, 'atmospherics' and most of the normal discussion of the causes and effects of events and the relationships between them, a chronology can include information which would find no place in an outline history of comparable length. At the same time, a chronology cannot attempt to give an adequate account of processes or trends or of the underlying social, ethnic, economic, ideological and historical factors which historians properly examine. This work is intended, therefore, not as a substitute for any of the excellent outline histories of the Soviet Union already in existence but as a useful complement to them.

No one would dispute that one of the most important changes which occurred in the Soviet Union between 1928 and 1940 was the transformation of the economy from that of a backward agrarian country into that of a major industrial power. But the industrialisation of the USSR was a long-drawn-out process of such immense complexity that it defies summary chronological treatment. Some 1,500 new industrial projects are said to have been launched in the first five-year plan alone. A convenient way of indicating the pace of industrial development would have been to quote each year from 1928 to 1941 an index figure for industrial production. On the other hand, there are general difficulties in the way of constructing reliable indices of production and special difficulties in the Soviet case. They have been well described, for instance, in chapter 5 of G. Warren Nutter's *Growth of Industrial Production in the Soviet Union*. In the light of these difficulties and of the substantial differences between the various western attempts to construct Soviet production indices, I have limited myself to giving some general indications from Nutter and other sources of industrial growth over the whole period 1928 to 1940. Most of these will be found at 20 May 1929, the date when the first five-year plan was officially adopted. I have also mentioned a small number of the largest of the five-year plan projects which must serve

1

to represent the host of medium and smaller projects. The fact that relatively little space has been given to industrialisation in the text is a reflection of the intractability of the subject, not of its historical significance. In general, the amount of space given to any particular entry in a chronology is not a good guide to its importance. Given the nature of a chronology, it is not surprising that the years of revolutionary change should occupy more space than the years of consolidation of the Stalinist dictatorship in the early 1930s. There are, of course, additional reasons for this disparity in chapter lengths such as the extreme secrecy of the Stalinist regime and the decreasing frequency of party congresses and other meetings in that period.

Some would argue that a chronology intended primarily as a work of reference should contain nothing but undisputed facts such as, for example, that Mirbach was assassinated on 6 July 1918 and Kirov on 1 December 1934. Strict application of this rule would eliminate reference to many important episodes in Soviet history in which the facts cannot be fully established. Furthermore, it has always seemed to me that a skeleton outline which gives no explanation of the events it records and no indication of their significance is of very little value to anyone who is not already fully conversant with the subject. I have therefore ventured to add a little flesh to the bare bones accepting that, in so doing, I have entered into areas of controversy.

Many of the best writers on Soviet history underline the limitations on western knowledge of the inner workings of the Soviet system. With the significant but limited exception of those parts of the Smolensk party records which fell into German hands in 1941 and into American hands in 1945, the archives of two of the most important elements in the Soviet system, the communist party and the state security service, remain closed to independent scrutiny. In the absence of adequate primary sources, more than one explanation of particular events is often possible. Attention can be drawn to this by quoting various opinions from different authors on the same subject. I have tried to do this, albeit for reasons of space, very selectively. For example, volumes have been written about the Zinoviev letter. I chose to single out Ruth Fischer's observation, not because it necessarily gives the right solution, but partly because the implied explanation is less familiar than some and mainly because of the suggestion that not even Zinoviev himself was sure of the correct answer. In general, in my choice of opinions to quote, I confess to a bias in favour of those authors who, on the basis of evidence, reasoned argument or insight born of personal experience, challenge generally accepted notions.

The emphasis throughout the text is, not surprisingly, on internal political developments. At the same time I have tried to include references to those elements of economic, social and military history which lend themselves to chronological treatment. I have not attempted to cover developments in the arts and sciences as such. Nevertheless, it seemed to me to be wrong to omit reference to some of the more conspicuous instances in which the political and cultural fields have impinged on one another.

As far as the USSR's external relations are concerned, the more important political and commercial treaties are mentioned; detailed agreements on such matters as posts, telegraphs, rail communications, navigation and health have been excluded. The Soviet role in establishing a communist regime in Outer Mongolia is outlined; subsequent internal developments in Mongolia are not. This pattern will be followed in the next volume in relation to Eastern Europe. The central apparatus of international communism, the Comintern, is outlined together with some of its more important known or believed operations and some of the communist front organisations to which it gave rise. The history of individual non-Russian communist parties is not included except where, as in the German and Chinese cases, it is directly relevant to the internal affairs of the Soviet party.

The first volume of this chronology has been compiled during a time of change in the USSR. Rehabilitations of Stalin's victims and 'revelations' about the past have been flowing thick and fast. I have not been at pains to include all the most up-to-date information in this first volume for several reasons. Inevitably my text will be out of date in this respect by the time it appears in print. More important, rehabilitations and 'revelations' belong as much to the history of the period in which they occur as they do to the period to which they relate. They can and should therefore be dealt with in greater detail later on in the chronology. By the time the chronology is finished, it will perhaps also be possible to see the 'revelations' in better perspective. As far as the present volume is concerned, I have restricted myself to a few references to Khrushchev's 'secret speech' and one or two items from *Moscow News* which it would have been artificial to ignore. I have referred to rehabilitations only in very general terms.

From the outset, the aim has been to produce an uncluttered text based on secondary sources which would be fully accessible to the non-specialist reader. I have therefore dispensed with footnotes altogether. A comprehensive list is given below of the works from which I have derived not only the facts but also the elements of judgement, opinion and interpretation which occur in the text. To have identified the works on which each entry has been based would have been not only inconsistent with the original aim of producing a streamlined text but virtually impossible given that many of the entries are based on a variety of sources. Authors have been mentioned by name only when I have drawn on them extensively or when the views expressed by them are controversial or, of necessity, speculative.

Unfortunately, secondary sources tend to be unreliable on dates. In general, I have relied when possible on the dates given in the various documentary compilations mentioned in the List of Sources. Even these are not free from discrepancies, some of which are noted in the text. Some dates are inherently ambiguous. For example, it is often difficult to identify the precise moment when a city changed hands in the course of a war or to say whether a military offensive should be deemed to have begun when the relevant orders were issued, when an artillery barrage was opened up or when troops began to move forward. In some cases, where it seemed there was no reason to prefer one version of a date to another, I have given a spread of dates for a particular event. The Soviet habit of issuing a number of decrees on the same subject at about the same time is another source of confusion as is the use of the expression 'the night of the 15th'. In general I believe the dates I have given are accurate enough for most practical purposes but certainty is often elusive. I can only recommend anyone who is, for example, seeking to develop a historical argument which depends on absolute precision over timings to verify his dates in the best available primary sources.

With one or two obvious exceptions, such as Comintern and Gosplan, I have used the English version of the names of Soviet organisations: e.g. 'Council of People's Commissars' rather than *Sovnarkom*'. I have prefaced the term 'Central Executive Committee' with the word 'Soviet' to underline the distinction from 'Central Committee' which always refers to the Central Committee of the communist party. The word 'Soviet' means 'council' but it has also become an indispensable noun and adjective for referring to the inhabitants and institutions of the multinational Soviet Union. To avoid any possible confusion with 'White Russian' in the sense of 'anti-communist Russian', I have used 'Byelorussia' and 'Byelorussian' rather than 'White Russia' and 'White Russian'. In a military context, the word 'front' is used, as in Russian, to denote a group of armies as well as a line of battle. The spellings of Russian names are, as far as possible, those given in the English translation of the Great Soviet Encyclopedia (GSE), the system of transliter-ation being the Library of Congress system with some modifications and exceptions like Trotsky, Gorky and Kerensky. Except where full names or initials are necessary to avoid confusion, I have given surnames only. Where place-names have not changed radically since 1917, I have used current spellings such as 'Batumi' and 'Bukhara'. Where place-names have changed completely, I have given the modern equivalent in the index if not in the text. The present volume contains an index of proper names only. To com-pensate in part for the lack of a subject index, I have included a certain number of internal cross-references in the text. It is intended that the final volume of the chronology will contain a comprehensive index covering the whole work; wherever possible, it will include the first names and patro-nymics of Russians mentioned in it.

Up to 13 February 1918, Russia used the Julian calendar which, in 1917–18, was thirteen days behind the Gregorian calendar in use elsewhere in Europe. All dates in the text from 1 January 1917 to 13 February 1918 are given both in old and in new style. Some White Russian authors continued to use old style dates after February 1918.

Unless otherwise stated, references in the text to the GSE are to the English translation of the third edition of the Great Soviet Encyclopedia. A reference in the text to an author by his or her name alone relates to the particular work of that author which figures in the List of Sources.

I would like gratefully to acknowledge my indebtedness to all the authors concerned. I am also much indebted to Professors John Barber, Ronald Hill and Peter Wiles and to Valeria Grainger for a number of helpful comments, criticisms, suggestions and corrections to various drafts of the text. Responsi-bility for whatever inaccuracies and inadequacies remain is entirely mine. I am grateful to Malcolm Mackintosh who kindly supplied the map of the Civil War in European Russia on page 83. I am also grateful to Martin Morgan and Heather McNeill for checking the references to *Pravda* and *Izvestiia* for me. Finally, I would like to express my sincere thanks for the unfailing patience and helpfulness of the staffs of the Kent County Library, the British Library, the Public Record Office, the libraries of the Foreign and Commonwealth Office, the School of Slavonic and East European Studies, University of London, the Royal Institute of International Affairs, Chatham House, the London School of Economics and Political Science and, for one brief visit, the Library of Congress.

# 1917

## January

According to the Great Soviet Encyclopedia (GSE), first edition, total membership of the bolshevik party in January 1917 was 23,600. The party was operating underground and its leaders were in exile abroad or in Siberia. Its full title was the All-Russian Social Democratic Labour Party (Bolsheviks) (RSDLP (B)). The RSDLP had split in 1903 into the so-called majority faction, the Bolsheviks, and the minority faction, the Mensheviks. A major factor in the split was Lenin's uncompromising authoritarianism combined with his belief in the necessity for a tightly knit, highly disciplined party of professional revolutionaries.

## 23 February/8 March

A Women's Day strike and demonstration by textile workers in protest at a shortage of bread quickly spread to other factories in the capital, Petrograd. It involved an estimated 80,000 workers and developed a militant, anti-regime character.

## 24 February/9 March

The number of strikers doubled and the demonstrations spread into the city centre. There were reports of clashes with the police leading to casualties.

## 25 February/10 March

The strike in Petrograd became general, involving over 200,000 workers. The crowds increased in size and there were more violent incidents involving the police. Cossacks and other troops deployed in their support showed signs of sympathy with the demonstrators whose principal demands were for bread and for the abolition of the Tsarist autocracy. There were also banners demanding an end to the war with Germany but these were not popular with the crowd and did not correspond with the mood of the country as a whole. *Note*: Cossacks were descendants of frontier settlers who, between the fifteenth and eighteenth centuries, had acquired or been granted land on the borders of the Empire and who held it in return for a perpetual obligation for military service. In the nineteenth century they became a mainstay of the Tsarist regime. They were organised in a dozen communities extending from the Don through central Asia to eastern Siberia, each community being presided over by an elected leader or *ataman*. (See E. H. Carr, *The Bolshevik Revolution 1917–1923*, vol. I, p. 294, footnote

2.) The twelve communities were the Don, Kuban, Terek, Orenburg, Yaitskii, Astrakhan, Siberian, Amur, Transbaikal, Semirech, Enisei and Ussur Cossacks. Kenez mentioned a thirteenth at Krasnoiarsk in 1917.

Tsar Nicholas II, who was visiting General Staff Headquarters at Mogilev, some 400 miles south of Petrograd, instructed General Khabalov, the commander of the Petrograd military district, to suppress the disorders in the capital from the following day. Khabalov issued orders to his troops to fire on aggressive crowds if they ignored three warning signals.

## 26 February/11 March

Troops fired on the crowds causing some sixty deaths. A company of the Pavlovsk regiment mutinied but the mutiny was suppressed.

The Council of Ministers headed by Prince Golitsyn issued an order on behalf of the Tsar proroguing the Duma (the lower house of Parliament).

## 27 February/12 March

The detachment of the Volynskii regiment which had taken part in firing on the crowds on the previous day mutinied and the mutiny spread rapidly to other units of the Petrograd garrison. Confusion, the absence of many officers from their posts and the lack of effective leadership from all but a few of those who remained contributed to the disintegration of the garrison as an effective force. Without military support, the police were overwhelmed and many of their buildings were set alight. Faced with anarchy in the streets and deprived of the means of restoring order, the government collapsed. Although not formally dismissed, the Tsarist Council of Ministers held its last meeting.

The Duma, without formally rejecting the prorogation decree, held a private session which commissioned the Council of Elders (an unofficial group of party leaders) to select a Provisional Committee to include representatives of all the political parties in the Duma other than the extreme Right and the Bolsheviks whose deputies were in exile. This Duma Committee established a Military Commission to restore order in the capital and set about the formation of a new government, thereby in effect assuming power.

Meanwhile, inspired by the example of the Petersburg Soviet (Council) set up in the unsuccessful revolution of 1905, a group consisting primarily of Mensheviks formed itself into a Temporary Executive Committee of the Petrograd Soviet. The committee called for the immediate election of delegates by all factories in the capital and by those military units which had mutinied. In the evening, a session of about 200 delegates with varying credentials decided to establish a united Soviet of Workers' and Soldiers' Deputies. (Kerensky claimed that it was at the suggestion of the Bolshevik, Molotov, that the soldiers were included.) The presidium of three members included Kerensky. (Kerensky had been the leader in the Fourth Duma of the Labour Group (*Trudoviki*), a caucus rather than a party including peasant deputies, members of the radical intelligentsia, the Peasants' Union and the Socialist Revolutionary (SR) party. From February/March onwards, Kerensky, who had had links with the SRs for over ten years, identified himself with them.) A secretariat of four members was also elected. The presidium and the secretariat in turn co-opted a further eight members, two of them Bolsheviks (Shliapnikov and Zalutskii), to form an Executive Committee. The committee was subsequently enlarged. Molotov and, at a later stage, Stalin were among the Bolsheviks who joined it but it remained under moderate socialist control until September.

At Mogilev, the Tsar appointed General Ivanov as commander of the Petrograd garrison and the transfer of reliable troops from the northern and western fronts to the capital was ordered.

## 28 February/13 March

Khabalov decided to cease operations in the capital and ordered the remnants of his force to deposit their arms in the Admiralty building and disperse to their barracks.

The Duma Committee, having arrested some former Tsarist ministers and police officials, appointed commissars to take over vacant ministries. A telegram was despatched on the nation-wide railway communications network stating that the Duma had taken upon itself the formation of a new government.

The Tsar left Mogilev by train with the intention of returning to his palace at Tsarskoe Selo near Petrograd but, warned correctly or otherwise that stations ahead had been taken over by revolutionaries, diverted his train to Pskov.

## 1 March/14 March

Control over the country's second city, Moscow, passed into revolutionary hands without violence.

The Petrograd Soviet issued 'Order Number One' whose provisions were as follows:

1. All military and naval units should elect committees representing the 'other ranks'.
2. Every military unit should send a representative to the Petrograd Soviet on the scale of one for each company.
3. All political activities of military units should be subordinate to the Soviet.
4. The Soviet's decisions should take precedence over competing orders from the Military Commission of the Duma.
5. The supply of arms should be controlled by the Soldiers' Committees and they should on no account be issued to officers even on demand.
6. While observing strict military discipline on duty, soldiers should enjoy the same civil liberties when off duty as other citizens. They should not be required to salute or stand to attention when off duty.
7. They should not use honorific titles when addressing officers or be addressed by them in familiar or disrespectful terms.

General Ivanov arrived at Tsarskoe Selo and received orders not to proceed with military action in Petrograd, pending further instructions.

## 2 March/15 March

The Tsar was persuaded by his senior generals to abdicate. Unable to contemplate separation from his haemophiliac son, he abdicated for himself and his son in favour of his brother, Grand Duke Michael.

The leader of the liberal Constitutional Democratic (Kadet) party, Miliukov, having negotiated on behalf of the Duma Committee a tentative agreement with the Soviet on the formation of a Provisional Government, informally announced the names of a new Council of Ministers as part of a proposed interim constitutional monarchy under the regency of Grand Duke Michael, pending the election of a Constituent Assembly.

## 3 March/16 March

Grand Duke Michael refused to accept the throne.

The General Staff's proposed transfer of reliable troops from the front to the capital was finally abandoned and General Ivanov was recalled to Mogilev, being replaced by General Kornilov as commander of the Petrograd military district.

The Provisional Government formally assumed office and declared that the Duma Committee had nominated a cabinet under the premiership of Prince Georgii Evgen'evich L'vov. The cabinet list included Miliukov as Foreign Minister and Kerensky as Minister of Justice. Kerensky alone managed to combine membership of the government with high office in the Soviet of which he was a deputy chairman.

The Provisional Government announced a programme which included

- complete and immediate amnesty for all political and religious offences, including terrorist attacks, military mutinies and agrarian disturbances;
- freedom of speech, freedom of the press and the right of assembly;
- the right to form trade unions and to stage strikes;
- the abolition of discrimination on class, religious or national grounds;
- the preparation of elections by direct, equal, secret and universal ballot for a Constituent Assembly charged with drawing up a new constitution;
- the replacement of the police by a people's militia;
- new democratic elections for local authorities;
- immunity for units of the Petrograd garrison which had mutinied from being disarmed or removed from the capital; and
- civil liberties for all military personnel subject to the needs of military discipline while on duty.

The programme made no reference to policy on the continuation of the war or to land reform.

The Petrograd Soviet declared its support for the Provisional Government in so far as it carried out its programme of democratic reforms and struggled decisively against the old order. In other words, the Soviet conceded state power to the Provisional Government but reserved its right to maintain a degree of control over it, thus introducing an inherently unstable system often referred to as the 'dual power' or 'dyarchy'. The Soviet decided that the former Tsar should be arrested. The Provisional Government reluctantly agreed on 7/20 March.

*Note on the February/March Revolution:* While there were numerous left-wing activists in the Petrograd factories in February 1917, non-communist western accounts generally agree that the leaders of the bolshevik and other revolutionary parties neither instigated the trouble nor appreciated in the early stages its revolutionary potential. Katkov, in *Russia 1917: The February Revolution*, argued that the nature of the disturbances indicated that they were organised and financed to an extent which had not been fully determined. He suggested that German agents might have been at least partly responsible as they appear to have been for a wave of strikes in Russia in 1916: he argued that the prominence of anti-war banners in the early stages of the demonstrations was consistent with this thesis. For evidence of the German effort to promote revolution in Russia, see also Zeman and the entry for 20 November/3 December below.

Hasegawa gave the total loss of life in Petrograd during the revolution as 433 with 1,514 wounded. Elsewhere in Russia, the revolution was unaccompanied by violence except for some instances of the murder of officers by other ranks notably in the naval bases at Helsingfors (Helsinki) and Kronstadt where Admiral Viren, the base commander, was killed by a mob of sailors.

## 4 March/17 March

The corps of gendarmes and the Tsarist secret police apparatus known as the *Okhrana* were abolished.

## 7 March/20 March

The Provisional Government restored the Finnish constitution giving Finland greater autonomy than it had enjoyed under the former Tsar.

## 8 March/21 March

The former Tsar was arrested at Mogilev and escorted back to detention with his family at Tsarskoe Selo.

## 9 March/22 March

The United States recognised the Provisional Government.

An independent bolshevik faction was established in the Petrograd Soviet. It consisted of about forty out of the total membership which had by this time swollen to about 2,000, the great majority of them supporters of the Mensheviks or SRs.

## 10 March/23 March

The Department of Police was formally abolished and replaced by a temporary police administration

## 11 March/24 March

Britain, France and Italy recognised the Provisional Government. Recognition was based on the new government's assurances that it accepted the treaty obligations undertaken by its predecessor.

General Alekseev was appointed supreme commander in place of Grand Duke Nikolai Nikolaevich.

## 12 March/25 March

Stalin, Kamenev and Muranov returned from exile to Petrograd and took control of *Pravda*, the Bolsheviks' party organ. At this time, Stalin rejected the bolshevik slogan 'down with the war': he called on the army and the public to stand firm against the Germans and advocated

# 1917

pressure on the Provisional Government to work for a negotiated settlement. He was also favourably disposed towards a restoration of menshevik–bolshevik unity. To some extent anticipating Lenin's 'April theses' (see 7/20 April), Stalin drew attention to the Soviets as organs of revolutionary struggle which could weld the capital's democracy to that in the provinces and, at the appropriate moment, convert themselves into instruments of revolutionary government.

The death penalty was abolished. Other liberal measures adopted in the following weeks on the lines of the programme of 3/16 March made Russia, as Lenin himself put it in April, the freest of all the belligerent countries in the world.

## 14 March/27 March

The Petrograd Soviet addressed an appeal to 'the Peoples of the Whole World' calling for proletarian solidarity with the new Russian democracy, particularly on the part of the German proletariat, in a struggle against the acquisitive ambitions of all governments and in a common effort to bring the war to an end. The German proletariat was urged to follow the Russian example and throw off the yoke of the semi-autocratic German regime.

## 16 March/29 March

The Provisional Government recognised the independence of Poland, then under occupation by the Germans and their allies.

## 23 March/5 April

Miliukov's statement to the press that Russia's war aims continued to include the acquisition of Constantinople and the Black Sea straits was rejected by the Soviet.

## 26 March/8 April

In a farewell letter to the Swiss workers on his departure for Russia, Lenin denounced the Provisional Government because it contained monarchists like Prince L'vov and Guchkov and was bent on continuing the imperialist war while refusing to publish the secret treaties with the allies on Russian acquisition of Constantinople, Armenia, Galicia, etc. (see 9/22 November). The slogan 'turn the imperialist war into a civil war', first put forward in November 1914 and ridiculed then, was, he wrote, correct: the transformation was becoming a fact.

## 27 March/9 April

The Provisional Government stated its war aims as the liberation of the country from the invading enemy and the establishment of a stable peace on the basis of the self-determination of peoples while at the same time observing all Russia's obligations towards her allies.

## 29 March–3 April/11–16 April

The movement to form Soviets of workers, soldiers and peasants having spread rapidly through the country, an all-Russian conference of workers' and soldiers' Soviets was held in Petrograd. The dominant parties were the Mensheviks and the non-Marxist SRs. The main plank of the SR programme was distribution of the land to the peasants. The Executive Committee of the Petrograd Soviet was expanded to a membership of about eighty to give it a nationally representative character. The conference passed by a large majority a resolution on war aims calling on all the belligerent peoples to exert pressure on their governments to renounce annexations and indemnities and urging the Provisional Government to negotiate an agreement with its allies on this basis.

## 3 April/16 April

Lenin arrived in Petrograd from Sweden having travelled, with other leading Bolsheviks, from exile in Switzerland through Germany in a 'sealed train' provided by the German authorities.

## 4 April/17 April

Lenin discussed his 'April theses' with bolshevik and, later, menshevik delegates to the all-Russian conference of Soviets.

## 7 April/20 April

*Pravda* published Lenin's 'April theses'. These rejected continuation of the war on the grounds that, being conducted by a capitalist Provisional Government, it remained an imperialist war. A truly democratic, non-oppressive peace could only be achieved through the overthrow of capitalism and the transfer of power to the proletariat and the peasantry. This view needed to be widely propagated in the army in the field, and fraternisation between Russian and German troops was to be encouraged. The theses called on the party to adapt itself to working with the masses in the new conditions of freedom. They rejected any form of support for the Provisional Government. They advocated a republic of nationwide Soviets of workers', soldiers' and agricultural workers' deputies. Recognising that the bolshevik party was in a small minority, the theses demanded the transfer of state power to the Soviets. They argued that the police, the army and the bureaucracy should be abolished and that the army should be replaced by a 'general arming of the people'. Officers, who were to be subject to election and removal, should be paid no more than the average wage of a skilled worker. Landlords should be expropriated and all the land should be nationalised, large estates being converted into model farms under the control of Soviets. All banks should be fused into one national bank. The immediate task was not the introduction of socialism but control by the Soviets over production and distribution. A party congress should be convoked immediately, the party's programme should be revised, the party's name should be changed to 'The Communist Party' and a revolutionary International should be revived.

## 8 April/21 April

*Pravda* published Kamenev's criticisms of Lenin's theses which were at first widely opposed in the party. Kamenev rejected the idea that the bourgeois-democratic revolution had been completed and that it could be immediately transformed into a socialist revolution.

## 14 April/27 April

The Petrograd and Moscow committees of the bolshevik party resolved to form a Red Guard. This was formed from workers recruited by bolshevik-organised factory committees and trained and armed by the Bolsheviks' Military Organisation, set up in March to promote bolshevik influence in the Petrograd garrison and the Kronstadt naval base. In April the Military Organisation was placed directly under the bolshevik Central Committee and its field of operation was widened to include troops at the front as well as in the rear.

### 18 April/1 May

The Russian Foreign Minister, Miliukov, sent a note to the allied powers, enclosing copies of the Provisional Government's declaration on war aims on 27 March/9 April, in which he reaffirmed the government's determination to pursue a decisive victory in the war while fully observing its obligations to its allies.

### 20 April/3 May

Miliukov's note of 18 April/1 May to the allied powers was published. In protest, the Finnish regiment and other military units (according to Kerensky at Lenin's instigation) led a demonstration of some 25,000 people demanding Miliukov's resignation.

### 21 April/4 May

More serious disturbances, including clashes between supporters and opponents of the government, involved bloodshed. When Kornilov ordered certain units to take up positions to protect the government, the units turned to the Soviet for instructions and Kornilov was prevailed on to withdraw the order. He was then transferred at his own request and

given command of the south-western front.

The Provisional Government issued a statement (published the following day) saying that it had unanimously approved the text of Miliukov's note of 18 April/1 May to the allies. The statement reiterated that the government's aim was a stable peace on the basis of the self-determination of peoples.

### 22 April/5 May

The Soviet accepted the government's statement as a renunciation of forcible annexation and called on the peoples of all the belligerent countries to compel their governments to begin peace negotiations on the basis of 'no annexations and no indemnities'.

### 24–29 April/7–12 May

The seventh all-Russian conference of the bolshevik party adopted Lenin's 'April theses'. Official Soviet estimates of party strength at this time vary from 40,000 to 79,000.

### 28–29 April/11–12 May

The Executive Committee of the Petrograd Soviet voted narrowly against participation by its members in the Provisional Government.

### 30 April–1 May/13–14 May

The War Minister, Guchkov, resigned.

### 1–2 May/14–15 May

Against opposition from the Bolsheviks and some SRs and left-wing Menshevik-Internationalists, the Executive Committee of the Petrograd Soviet voted to allow its members to join the government in a coalition including socialists.

## 3 May/16 May

Miliukov resigned. He was succeeded as Foreign Minister by Tereshchenko.

## 4 May/17 May

Trotsky returned to Russia and, although not a member of the bolshevik party, co-operated closely with Lenin.

## 4–28 May/17 May–10 June

Of the 1,115 delegates to the All-Russian Congress of Soviets of Peasants' Deputies, 537 were SRs and fourteen Bolsheviks.

## 5 May/18 May

The second Provisional Government (also known as the first coalition government owing to the participation of socialists in it) was formed with Kerensky as War Minister and two SRs, two Mensheviks and one Populist Socialist as members. The new government's programme, while rejecting the idea of a separate peace with the Germans, included the formula of peace without annexations or indemnities.

## 10 May/23 May

In *Pravda*, Lenin denounced the government's attempts to deceive the soldiers and workers into believing that they were defending freedom and the revolution; in reality they were defending the sordid, secret Tsarist treaties which the government refused to publish. He urged Russian soldiers to fraternise with the Germans at the front and to persuade them that a workers' revolution was the only way of terminating the war and overthrowing capitalism.

## 21 May/3 June

The special US mission to Russia headed by Senator Elihu Root arrived in Vladivostok and reached Petrograd ten days later. Its brief was to discuss US co-operation with the Provisional Government in the prosecution of the war. It left Vladivostok for the United States on 8/21 July.

## 22 May/4 June

General Brusilov was appointed supreme commander in place of General Alekseev.

## 31 May/13 June

The workers' section of the Petrograd Soviet, reflecting the rising tide of bolshevik influence among the Petrograd industrial workers, voted 173 to 144 in favour of the bolshevik slogan 'all power to the Soviets'.

## Late May/early June

John F. Stevens, an American railway engineer, arrived at Vladivostok at the head of a US railway mission intended to help revive the Trans-Siberian railway which had deteriorated so much that it was incapable of transporting allied war supplies to Russia.

## 3–24 June/16 June–7 July

The first All-Russian Congress of Soviets of Workers' and Soldiers' Deputies was held in Petrograd. It was attended by 822 voting delegates, of whom 777 declared their party allegiance. Of these, 105 were Bolsheviks, 285 SRs, 248 Mensheviks, thirty-two Menshevik-Internationalists (occasional allies of the Bolsheviks) and seventy-three miscellaneous socialists. Lenin declared that the Bolsheviks, unlike the other parties, were ready at any moment to assume full power. The congress elected a new All-Russian Central Executive Committee (VTsIK) to act as the highest national Soviet authority between congresses. It consisted of 104 Mensheviks, ninety-nine SRs, thirty-five Bolsheviks and eighteen others.

## 10 June/23 June

With some difficulty, bolshevik party discipline being far from established, Lenin called off a bolshevik demonstration planned for that day, the Congress of Soviets having voted against it.

In the Ukraine, the Central *Rada*, a representative body which had been formed on 6/19 April at an all-Ukrainian National Congress in Kiev, issued its first 'Universal', a message to the Ukrainian people calling for the right of the Ukraine, without separating itself from Russia, to manage its own life: it demanded the creation of a freely elected Ukrainian Assembly (*Sejm*) responsible for maintaining order and supervising the distribution and management of the land within its borders. The 'Universal' envisaged that its proposals would be subject to ratification by the All-Russian Constituent Assembly.

## 18 June/1 July

The Congress of Soviets organised a demonstration which was largely taken over by the Bolsheviks using slogans and banners originally prepared for 10/23 June against the war, the government and the allies and in favour of 'bread, peace and freedom'.

Under Kerensky's direction and partly as a result of allied urging, the Russian army launched an offensive on the Galician front and achieved some early successes.

## 19 June/2 July

Patriotic demonstrations took place in Petrograd in support of Kerensky and his offensive.

## 2–3 July/15–16 July

Against a background of mounting war-weariness and indiscipline in the armed forces in Petrograd, labour disturbances in industry and land seizures by the peasantry, four Kadet ministers resigned in protest against the government's concessions to the demands of the Ukrainian *Rada* for autonomy (see 3/16 July). The failure of the socialist ministers either to exert a moderating influence on the workers or to help restore discipline in the army were probably contributory factors. The resignations in effect brought the coalition to an end.

## 3 July/16 July

The First Machine-Gun Regiment, at the instigation of members of the Bolsheviks' Military Organisation but apparently without the approval of the bolshevik Central Committee, led a demonstration of soldiers and workers to the seat of the Soviet in Petrograd.

The Bolsheviks' Military Organisation at this time claimed 26,000 members. It was primarily concerned with subverting the Russian army and agitated through its newspapers for land seizures (calculated to appeal to the 'other ranks' who were drawn largely from the peasantry) and for fraternisation between Russian and German troops at the front. The Germans also encouraged fraternisation which they found a useful means of demoralising the Russian army.

The Ukrainian *Rada* issued its second 'Universal' after negotiations with Kerensky and two other representatives of the Provisional Government. It declared that the Provisional Government recognised the right of the Ukrainian people to self-determination but included a clause rejecting any attempt to implement Ukrainian autonomy before convocation of the All-Russian Constituent Assembly.

## 4 July/17 July

Armed sailors from Kronstadt, where bolshevik and anarchist influence were both strong, numbering between 10,000 and 12,000 according to Getzler, arrived in the capital in the morning. As they marched through the streets to the headquarters of the Soviet, accompanied by some thousands of workers, there was considerable random violence. The SR Minister of Agriculture, Chernov, who tried to address the crowd, was seized and bundled into a car by some sailors. Trotsky displayed considerable courage in rescuing him.

The bolshevik Central Committee issued a proclamation demanding that the all-Russian Soviet should take power into its own hands, the provisional coalition government having 'collapsed'.

Units of the Petrograd garrison proved to be either neutral or sympathetic towards the demonstrations. The government therefore ordered up reinforcements from outside the capital. In the evening, the Ismailov regiment arrived, having decided to defend the Soviet which had rejected the idea of seizing power. The Preobrazhenskii regiment, influenced by a communiqué from the Ministry of Justice claiming that Lenin and his associates were German agents, also came out actively against the demonstrators. (For a discussion of the evidence of German funding of the bolshevik party, see Katkov, *The February Revolution*, chapter 5.)

Chamberlin gave the total casualties in these 'July Days' as about 400.

While the government and Soviet were both defenceless during the afternoon of 4/17 July and a coup might well have been possible, Lenin seems to have calculated correctly that a premature attempt would drive the moderate elements of the Soviet into firmer collaboration with the government in resisting bolshevik influence and that a bolshevik seizure of power in the capital would not have survived opposition from the provinces. At this time, as a result of elections in May and June, the Bolsheviks had captured about half the seats in the workers' section of the Petrograd Soviet and a quarter of those in the soldiers' section.

The 'July Days' provoked a marked public reaction against the Bolsheviks except in the working-class districts of the capital.

## 5 July/18 July

*Pravda* called off the demonstrations.

Government troops raided the offices of *Pravda* and destroyed equipment.

## 6 July/19 July

In the early hours government troops turned the Bolsheviks out of their party headquarters. In the afternoon they reoccupied the Peter and Paul fortress, the last stronghold of leftist resistance. Measures, only partially effective, were taken to disband and disarm the rebellious troops and Red Guards. On the following day the arrest of Lenin and other Bolsheviks was ordered. Lenin evaded arrest and remained in hiding, mainly in Finland, until the eve of the October/November revolution.

Government action against the Bolsheviks proved inadequate to destroy their organisation but severe enough to win them additional working-class sympathy during the following weeks at the expense of the moderate socialists.

## 8 July/21 July

Price L'vov found himself unable to go along with the proposals of his socialist ministers on land reform, which he considered dangerous in themselves and a usurpation of the functions of the forthcoming Constituent Assembly. He resigned the premiership and handed over to Kerensky who set about forming the second coalition (third provisional) government.

## 9 July/22 July

The news broke in Petrograd that

after some initial Russian successes in their offensive against Austrian troops on the Galician front, a German counter-attack had begun on 6/19 July and had broken through the Russians. Ternopol' was abandoned on 11/24 July without a fight and discipline in a number of Russian units appeared to have broken down. News of the disaster stimulated a reaction against the extremist leaders of the disturbances of the 'July Days' in Petrograd.

## 12 July/25 July

The death penalty was restored for offences against military discipline at the front. The Petrograd Soviet protested against the measure.

## 13 July/26 July

His ministers having put their portfolios at his disposal, Kerensky began to reconstruct his government.

## 16 July/29 July

Kerensky and Tereshchenko attended a conference of the general staff at Mogilev to discuss the breakdown of discipline in the army and measures needed to restore it.

## 18 July/31 July

General Kornilov was appointed by Kerensky to replace General Brusilov as supreme commander.

## 21–22 July/3–4 August

Kerensky resigned as Premier declaring that he was unable to form a government. A hastily assembled conference of ministers and party leaders decided to give him a free hand in the construction of a govern-

ment and he withdrew his resignation.

## 23 July/5 August

Trotsky was arrested.

## 25 July/7 August

The list of members of the third provisional (second coalition) government was announced. It consisted of
eight socialist and seven 'bourgeois'
ministers. Kerensky retained the
Premiership and the War Ministry.

## 26 July–3 August/8–16 August

The Sixth Congress of the bolshevik
party was held semi-clandestinely in
Petrograd. In Lenin's absence but at
his instigation, the congress abandoned the slogan of 'all power to the
Soviets' in favour of the 'dictatorship
of the proletariat' which, with the
support of the poorest peasantry, was
described as the only force capable
of breaking the resistance of the
counter-revolutionary bourgeoisie
and seizing power. In practice this
meant that the party was to seek to
achieve exclusive power through an
armed uprising procured by a combination of legal and illegal activity,
using Soviets and factory committees
as their means of access to the masses
in general and the armed forces in
particular.

Sverdlov, a leading party organiser, estimated the party's membership at 200,000. A Central Committee of twenty-two members was
elected including Trotsky who, together with his hitherto independent
group of followers, the *Mezh-
raiontsy*, formally joined the party.
New rules were adopted to tighten
party discipline. At that time the
party was publishing forty-one newspapers in Russian and minority languages with a total daily circulation
of 320,000. Much of this propaganda
effort was directed at the army.

## 1 August/14 August

Largely because of the July disturbances in Petrograd, the government
moved the former Tsar and his family
to Tobol'sk in Siberia for their
greater safety.

## 3 August/16 August

Kornilov visited Petrograd from
Mogilev and presented Kerensky
with a memorandum containing draft
measures which he and other senior
officers considered essential to counter bolshevik subversion of the Russian army, to restore its fighting
capacity and to save the country from
collapse. These measures included
the reintroduction of the death penalty for seditious activities in the rear
as well as at the front.

## 4 August/17 August

On return to Mogilev, Kornilov set
about organising a force under a cavalry officer, General Krymov, to be
deployed around Petrograd which
was indirectly threatened by the
German army on the Riga front 550
miles to the south-west. In view of
the certain opposition of the Bolsheviks and the Soviet to the introduction of the harsh measures envisaged
by Kornilov, it was intended that the
force should be available to deal with
disturbances in the capital. Kornilov
is said to have received reports that
a bolshevik uprising there was
planned to occur on or about 28
August/10 September.

## 9 August/22 August

The Provisional Government announced that elections to the Constituent Assembly would be postponed from 17/30 September to 12/25 November and that the Constituent Assembly would convene on 28 November/11 December.

## 10 August/23 August

At a further meeting between Kerensky and Kornilov in Petrograd, Kerensky temporised over the introduction of Kornilov's proposed measures.

## 12–15 August/25–28 August

In accordance with a decision taken on Kerensky's initiative in July, the Moscow State Conference was held, bringing together delegates from a variety of public organisations representing all shades of political opinion apart from the Bolsheviks who chose not to attend and who promoted a strike of transport and other workers in Moscow to coincide with the opening of the conference. The conference's object was to obtain for the government a popular mandate for prosecuting the war while preserving the gains of the revolution. Instead the conference underlined the depth of the division between those on the right who wished to see firm government and a successful end to the war and who looked increasingly to Kornilov as the only leader strong enough to realise these aims and those on the left who thought that the safeguarding of the revolution was the paramount consideration and who saw in Kornilov the paladin of counter-revolution.

## 17 August/30 August

Kerensky told Savinkov, the Deputy War Minister, that he accepted Kornilov's proposed measures.

## 19–21 August/1–3 September

Riga fell to the Germans.

## 20 August/2 September

In elections for a new Petrograd City Duma, the SRs won seventy-five seats, the Bolsheviks sixty-seven (an increase of thirty), the Kadets forty-two and the Mensheviks eight (a loss of thirty-two).

## 24 August/6 September

Savinkov saw Kornilov in Mogilev and told him that the government would approve his measures and that, in view of the likelihood of violent opposition, force should be available to the government in Petrograd. According to Kornilov's subsequent deposition to the Commission of Investigation, Savinkov persuaded Kornilov that because of Kerensky's following on the Left, he should continue to participate in the government; Kornilov promised full support for Kerensky if this was required for the good of the country.

## 25 August/7 September

Vladimir Nikolaevich L'vov, who had served as Procurator of the Holy Synod in the first Provisional Government, visited Kornilov at Mogilev. Apparently misrepresenting himself as an emissary with authority to speak for Kerensky, he discussed with Kornilov alternative solutions to the problem of forming a strong government. Kornilov expressed himself in favour of a dictatorship under the supreme commander, whoever that might be, provided that Kerensky and Savinkov also joined the government. Through L'vov, Kornilov invited Kerensky to Mogilev so that they could reach a definite understanding.

## 26 August/8 September

On the basis of L'vov's reports to him on his return to Petrograd, Kerensky concluded that Kornilov was engaged in a full-scale conspiracy against him and that his, Kerensky's, life would be in danger if he were to visit Mogilev. After an ostensibly friendly teleprinter conversation in which he told Kornilov he would ·be leaving for Mogilev the following day, Kerensky sent Kornilov a telegram dismissing him from his post.

## 27 August/9 September

In the early morning, Kerensky informed his cabinet of Kornilov's 'treachery' and asked for emergency powers; most of his ministers agreed to offer their resignations.

Kornilov refused to accept his dismissal. Other senior officers refused to take over command from him. Kerensky ordered a cessation of troop movements towards Petrograd. The order was not obeyed.

Despite attempts at mediation between Kerensky and Kornilov by Savinkov and others, the government publicly announced that Kornilov had been dismissed. Kornilov replied with a denunciation of the government (published on 29 August/11 September) in which he accused it of acting under bolshevik pressure in the German interest. He ordered General Krymov to proceed with his force towards the capital as planned. Thereafter communications between Krymov and the general staff were cut.

The Soviet Central Executive Committee pledged its support for Kerensky and issued directives to army committees, provincial soviets, postal and railway workers and the garrison to impede the movements of 'counter-revolutionary troops'. The Soviet formed a Committee for Struggle with Counter-Revolution which attracted widespread support. The committee approved a bolshevik move to create an armed workers' militia. In practice this led to the revival of the bolshevik Red Guard which had been partially suppressed after the 'July Days'.

## 29 August/11 September

Kerensky appointed a Commission of Investigation and despatched its members to Mogilev to interrogate Kornilov.

## 29–30 August/11–12 September

Finding the approaches to Petrograd blocked by torn-up railway lines and subjected to a barrage of pro-government and pro-Soviet propaganda, Krymov's forces disintegrated; many of his units declared their allegiance to the government and the Soviet.

## 30 August/12 September

Lenin addressed a letter to the Central Committee, rejecting the idea of supporting Kerensky and the Provisional Government against Kornilov and his supporters. Lenin demanded a stepping-up of propaganda in favour of an immediate peace with the Germans, immediate transfer of land to the peasantry, workers' control over industry and bread supplies, the arming of the workers, arrests of leading bourgeois political figures, suppression of various bourgeois newspapers and dispersal of the State Duma. As he put it: 'A more active and truly revolutionary war against Kornilov alone can lead us to power but we must speak of this as little as possible in our propaganda (remembering very well that even tomorrow events may put power into our hands and then we shall not relinquish it).'

Kerensky assumed office as supreme commander with General Alekseev as his chief of staff.

Kerensky's ministers placed their offices at his disposal to give him freedom to reconstruct his government.

## 31 August/13 September

After a bitter meeting with Kerensky in Petrograd, Krymov shot himself.

## 1 September/14 September

Kerensky set up a temporary Directory of five ministers and proclaimed Russia to be a republic.

Alekseev arrived at Mogilev and arrested Kornilov and his senior aides who surrendered without protest.

*Note on the Kornilov affair:* A commonly held view is that Kornilov headed an unsuccessful right-wing, counter-revolutionary conspiracy. Katkov, in *The Kornilov Affair* (1980), which contains the text of Kornilov's deposition to the Commission of Investigation, questioned whether Kornilov personally was party to anything like a conspiracy in

the normal sense of the word. Katkov laid the blame for the crisis primarily on the indecisiveness and hysterical reactions of Kerensky. While the degree of blame to be accorded to Kerensky and Kornilov respectively is disputed, there is common agreement that the crisis, together with the Bolsheviks' readily intelligible demands for peace, land and bread, enabled them to gain more public support than they had lost after the 'July Days' and opened the way for the bolshevik coup two months later.

## 4 September/17 September

Trotsky and a number of other Bolsheviks were released from prison.

## 5 September/18 September

The Bolsheviks obtained majorities in the Moscow and Krasnoiarsk Soviets amid a general swing to the Left in the provinces. The bolshevik slogan 'all power to the Soviets' was revived.

## 7 September/20 September

Georgia, Armenia and Azerbaijan formed a Transcaucasian Federal Republic.

## 9 September/22 September

In the Petrograd Soviet, which had already voted in favour of a bolshevik motion on 31 August/13 September, a further bolshevik motion to re-elect the Soviet's menshevik- and SR-controlled presidium on the basis of proportional representation (i.e. to include Bolsheviks) was narrowly carried.

## 10 September/23 September

General Dukhonin replaced General Alekseev (who had asked to be relieved of his post) as chief of staff.

## 12 September/25 September

The Soviet Central Executive Committee voted in favour of the principle of a coalition government but one from which the Kadets would be excluded.

## 12–14 September/25–27 September

Lenin's letters to the Central Committee demanded that, the Bolsheviks having achieved majorities in both metropolitan Soviets, an armed uprising in Petrograd and Moscow be placed on the party's 'order of the day'.

## 14–22 September/27 September–5 October

About 1,200 delegates assembled in Petrograd for the Democratic Conference which had been proposed by the Soviet Central Executive Committee on 2/15 September as a means of deciding on the future form of government. The Kadets and other representatives of the property-owning classes were excluded from the conference. The conference discussed at length and voted inconsistently on whether a socialist government or a coalition government of socialists and Kadets should be formed. In the end the conference appointed a new body, the Provisional Council of the Russian Republic or Pre-Parliament, composed of 388 delegates from the parties represented in the Soviets together with 167 delegates from the propertied classes including the Kadets, the Cossacks, the national minorities and other groups. The Pre-Parliament was to represent the popular will until the Constituent Assembly had met and the new Provisional Government was to be responsible to it. It was, however, left to the new government to draft a statute for the Pre-Parliament.

## 21 September/4 October

A bolshevik party conference rejected a Lenin-Trotsky motion to boycott the Pre-Parliament.

The Petrograd Soviet demanded the holding of the Second All-Russian Congress of Soviets.

## 25 September/8 October

The third coalition (fourth provisional) government, under Kerensky's leadership and containing Kadets as well as socialists, was announced.

Trotsky was elected chairman of the Petrograd Soviet, the reconstructed presidium of which contained three other Bolsheviks, two SRs and one Menshevik.

## 26 September/9 October

The Mensheviks and others, fearing that the proposed Congress of Soviets would interfere with elections to the Constituent Assembly and challenge the authority of the Provisional Government, opened a campaign for postponement of the congress.

## 29 September/12 October

*Izvestiia* published a Soviet Central Executive Committee decision to convoke the Congress of Soviets on or about 20 October/2 November.

Lenin threatened to resign from the bolshevik Central Committee if it did not agree to prepare for an immediate insurrection.

## 1–6 October/14–19 October

The Germans occupied islands in the Gulf of Riga and established naval control over the gulf.

## 7 October/20 October

The Provisional Government having issued a law on the previous day dissolving the Fourth Duma, the Pre-Parliament held its opening session. Trotsky led a bolshevik walk-out having first denounced the Pre-Parliament as unrepresentative. He accused the government of needlessly prolonging the war and planning to delay convocation of the Constituent Assembly. He said that the government sought to destroy the revolution by surrendering Petrograd to the Germans while establishing a counter-revolutionary regime in Moscow. He demanded immediate peace, all power to the Soviets, all land to the people and convocation of the Constituent Assembly.

Lenin secretly arrived in Petrograd from Finland.

## 9 October/22 October

A menshevik proposal in the Petrograd Soviet to set up a Committee of Revolutionary Defence to act as a liaison between the Soviet and the staff of the Petrograd Military District on matters affecting the defence of Petrograd from the Germans was taken up by the Bolsheviks. (Trotsky claimed to have seen it from the start as a potential instrument for organising an armed insurrection against the

government although the party as a whole do not seem to have viewed it in this light until a week later.) The tasks of the committee were worked out under Trotsky's guidance by a Left SR and included a number of liaison and information-gathering functions which were equally relevant to the defence of Petrograd or to the preparation of an insurrection. Three days later, the new name, Military Revolutionary Committee, was adopted. The committee was to become in fact the headquarters organisation of the insurrection. It set up a Permanent Conference of the Garrison which was to keep the committee informed of the state of morale and the allegiance of the different units of the garrison and of the forces round the capital. In the name of the Military Revolutionary Committee, the Bolsheviks made a successful bid for the goodwill of the Petrograd garrison during the next ten days by protecting it from the government's attempts to transfer a number of units to the front and also by alleging, falsely, that the government was proposing to abandon Petrograd to the Germans.

## 10 October/23 October

Lenin attended a clandestine meeting of the Central Committee in Petrograd at which his motion in favour of making armed insurrection the 'order of the day' was passed by ten votes to two, those of Zinoviev and Kamenev who made their opposition public on 18/31 October. Lenin's majority would probably have been proportionately smaller had all committee members been present. A Political Bureau of seven members was formed (Lenin, Trotsky, Stalin,

Zinoviev, Kamenev, Sokol'nikov and Bubnov) but there is no evidence that it functioned as such. According to Trotsky in his *History of the Russian Revolution* 15/28 October was tentatively set as the date for the insurrection which Lenin was most insistent should take place before the opening of the congress of Soviets then scheduled for 20 October/2 November.

## 11–13 October/24–26 October

As part of their campaign in favour of the holding of the Second All-Russian Congress of Soviets and in order to strengthen their military influence in Petrograd, Moscow and the military and naval bases near the capital, the Bolsheviks convened an unofficial Congress of Soviets of the Northern Region, attended by ninety-four delegates under the presidency of a Bolshevik, Krylenko.

Some bolshevik leaders thought that this northern regional congress would be the opening shot in the Bolsheviks' bid for power, but it appears that the bolshevik Military Organisation did not consider that their forces were ready at that stage or that they would receive popular backing for a coup in advance of the All-Russian Congress of Soviets.

From the bolshevik point of view, the purpose of the All-Russian Congress was, in Trotsky's words, 'to screen the semi-conspirative, semi-public preparation of an insurrection. . . . Having thus promoted the assembling of forces for the revolution, the Congress of Soviets was afterward to sanction its results and give the new government a form irreproachable in the eyes of the people.'

## 13 October/26 October

The Soviet Central Executive Committee announced the formation of a special department of the Red Guard. As Trotsky put it, 'Arming the workers . . . had become one of the most important tasks' of the bolshevik-controlled Soviet. At about this time, the Sestroretsk armaments factory delivered to the Soviet 5,000 rifles which Trotsky had ordered. According to the GSE, second edition, the strength of the Red Guards was then 10,000 to 12,000. A figure of about 20,000 is quoted by Chamberlin and other western historians.

## 14 October/27 October

The Bolsheviks' Moscow regional committee decided to follow the Central Committee's decision of 10/23 October and 'to organise armed insurrection for the seizure of power'.

## 16 October/29 October

A plenary session of the Soviet approved the proposed regulations for the Military Revolutionary Committee by a large majority against Menshevik opposition.

## 18 October/31 October

The Soviet Central Executive Committee postponed the Second All-Russian Congress of Soviets from 20 October/2 November to 25 October/7 November.

The Garrison Conference was called together for the first time. As part of the Soviet's effort to gain control over the garrison, units were instructed to obey only those orders from their headquarters which had been countersigned by the soldiers' sections.

The writer, Maxim Gorky, challenged the bolshevik Central Committee to deny the allegation that it was planning an uprising for 20 October/2 November. Trotsky denied the allegation on behalf of the Soviet.

## 18 and 19 October/31 October and 1 November

In letters to party members and to the Central Committee, Lenin accused Zinoviev and Kamenev of strike-breaking and treachery for revealing the party's plans for insurrection: he demanded their expulsion from the party.

## 20 October/2 November

The Military Revolutionary Committee was officially constituted by the Soviet. Boycotted by the Mensheviks, it consisted almost entirely of Bolsheviks and Left SRs, the latter included largely for the purpose of camouflage. It appointed commissars, chosen largely from the Bolsheviks' Military Organisation, to units of the garrison and to key arms and communications facilities with a view to gaining control over them.

## 21–22 October/3–4 November

The three commissars appointed by the Military Revolutionary Committee to district headquarters called on the garrison commander, Colonel Polkovnikov, and told him that his orders were to become effective only if countersigned by one of the three of them. Polkovnikov refused to recognise the commissars' authority. The Military Revolutionary Committee called an emergency conference of the regimental committees as a result of which it decided to issue a proclamation denouncing district headquarters as an instrument of the counter-revolutionary forces and reaffirming that no orders to the garrison which were not signed by the committee were valid.

## 22 October/4 November

'The Day of the Petrograd Soviet'. The bolshevik press summoned a massive, non-violent demonstration of support for the Soviet to give the many thousands involved confidence that the government was powerless to oppose them as it had succeeded in doing during the 'July Days'.

## 23 October/5 November

The commandant of the strategically vital fortress of Peter and Paul and its adjoining Kronwerk arsenal having refused to recognise the authority of the Military Revolutionary Committee's commissar appointed to the fortress, Trotsky addressed the troops there and persuaded them to throw in their lot with the Military Revolutionary Committee.

The staff of the Petrograd military district agreed to accept Soviet countersigning of its orders on condition that the Military Revolutionary Committee cancelled the order describing the staff as counter-revolutionary. The committee agreed 'in principle' while in fact pressing ahead with plans for an insurrection.

The government decided to close the bolshevik press, to rearrest the bolshevik leaders who had been arrested after the 'July Days' and subsequently released and to take proceedings against the Military Revolutionary Committee.

According to the GSE, bolshevik party membership on the eve of the October/November revolution had risen to 350,000.

## 24 October/6 November

In the early morning government troops raided and closed the bolshevik printing-works. The cruiser *Aurora*, moored in the River Neva near the centre of Petrograd, was ordered to put to sea.

Within hours, the Bolsheviks recovered their printing-works and restarted publication of their newspapers. The orders to the *Aurora* were successfully countermanded by the Military Revolutionary Committee.

Around noon Kerensky informed the Pre-Parliament that Petrograd was in a state of insurrection. He sought, but did not receive, unqualified support from the Pre-Parliament in dealing with the situation. Martov's group of Menshevik-Internationalists and some SRs took the view that the insurrection could not and should not be suppressed by force. In the evening, their resolution having been passed by the Pre-Parliament, they tried but failed to persuade Kerensky that the government should meet the insurrection by announcing at once that it was seeking allied agreement to peace negotiations, that ownership of private land was being transferred to the local land committees and that convocation of the Constituent Assembly was being brought forward. The Left SRs in the Pre-Parliament agreed to join forces with the Military Revolutionary Committee.

In a speech to the Petrograd Soviet at about 7 p.m., Trotsky continued to camouflage the Bolsheviks' intended seizure of power by speaking in terms of defending the revolution against the government rather than taking direct action to overthrow it.

## 24–25 October/6–7 November

In the course of the night and early morning, Red Guards and elements of the garrison loyal to the Military Revolutionary Committee occupied the railway stations, the central telephone exchange, the central telegraph office, the State Bank and various public utilities and · printing-works, all without violence. Government attempts to close the bridges in the capital were mainly unsuccessful.

Three Cossack regiments failed to carry out orders issued by the Petrograd military district headquarters on Kerensky's behalf to turn out in defence of the Soviets and the Provisional Government.

A joint session of the Central Executive Committees of the Soviets of Workers' and Soldiers' Deputies and of the Soviets of Peasants' Deputies adopted a resolution condeming the bolshevik insurrection and calling on the government to take immediate action on peace and land reform.

## 25 October/7 November

Sailors from the *Aurora* chased away the army cadets under government orders who were guarding one of the bridges between the working-class district of the capital and the centre.

At 10 a.m. the Military Revolutionary Committee, on behalf of the Petrograd Soviet, announced that the Provisional Government had been overthrown and that power had passed into its hands.

At about 11.30 a.m. Kerensky left the capital for the front in the hope of returning at the head of loyal units willing to defend the regime.

Shortly after 1 p.m. the Pre-Parliament's building was surrounded and its members were obliged to leave.

The Petrograd Soviet assembled at 2.35 p.m. At abut 3 p.m. Lenin addressed the Soviet. He announced that the workers' and peasants' revolution had occurred and called for an immediate peace with the Germans, the abolition of private ownership of land, workers' control of production and world socialist revolution.

At 7.40 p.m. Petrograd military district headquarters, finding itself without troops, surrendered to the Revolutionary Military Committee.

At 8.30 p.m. the Provisional Government in the Winter Palace received an ultimatum from the Petrograd Soviet to surrender or face bombardment, in particular by the cruiser *Aurora*. This began the so-called siege of the Winter Palace, which had been delayed by the late arrival of sailors ordered up from Kronstadt by the Military Revolutionary Committee.

At 10 p.m. General Cheremisov, commander of the northern front, countermanded all Provisional Government orders for troops to move to the capital from his front.

In Moscow the Soviet approved a bolshevik motion to form a Military Revolutionary Committee. In opposition to this, the Moscow City Duma set up a Committee of Public Safety.

In the Don region General Kaledin, who had been elected *ataman* (leader) of the Don Cossacks in June, announced that a Cossack government had temporarily assumed power until order and the Provisional Government had been restored. An All-Cossack Congress in Kiev denounced the Bolsheviks. Similar declarations were made by Dutov, Karaulov and Filimonov, the *atamans* of the Orenburg, Terek and Kuban Cossacks.

In Petrograd the Second All-Russian Congress of Soviets opened at 10.40 p.m. Of about 650 voting delegates, about 390 were Bolsheviks, eighty were Mensheviks, and between 160 and 190 SRs of whom 60 per cent were Left SRs. Fourteen Bolsheviks and seven Left SRs were elected to the presidium and Kamenev took the chair. The three questions on the agenda were the formation of a government, the subject of war and peace and the convocation of a Constituent Assembly. After a stormy debate, the moderate socialists and the peasants' deputies walked out in protest at the seizure of power by the Military Revolutionary Committee, leaving the floor to the Bolsheviks and their sympathisers, mainly the Left SRs. This marked the final break between the Left SRs and the bulk of the SR party.

## 26 October/8 November

The siege of the Winter Palace, which had cost no more than a handful of casualties on either side, concluded at 2 a.m. with the arrest of the ministers of the Provisional Government (excluding Kerensky) by Antonov-Ovseenko and other Bolsheviks.

At about 5 a.m. at the Congress of Soviets, the Bolshevik Lunacharskii read a proclamation written by Lenin stating that the authority of the existing Soviet Central Executive Committee was at an end, that the Provisional Government was deposed and that the congress had assumed power. The proclamation was approved, with minor amendments, by an overwhelming majority, the congress setting itself a programme of immediate armistice, a democratic peace, transfer of all land without compensation to peasant committees, democratisation of the army, workers' control over industry, convocation of the Constituent Assembly, organisation of the bread supply, application of the right of self-determination to all nationalities in Russia and the transfer of all local authority to Soviets of Workers', Soldiers' and Peasants' Deputies. The congress appealed to the soldiers to resist Kerensky and to the railwaymen to prevent troop movements against Petrograd.

A Committee for the Salvation of the Country and the Revolution was formed by members of the Petrograd Duma, the old Central Executive Committee of the Soviets, the Pre-Parliament, the Kadets, the moderate socialist parties, co-operatives, trade unions, etc. in opposition to the Bolsheviks. Affiliated committees were set up in Moscow and elsewhere.

In the course of this and the following day, a number of centre and right-wing newspapers were closed down by the Military Revolutionary Committee.

In Moscow a conference of the garrison voted in favour of the seizure of power by the Soviets. Troops of the Military Revolutionary Committee occupied the arsenal and the Kremlin.

The Congress of Soviets reassembled in Petrograd at 9 p.m. Lenin read a proclamation to the peoples and governments at war proposing an immediate peace without annexations or indemnities, the abolition of secret diplomacy and the publication of secret treaties between the Tsarist government and its allies (see 9/22 November). Peace was to be negotiated in the course of a three-month armistice. The workers of Britain, France and Germany were urged to take decisive action to secure peace and put an end to slavery and exploitation. The proclamation was approved unanimously.

Lenin then read out a short Decree on Land. This abolished the landlords' right to own land immediately and without compensation. Landlords' estates and crown, monastery and church land, together with the associated buildings, machinery and livestock, were to be held, until the meeting of the Constituent Assembly, by the Land Committees in the towns and by the Soviets of Peasants' Deputies in the countryside. Attached to the decree was a much longer resolution, drafted largely by SRs and originally published by the All-Russian Soviet of Peasants' Deputies on 19 August/1 September. This was to serve as guidance in carrying out the land reform. In outline, the resolution

•• prohibited the purchase, sale or leasing of land; nationalised all major mineral resources, forests and water resources;

•• protected from confiscation land held by small peasants and Cossacks;

•• conferred the right to use land on those who wished to cultivate it

with their own or their families' labour or in co-operative groups;
- ●●prohibited the use of hired labour;
- ●●decreed that land should be distributed by local authorities in accordance with local conditions on an equal basis between those who worked on it; and
- ●●provided for the transfer by the state of surplus population from areas of land shortage.

(As Lenin himself admitted, this resolution was not wholly in accordance with bolshevik ideology, but, together with the proclamation on peace, it served very well to gain support for the Bolsheviks from the peasants including the millions still under arms. Given persistent rural over-population, the practical effect of the measure on average landholdings during the next three years was, according to the Commissar for Agriculture, less than expected, amounting in the large majority of cases to a *per capita* increase of less than an acre.)

## 27 October/9 November

The Congress of Soviets approved the nomination of a team composed exclusively of Bolsheviks to form a Council of People's Commissars (*Sovnarkom*) or government responsible to the Congress of Soviets and its Central Executive Committee. The members were Lenin – its President, Rykov – internal affairs, Miliutin – agriculture, Shliapnikov – labour, Nogin – trade and industry, Lunacharskii – education, Skvortsov (replaced by Menzhinskii after two days) – finance, Trotsky – foreign affairs, Lomov – justice, Teodorovich – supply (mainly of food), Avilov – posts and telegraphs, and

Stalin – nationality affairs. Military and naval affairs were given to a committee consisting of Antonov-Ovseenko, Krylenko and Dybenko. Transport was left open pending negotiations with the politically moderate railway trade union.

A new Soviet Central Executive Committee of about 110 members, including sixty-one Bolsheviks and twenty-nine Left SRs, was elected with Kamenev as president. Zinoviev was given the editorship of the Soviet's official organ, *Izvestiia*.

The session of the congress closed at 5.15 a.m.

The Council of People's Commissars passed a decree closing all newspapers which called for open opposition or disobedience to the Provisional Workers' and Peasants' Government. The measure was described as temporary pending the restoration of normal conditions. Hostile papers continued to appear after the decree.

There was widespread non-co-operation with the new government on the part of government officials in line with a proclamation by the Committee of Salvation urging disobedience. The Union of Unions of State Employees of Petrograd declared a strike which continued until the dissolution of the Constituent Assembly in January but was gradually broken, in part by the government's increasing control over the banking system. In Petrograd most teachers struck until 5/18 January 1918 and in Moscow until March 1918. The strikes were one of the factors which led to the creation of the Cheka on 7/20 December and the inclusion of the word 'sabotage' in its title.

In Moscow fighting broke out

between troops of the Military Revolutionary Committee and officers and cadets of the Committee of Public Safety. The fighting continued for a week.

## 28 October/10 November

A decree called for the organisation of workers' militias by all workers' and soldiers' Soviets.

In Moscow the Military Revolutionary Committee's troops occupying the Kremlin surrendered to the officers and cadets under the orders of the Committee of Public Safety by whom they were surrounded.

The All-Russian Executive Committee of Peasants' Soviets condemned the seizure of power by the Bolsheviks and the Petrograd Soviet.

## 29 October/11 November

A force of 700 Cossacks under General Krasnov, who had linked up with Kerensky in Pskov, occupied Tsarskoe Selo during the morning, meeting little resistance.

In the course of the preceding night in Petrograd, cadets under Colonel Polkovnikov, instigated by the Committee for Salvation, had seized the State Bank and the central telephone exchange and captured Antonov-Ovseenko. Fighting during the day caused a total of about 200 casualties before the cadets surrendered. Their action had been intended to coincide with the arrival in Petrograd of Kerensky and Krasnov's Cossacks but the Cossacks had spent the whole of 29 October/11 November in Tsarskoe Selo and the rising was in any case precipitated by a warning that the Bolsheviks were about to disarm the cadets.

The railway workers' union threatened a railway strike if a government embracing all socialist groups was not formed.

A Council of People's Commissars decree established a maximum working day of eight hours and a working week of forty-eight hours.

## 30 October/12 November

Krasnov's Cossacks retired towards Gatchina from the Pulkovo Heights outside the capital in the face of superior Red forces.

By decree the Council of People's Commissars conferred legislative powers on itself until the convocation of the Constituent Assembly; the Soviet Central Executive Committee was given the right to 'defer, modify or annul' enactments of the Council but this was negated in practice by the Council's right to issue urgent decrees without submitting them to the Soviet Central Executive Committee.

## 1 November/14 November

Faced with his failure to muster any substantial force and narrowly escaping arrest by the Bolsheviks, Kerensky went into hiding.

General Dukhonin, Kerensky's chief of staff, abandoned attempts to move troops to Petrograd.

## 2 November/15 November

His Cossacks having reached an agreement with the Bolsheviks, Krasnov was arrested and taken to Petrograd but was released shortly afterwards.

At a meeting of the party's Central Committee, a resolution drafted by Lenin attacking the 'vacillators' (including Kamenev and Zinoviev) who had been advocating a coalition government including other Soviet parties (principally the SRs and Mensheviks) was carried by ten votes to five.

In Moscow the Committee of Public Safety conceded victory to the Military Revolutionary Committee and ceased to exist. In the week's fighting, the Red forces had lost about 500 dead.

Elsewhere in Russia there was wide variation in the speed of the bolshevik take-over.

A Declaration of the Rights of the Peoples of Russia, signed by Lenin and Stalin, proclaimed the equality and sovereignty of the peoples of Russia and the right to free self-determination of peoples even to the point of separating and forming independent states.

## 4 November/17 November

The Soviet Central Executive Committee passed a bolshevik resolution to confiscate all private printing-presses and stocks of paper. At the end of the discussion of this resolution, Rykov, Nogin, Miliutin and Teodorovich resigned from the Council of People's Commissars in protest against Lenin's refusal to form a coalition government with the socialist parties represented in the Soviet: they said that a purely bolshevik government would alienate the masses and could only sustain itself by the use of terror. Shliapnikov agreed with their views but did not think it right to resign. Rykov, Nogin and Miliutin, together with Zinoviev and Kamenev, also resigned from the bolshevik Central Committee. Kamenev and others were prepared to contemplate a coalition govern-

ment from which Lenin and Trotsky would be excluded. In due course all who resigned returned to senior government or party posts. The Left SRs withdrew from the Military Revolutionary Committee.

## 6–15 November/19–28 November

The Left SRs held their first independent conference.

## 7 November/20 November

A state monopoly of advertising was decreed as a means of further curbing the hostile press.

The Ukrainian *Rada* issued its third 'Universal' proclaiming the Ukraine a People's Republic which would form part of a Russian federation. The *Rada* declared itself the sole authority in the Ukraine until the convocation of the Constituent Assembly.

## 8 November/21 November

Dukhonin received an order from the bolshevik government to propose an armistice with the Germans.

Trotsky addressed a note to the allied ambassadors, informing them of the establishment of the Council of People's Commissars as the new government of Russia and the appointment of himself as Commissar for Foreign Affairs. He requested the ambassadors to treat the peace declaration of 26 October/8 November as a formal proposal for an immediate armistice on all fronts.

## 9 November/22 November

Dukhonin refused to carry out the order received by him on the previous day on the grounds that the government was not recognised by the army and the people. He was dismissed and Krylenko was appointed commander-in-chief.

Publication of the secret treaties began in *Izvestiia* with an article 'Secret Diplomacy and the Palestinian Problem'.

*Note:* Among the treaties were the Constantinople Agreement of 18 March 1915 between Britain, France and Russia concerning the future of Constantinople, the Black Sea straits and Persia, the Secret Treaty of London of 26 April 1915 between Britain, France, Italy and Russia which dealt with Italian territorial demands on Austria-Hungary and under which Italy entered the war and the Sykes-Picot Agreement of 16 May 1916 relating mainly to the Arab regions of the Ottoman Empire.

## 10 November/23 November

The British, Romanian, Italian, Japanese, French and Serbian military missions at Mogilev, acting on instructions from their governments, reminded Dukhonin of Russia's treaty obligation not to conclude a separate armistice or peace treaty with the Germans. The Americans followed up with a similar communication on 14/27 November.

A decree on the gradual demobilisation of the army aimed to avoid dislocation of transport and precipitate weakening of the front.

## 11 November/24 November

A decree abolished Tsarist civil ranks, such as privy councillor, and class distinctions and privileges as between nobility, merchants, com-moners and peasantry and created a single legal category of citizens of the Russian Republic.

## 11–15 November/24–28 November

An interim government known as the Transcaucasian Commissariat was formed in Tiflis by a group of Georgians, Armenians and Azerbaijanis representing the non-bolshevik Left. Elections were held throughout Transcaucasia from 26 to 28 November/9 to 11 December. The Constituent Assembly met from 5 to 6/18 to 19 January 1918 but bolshevik opposition, mainly from Baku, prevented further sessions. An assembly or *seim* was then constituted and met for the first time on 23 February 1918.

## 12 November/25 November

Voting began in Petrograd on the date fixed by the Provisional Government for elections to the Constituent Assembly under a system of universal suffrage. The Kadets in particular suffered from suppression of their newspapers and the arrest of their leaders. The partial nation-wide results quoted by Chamberlin, which Lenin accepted, gave the Bolsheviks about 25 per cent of the total vote, the SRs and moderate socialists about 62 per cent and the conservative and liberal parties, including the Kadets, about 13 per cent. The Bolsheviks, however, had majorities in the strategic key points of Petrograd, Moscow, the northern and western fronts and the Baltic fleet. In the bolshevik-dominated regions of Latvia unoccupied by the Germans, the Bolsheviks polled 72 per cent of the votes.

## 13–14 November/26–27 November

Three Soviet emissaries made initial contact with the German army near Dvinsk and proposed an armistice. It was agreed that talks should take place at German headquarters at Brest-Litovsk.

## 14 November/27 November

At a Left SR-dominated Peasants' Congress, an agreement was reached between the Bolsheviks and the Left SRs under which the Peasants' Congress elected 108 delegates to the Soviet Central Executive Committee. Thenceforward this body officially represented the peasants as well as the workers and soldiers.

The government issued a decree on workers' control over all enterprises employing hired labour or giving out work at home. Enterprises were to elect factory committees or other representative bodies which would send delegates to councils of workers' control in all large cities. An All-Russian Council of Workers' Control was to be established in Petrograd. Owners of enterprises were obliged to submit all accounts and correspondence to the committees and to accept their decisions subject to a right of appeal within three days to a higher-level committee of workers' control.

Workers' committees had sprung up in many factories in the wake of the February/March revolution and had been recognised by the Provisional Government. They were welcomed by Lenin and the Bolsheviks who used them for their revolutionary purposes. At the same time Lenin recognised their anarchic and syndicalist tendencies. After the revolution their influence proved largely destructive and resulted in much industrial chaos and severe losses in production. The decree of 14/27 November was described by Carr as a dead letter: it is doubtful if the All-Russian Council of Workers' Control ever met.

## 15 November/28 November

Krylenko ordered an immediate cease-fire and fraternisation on all fronts.

A few minutes before being dissolved in the course of a bolshevik take-over, the Estonian National Council proclaimed Estonia independent.

## 18 November/1 December

The allied military missions left Mogilev for Kiev.

During the night Kornilov, Denikin and three other generals were unofficially released from imprisonment near Mogilev by Dukhonin and made their way to Novocherkassk near Rostov in the Don basin which General Alekseev, the former commander-in-chief, had reached on 2/15 November. Alekseev was in the early stages of forming what became the Volunteer Army with less than whole-hearted support from the divided and ill-disciplined Don Cossacks under General Kaledin.

A decree was issued setting severe limits on the salaries of commissars and senior officials.

## 19 November/2 December

A Russian peace delegation led by the Bolshevik, Ioffe, had its first meeting with the German High Command at Brest-Litovsk. The allies had ignored Trotsky's invitation to participate in the negotiations.

## 20 November/3 December

Krylenko, who had left Petrograd on 10/23 November with a posse of sailors and had taken over control of army headquarters in Pskov and Dvinsk, arrived at Mogilev where he encountered no resistance. Dukhonin was taken prisoner and, despite orders to the contrary from Krylenko, was lynched by a mob.

In a telegraphic report to the Kaiser, the German Foreign Ministry liaison officer defined the purpose of the subversive activity which the Germans had carried out behind the front in Russia as the removal of what appeared to be the weakest link in the allied chain, namely Russia. He continued: 'It was not until the Bolsheviks had received from us a steady flow of funds through various channels and under different labels that they were . . . able to build up their main organ, *Pravda*, to conduct energetic propaganda and extend the originally narrow basis of their party. . . . It is in our interests to exploit the period while [the Bolsheviks] are in power . . . to attain . . . an armistice and then if possible peace . . . [which] would mean the achievement of the desired war aim, namely a breach between Russia and her allies. Once cast off by [them], Russia will be forced to seek our support . . . and our aid . . . could bring about a *rapprochement* between the two countries.' The Kaiser agreed.

## 22 November/5 December

A provisional cease-fire until 17/30 December was signed between the armies of Russia and the Central Powers (Germany, Austria-Hungary, Bulgaria and Turkey).

The armistice negotiations were then interrupted for a week to allow the Soviet delegation to return to Petrograd for consultation on whether they should sign a separate armistice. Meanwhile the distribution of Bolshevik propaganda to the German armed forces was stepped up. The Soviet delegation used delaying tactics throughout the ensuing peace negotiations to give their propaganda time to make its impact.

A Council of People's Commissars' decree abolished the existing system of courts and introduced local courts (later known as People's Courts) to deal with civil and criminal cases and Revolutionary Tribunals of Workers and Peasants consisting of a chairman and six jurors or assessors to deal with counter-revolutionary acts against the state. According to an instruction dated 19 December 1917/1 January 1918, these acts included insurrection, active opposition or disobedience to the workers' and peasants' government or incitement to such opposition or disobedience, misuse of public office to hamper the work of the public service or concealment of property documents, stopping or curtailing the production of articles of general use without good reason and violations of the decrees and orders of the government. In People's Courts, trials were to be conducted by one professional and two lay assessors. They were to be guided in their judgments by the laws of the deposed government only in so far as those laws had not been annulled by the revolution and did not contradict the revolutionary conception of right.

*Pravda* published an 'Appeal to the Working Muslims of Russia and the East', drafted by Stalin and signed by Lenin, promising them national, religious and cultural freedom. It reaffirmed that the secret treaties were null and void, that Constantinople would remain in Muslim hands and that troops would be withdrawn from Persia which would be free to determine its own destiny as would Armenia. Indian Muslims and Hindus were encouraged to throw off the imperialist yoke and all Muslims were enjoined to defend the revolution and the building of a new world.

## 23 November/6 December

The right to own large houses was abolished. Ownership was transferred to local authorities.

The Finnish Diet proclaimed Finnish independence of Russia. (Finland had been a province of Sweden until conquered by Russia in 1809.)

## 25 November/8 December

The Military Revolutionary Committee declared that state and public officials who went on strike were enemies of the people.

## 26 November/9 December

A proclamation by the Council of People's Commissars denounced as counter-revolutionaries Kaledin, *ataman* of the Don Cossacks, Dutov, *ataman* of the Orenburg Cossacks, Kornilov, the Kadets and the Ukrainian *Rada*. The Don, Ural and other areas were declared to be in a state

of war. Dutov's seizure of Orenburg was significant in that it interrupted direct communications between the capital and the non-Muslim, Bolshevik and Left SR-dominated Turkestan Soviet which had established itself in Tashkent a week or so before the October/November revolution.

An All-Muslim Congress in Kokand, in opposition to the exclusively Russian Tashkent Soviet, declared Turkestan autonomous and established a Muslim government in Kokand.

The Third All-Kirghiz (Kazakh) Congress in Orenburg in December proclaimed an autonomous Kazakh region. Although various cities such as Orenburg, Semipalatinsk and Alma-Ata were occupied by the Bolsheviks between January and March 1918, by the summer they had been driven out of virtually all the Kazakh steppe by the Ural and Orenburg Cossacks.

## 26–27 November/9–10 December

With the help of sailors from the Black Sea fleet, a Revolutionary Military Committee took control of Rostov, the principal city of the Don basin.

## 27 November/10 December

Bukharin became editor of *Pravda*, a post which he held with one interruption from February to July 1918, for twelve years.

## 28 November/11 December

An attempt was made to convene the Constituent Assembly on the date originally fixed by the Provisional Government. In consequence the

Council of People's Commissars issued a decree for the arrest of the leading Kadets. Among those arrested were Shingarev and Kokoshkin who were murdered in hospital by a group of Kronstadt sailors during the night of 6/19–7/20 January 1918 after the closure of the Constituent Assembly to which the two Kadets had been elected.

Lithuania declared itself independent but in terms which provided for a virtual German protectorate over it.

## 30 November/13 December

Lenin gave Antonov-Ovseenko command of operations against General Kaledin in the Don basin. Murav'ev, a Left SR, was put in charge of the drive against Kiev.

## 1 December/14 December

A decree setting up the Supreme Council of National Economy (VSNKh or *Vesenkha*) described its function as the organisation of the economic activity of the nation and the financial resources of the state. It was given powers to confiscate, requisition, sequester or consolidate various branches of production or commerce but it used these powers sparingly during the first few weeks, wholesale nationalisation of industry not having been part of the original bolshevik programme. The council absorbed and superseded the All-Russian Council of Workers' Control and devoted the main thrust of its activity towards centralising control over the industrial sector of the economy.

The Provisional Revolutionary Committee, which had taken over general staff headquarters at Mogi-

lev, issued an order making officers elective and abolishing titles and epaulettes. The stream of land-hungry peasant soldiers returning to their villages from the front had by this time developed into a flood.

## 2 December/15 December

The Soviet–German armistice agreement was signed in Brest-Litovsk. The armistice was to last until 1/14 January unless either side gave seven days' notice. Organised fraternisation and the exchange of newspapers between members of the opposing armies were permitted, concessions of which the Soviet side were quick to take advantage.

Despite the refusal of most of the Don Cossacks to fight, troops of the Volunteer Army regained control of Rostov.

## 4 December/17 December

The Soviet government issued an ultimatum to the Ukrainian *Rada* demanding that it desist both from disarming Soviet troops in the Ukraine and from permitting free passage to armed forces seeking to join General Kaledin in the Don territory. The ultimatum was rejected on 6–7/19–20 December.

## 5 December/18 December

The Military Revolutionary Committee, which had functioned as an interim administrative body while the new people's commissariats were being formed and had been particularly active in combating counter-revolution, profiteering and strike activity (described as sabotage), was dissolved.

**1917**

## 6 December/19 December

Kornilov arrived at Novocherkassk. His arrival caused complications over the command of the Volunteer Army. It was eventually agreed that Kornilov should take over command, leaving Alekseev in charge of political and financial matters and Kaledin in charge of internal affairs in the Don region. An attempt was made to re-form a provisional government around the three generals consisting of representatives of the Kadets, the Cossacks, the SRs and various interest groups. According to Carley, among other credits made available by the French government for political action in the Ukraine, Romania and southern Russia was one for 100 million francs to Alekseev.

## 7 December/20 December

The VCHEKA (All-Russian Extraordinary Commission for Combating Counter-Revolution and Sabotage, usually known as the Cheka), was set up by a resolution of the Council of People's Commissars as a political police and security service responsible to the Council of People's Commissars and under the leadership of the Polish Bolshevik, Dzerzhinskii. The words 'Speculation' and 'Misconduct in Office' were later added to its title.

## 9 December/22 December

Three Left SRs joined the government as commissars for agriculture, justice and posts and telegraphs.

The first session of the peace conference took place at Brest-Litovsk.

Romanian troops entered Bessarabia.

## 10 December/23 December

The military representatives of the allied Supreme War Council passed a resolution recommending that all national groups in Russia which were determined to continue the war with Germany should be supported by all available means. At this time the outcome of the war on the western front was completely uncertain; there was nothing to indicate the likelihood of a German collapse as early as the autumn of 1918. Although Carley found that, in the French case, the desire to recoup some of the losses inflicted on French capital by the revolution and the determination to protect long-term French political and economic interests in Russia had an important bearing on French policy on intervention, the requirements of the war effort were the principal determinant of allied policy as a whole. The allies' main aims in Russia at this stage were to dissuade the Germans from transferring further troops to the western front by creating some form of revived front in the east and to deny to the Germans the economic resources of Russia including Siberia. Subsidiary motives were the desire to maintain contact with all anti-German elements in Russia, to deny to the Germans the possibility of building submarine bases on the Russian Arctic coast, to deny to the Germans the allied war stores which had accumulated in north Russia and Vladivostok, to protect and use in the allied cause the Czechoslovak troops in Russia and to regenerate the Russian economy. Further arguments used in the British War Office in relation to intervention in Siberia were that it was the only area in which the Japanese army could be deployed on behalf of the allies and, perhaps, a suitable area for US deployment if the unsolved problem of German submarine activity in the Atlantic should prevent US military strength from being fully brought to bear in Europe. It was considered undesirable, particularly by the Americans, that the Japanese should be allowed to intervene alone in the Far East.

An Anglo-French convention was signed under which the British were to direct military activities against the Germans and their allies in the Cossack territories, the Caucasus, Armenia, Georgia and Kurdistan, while the French were to do the same in Bessarabia, the Ukraine and the Crimea.

## 11 December/24 December

The Commissariat of Education took over control of ecclesiastical seminaries and other church schools.

The Ukrainian *Rada* addressed a note to all relevant belligerent and neutral powers complaining that it had not been consulted about the armistice of 2/15 December and declaring that it would not necessarily be bound by any peace treaty between the Soviet government and the Central Powers. On 13/26 December the latter invited the *Rada* to send a separate peace delegation to Brest-Litovsk.

## 13 December/26 December

The Council of People's Commissars allotted 2 million rubles to the representatives abroad of the Commissariat for Foreign Affairs to support the left, internationalist wing of the working-class movement in all countries whether at war or in alliance with Russia or neutral.

## 14 December/27 December

The government declared a state monopoly of banking and used its armed forces to take physical control of all private banks in Petrograd. The Moscow banks were occupied on the following day. The banks were then nationalised and fused with the State Bank which had been occupied by troops since 7/20 November. The state took over private gold holdings. Banks of the co-operatives, such as the Moscow Narodny Bank, were exempted from these measures.

## 15 December/28 December

The peace negotiations in Brest-Litovsk were suspended until 27 December/9 January 1918.

## 16 December/29 December

The government recognised the Ukrainian Soviet government which, in opposition to the *Rada*, had announced its formation on 14/27 November in Kharkov in the eastern Ukraine where Antonov-Ovseenko had established his headquarters.

The Commissariat of Justice decreed that the Cheka should have power to arrest.

German economic and naval missions arrived in Petrograd to discuss exchanges of prisoners and other matters. They left on 18 February 1918.

## 16 and 17 December/29 and 30 December

Decrees of the Council of People's Commissars declared that the army was subordinate to the Council of People's Commissars, that full power in every military unit belonged to the relevant soldiers' committee and that commanders up to regimental level were to be elected by ballots in their units and, above that level, by conferences of delegates from the relevant committees. All ranks and titles from corporal to general inclusive and all privileges and badges of rank were abolished as were saluting, decorations, officers' organisations and orderlies.

## 18 December/31 December

The Soviet government recognised the independence of Finland.

A decree established a Revolutionary Tribunal on the Press to try cases of misuse of the press, such offences being punishable by fines or closure of the offending newspaper.

On this and the following day, decrees were issued giving men and women equal rights, recognising civil marriages only, granting full rights to illegitimate children and providing for divorce on demand by either party.

# 1918

## 19 December 1917/1 January 1918

Party membership was given as 115,000 by Bubnov in the GSE, first edition, but *Partiinaia Zhizn* in 1967 gave a revised total of 390,000 in March 1918. Figures for the civil war period are no more than approximations.

## 26 December 1917/8 January 1918

Reacting in part to the peace talks in Brest-Litovsk, President Wilson, in an address to Congress, enunciated the 'fourteen points' of his programme for peace.

## 27 December 1917/9 January 1918

The peace talks at Brest-Litovsk were resumed with Trotsky leading the Soviet delegation.

A proclamation setting out the aims of the Volunteer Army brought little response in the shape of volunteers. Many of the younger Don Cossacks who had served at the front had become radicalised and supported the Bolsheviks.

## 28 December 1917/10 January 1918

In a drive against the Ukrainian *Rada*, bolshevik forces which had set out from Kharkov captured Ekaterinoslav.

## 29 December 1917/11 January 1918

A decree stopped payment of interest or dividends on bonds or shares and prohibited dealings in them.

## 30 December 1917/12 January 1918

Latvia proclaimed its independence.

In response to growing allied concern over the situation in Vladivostok, the Pacific terminal of the Trans-Siberian and Chinese Eastern railways, a Japanese warship, the *Iwami*, arrived off Vladivostok, followed by a British warship, HMS *Suffolk* on 1/14 January and another Japanese warship, the *Asahi* on 5/18 January. The reasons for concern were the growth of bolshevik influence in Vladivostok and the possibility that the 648,000 tons of allied war supplies, which had been provided to the Tsarist government and had accumulated there, might be shipped westwards by the Bolsheviks and fall into the hands of the Germans and their allies with or without the help of the 800,000-odd Austro-Hungarian and German prisoners of war virtually at large in Siberia.

## 31 December 1917/13 January 1918

Diamandi, the Romanian ambassador in Petrograd, was arrested in reprisal for the disarming of some Russian troops in Romania. He was released the following day after energetic protests by the diplomatic corps.

## 1 January/14 January

A Soviet note to Persia repudiated the Anglo-Russian Convention of 1907 which had divided Persia into Russian and British spheres of interest and promised to help the Persians expel Turkish and British troops from their country.

Lenin was shot at but was shielded by the Swiss communist Platten who received a bullet in the hand.

## 3 January/16 January

The Soviet Central Executive Committee adopted the 'Declaration of the Rights of the Toiling and Exploited People' as its submission to the Constituent Assembly. The declaration said that Russia was a Republic of Soviets of Workers', Soldiers' and Peasants' Deputies to whom all power in the centre and the localities belonged. The Soviet Russian Republic was a federation of Soviet national republics established on the basis of a free union of free peoples. Describing the victory of socialism in all countries as the fundamental task, the declaration endorsed measures which had already been taken on land, workers' control, banks and the formation of a Supreme Council of National Economy. It foreshadowed the cancellation of state loans and spoke of a 'general liability to labour service' and the 'organisation of a socialist Red Army of Workers and Peasants'. (This was intended to be a new sort of army based on the volunteer system and 'mutual comradely respect'.) The declaration called for the tearing-up of secret treaties and the achievement of peace without annexations or indemnities on the basis of national self-determination. It condemned imperialism in Asia, the colonies and other small countries and endorsed the independence of Finland, the withdrawal of troops from Persia and self-determination for Armenia. It approved the repudiation of the Tsarist government's debts. It declared that it would be wrong for the Constituent Assembly to set itself up in opposition to the Soviets, that the government belonged wholly to the representatives in the Soviets of the toiling masses and that the Constituent Assembly had no powers beyond working out some of the fundamental problems of reorganising society on a socialist basis and formulating the principles of a federation of the Soviet Republics of Russia, leaving it to each nation to decide whether and on what conditions to enter the federation.

## 5 January/18 January

The Constituent Assembly met, the SRs having already decided against using such armed force as they could still command in a demonstration in defence of the Assembly. Out of an incomplete list of 707 members, 370 were Right SRs, forty Left SRs, 175 Bolsheviks, sixteen Mensheviks, seventeen Kadets, two Socialist-Populists and the rest undetermined.

When the assembly refused by 237 votes to 136 to accept the 'Declaration of the Rights of the Toiling and Exploited People', the bolshevik delegates, followed by the Left SRs, withdrew and did not return.

## 6 January/19 January

The Bolsheviks forcibly prevented delegates to the Constituent Assembly from meeting and on 7/20 January the Soviet Central Executive Committee endorsed a Council of People's Commissars' decree declaring the assembly dissolved.

## 7 January/20 January

Trotsky arrived in Petrograd from Brest-Litovsk to seek further instructions on the peace negotiations which had been broken off two days earlier when the German General Hoffmann had indicated the line behind which the German army would not withdraw. Opinion in the bolshevik party was divided into three groups: those led by Bukharin who wished to pursue a 'revolutionary war' aimed at unseating the German and other governments in the immediate future; those led by Lenin who thought that in order to win a breathing space for the bolshevik regime, even an unfavourable peace with the Germans should be signed; and those who agreed with Trotsky that the Russians should discontinue the war but refuse to sign an 'annexationist' peace treaty.

## 7–14 January/20–27 January

The First All-Russian Congress of Trade Unions met. Bolshevik delegates were in the majority. Trade unions had developed since the February/March revolution largely under menshevik and SR control and in opposition to the more radical workers' or factory committees. Thus in 1918 they became natural allies of the economic organs of the state working for a restoration of order in industry. In addition they were given responsibility for administering social insurance measures decreed during the previous month. The main congress resolution, passed in spite of considerable opposition from some Bolsheviks as well as socialists, envisaged the trade unions becoming 'instruments of state authority'. Another resolution recorded a decision that factory committees should become local organs of the trade unions and subordinate to them.

A bolshevik majority was elected to the new All-Russian Central Council of Trade Unions.

## 8 January/21 January

A significant number of Left SRs joined the Cheka up to the level of deputy chairman.

Local incidents in Vyborg (Viipuri) and elsewhere led to the outbreak of civil war in Finland. Baron General Carl Gustav von Mannerheim, a native of Finland who had served for thirty years in the Russian army, soon gained control over the north of the country. With his 'White' Finnish army, supplied with German arms from 17 February onwards, he set about eliminating local pockets of Finnish Red Guards and the demoralised and undisciplined units of the 40,000-strong Russian army still in Finland. Meanwhile, Finnish Red Guards, with some assistance from the bolshevised minority of the Russian army in Finland, seized Helsingfors on 14–15/27–28 January and later extended their control to most of the industrial centres in the south with encouragement and arms supplies from the Soviet government.

## 8–29 January/21 January–11 February

The intensely anti-bourgeois Symbolist poet, Aleksandr Blok, wrote his poem *The Twelve* celebrating, not without irony and ambiguity, the cataclysmic nature of the revolution. The poem was published in the Left SR journal *Znamia Truda* on 3 March.

## 9 January/22 January

By nine votes to seven, the bolshevik Central Committee voted to adopt Trotsky's line on the peace negotiations, and by twelve votes to one, to spin out the negotiations for as long as possible. The proposal in favour of revolutionary war was lost by eleven votes to two.

In its fourth 'Universal', the Ukrainian *Rada* proclaimed Ukrainian independence.

## 10 January/23 January

A United Government of the Don, formed by Cossack and non-Cossack elements on 5/18 January, issued a policy declaration opposing the extension of bolshevism into the region and purporting to supervise the efforts of the Volunteer Army in defence of the Constituent Assembly. On the same day a congress of Cossacks from the front formed a Military Revolutionary Committee which promptly challenged the United Government.

## 10–18 January/23–31 January

The Third All-Russian Congress of Soviets approved the forced abolition of the Constituent Assembly and the line being taken by the Russian delegation in Brest-Litovsk.

It instructed its Central Executive Committee to prepare for the next congress a draft constitution for the Russian Federal Soviet Republic.

On 15/28 January, Stalin, the Commissar for Nationalities, spoke of the principle of self-determination of small nations being limited in such a way as to make it applicable only to the toilers and not to the bourgeoisie; it had to be a means of attaining socialism. In the Ukraine, for example, the chauvinistic bourgeoisie was using the slogan of self-determination 'for class purposes'.

Lenin told the congress that events in Finland, where the workers had seized power and proclaimed their loyalty to proletarian internationalism, had proved that bolshevik policy on self-determination was correct.

The final session of the congress unanimously decided to drop the word 'Provisional' from the government's title and to refer to it in future as the Workers' and Peasants' Government of the Russian Soviet Republic. (The word had been included at the outset in view of the bolshevik commitment to hold elections for the Constituent Assembly.)

## 11 January/24 January

At a meeting of the Central Committee on the question of peace with the Germans, Stalin commented, 'There is no revolutionary movement in the

West: . . . it exists only in potential and in our practical activities we cannot rely merely on potentials.' Lenin took issue with him: 'There is a mass movement in the West but the revolution there has not yet begun. If, however, on the strength of this we were to alter our tactics, we should be traitors to international socialism.'

## 13 January/26 January

Romanian troops completed their occupation of Bessarabia. The Council of People's Commissars broke off relations with Romania.

## 14 January/27 January

The Council of People's Commissars instructed the Cheka to form an armed unit. On 31 March, this was merged with other units to form the Cheka's Combat Detachment.

## 15 January/28 January

A Council of People's Commissars' decree on the creation of a volunteer 'Workers' and Peasants' Red Army' was published. Admission to the army was open to all Russian citizens of 18 years or more on the recommendation of at least two members of army committees or organisations supporting the Soviet government. Soldiers' pay was to be fifty rubles a month over and above their keep. The bolshevik armed forces consisted at this time of a wide variety of unco-ordinated and ill-disciplined local units.

## 16 January/29 January

Chicherin, who had returned to Russia from imprisonment in England, took over as Trotsky's deputy in the Commissariat for Foreign Affairs. Chicherin's release had been procured in effect by Trotsky who in December had stopped exit visas for British subjects in Russia until the release was agreed.

Fighting broke out in and around Kiev between pro-*Rada* and pro-bolshevik forces and continued for ten days.

## 17 January/30 January

Robert Bruce Lockhart arrived in Petrograd as the emissary of the British government. Unlike Raymond Robins of the American Red Cross and Captain Jacques Sadoul of the French military mission and a confidant of the French socialist leader, Albert Thomas, who also acted as unofficial contacts with the Soviet leaders, Lockhart had direct cypher communications with his government. Robins had been in contact with Trotsky since December and kept in close touch also with the US ambassador, David R. Francis. Litvinov acted as Lockhart's Soviet counterpart in London.

The peace talks in Brest-Litovsk were resumed.

Bolshevik forces occupied Odessa.

## 19 January/1 February

Tikhon, Patriarch of Moscow and All-Russia, anathematised the Bolsheviks for their brutality, lawlessness and persecution of the Orthodox Church.

## 20 January/2 February

A Council of People's Commissars decree separated the church from the state and school from the church; it prohibited religious instruction in schools and declared all church property nationalised. Buildings and objects needed for religious services were to revert to the free use of religious organisations by arrangement with central or local Soviet authorities.

## 22 January/4 February

Bolshevik forces took Nikolaev, seventy miles north-east of Odessa.

## 26 January/8 February

The capital assets of private banks were confiscated.

Merchant shipping was nationalised.

## 27 January/9 February

The Germans and their allies signed a separate peace in Brest-Litovsk with the delegation from the Ukrainian *Rada*.

Pro-bolshevik forces under Murav'-ev having finally gained control of Kiev, the Ukrainian Soviet government took up residence there, replacing the *Rada* government which had retired to Zhitomir on 25 January/7 February.

## 28 January/10 February

Trotsky walked out of the Brest-Litovsk talks having declared that Russia, while refusing to sign an unjust 'annexationist' peace, was abandoning the war with Germany and her allies and demobilising all the troops opposed to them.

A decree of the Council of People's Commissars repudiated all foreign loans unconditionally and without exception. Internal state loans made by the Tsarist regime were also annulled with some compensation for individual small bond-holders, co-operatives, organs of local self-government and other public service or democratic institutions.

According to Stephen White quoting an official French estimate dated February 1922, France held 43 per cent of all Russian foreign debt, Britain 33 per cent, Belgium and Germany 6 per cent and the United States 3.4 per cent. About three-quarters of the British debt but less than a quarter of the French debt was government debt, the rest of the French debt being owed to 1.2 million individual French citizens.

According to R. W. Davies in *The Development of the Soviet Budgetary System*, much of the revenue required to keep the administration going during the first six months after the revolution was raised by local taxation of the richer classes.

The British consul in Archangel reported that the town had come under bolshevik control. Shortly afterwards, the bolshevik Soviet began shipping allied war stores southwards by rail to Vologda. (By the end of 1917, 162,000 tons of war material supplied by the allies to the Tsarist government had accumulated in Archangel.) At the end of March 1918, shipments southwards were reported to be running at about 3,000 tons a week.

## 29 January/11 February

Faced with the failure of his attempts to achieve unity among his own Cossacks against the threat of the advancing bolshevik forces and confronted with the decision of the Volunteer Army to withdraw from the Don into the Kuban region, Kaledin resigned as *ataman* and committed suicide. (Date as given in GSE.)

### 31 January/13 February

The last day on which the old style Julian calendar was used in Russia.

### 14 February

Russia adopted the new style Gregorian calendar.

A decree formally established the Red Navy.

### 14–20 February

Red Guards and impressed Austrian and Romanian war prisoners operating on behalf of the Tashkent Soviet occupied Kokand destroying the autonomous Muslim government. The Tashkent Soviet maintained that the conflict with the Kokand government had arisen on class not national grounds. Estimates of the number of Kokand's inhabitants who were killed vary between 5,000 and 14,000. The massacre finally extinguished Muslim hopes that the October/November revolution would give them a genuine opportunity for self-determination and relieve them of Russian domination: it gave rise to the fragmented Muslim freedom movement referred to by the Soviets as the *Basmachi*, a somewhat disparaging term roughly equivalent to 'bandits'. By the end of 1919, the movement counted over 20,000 fighters.

### 16 February

General Hoffmann, leader of the German delegation to the Brest-Litovsk peace talks, sent the Russians a message to the effect that the armistice would expire on 18 February and that war would be renewed on that day.

Lithuania again proclaimed its independence (cf. 28 November/11 December 1917) omitting any reference to a German protectorate.

### 18 February

The German army began a general advance in Russia occupying the whole of the Baltic states by 25 February.

### 18–19 February

The Council of People's Commissars sent a message to the Germans saying that they were willing to sign a peace on the terms originally offered early in January.

### 19 February

A Soviet Central Executive Committee decree on the socialisation of land was issued. All private ownership of land, minerals, water, forests and natural resources in the republic was abolished for ever, the land being handed over without compensation to those who cultivated it with their own labour and the other resources to the Soviets. Privately owned livestock, agricultural implements and buildings on estates worked by hired labour were to be taken over by land departments set up by the Soviets. These land departments were also to be responsible for the distribution of land. They were intended to absorb or replace the Land Committees which had been largely under Right SR control. They were instructed to encourage the collective system of agriculture at the expense of individual farming on the grounds that the former was the more economical and led to a socialist economy. The immediate practical effects of this measure were probably slight in most areas. It certainly contributed nothing to the solution of the pressing food supply crisis arising from four main causes: the peasants' reluctance to part with grain for inflated paper currency, the shortage of manufactured goods to be used in barter with them, the government's inability to organise forcible grain collections and the dislocation of transport.

## 20 February

The Left SR journal, *Znamia Truda*, published Blok's poem, *The Scythians*, written between 15 and 17/28 and 30 January. Described by Schapiro as a 'Left SR pamphlet rather than a poem', it expressed defiance of the Germans and reflected Slavophil faith in peasant Russia. According to Carr, its allusions to the hordes of Asia were to provide part of the inspiration for the Eurasian movement (see July 1921). Deutscher saw in the poem an expression of the Russian attitude to the outside world with its vision of Russia eternally facing both East and West, indifferent to the struggles between the western powers, conscious of its inferiority to the West yet appealing to the West to follow its revolutionary example, and ready, if rejected by the West, to show its Asiatic colours.

## 21 February

German troops occupied the Byelorussian capital, Minsk.

Lenin signed a decree, 'The Socialist Fatherland is in Danger', warning the country of the threat of German invasion. It called for labour battalions to dig trenches and instructed Soviets to deny rail communications and food stocks to the Germans by destruction where necessary. Members of the bourgeoisie who resisted being drafted into the labour battalions were to be shot as were enemy agents, speculators, thugs, hooligans and counter-revolutionary agitators.

Trotsky enquired of the allied representatives what support the allies would give if the Soviets declared war on the Germans. The French ambassador, supported by the US, Japanese and Italian ambassadors and the British chargé d'affaires, offered military and financial support.

## 22 February

The Central Committee voted by six to five in favour of a motion to accept the assistance of 'the brigands of Anglo-French imperialism against the German brigands' despite vigorous protests from Bukharin.

## 23 February

The German reply dated 21 February to the Soviet message of 18–19 February was received in Petrograd. The terms were stiffer than those offered in January and acceptance was demanded within forty-eight hours. The Central Committee, threatened by Lenin with his resignation if they refused to accept, voted to do so by seven to four with four abstentions including Trotsky's. The 'left communists' who voted against (Bubnov, Uritskii, Lomov and Bukharin) handed in their resignations.

In the light of reports (which were later regarded as greatly exaggerated) of the arming by the Bolsheviks of thousands of German and Austrian prisoners of war in Siberia, the British government authorised the funding of the anti-bolshevik Cossack leader, Grigorii Semenov, who was operating in the Manchurian border area and controlling the western end of the Chinese Eastern railway and its link with the Trans-Siberian railway. The French also provided some support for Semenov. In March it became apparent that the Japanese were already supplying Semenov with funds, arms and personnel on a much more generous scale. This, together with the difficulty of exercising any form of restraint over his savage and disorderly campaigning, led to British disenchantment with him.

*Note:* Fic maintained that German and Austro-Hungarian prisoners of war made up over half the strength of many of the bolshevik armed units especially in Siberia and that they made a significant contribution to the survival of the regime.

Kamenev arrived in Britain on his way to take up a post in Paris analogous to that of Litvinov in London. His mission was ostensibly to enlist allied aid against the Germans. The French government decided to refuse him entry and the British therefore obliged him to return to Russia.

This date was subsequently adopted as the official date of birth of the Red Army, the claim being made that the advance of the Germans and their allies was halted on this day by Soviet troops at Pskov, Reval (Tallinn) and Narva.

The Transcaucasian *seim* assembled in Tiflis. Georgia was controlled by Mensheviks strongly tinged with nationalism, Armenia by the Dashnak party loosely affiliated with the SRs, and Azerbaijan by the Musavat (Equality) party of the educated Turkish-oriented inhabitants.

## 24 February

The Soviet Central Executive Committee voted at 4.30 a.m. by 116 to eighty-five and twenty-six abstentions to sign the peace. The Council of People's Commissars immediately notified the Germans who refused to renew the armistice until the peace treaty had been signed. The bolshevik peace delegation left for Brest-Litovsk at 10 p.m.

Bolshevik troops occupied Rostov which had been evacuated by the Volunteer Army under General Kornilov. At this time the Volunteer Army was not more than 3,000 or 4,000 strong. It embarked on a long winter march south towards Ekaterinodar, entering the Kuban province on 9 March.

The Cheka carried out its first recorded summary execution, the victim being a blackmailer and bandit known as Prince Eboli. Summary executions for political reasons did not begin until July.

The Bolsheviks having abandoned the Estonian capital, Reval (Tallinn) on 23 February, Estonian nationalists issued a new declaration of independence. However, on the following day the Germans took over the capital and installed an occupation regime which lasted until November.

## 24–28 February

The military missions and members of the diplomatic corps, who had kept their official contact with the Soviet regime to a minimum, left Petrograd. Some of the military went to Murmansk; the US, Italian,

Japanese, Brazilian, Siamese, Chinese and some of the Serbian diplomats went to Vologda. The British, French, Greeks, Portuguese and some of the Serbians left via Finland which was still in the throes of civil war. The British got through to Sweden but the French were held up and eventually made their way to Vologda.

## 25 February

Bolshevik troops occupied Novocherkassk and set up a Soviet government. The newly elected *ataman*, General Nazarov, was shot by radical Cossacks.

## 26 February

On the northern front, the German advance was halted at Narva. The German and Austrian advance in the Ukraine continued.

## 28 February

The Soviet peace delegation arrived at Brest-Litovsk having been given three days by the Germans in which to sign the peace treaty.

## March

The Terek People's Soviet Socialist Republic was formed at Vladikavkaz, the Bolsheviks having agreed to form a temporary coalition with Mensheviks, SRs and local parties. This prototype 'people's republic' lasted only until August when it was overthrown by Terek Cossacks.

## 1 March

For some hours, owing to telegraphic confusion, Lenin and Trotsky were under the mistaken impression that negotiations with the Germans at Brest-Litovsk had been broken off and that war with Germany would continue. During this time Trotsky instructed the non-bolshevik Murmansk Soviet to accept 'any and all assistance' from the allied missions in the face of the German/Finnish threat to Murmansk and the railway running southwards from there to Petrograd.

The USS *Brooklyn* arrived at Vladivostok.

The Council of People's Commissars signed a treaty with the 'Red' Finnish government, the Finnish People's Deputation, described by Lenin as the Finnish Socialist Workers' Republic. The treaty covered mutual transfers of immovable property, the rights of citizens of each country resident or working in the other, the evacuation of Russian troops from Finland (most of whom had refused to fight for the 'Red' cause), the delineation of the frontier in the extreme north giving the Finns access to the Arctic through Pechenga (Petsamo) and the return of Finnish ships to Finland.

## 2–3 March

German troops entered Kiev, which had been abandoned by the Ukrainian Soviet government, and restored the *Rada* government.

## 3 March

The treaty of Brest-Litovsk was signed. Under the treaty Soviet Russia in effect lost control over most of the Baltic provinces, Finland, part of Byelorussia, the Ukraine and the districts of Kars, Ardahan and the oil-port of Batumi on the Turkish frontier. In economic terms this meant the loss of over a quarter of the country's population, sown area and railways and about three-quarters of its coal, iron and steel. The Russian army was to be completely demobilised and the navy disarmed and its warships detained in Russian ports. The Soviets were obliged to make peace with the Ukrainian *Rada* and to recognise the *Rada*'s separate treaty with Germany and her allies. Estonia, Livonia, Finland, the Aaland Islands and the Ukraine were all to be evacuated by Soviet troops. The independence of Persia and Afghanistan was to be recognised. Both sides renounced compensation for war expenditure. Diplomatic and consular relations were to be resumed. Agitation and propaganda by one party to the treaty against the government or military institutions of the other party were forbidden.

When challenged about this last clause at the meeting of the Petrograd Soviet on 23–24 February, Lenin replied: 'The Central Executive signs the peace, the Council of Commissars signs the peace, but not the Central Committee of the party. For the behaviour of the latter, the Soviet government is not responsible.' After signature of the treaty, the Bureau of International Revolutionary Propaganda, originally part of the Commissariat of Foreign Affairs, was disbanded but was replaced by a Bureau of Foreign Political Literature employing the same staff under party auspices.

Internally, signature led to the resignation of the Left SRs from the Council of People's Commissars (but not from the Soviet Central Executive Committee or the Cheka) and to the formation within the bolshevik party of a faction of 'Left Communists' under Bukharin. But by signing a separate peace with the Germans, the regime gained a breathing-space and, as Carr pointed out, established a basic principle of Soviet foreign policy, the encouragement and exploitation in the Soviet interest of differences, divisions and enmities in the capitalist world.

*Note:* After the bolshevik coup in October/November 1917, the German government authorised the expenditure of considerable sums for propaganda in Russia largely for the purpose of keeping the Bolsheviks in power. There is insufficient evidence to determine whether or not German money had any influence on Russian signature of the treaty (see Schapiro, *The Communist Party of the Soviet Union*, chapter x). The so-called Sisson papers, a number of documents obtained in Petrograd in February and March by Edgar Sisson, the representative of the US propaganda organisation, the Committee on Public Information, were shown to be almost certainly forgeries. Many of the documents ostensibly emanated from the bolshevik party's headquarters and purported to demonstrate the subservience of the bolshevik leaders to the German general staff.

## 5 March

Trotsky gave Robins a memorandum enquiring what aid the Americans, British and French would give the Soviet government if the Brest-Litovsk treaty were not ratified by the congress of Soviets or if, despite ratification of the treaty, the German advance continued or if the Soviets were obliged to renounce the treaty.

He also enquired what steps would be taken to prevent a Japanese landing in the Far East followed by Japanese occupation of the Trans-Siberian railway. The memorandum in no way committed the Soviet government to co-operation with the allies and stated that the internal and foreign policies of the Soviet government would continue to be based on the principles of international socialism and would retain their complete independence of all non-socialist governments. Trotsky spoke along similar lines to Lockhart.

In a telegram to London, Lockhart wrote: 'Empower me to inform Lenin that the question of Japanese intervention has been shelved, that we are prepared to support the Bolsheviks in so far as they will oppose Germany and that we invite his suggestions as to the best way in which this help can be given. In return for this, there is every chance that war will be declared.'

## 6–8 March

The bolshevik party's Seventh Congress voted decisively in favour of the Brest-Litovsk Treaty. Lenin spoke strongly in favour of ratification. Kennan pointed out in *Russia Leaves the War* that there was no evidence that he mentioned the possible alternative course of accepting allied aid to continue the war against Germany. Lenin made it plain that the Soviet government had no intention of abiding by the terms of the treaty.

The congress resolution on war and peace called for draconian measures to improve the discipline of the workers and peasants and for the systematic general military training of the whole adult Russian population.

This was incompatible with the treaty and the resolution was not published until 1 January 1919.

The congress changed the name of the party to the All-Russian Communist Party (Bolsheviks) – RKP (B) – symbolising the party's final break with all other socialist groups, particularly the Mensheviks, and agreed that a new party programme should be drawn up.

## 7 March

German forces landed on the Aaland Islands in the Gulf of Bothnia. This was the first step in direct German intervention in the Finnish civil war. It was welcomed by some members of the 'White' Finnish government but not by Mannerheim whose outlook was not pro-German but Scandinavian and anti-bolshevik: he considered that Finland should fight its own war of liberation independently.

## 9 March

The British Admiral Kemp who, since 1916, had had the major responsibility for anti-submarine and mine-sweeping operations off the Murmansk coast, acting apparently on his own initiative in the light of the local situation and, perhaps, in the light of intelligence on German naval and troop movements towards Finland, landed a company of marines, about 130 men, at Murmansk. About 100 French marines were also landed from the cruiser *Amiral Aube*.

## 10–12 March

Petrograd being too exposed in the event of a further German advance, the Soviet government moved to

Moscow which thenceforward became the capital. Trotsky left Petrograd for Moscow on 16 March taking Lockhart on his train.

Evacuation of industry from Petrograd exacerbated the severe unemployment problem caused by the reversion from war to peacetime production and the post-revolutionary dislocation.

## 12–14 March

German troops occupied Odessa.

## 13 March

Trotsky became People's Commissar for War and chairman of the Supreme War Council (VVS) which had been set up on 4 March. He immediately set about the creation of a disciplined, conscript Red Army commanded largely by 'military specialists', i.e. former Tsarist officers, nearly 50,000 of whom were recruited into the Red Army in the next two years, exceeding the number of newly trained Red Army commanders who graduated in that period. Political commissars provided by the party served to check on the loyalty of the 'military specialists' and to carry out party propaganda work among the rank and file. The Supreme War Council, staffed by 'military specialists', drew up plans for defence against further German and Finnish advances. The conduct of the civil war remained for the time being the responsibility of the War Commissariat.

## 13–14 March

Red troops from Novorossiisk occupied the capital of the Kuban, Ekat-erinodar, its Cossack government having fled.

## 13–17 March

Red Troops controlled by the Tashkent Soviet made an unsuccessful attack on Bukhara.

## 14–18 March

The Fourth All-Russian Congress of Soviets met in Moscow and on 16 March ratified the Brest-Litovsk Treaty by a majority of 784 to 261 with 115 abstentions. Among the abstainers were 64 'Left Communists'.

The congress set as the main task for the immediate future the raising of the levels of production and workers' self-discipline. The reaction against 'workers' control' (which had proved destructive to production but was still being advocated by some of the 'Left Communists') and in favour of nationalisation and centralised direction was already being reflected in appointments in and by the Supreme Council of National Economy. Bukharin, while quarrelling with Lenin over 'state capitalism', was less contentious over practical issues of economic policy and began to distance himself from the other 'Left Communists'. By July 'left communism' was a spent force.

## 15 March

The Soviet government agreed that the Czechoslovak corps located near Kiev should be allowed to cross Siberia and leave Russia through Vladivostok provided that it surrendered a large proportion of its arms to the Soviets. The corps had been formed earlier in the war from

Czechs and Slovaks resident in Russia who were prepared to fight the Germans and their Austrian allies in the hope of establishing a Czechoslovak national state after the war. The Russian war effort having collapsed in 1917, Thomas Masaryk, the future president of Czechoslovakia, negotiated the corps' departure from Russia in order that it should take part in the fighting on the western front. From January 1918 the corps formed part of the Czechoslovak army subordinated to the French high command. The corps was expanding rapidly through recruitment of Czechs and Slovaks from the Austrian army who had been taken prisoner by the Russians. By March 1918 it had reached a strength of about 40,000. After much wrangling over the terms under which they were allowed to travel, the first Czechoslovak units left Penza by train for Vladivostok on 27 March but soon encountered further obstruction from both the central and local Soviet authorities. The first train did not reach Vladivostok until 28 April.

## 21 March

Trotsky told the Moscow Soviet that there was a requirement for a modern army of 300,000 to 500,000 men. On 19 March he had asked Robins for five US army officers to act as inspectors of the Soviet army and for American railway specialists. Trotsky also discussed the possible attachment of British, French and Italian army officers for the training and inspection of the new army. A week later he asked for British help with the reorganisation of the Black Sea fleet. Little or nothing came of these approaches. In *Russia and the West under Lenin and Stalin*, Kennan took the view that the bolshevik leaders had two purposes in mind in their dealings with the allied representatives between March and May: one was to prepare the ground for the acceptance of support from the western allies if the Germans should decide to pursue their advance on Petrograd and Moscow with a view to overthrowing the bolshevik regime; the second was to foster the illusion of bolshevik willingness to collaborate with the western allies against Germany as a means of inducing them to keep the Japanese in check in the Far East.

## 25 March

The Soviet government signed a treaty with the Emir of Bukhara recognising his independence.

## 26 March

A decree ended the system of workers' control on the railways, which had been established on 23 January and which had reduced the railway network to a shambles. The Commissar of Communications was given dictatorial powers in matters relating to rail transport.

## 27 March

*Izvestiia* announced that all newspapers were required to submit three copies of each issue to the Cheka which had ill-defined responsibility for countering 'misuse' of the press.

Arskii, a bolshevik economist, drew attention to some of the chaotic consequences of workers' control.

## 31 March–2 April

Fighting in Baku between Muslim Azerbaijani Musavatists and the forces of the Baku Soviet (in which the influence of the bolsheviks was greater than their formal representation), supported by the Armenian Dashnaks, ended in victory for the Soviet which extended its influence through much of the province. An estimated 3,000 people were killed, many of them Muslims. The Musavat leaders fled from the city.

## 1 April

The Soviet Central Executive Committee appointed a commission under Sverdlov to draft a constitution.

## 3–5 April

German troops under General Graf Rüdiger von der Goltz landed at Hangö (Hanko) in Finland and advanced towards Helsingfors.

The All-Russian Central Council of Trade Unions, of which Tomskii had become president in the previous month, issued a regulation under which the trade unions accepted responsibility for improving labour discipline and increasing productivity.

## 4–5 April

The Germans occupied Kharkov.

## 5 April

In response to westward shipment by the communists of allied war stores in Vladivostok, the deteriorating security situation there and the murder of two or three Japanese citizens, the Japanese admiral in command, apparently acting on his own authority but within his standing instructions, landed a force of about 500 marines. The British followed suit with a force of about fifty marines who were deployed round the British consulate. The Soviet government protested vigorously against the landings.

## 6 April

Mannerheim completed the capture of Tampere, inflicting heavy casualties on the Reds and severely damaged their morale.

## 8–9 April

The military representatives of the allied Supreme War Council again recommended that effective military support should be given to every element of the Russian people able and willing to resist German penetration and advocated Japanese intervention extending as far west as Omsk or Cheliabinsk and preferably as far as Samara.

The Bessarabian Council voted for political union with Romania on certain conditions. The Soviets refused to recognise this union and the western allies also withheld recognition.

## 10 April

A decree on consumers' co-operatives (which had expanded rapidly in the prevailing economic chaos) gave them a degree of government protection and some privileges (e.g. over tax) while subjecting them to financial control by the State Bank and supervision by the Supreme Council of National Economy.

## 11–12 April

The Cheka carried out a raid on twenty-six anarchist centres in Moscow, killing over 100 people.

## 12–14 April

Von der Goltz's troops captured Helsingfors.

## 13 April

General Kornilov, who had led the Volunteer Army on its winter march from the Don, was killed by a shell which hit his headquarters in the course of his unsuccessful attempt to storm Ekaterinodar. Denikin assumed command, abandoned the assault on Ekaterinodar and marched the Volunteer Army northwards again towards Novocherkassk in the Don region, picking up recruits and equipment on the way. The brutality of the regime in the Don Soviet republic had antagonised the local Cossacks and revived their fighting spirit.

## 14–15 April

The Turks occupied Batumi.

## 22 April

The Transcaucasian assembly proclaimed an independent Transcaucasian Federal Republic, a move urged by the Turks and supported enthusiastically by the Azerbaijani Musavatists but reluctantly by the Armenian Dashnaks and Georgian Mensheviks. The republic lasted only until 26 May.

A decree of the Soviet Central Executive Committee introduced compulsory military training for all workers and peasants aged between 18 and 40 other than those who employed hired labour. The bourgeoisie were precluded from bearing arms. Training courses were to be continuous for eight weeks at not less than twelve hours a week.

A decree nationalised all foreign trade and ruled that all commercial transactions with foreign states and trading concerns abroad were to be conducted exclusively in the name of the Russian Republic by organs specially authorised by the Commissariat of Trade and Industry.

## 25 April

The Japanese marines were withdrawn from Vladivostok, the British force having already re-embarked.

The Baku Soviet set up a bolshevik-dominated Council of People's Commissars including Left SRs. The regime, which lasted until July, is often referred to as the 'Baku Commune'. The oil industry was nationalised on 1 June.

## 25–27 April

The Turks occupied Kars.

## 26 April

The German minister, Count von Mirbach, presented his credentials to Sverdlov, the President of the Soviet Central Executive Committee. Ioffe had been appointed Soviet representative in Berlin.

Chicherin, Acting Commissar for Foreign Affairs, protested without success against German advances beyond the line agreed at Brest-Litovsk.

## 27 April

The military representatives of the

allied Supreme War Council recommended that all the Czechoslovak
troops which had not already passed
through Omsk on their way to Vladivostok should be diverted to Archangel and Murmansk. On 30 April,
probably for quite different reasons,
Moscow issued instruction on these
lines to the Omsk Soviet.

A decree abolished inheritance
either by law or by testament except
for estates under 10,000 rubles and
certain possessions required for productive purposes. Subject to certain
provisions for dependent relatives,
property of the deceased passed to
the local Soviet.

## 29 April

The former Tsarist officer and land-
owner, General Skoropadskii, was
proclaimed *Hetman* (leader) of the
Ukraine, having reached a prior
agreement with the Germans. The
*Rada*, which had proved insufficiently co-operative in procuring
grain supplies for the Germans,
collapsed.

Elections to posts of command in
the army were forbidden. In practice
they seem to have continued in some
units until about the end of the year.
'Soldiers' Committees' were also
gradually eliminated.

Vyborg (Viipuri), to which the
rump of the 'Red' Finnish government had withdrawn, fell to Mannerheim's forces.

## 30 April

A Turkestan Autonomous Soviet
Socialist Republic was proclaimed in
Tashkent.

## 1 May

The Germans occupied Taganrog,
fifty miles to the west of Rostov, and
Sevastopol in the Crimea.

## 2 May

The US ambassador, Francis, having
given up hope of stimulating a Soviet
request for allied intervention against
the Germans on Russian territory,
sent a telegram to Washington, advocating intervention without Soviet
consent. His main ground was his
belief in the growth of German
influence in Russia.

The Vladivostok Soviet took control of the city in which 6,000 men of
the Czechoslovak corps had arrived.

## 4 May

The Finnish Senate reassembled and
on 18 May the conservative nationalist leader, Svinhufvud, was sworn in
as Regent under the Swedish constitution of 1772. The last Red Guard
units surrendered on 5 May.

## 6 May

Anti-Soviet Cossacks occupied
Novocherkassk.

## 7 May

A decree set up a Central Board of
Universal Military Training (*Vsevobuch*) to supply the Red Army with
'trained conscripts'. To this end, it
was given control of all sports clubs
and made responsible for the physical training of all those between the
ages of 16 and 40, becoming the principal agency for what Riordan
described as the militarisation of
sport in the civil war period.

## 8 May

German troops occupied Rostov.

## 9 May

The Soviet Central Executive Committee approved a decree giving the Commissariat of Supply (*Narkomprod*) extraordinary powers, including the use of armed force, in the struggle with the 'rural bourgeoisie' which was accused of concealing and speculating in grain stocks. The commissariat was recognised as the single institution in which all orders relating to food supply should be centralised.

## 10–14 May

A number of papers, some of them menshevik or SR, were closed down.

## 11 May

The Mountain Republic of the North Caucasus declared its independence.

## 14 May

Robins left Moscow for Washington via Vladivostok, carrying a paper from Lenin outlining Russia's economic needs and the commercial opportunities they presented for US business, particularly in Siberia and the Far East. In the light of a speech by Lenin a day or two earlier on exploiting contradictions between the imperialist powers, Kennan interpreted Lenin's paper as an attempt to induce US business interests to restrain the Japanese from intervening in Siberia.

Chicherin wrote to the Germans offering economic concessions under the terms of the Brest-Litovsk treaty. Mirbach, the German minister in Moscow, reported to his Foreign Ministry on 13 May that the Bolsheviks were all of a sudden much more co-operative on economic affairs. He saw it as still in the German interest to keep them in power.

In an atmosphere of deepening mutual suspicion between the Czechoslovak corps and the Soviets, an incident occurred at Cheliabinsk, east of the Urals, between Czechoslovak soldiers travelling to Vladivostok and Hungarian prisoners of war returning to Hungary. Some Czechoslovaks were arrested by the local Soviet but the matter was settled amicably on the spot within a few days.

The newly promoted US consul-general in Moscow, DeWitt C. Poole, called on Chicherin, opening a short-lived semi-official link between the US and Soviet governments.

## 14–16 May

Two German submarines appeared off the Murman coast.

## 15 May

Trotsky, who had little or no knowledge of the previous day's incident at Cheliabinsk, reaffirmed his willingness to facilitate the departure of the Czechoslovak corps from Russia using, by agreement with the allies, Archangel as the port of departure for those Czechoslovaks who had not already passed Omsk on their way to Vladivostok. Fic contended however that there was evidence to show that Trotsky had already decided to dissolve the Czechoslovak corps and retain its members in Russia for service in the Red Army or in labour battalions.

## 16 May

Krasnov was elected *ataman* of the

Don Cossacks in Novocherkassk and sought German recognition of an independent Don republic. A working agreement with the German General von Eichhorn was reached in June. Krasnov undertook to remain neutral in the event of hostilities between the Germans and the Czechoslovaks who would be denied access to Don territory.

## 16–18 May

Turkish troops occupied Aleksandropol' and began an advance towards Tiflis in Georgia and Erevan in Armenia.

## 21 May

Trotsky, having received a report on the Cheliabinsk incident on or about 18 May, made use of it, according to Fic's account, in two separate ways to procure the total disarmament of the Czechoslovaks: he used it as one of the means of persuading two members of the Czechoslovak political leadership who were under arrest in Moscow to sign an order to their troops calling on them to give up all their arms; and he used it in argument with the allies to induce them to bring pressure to bear on the Czechoslovak troops to comply. On the same day Trotsky secretly instructed local Soviets to approach all Czechoslovaks travelling on the railway with invitations to join labour battalions or the Red Army.

## 21–27 May

An All-Russian Menshevik Conference was held in Moscow.

## 23 May

The British government decided to despatch a 560-strong military mission to Archangel and an expeditionary force of 600 to Murmansk. The original objectives were to forestall an expected German–Finnish attack on Murmansk or the Murmansk–Petrograd railway, to prevent the Germans from establishing submarine bases at Murmansk or Pechenga (Petsamo), to tie down German troops in Finland and to protect allied war stores in Archangel. The mission, which was not intended primarily as a fighting unit, was to equip and train any Czechoslovaks who might reach Archangel and a locally recruited Russian force which was expected to reach 30,000 men. This force was intended to link up with pro-allied forces in Siberia and thus to open a new eastern front against the Germans. Allied troops in northern Russia were to be under the command of the British General Poole and the Murmansk force was to be commanded by General Maynard.

The Council of People's Commissars instructed the Cheka to undertake surveillance of the menshevik and SR leadership.

The Czechoslovak corps decided to repudiate their political leadership, to defy any orders to disarm totally and to refuse to allow any part of their force to be diverted via Archangel. They resolved to make their way as a body to Vladivostok using peaceful persuasion or if necessary force. Moscow ordered the movement of Czechoslovak trains to be halted, their occupants to be disarmed and their units to be dissolved.

## 24 May

General Poole arrived at Murmansk on board the US cruiser *Olympia*.

In a Soviet–Czechoslovak clash west of Omsk, 250 Bolsheviks and eighteen Czechoslovaks were killed. Trotsky ordered local Soviets to shoot on the spot any armed Czechoslovaks found on the railway: anyone helping the eastward movement of the Czechoslovaks was to be court-martialled. Few of the Soviets concerned were in a position to carry out these orders and, within two weeks, the Czechoslovaks, assisted in places by anti-communist Russian groups, were in control of the line between Samara and a point west of Irkutsk. At this stage nearly 14,000 Czechoslovaks had reached Vladivostok, about 8,000 were in the Penza area, nearly 9,000 in the Cheliabinsk area and between 3,000 and 4,000 near Novonikolaevsk.

## 25 May–4 June

The first All-Russian Congress of Councils of National Economy in Moscow was attended by over 100 delegates from the Supreme Council of National Economy, its local offshoots and other economic organisations including the trade unions. The vice-chairman of the Supreme Council of National Economy reported that 304 enterprises, mainly in the mining, metallurgy and metal-working industries, had been nationalised or sequestered up to 15 May in an unplanned fashion and often for 'punitive' reasons. A resolution endorsed wholesale nationalisation beginning with the key industries of metal-working, machine-building, chemicals, oil and textiles. Bukharin joined the 'Left Communists' in an unsuccessful protest against this tendency towards state capitalism.

## 26 May

The Transcaucasian Federation broke up into the three independent republics of Georgia, Armenia and Azerbaijan.

The SRs held their eighth conference and adopted a programme on the same lines as that of the French-funded Union for the Regeneration of Russia (SVR), consisting of backing for allied intervention in Russia, the formation of a Russian national army, the election of a new Constituent Assembly and the restoration of democracy.

## 27 May

A decree confirmed the monopoly of the Commissariat of Supply over the distribution of all objects of prime necessity. It also provided for the recruitment of armed 'workers' detachments' to go out into the countryside and organise the working peasants against the rich peasants and force the latter to disgorge their grain surpluses.

## 28 May

A meeting near Novocherkassk between the Don Cossack leader, General Krasnov, and General Denikin, leader of the Volunteer Army, failed to improve relations between the two men. Denikin mistrusted Krasnov's close relations with the Germans and was more concerned with securing the Kuban to the south than with helping Krasnov to capture Tsaritsyn to the north. No agreement was reached on a unified command. Apart from Denikin's loyalty to Russian commitments to the allied cause, collaboration with the Germans was for him incompatible both with his anti-bolshevism and, given German support for separatist movements in the Ukraine, the Don and Georgia, with his aim of a reunited, democratic, 'Great Russia, One and Indivisible'.

A German-Georgian treaty was signed at Poti implying German recognition of Georgian independence and opening the way for German access to Georgian raw materials including manganese, and to the western end of the Transcaucasian railway which transported oil from Baku to the Black Sea. As a welcome counterweight to the Turks, the Georgians agreed to receive a contingent of German troops who arrived, on 10 June and stayed until November.

The US consul-general in Moscow reported Chicherin as saying that the Soviet government had decided under German pressure to cede the Pechenga (Petsamo) area west of Murmansk to Finland.

## 28–30 May

Lockhart visited Vologda and was persuaded by the US ambassador, Francis, and the French ambassador, Noulens, of the need for allied intervention without Soviet consent.

## 29 May

The Council of People's Commissars decided to declare martial law in Moscow where the Cheka arrested thirteen members of the anti-bolshevik Union for Defence of the Motherland and Freedom (SZRiS). The union was organised by Savinkov who had returned to Moscow at the end of January on behalf of the Volunteer Army.

The Soviet Central Executive Committee introduced partial conscription for the nascent Red Army. Conscription was limited to workers and peasants, members of the bourgeoisie being disqualified from bearing arms.

## 30 May

Chicherin was appointed Commissar for Foreign affairs.

## 31 May

Coeducation of the two sexes from elementary school to university was decreed.

## 1 June

A new government, the West Siberian Commissariat, was formed at Omsk and pronounced itself in favour of a revival of the Constituent Assembly.

A trade agreement was signed in Moscow between Soviet Russia and a Swedish trade delegation.

## 3 June

Mirbach, the German minister in Moscow, asked his government for 3 million marks a month to be spent for political purposes in Russia in the face of strong competition from the western allies. He warned that larger sums would be required in the event of any change in the German political line. On 8 June the German Foreign Minister asked the treasury for a fund of at least 40 million marks.

## 4 June

Stalin left Moscow for Tsaritsyn on appointment as General Director of Food Affairs in South Russia to organise food supplies, mainly from the North Caucasus, for Moscow and Petrograd.

A decree abolished the diplomatic ranks of ambassador and minister and substituted the term 'plenipotentiary representative' (*polpred*) for the head of a diplomatic mission. In practice it proved impossible altogether to avoid use of the traditional terms.

Georgia and Armenia signed peace treaties with Turkey at Batumi. Thereafter, the Germans consolidated their position in Georgia while the Turks, having already occupied parts of Armenia, focused on Azerbaijan taking advantage of Muslim Azerbaijani hostility to the Baku Soviet. The Turks' advance towards Baku and their control over the eastern sectors of the Transcaucasian railway aroused German as well as British apprehensions.

A decree published in *Izvestiia* recognised the Geneva Convention for the amelioration of the condition of sick and wounded soldiers in the field, both in its original and later versions and other agreements concerning the Red Cross which were recognised by Russia before 1917.

## 7 June

Trotsky sent a telegram to Murmansk, saying that 'conniving with foreigners' was not permissible. The Murmansk Soviet chose to ignore the message.

The Czechoslovaks captured Omsk.

## 8 June

The Czechoslovaks occupied Samara, enabling SR members of the Constituent Assembly to form an anti-bolshevik government there, the Committee of Members of the Constituent Assembly (*Komuch*).

## 11 June

A decree established township and village 'Committees of the Poor' which, under the general direction of the local Soviets and the Commissariat of Supply and in conjunction with the 'workers' detachments', were to extract grain stocks from the well-to-do peasants and distribute them. The poor peasants were to be rewarded for their collaboration with grain supplies free or at discounted prices. The effect on overall production was disastrous: the more efficient peasants capable of producing a surplus over and above their own needs had every incentive not to do so. In some areas the 'Committees of the Poor' challenged the authority of local Soviets. The problem was tackled in November by abolishing the committees and re-electing the local Soviets so as to include the committees' most active members.

The USS *Olympia* landed about 150 US marines in the Murmansk area to replace British and French troops which had been sent down the Murmansk railway to deal with a reported advance by 'White' Finns towards Kem.

## 11–14 June

The first conference of Chekas (i.e. subordinate units of the VCHEKA) decided to form Frontier Chekas, Railway Chekas and a corps of Cheka troops.

## 13 June

Trotsky set up an eastern front (or army group) under the Latvian Vatsetis, the Red forces in the Volga area being reorganised into the First, Second, Third, Fourth and Fifth Red Armies. Tukhachevskii was given command of the First Red Army.

## 14 June

The Soviet Central Executive Committee decided to exclude Right SRs and Mensheviks from its ranks on the grounds of their association with counter-revolutionaries and recommended all local Soviets to do likewise.

Chicherin, the Commissar for Foreign Affairs, sent messages to British, French and American representatives saying that the presence of their warships in Russian ports was unacceptable.

## 16 June

The death penalty was legally reintroduced despite Left SR opposition.

## 17–19 June

An unsuccessful rebellion against the Soviet regime occurred in Tambov.

## 18 June

Part of the Russian Black Sea fleet scuttled itself at Novorossiisk on secret orders from Trotsky to avoid being handed over to the Germans. The rest of the fleet sailed to the Crimea and surrendered to the Germans there.

The US consul-general in Moscow instructed the US vice-consul at Samara to advise the Czechoslovaks that they should hold their present positions and secure control of the Trans-Siberian railway. At about the same time, the French ambassador at Vologda gave the Czechoslovaks to understand that they should regard themselves as the advance guard of an allied intervention force.

## 20 June

Volodarskii, the commissar for press, agitation and propaganda in the Petrograd regional government, was assassinated by an SR in Petrograd.

## 22–23 June

Denikin began his second offensive southwards from Novocherkassk into the Kuban territory with about 9,000 men, capturing Torgovaia on 25 June and thereby severing rail communications between the North Caucasus region and central Russia.

## 23 June

The British expeditionary force under General Maynard and the training mission for Archangel arrived at Murmansk. The allied forces already deployed in Pechenga, Murmansk and 350 miles to the south along the Murmansk railway amounted to about 500 British and French marines and about 2,000 Serbian, Finnish, Russian, Polish and French troops. The Serbs and the French had arrived at Murmansk from the south with a view to embarking for France.

## 25 June

In a letter to the German State Secretary, Mirbach, the German minister in Moscow, described the bolshevik regime as dangerously ill and drew attention to the danger to German interests of a possible takeover by the SRs backed by the Czechoslovaks and the western allies. He argued that the Germans should reinsure by supporting moderates from the right wing, Octobrists and Kadets, drawing in the Siberians if possible. He expressed reservations about the Monarchists with whom Ludendorf, the German 'First Quartermaster General', had on 9 June advocated taking up contact. Miliukov was the most prominent of the Kadets who, disillusioned with the vacillations in allied policy, entered into talks with the Germans to explore the possibilities of collaboration with them against the Bolsheviks. (For details, see Brinkley, chapter 2.)

## 26 June

Lenin urged the use of mass terror in Petrograd.

A decree rendered members of the bourgeoisie of military age liable to labour service.

## 27 June–3 July

Maynard and an escorting party travelled over 300 miles south on the Murmansk railway encountering three train-loads of Soviet troops, the advance guard of a larger force intended to expel the allies from Murmansk. The advance guard were disarmed and sent back to the south of Kem.

## 28 June

A decree nationalised, without compensation to the owners, the mining, metallurgical, textile, electrical, timber, tobacco, resin, glass and pottery industries, steam-driven mills, local utilities and private railways. The timing of this decree was dictated largely by the desire to prevent substantial parts of Russian industry

falling under German ownership under the terms of a supplementary agreement to the Brest-Litovsk treaty.

Krasnov again appealed to the Kaiser for support. He controlled much of the Don territory during the summer but his repeated attempts to capture Tsaritsyn, in the defence of which Stalin and Voroshilov played a prominent role, were unsuccessful. (The city was renamed Stalingrad on 10 April 1925.)

## 29 June

The Czechoslovak forces in Vladivostok took over control of the town from the local Soviet as a preliminary to a westward move aimed at regaining contact with their colleagues still in western Siberia, the Urals and the Volga area, from whom they were separated by bolshevik forces on the Trans-Siberian railway near Irkutsk and Lake Baikal. These forces held out until 20 August. The Czechoslovaks appealed to the western allies for support. The threat to the Czechoslovaks was almost certainly the most important single factor in persuading a hitherto consistently reluctant President Wilson to authorise intervention by US troops in Siberia: fear of unilateral Japanese intervention was probably also a factor.

The Czechoslovak seizure of Vladivostok was followed immediately by small-scale landings of troops from the Japanese, British, Chinese and American warships in the harbour.

## 30 June

The Murmansk Soviet decided to defy Moscow and continue its collaboration with the allies. On 1 July its president was denounced as an enemy of the people by the Council of People's Commissars.

The Siberian Commissariat in Omsk was replaced by a new Siberian government which moved steadily to the right. On 4 July it annulled all Soviet decrees. On 6 July it ordered the suppression of all Soviets and embarked on the restoration of private property in every form. Its relations with the Samara government (*Komuch*) became increasingly strained.

## 3 July

The draft constitution of the Russian Soviet Federated Socialist Republic (RSFSR) was published and submitted for approval to the party Central Committee. It began with the Declaration of Rights of the Toiling and Exploited People (see 3/16 January 1918). It referred to

1. the separation of church from state and school from church;
2. freedom of speech, opinion and assembly for workers;
3. the obligation for all citizens to work on the principle that 'he that does not work, neither shall he eat';
4. the obligation of military service for all workers; citizenship for all workers living on Russian territory and right of asylum for foreigners persecuted for political or religious offences; and
5. the abolition of discrimination on grounds of race or nationality.

Soviets of regions with special national characteristics were to be allowed to form autonomous, regional unions which would enter the RSFSR on a federal basis. The All-Russian Congress of Soviets (heavily weighted in favour of the cities at the expense of the countryside) was declared the supreme authority: the All-Russian Central Executive Committee (VTsIK) of not more than 200 members which the congress elected was to exercise all its powers between congresses. This committee appointed the Council of People's Commissars which was entitled to issue urgent decrees without reference to the committee. The All-Russian Congress of Soviets formed the apex of a pyramid of regional and local Soviets extending down to the village Soviets. The Soviets had both legislative and executive powers. Excluded from the franchise were those who employed labour, *rentiers*, private traders, priests and monks, members of the former Royal Family, criminals, the insane and officials and agents of the former police service. The constitution made no reference to the party, the Cheka or the revolutionary tribunals. Matthews gives a full English translation.

## 4–10 July

The Fifth All-Russian Congress of Soviets was attended by 1,132 voting delegates of whom 745 were Bolsheviks and 352 Left SRs. A clash soon developed between the two parties, mainly over the Brest-Litovsk treaty but also over bolshevik provocation of class war in the countryside, the suppression of other parties and the use of the death penalty. The congress was interrupted for two days by the events of 6 and 7 July. The congress officially adopted the RSFSR Constitution on 10 July.

**1918**

## 6 July

Two Left SR members of the Cheka, Bliumkin and Andreev, apparently acting on the orders of the Left SR Central Committee, assassinated the German minister, Count von Mirbach, with a view to provoking a resumption of hostilities between Russia and Germany.

Other Left SRs, who controlled the Cheka's Combat Detachment, arrested Dzerzhinskii, the head of the Cheka, and one of his deputies, Latsis, and took control of Cheka headquarters for a few hours. The headquarters of the Combat Detachment was retaken by loyal bolshevik forces on 7 July and thirteen of the leading Left SRs, who maintained that their object had been to procure changes in government policy, not to overturn the government, were summarily shot on the same day. Many of the Left SR delegates to the Soviet Congress were arrested.

*Note*: In *The Assassination of Count Mirbach* Katkov offered a different interpretation of the incident. He cited the evidence (see 3 and 25 June) that Mirbach had become increasingly dubious about the Bolsheviks' prospects and was advocating switching German support to the moderate right. In all probability, Lenin and his close associates would have received information on this and would have seen it as a serious threat to their precarious hold on power. By using Bliumkin for the assassination the bolshevik leaders succeeded in pinning the blame for it on the Left SRs, thereby avoiding any serious German retaliation and providing themselves at the same time with an opportunity to destroy the Left SRs as an opposition force.

Katkov argued that the fact that Bliumkin escaped punishment and resumed his career in the Cheka until he was shot in 1929 supported the thesis that the assassination had bolshevik backing. According to Agabekov, Bliumkin was shot because while serving in Constantinople, he made common cause with Trotsky and conveyed letters from Trotsky to his supporters in the USSR through OGPU channels.

In an apparently unconnected uprising, Savinkov's Union for the Defence of the Motherland and Freedom (SZRiS), which received French financial backing, seized control in Yaroslavl' and held it for two weeks. Short-lived revolts also occurred at Rybinsk on 7 July and Murom on 8 July. As a result, the Cheka effectively wound up the SZRiS. The risings were intended to coincide with allied intervention: Kennan suggested (*The Decision to Intervene*, pp. 436–7) that false information spread by the Bolsheviks may have provoked their premature occurrence.

These events in early July led to the gradual elimination of Left SRs from the Cheka and the intensified use of mass terror as a political weapon.

An agreement on co-operation was signed between the presidium of the Murmansk Soviet and allied forces there: it came into force on 7 July. Its declared purpose was the defence of the region against the Germans. It stated that the Murmansk Regional Soviet was the supreme authority in the internal affairs of the region and provided for the creation of a Russian army under Russian command to be supplied by the allies. The allies also undertook to supply the civilian population with food.

President Wilson informed his Secretaries of State, War and the Navy of his decision that a force of 7,000 Japanese followed by a US force of equal numbers should be landed at Vladivostok with a view to safeguarding the Czechoslovak corps' lines of communication.

British, French, Japanese, US, Chinese and Czechoslovak representatives signed a proclamation that the Vladivostok area had been taken under temporary allied protection.

## 7 July

Lindley, the British chargé d'affaires who had left Russia via Finland in February, arrived at Vologda.

## 8 July

Vatsetis was appointed commander-in-chief of the Red Army.

The allied diplomats in Vologda pleaded for intervention in Archangel to be speeded up.

## 10 July

The British War Cabinet decided to despatch a British battalion to Vladivostok and to ask the French to do the same. The stated purpose of the British move was to ensure order in Vladivostok, to secure Czechoslovak communications and to safeguard allied war stores.

## 11 July

The Czechoslovaks took Irkutsk.

## 12 July

The Council of People's Commissars declared that Murav'ev, the Left SR commander-in-chief of Soviet troops on the Volga front, was a traitor and an enemy of the people. On 11 July Murav'ev had declared an armistice with the Czechoslovaks and war against the Germans and had broken up the Simbirsk Soviet. His attempt to win over the provincial Soviet Executive Committee failed and he either shot himself or was shot.

## 14 July

Discontent in Transcaspia with the Tashkent Soviet government culminated in a revolt in Ashkhabad resulting in the formation of a Menshevik–SR 'Ashkhabad Committee' which, early in August, appealed for British support.

## 14–15 July

Denikin's Volunteer Army captured the important rail junction at Tikhoretskaia.

## 16 July

Maxim Gorky's independent but menshevik-inclined paper, *Novaia Zhizn'*, was closed down on Lenin's orders. By the end of the year, however, Gorky was taking a pro-bolshevik line.

## 16–17 July

According to a widely accepted version of events, the former Tsar, his wife, son, four daughters and four attendants were executed in the house in which they were held in Ekaterinburg by members of the Cheka acting on the instructions of the local Soviet, very probably with the consent of Moscow. At the time, Ekaterinburg, to which the former Tsar had been moved from Tobol'sk in April, was threatened by advancing Czechoslovak and 'White' forces. Lenin is reported to have said that the 'Whites' should not be left a live banner to rally around.

*Note*: In *The File on the Tsar*, Anthony Summers and Tom Mangold raised doubts about this story and described the evidence that while the former Tsar and probably his son were killed in or near Ekaterinburg in July, his widow and daughters were subsequently held for several months at Perm' and probably survived at least until November 1918. On 16 April 1989 *Moscow News*, the weekly publication of the Union of Soviet Societies for Friendship and Cultural Relations with Foreign Countries and *Novosti* press agency, published an account of the alleged discovery in 1979 of the bodies of the Tsar and his family near Ekaterinburg (Sverdlovsk).

## 19 July

Having been unanimously approved on 10 July by the Fifth All-Russian Congress of Soviets, the constitution of the RSFSR came into force on its publication in *Izvestiia*.

Stalin was made head of the War Council of the North Caucasus military district at Tsaritsyn which was threatened by Krasnov's Don Cossack army. Between them, Krasnov and Denikin had cut Tsaritsyn's rail connections to the south.

## 25 July

The allied diplomats left Vologda for Archangel whence they were shipped to Murmansk on 29 July. Some of them, including the US ambassador, Francis, returned to Archangel in August.

With the Turkish army threatening Baku, the local Soviet carried a motion against the opposition of local Bolsheviks supported by Lenin and Stalin to invite the British to help in the defence of the city.

The Czechoslovaks occupied Ekaterinburg.

## 26 July

A French colonial infantry battalion arrived at Murmansk.

## 28 July

Karl Helfferich arrived in Moscow as German minister. He stayed only ten days, but during that time he received a suggestion from Chicherin, Soviet Commissar for Foreign affairs, that German troops should be sent into Russia from Finland to counter the allies' southward advance from Archangel and Murmansk and that German troops in the Ukraine should fight Denikin's Volunteer Army.

## 29 July

Trotsky announced that former officers who refused to serve in the Red Army would be sent to concentration camps.

## 30 July

A young Left SR, Boris Donskoi, assassinated Field-Marshal von Eichhorn, the German commander in the Ukraine, in Kiev.

## 31 July

Faced with a Turkish demand for surrender and the apparently imminent fall of the city, the communist members of the Baku Soviet left by sea for Astrakhan but were forced by an anti-communist gunboat to return to Baku where a new government known as the Centro-Caspian Directorate, a coalition of Right SRs, Right Dashnaks and Mensheviks, was formed on 1 August.

## 1 August

An anti-bolshevik coup was carried out in Archangel in co-operation with the allies by a White Russian naval officer, Captain Chaplin.

## 1–7 August

Three decrees called on the larger trade unions, factory committees and city Soviets to form 'workers' detachments' to go out into the grain-producing areas to help with the harvest where necessary and to obtain grain either by purchase at fixed prices or by requisition. More often than not, requisitioning was necessitated by the reluctance of peasants to part with grain in return for money which would buy them nothing they wanted.

## 2 August

An allied force of about 1,500 French, British and Americans under General Poole landed at Archangel and was welcomed by the Supreme Administration of the Northern Region which had been formed during the night under the veteran socialist, Chaikovskii, who was also a leading member of the Union for the Regeneration of Russia (SVR), a pro-allied, largely socialist, anti-bolshevik movement.

A decree opened universities to anyone over the age of 16: fees, entrance examinations and minimum educational requirements for entry were abolished. 'Workers' faculties' were set up to provide workers with the background education necessary for university study. The first of them opened on 2 February 1919. In practice, entry to them was normally controlled by the unions, local Soviets or party organisations.

## 3–10 August

About 12,000 Japanese and a small contingent of British troops landed at Vladivostok. They were followed in the next three months by a further 50,000 Japanese deployed in Siberia and 12,000 deployed along the Chinese Eastern Railway in Manchuria. The French, Italians and Canadians also sent small detachments.

## 4 August

The first contingent of British troops from northern Persia under the command of General Dunsterville landed at Baku with the object of denying to the Turks and their German allies control over the Baku oilfields and the Caspian Sea.

In Russia proper, the remaining 'bourgeois' newspapers were suppressed. Some socialist papers continued to appear intermittently on sufferance.

## 5 August

In retaliation for the allied landings, the Cheka arrested about 200 British and French subjects in Moscow and Petrograd, including staff of the consulates and military missions who were described by Chicherin to the US consul-general as 'hostages'. Most were released after a few days when it became clear that the landings at Archangel were on a much smaller scale than had been expected.

## 6 August

A small British mission from northern Persia reached the port of Krasnovodsk on the eastern shore of the Caspian.

## 6–7 August

The Czechoslovaks and Russian troops of the Samara Constituent Assembly government occupied Kazan and captured the state gold reserve which had been moved there. The gold was later handed over to Admiral Kolchak.

## 7 August

Trotsky left Moscow for the front near Kazan in his special headquarters train.

## 8 August

Rich peasants (kulaks) who refused to give up their surplus grain were declared enemies of the people liable to ten years' imprisonment, banishment and confiscation of property.

## 10 August

The first detachment of British and Indian troops under the command of General Malleson crossed into Transcaspia from northern Persia in response to the Ashkhabad Committee's appeal for support. They were soon in action against Red troops sent by the Tashkent Soviet to drive the Ashkhabad Committee's forces back along the Central Asian railway from the Merv oasis. Malleson's objective was to gain control over the port of Krasnovodsk and the Central Asian railway so as to be able to render both of them useless in the event of a Turkish or German attempt to advance eastwards from the Caucasus. Such an advance would have given them access both to the large stocks of cotton in Turkestan and to the north-western approaches to India.

## 12 August

Trotsky began his counter-attack on the Volga front.

## 14 August

Fifteen ships carrying the members of the former Baku Council of People's Commissars, their Left SR and Left Dashnak supporters and troops loyal to them left Baku for Astrakhan but were forced to return to Baku by warships of the Centro-Caspian Directorate.

## 15 August

Two Cheka provocateurs, one of whom bore a letter of introduction from Captain Cromie, the British naval attaché in Petrograd, called on Lockhart in Moscow. They claimed to be unwilling to fight against the allied troops who had landed at Archangel and said they would surrender if ordered to fight on that front. They asked Lockhart to arrange with General Poole that they would not be shot down by allied troops if they approached their lines. According to his memoirs, Lockhart gave them an introduction to Sidney Reilly, a British intelligence agent in Moscow, and some *laissez-passer* forms addressed to 'British Military Authorities in Russia'. This was, in part, the origin of the 'Lockhart Plot' (see 1 September).

## 15–18 August

Denikin's Volunteer Army captured Ekaterinodar.

## 16 August

The first US army units arrived at Vladivostok. General Graves, the commander of the US expeditionary force, arrived with the bulk of the US troops at the beginning of September. Throughout his time in Siberia, Graves strove conscientiously to comply with his orders not to intervene in internal Russian affairs, the duties of his troops being confined almost exclusively to protecting sections of the Trans-Siberian railway.

## 17 August

General Dunsterville arrived at Baku with reinforcements for his advance party which had landed on 4 August.

## 19 August

General Malleson initialled a protocol with the Ashkhabad Committee covering co-operation against the common dangers from bolshevism and Turko-German invasion.

## 20 August

Tsiurupa, the Supply Commissar, signed a regulation to the effect that food-requisitioning detachments should consist of not less than seventy-five men and two or three machine-guns. Political commissars in the detachments were responsible for imbuing them with revolutionary zeal and discipline and for organising local committees of the poor in the countryside.

A Council of People's Commissars' decree abolished the right to own land or buildings in cities with a population of over 10,000, ownership being turned over to local authorities.

## 22 August

The Czechoslovaks occupied Verkhneudinsk on the Trans-Siberian railway.

## 26 August

The Volunteer Army gained access to the Black Sea by occupying the port of Novorossiisk. The army's strength increased rapidly to over 35,000.

A telegram was sent from London to General Knox in Tokyo appointing him head of the British military mission attached to the headquarters of the allied expeditionary forces in Siberia. Knox was intended to assist the local governments in distributing arms and war material from British sources and in training their troops. Equipment for 100,000 men was approved on 25 September and for a second 100,000 on 6 December.

## 26–27 August

All but a few of the American residents in Moscow left for Petrograd and Finland.

## 27 August

Supplementary agreements to the Brest-Litovsk treaty were signed in Berlin. The Soviet government agreed to pay 6 thousand million marks compensation to the Germans. They renounced Soviet claims to sovereignty over Livonia and Estonia and accepted German recognition of Georgian independence, in return for which the Germans agreed to prevent any third power invading the Baku area. The Soviets agreed to sell to Germany 25 per cent of the production of the Baku oilfield. Germany agreed to evacuate Byelorussia, the Black Sea territory, Rostov and part of the Don basin and to give the Soviets access to the Baltic through Reval, Riga and Windau. In a secret exchange of notes (the first communist recourse to a secret diplomatic agreement), the Soviets agreed that if their efforts to expel allied forces from Archangel and Murmansk were unsuccessful, they would, under certain conditions, allow the Germans and Finns to do so.

## 30 August

Uritskii, the head of the Petrograd Cheka, was assassinated by Kanegiesser, a military cadet with SR associations.

In the evening, Lenin was shot and wounded by a young SR, Fanny (Dora) Kaplan. There is no known evidence of co-ordination between this attack and Uritskii's assassination.

## 31 August

The Cheka stormed the British embassy building in Petrograd, killing the naval attaché, Captain Cromie.

## 31 August–1 September

Czechoslovak forces moving eastwards on the Trans-Siberian railway linked up near Chita with Semenov's forces and their fellow-nationals from Vladivostok.

The Cheka shot over 500 political prisoners in a wave of terror. Provincial Chekas were instructed to shoot hostages in reprisal for opposition activities and to shoot 'White Guards' on sight.

## 1 September

In the early hours, Lockhart and his assistant were arrested by the Cheka who tried to establish whether they were linked to the attempt on Lenin's life. They were released later in the day.

## 2 September

A supreme military command, the Revolutionary Military Council of the Republic (*Revvoensovet*) was set up with Trotsky as chairman and Vatsetis as commander-in-chief. Its establishment was confirmed by a decree of the Soviet Central Executive Committee on 30 October.

## 4 September

US reinforcements arrived at Archangel bringing troop strengths there up to over 5,000 Americans, 2,420 British, 900 French and 350 Serbs.

Lockhart was again arrested and imprisoned, first in Cheka headquarters for four days and then in the Kremlin. He was publicly accused of complicity in a variety of counter-revolutionary plots.

The Commissar for Internal Affairs, Petrovskii, instructed all local Soviets to arrest all Right SRs known to them, to take numerous hostages from the bourgeoisie and former officers and to shoot all those engaged in 'White Guard' activities.

## 5 September

A decree on Red Terror gave the Cheka sweeping repressive powers including the incarceration of 'class enemies' in concentration camps.

The Japanese occupied Khabarovsk.

## 5–6 September

Chaplin staged a coup against the SR Supreme Administration of the Northern Region in Archangel and imprisoned Chaikovskii and some of his ministers: they were released by the allies in the next three days and the government was gradually and partially reinstated.

## 8–23 September

A State Conference at Ufa brought together representatives of the predominantly SR Constituent Assembly government of Samara (*Komuch*), the right-wing Siberian provisional government at Omsk and a number of other groups. Out of it emerged an All-Russian Provisional Government with a five-member Directorate (including two SRs) which established itself in Omsk on 9 October alongside and at odds with the Siberian government.

## 10 September

The Red Army under Trotsky's personal direction recovered Kazan. This marked a turning-point in the Volga campaign and the beginning of a long retreat by the Czechoslovaks eastwards to the Pacific coast along the Trans-Siberian railway.

Trotsky issued an order that the families of former Tsarist officers who deserted from the Red Army should be arrested.

## 12 September

The Red Army recaptured Simbirsk.

## 14–15 September

The Turkish army penetrated the defences of Baku. General Dunsterville embarked his 1,300-odd British troops by night for Persia. Azerbaijani and Turkish irregular troops then massacred an estimated 9,000 Armenians before the Turkish army occupied the city on the following day.

## 15 September

Twenty-six bolshevik commissars from the former Baku Soviet, who had escaped by sea from Baku, arrived at Krasnovodsk. They were arrested and, during the night of 19–20 September, were taken out into the desert and shot on the orders of the Ashkhabad Committee. Ill-founded attempts were subsequently made in Soviet propaganda to hold General Malleson's mission responsible for these shootings.

## 19 September

The Japanese occupied Blagoveshchensk and by 22 September controlled the Amur section of the Trans-Siberian railway, later extending their control over the Trans-Baikal section. The British, French and Italian contingents moved up into western Siberia early in October while most of the Americans and all the Canadians remained in the Maritime Province.

## 20 September

The Cheka declared that it was autonomous in its activities, carrying out searches, arrests and executions, reporting after the event to the Council of People's Commissars and the Soviet Central Executive Committee. The declaration evoked protests from the Commissariat of Justice which were overruled by Lenin.

## 1 October

A Council of People's Commissars' decree abolished academic titles and ranks and advanced degrees. Up to 1925 advanced training was given in the form of 'professorial scholarships': promising students were chosen to stay on for further study and research at university. After 1925 they were known as 'aspirants'.

The decree seems to have been largely ignored throughout the civil war by Moscow university. Fitzpatrick pointed out in *The Commissariat of Enlightenment* that by and large the Commissariat of Education respected the principle of university autonomy at this time.

## 2–3 October

Lockhart, having been released from imprisonment on the previous day, left Moscow for Finland and the West with a group of British and French officials. In exchange the British government had released Litvinov, Lockhart's Soviet equivalent in London, to enable him to return to Russia.

## 4 October

Partly with an eye on the impending German military collapse on the western front and the possibility of the revolution spreading to Germany and beyond and partly with an eye on the possibility of serious allied intervention against the Soviet regime, Lenin called for a Red Army of three million men. Chamberlin gave Red Army strength as 331,000 in August 1918, 550,000 in September 1918, 800,000 in January 1919, 3,000,000 in January 1920 and 5,500,000 in January 1921. In 1919 and 1920 there were 2,846,000 desertions.

## 7 October

Chaikovskii formed a Provisional Government of the Northern Region from which socialists other than himself were excluded. Shortly afterwards, he was made a member of the Directorate of the All-Russian Provisional Government at Omsk (see 8–23 September).

Trotsky issued an order that deserters from the army who surrendered and carried out their service would be pardoned; those who resisted would be shot. The chairmen of local Soviets would be arrested if deserters were found in their villages.

Following disagreements over strategy, Sorokin, the commander of the North Caucasian Red Army, persuaded the other four members of his Military Revolutionary Soviet to arrest and execute Matveev, the next most senior commander.

## 7–8 October

The Red Army captured Samara, the members of the Constituent Assembly government having left for Ufa. Thereafter the SR party progressively disintegrated while making ineffective attempts to fight a 'war on two fronts' against bolshevism and against reaction in Siberia. Armed struggle against the communist regime was finally abandoned by them in June 1919.

## 8 October

General Alekseev's death after a long illness allowed Denikin to assume the supreme command of the Volunteer Army in title as well as in effect.

## 10 October

With German support a Northern Corps was established at Pskov, composed of former Tsarist officers who had escaped from Petrograd, local Russians and former Russian prisoners of war repatriated from Germany. By the end of October the corps had reached a strength approaching 3,000. It later formed the basis of General Iudenich's North-Western Russian Army.

## 14 October

General Poole left Archangel and was succeeded by General Ironside. By the end of the year, the forces under the latter's command included about 6,300 British, 5,200 Americans, 1,700 French and 2,700 locally recruited Russians.

## 16 October

A decree announced that all schools at all levels in the RSFSR except institutions of higher learning should be known under the name of the Unified Labour School. All pupils would have the right to go up through the system to the highest level. Productive labour was to be the core of school life. Conventional subjects were to be taught as far as possible by activity methods. Work was to be 'creatively joyful, free from com-

pulsion . . . systematic and socially organised'. The 'old discipline' was discarded. Education was to be of a 'general and polytechnic nature . . . with special emphasis on physical and aesthetic development'. Punishment of schoolchildren was prohibited and homework and examinations were abolished. Education from 8 to 17 was to be free, compulsory, secular and co-educational. Teachers were to be subject to election. The responsible organs of school self-government were to be school Soviets consisting of all school-workers, representatives of local labour, representatives of pupils aged 12 and over and one representative of the local education department. (See 18–23 March 1919 for a *Note* on the educational system in the 1920s.)

## 17 October

A Code of Laws concerning the Civil Registration of Deaths, Births and Marriages codified existing bolshevik legislation on family law including the conditions for marriage and divorce, the rights and duties of spouses, children and relatives.

## 18 October

At Trotsky's insistence, Lenin recalled Stalin from the beleaguered city of Tsaritsyn. Trotsky had been outraged by Tsaritsyn's undisciplined resistance to orders and, in a telegram dated 4 October to Lenin, described Voroshilov, the commander of the Tenth Army and a former associate of Stalin in Baku, as capable of commanding a regiment but not an army of 50,000. Voroshilov and his associates like Budennyi (another former NCO in the Tsarist army) and Ordzhonikidze (political commissar with the Tenth Army and a colleague of Stalin in his Baku days) resented Trotsky's efforts to impose centralised control over the Red Army and his use of former Tsarist officers like Sytin whom Trotsky had appointed commander of the southern front covering Tsaritsyn. In Deutscher's opinion, Stalin was already bitterly jealous of Trotsky and played on the Tsaritsyn group's feelings of resentment against him. Coinciding with Stalin's recall, Tsaritsyn was relieved by the transfer of a Red Army division from the North Caucasian front. Stalin claimed credit for the victory, a claim hotly contested by Trotsky.

## 21 October

Sorokin, the commander of the North Caucasian Red Army, anticipating a move against himself, arrested and shot the four other members of his Military Revolutionary Soviet. The ensuing blood-bath ended in Sorokin's own execution on 2 November.

## 29 October

Disheartened by the failure of the allies to come to their assistance in the Volga area, the Czechoslovak command ordered a general withdrawal.

## 29 October–4 November

The First All-Russian Congress of Workers' and Peasants' Youth Leagues, from March 1926 known as the All-Union Leninist Communist League of Youth (Komsomol), was held in Moscow. It was attended by 175 delegates representing 22,100 members.

## 30 October

An armistice was signed between Turkey and the allies at Mudros which transferred naval control of the Black Sea straits from Turkey to the allies.

An extraordinary tax for the defence of the Russian and international revolutions, designed to levy 10 thousand million rubles, was imposed on the well-to-do. In fact only about a tenth of this amount was collected before the end of 1919.

## 31 October

The Soviet Central Executive Committee decreed that all healthy able-bodied citizens of the RSFSR between the ages of 16 and 50, other than students, were subject to compulsory labour. Those not engaged in socially useful work could be summoned by local Soviets to undertake public work.

## 1 November

British and Indian forces in Transcaspia, by then numbering about 1,000 men, fighting alongside troops of the Ashkhabad Committee, recaptured the Merv oasis which had been taken by Tashkent Soviet forces in August. The British and Indian force received orders not to pursue their eastward advance.

## 1 November and 8 December

Decrees covered the dual subordination of finance departments to their local Soviets and to the Commissariat of Finance. They also regulated the sources of revenue, laying down distinctions between local and central taxation. In practice, with the onset of the civil war, the printing-press continued to be the main source of revenue and by the end of the year currency circulation was some forty times its pre-war level. The monetary system was increasingly replaced by state allocation of resources, by the spread of barter and by the compulsory requisitioning of agricultural produce.

## 5 November

In Omsk the Directorate and the Siberian government merged.

## 6 November

The Soviet envoy in Berlin, Ioffe, was expelled from Germany for his subversive activities.

## 6–9 November

The Sixth All-Russian Congress of Soviets was held.

## 9–10 November

The abdication of the Kaiser and the formation of a social-democratic provisional government in Germany aroused intense enthusiasm and revolutionary expectations in the Russian communist party.

## 11 November

The armistice between the allies and Germany which ended the First World War came into effect.

Allied troop strengths in Siberia in the next few months were 70,000 Japanese concentrated in eastern Siberia with only minor components as far west as Irkutsk; 60,000 Czechoslovaks, virtually non-combatant by this stage; 9,000 Americans; 2,000 British; and smaller contin-

gents from France, Italy and Poland. Of these, only two small British units penetrated briefly to the west of the Ural mountains.

## 13 November

The Soviet Central Executive Committee unanimously agreed to annul the Brest-Litovsk treaty.

Ukrainian nationalists led by Petliura raised a revolt against Skoropadskii in Belaia Tserkov' but were prevented by the German army from reaching Kiev.

The Estonian National Council proclaimed an Estonian republic.

The British War Cabinet confirmed the Anglo-French convention of 23 December 1917.

## 14 November

The British War Cabinet decided to assist Denikin with arms and ammunition, to send additional officers and equipment to Siberia and to grant *de facto* recognition to the Omsk government.

## 15 November

Denikin's Volunteer Army captured Stavropol'.

## 17 November

About 2,000 British and Indian troops under General Thomson reoccupied Baku. Mistrusting Turkish intentions in Azerbaijan, the British government decided to 'police the area between the Caspian and the Black Sea . . . to maintain order and enforce the terms of the armistice pending the final settlement at the Peace Conference of the various territorial questions involved'.

## 17–18 November

A group of right-wing officers arrested the two SR members of the government in Omsk, Avksentiev and Zenzinov, and two other leading SRs. The Council of Ministers decided to dissolve the government and offered the post of Supreme Ruler (i.e. dictator) and commander-in-chief of 'all the land and naval forces of Russia' to Admiral Kolchak who had served for the previous four weeks as Minister of War in Omsk. Kolchak accepted. Avksentiev and Zenzinov were escorted to Vladivostok whence they travelled to Paris. The removal of the SRs from the government alienated both the Siberian peasantry and the Czechoslovaks. The peasantry displayed a marked reluctance to accept recruitment into Kolchak's forces. When Kolchak's officers adopted forcible recruitment methods, increasing numbers of peasants left their villages to join partisan detachments. According to Footman in his paper on the Siberian Partisans the peasant groups began to form spontaneously before Kolchak's accession to power in reaction against urban interference in their affairs. Some of the groups were led by Bolsheviks acting as individuals, the Whites having effectively destroyed the bolshevik underground in Siberia by May 1919. The partisans made a significant contribution to Kolchak's defeat after which some of their units dispersed, some joined the Red Army and some ended up fighting against it. Three days after the Kolchak coup, the Czechoslovaks condemned it as contrary to the principles for which they were fighting and rapidly lost any remaining enthusiasm for participating in the civil war. Semenov did not acknowledge Kolchak's authority and he and another Cossack leader, Kalmykov, caused much havoc on the Trans-Siberian railway and in eastern Siberia generally. Allied policy towards the intervention after the armistice with Germany was undecided. Thoughts of unseating the bolshevik regime foundered on the lack of willing and reliable allied troops. Since it was impossible to evacuate the allied forces in northern Russia before winter, there was a military argument for continuing allied support to Kolchak in Siberia in order to relieve bolshevik pressure on northern Russia. Secondly there was a moral argument for not abandoning those who had rendered assistance against the Germans and who had been encouraged to expect assistance against the Bolsheviks in whose eyes they had compromised themselves. There was also an economic argument for preserving and opening up Siberia's economic resources to world trade. Some details of British and French support of Kolchak in 1919 are given below. The determined non-involvement of General Graves, the commander of the US expeditionary force (see 16 August), brought him into conflict with his allies and some of his American diplomatic compatriots. Graves soon concluded that the Japanese were primarily concerned with pursuing their own interests in eastern Siberia and he was revolted by the atrocities of Semenov and Kalmykov, both of them backed by the Japanese. Graves was equally revolted by the behaviour of many of Kolchak's officers. Disagreements among the allies over the purposes of intervention were a factor in Kolchak's failure to establish his authority, especially in eastern Siberia.

## 18 November

The Latvian National Council proclaimed a Latvian Republic.

## 20 November

Denikin's forces defeated the North Caucasian Red Army in the Stavropol' area. In the following weeks, political disunity, typhus and Denikin's forces between them brought about the disintegration of this army which had already been weakened by the Sorokin affair. By February 1919 Denikin had gained control over virtually the whole of the area north of the Caucasus and west of the Caspian, allowing him to plan a northward drive on Moscow.

## 21 November

The Soviet government nationalised internal trade. The Commissariat of Supply became the sole institution authorised to supply consumer goods. It was given the right to confiscate stocks of goods still in private hands. It was required to put an end to the remnants of workers' control on the railways. The role of the co-operatives was recognised but in effect they became even more closely incorporated into the state system.

The British Cabinet decided to despatch a naval force to the Baltic. Its aims were: to 'show the flag'; to enforce the articles of the armistice agreement with the Germans covering the maintenance of a blockade until a peace treaty had been signed and until German troops had been withdrawn from former Russian territory; and to shore up the newly won

independence of Finland and the Baltic states from bolshevik control. The British admiral in command was instructed that bolshevik warships encountered off the coast of the Baltic states should be assumed to be operating with hostile intent and should be treated accordingly.

## 23 November

The French cruiser, *Ernest Renan*, and the British cruiser, *Liverpool*, arrived at Novorossiisk.

## 24 November

A division of British troops based on Salonika and under the command of General Forestier-Walker occupied Batumi. Control was established over the Baku–Batumi railway and pipeline and a British garrison was established in Tiflis. The withdrawal of the Turkish army from the Erevan province was completed in December.

## 25 November

Allied ships arrived in Sevastopol' to receive the surrender of those ships of the Russian navy which had been acquired by the Germans.

## 26 November

The Council of People's Commissars decreed that every published or unpublished scientific, literary, musical or artistic work might, on the decision of the Commissariat of Education, be declared the property of the RSFSR.

## 26–30 November

British and French military missions arrived at Denikin's headquarters in

Ekaterinodar. This marked the beginning of substantial British material and training support for Denikin's army which included nearly 200,000 rifles, over 6,000 machine-guns, 800 field guns of various calibres, 400 lorries and large quantities of uniforms. By October 1919 eighty-seven aircraft and twelve tanks had been handed over to Denikin's forces; thirty-seven aircraft and forty-four tanks were awaiting issue to them. According to Soviet archives quoted by Kenez in *Civil War in South Russia 1919–20*, total allied aid to Denikin between February and October included 102 tanks, 194 aircraft and 917 'cannons'.

## 27 November

A provisional Soviet government of the Ukraine was proclaimed as a first step towards a new bolshevik occupation of the Ukraine.

## 28 November

Insurance was declared a state monopoly and the insurance companies were nationalised.

## 28 November–3 December

The Supreme Revolutionary Tribunal heard the 'Lockhart case' and the case of the 'envoys' plot'. Lockhart, Reilly, Grenard, the French consul-general, and the French Colonel de Vertement were sentenced to be shot if apprehended; the US intelligence representative, Kalamatiano, and the Russian Colonel Friede were sentenced to death for spying. The latter was executed on 14 December 1918. Kalamatiano was twice reprieved at the last moment, then held as a potential hostage. He

was released in 1921 and returned to the United States. Although the role of Lockhart in particular was grossly distorted, there was some foundation for some of the charges against the accused. Both British and French representatives were engaged in financing anti-bolshevik organisations; by his own account, Reilly was interested in overturning the bolshevik government; and the account given to the Cheka by the French journalist Marchand of a meeting of US, British and French intelligence representatives at the US consulate on 25 August may well have had some basis in fact. The representatives allegedly discussed arrangements for staying behind in Moscow after the departure of official allied representatives and, for example, contingency plans for the blowing-up of bridges.

## 30 November

The Council of Workers' and Peasants' Defence was established to harness all the economic and, later, manpower resources of the country to the war effort. Its members included Lenin, Trotsky and Stalin and its authority extended beyond the RSFSR to the borderlands of Lithuania, Latvia, Byelorussia and the Ukraine which were falling rapidly under communist control.

The Soviet Central Executive Committee repealed the ban on Mensheviks which had been imposed on 14 June. In practice they remained thinly represented in the Soviets and liable to arbitrary arrest but their popularity in the trade unions and proletariat as a whole flourished as disillusionment with the communists deepened.

## 2 December

The largely bolshevik-led committees of poor peasants having in many cases clashed with the less radical local Soviets, the government decreed that the committees should be disbanded. In part, this decree was aimed at placating the middle peasants whose support the regime needed to survive the civil war.

A decree deprived the Moscow Narodny Bank, the central bank of the co-operatives which had hitherto escaped nationalisation, of its independent status. All foreign banks operating in the RSFSR were liquidated.

## 5 December

A decree of the Soviet Central Executive Committee set up a Soviet propaganda department connected with the Commissariat of Foreign Affairs. One of its functions was to organise foreign bureaux of the Russian Telegraphic Agency (*Rosta*).

## 8 December

A Council of People's Commissars' decree recognised the Estonian Soviet Republic which had been proclaimed on 29 November.It collapsed in the following month. Similar decrees recognised the Latvian and Lithuanian Soviet Republics.

## 12 December

The British navy delivered small arms to the Estonian army at Reval and a week later to the Latvian government at Riga.

## 12–14 December

The German army having agreed to withdraw from Kiev, Ukrainian nationalist forces which had revolted in Belaia Tserkov' on 13 November, entered the city on 14 December. The formerly German-backed Ukrainian leader, Skoropadskii, resigned and fled. The Ukrainian nationalist leader, Petliura, arrived in Kiev a few days later and a new government known as the Directory was formed.

## 13 December

British naval forces bombarded the lines of communication of the bolshevik forces near Narva, impeding their westward advance on Reval which was defended by the newly reformed Estonian army stiffened by Finnish volunteers and part of the Northern Corps (see 10 October).

## 14 December

The Red Army, moving westwards into the former zone of German occupation, entered Minsk, the capital of Byelorussia.

## 16 December

The formation of a Provisional Revolutionary Workers' and Peasants' Government of Lithuania was announced.

## 17–24 December

About 1,800 French troops landed at Odessa which the Germans had left a few days earlier. They were followed by further French, Greek, Polish, Senegalese and Algerian detachments totalling over 60,000 men. They occupied the Black Sea coast from the Bessarabian frontier to Kherson, 100 miles east of Odessa. In January French and Greek troops also occupied Sevastopol' in the

Crimea where they had first landed on 25 November.

## 19–31 December

Clashes occurred between Georgian and Armenian troops. This fighting and other squabbles between the three Transcaucasian republics severely damaged their cause at the Paris Peace Conference.

## 23 December

As the Red Army advanced into the Baltic states, the Soviet Central Executive Committee confirmed Soviet recognition of the independence of the short-lived Soviet Republics of Estonia, Latvia and Lithuania.

The Soviet Central Executive Committee dissolved the All-Russian Teachers' Union (VUS) which it accused of counter-revolutionary activities. The VUS was replaced by a communist Union of Workers in Education and Socialist Culture (*Rabpros*) in the summer of 1919.

## 24–25 December

Kolchak's Northern Army captured Perm'.

## 25 December

British troops occupied Tiflis.

## 26–27 December

Two Soviet destroyers surrendered to the British navy in the Baltic.

## 27 December–1 January 1919

An All-Russian Menshevik Conference was held in Moscow.

## 31 December

The Czechoslovak and Kolchak forces abandoned Ufa.

# The Civil War in European Russia 1918-19

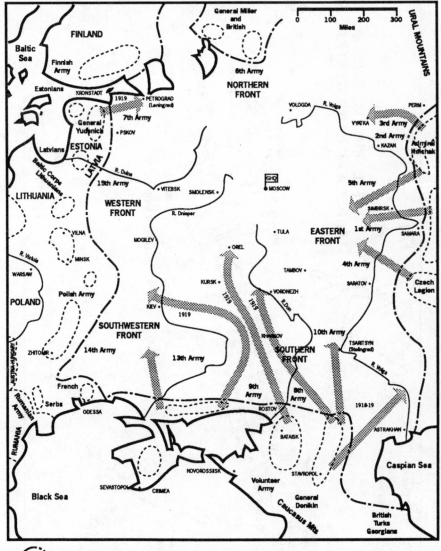

| | |
|---|---|
| Central area of European Russia generally controlled by the Soviet Regime, 1918-1919 |
| White Russian forces and their allies |
| Main White Russian raids into Soviet-controlled territory (with dates) |
| Area remaining under White Russian control in January 1920 |

**1918**

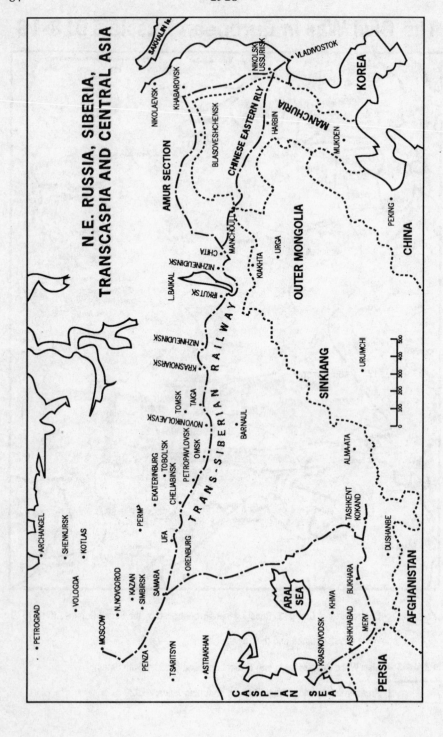

N.E. RUSSIA, SIBERIA, TRANSCASPIA AND CENTRAL ASIA

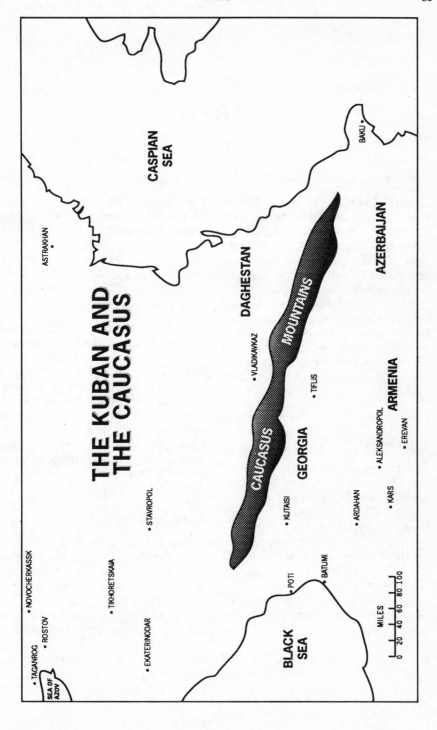

THE KUBAN AND
THE CAUCASUS

# 1919

## January

General Janin, head of the French military mission in Siberia, was appointed commander-in-chief of allied and Czechoslovak troops to the west of Lake Baikal and was given responsibility for advising Kolchak on operational matters and for co-ordinating Russian and allied actions. General Knox, head of the British military mission in Siberia, was given responsibility for handling supplies from abroad and for training and organising all troops raised in the rear zone.

## 1 January

Party membership was given as 251,000 in one Soviet estimate: another gave 350,000 in March.

The Cheka's central Special Department (OO) was established and began to take over responsibility for the security of the armed forces and their counter-espionage and counter-subversion work.

In Minsk a Provisional Workers' and Peasants' Government of Byelo-russia proclaimed the formation of the Byelorussian SSR. The consti-tution of the republic was adopted by the First Byelorussian Congress of Soviets on 3 February.

## 3 January

Continuing their westward and southward advances into the area formerly occupied by the Germans, Soviet troops took Riga and Khar-kov, driving Petliura's nationalist forces out of the latter.

## 4–6 January

The Red Army occupied Vilna (Wilno, Vilnius) which had recently been proclaimed capital of indepen-dent Lithuania. The provisional Lithuanian government which had emerged under the German occu-pation had fled to Kaunas on 2 Jan-uary. A Soviet regime was estab-lished in Vilna; it enjoyed little popular support and collapsed when the Red Army was driven out on 19 April.

## 6–15 January

A rising in Berlin by the Revolution-ary Shop Stewards and the extreme left Spartacus League, which had involved considerable street violence in December and January, collapsed after Karl Liebknecht and Rosa Lux-emburg, the two outstanding Sparta-cist leaders, were 'shot while trying to escape' from the security forces. Luxemburg had opposed Lenin's proposal to found an exclusively bolshevik International on the grounds that it would repel important sections of the international revolutionary movement.

## 8 January

The withdrawal of the German army from the Ukraine, military pressure from the Red Army and diplomatic pressure from the allied missions obliged Krasnov to accept unified command of the Don Cossacks and the Volunteer Army. Denikin proclaimed himself commander-in-chief of the Armed Forces of South Russia.

## 13 January

General Evgenii Karlovich Miller arrived in Archangel at Chaikovskii's invitation to take over command of White Russian forces in the area.

## 16 January

A Red Army attack on the combined Transcaspian and British–Indian force on the north-east side of the Merv oasis was beaten off.

Although weak and divided, the Ukrainian Directory declared war on Soviet Russia.

## 16–25 January

At the Second All-Russian Congress of Trade Unions, the party, in the person of Tomskii, imposed on the unions the responsibility for preventing or, when necessary, terminating strikes. The right to strike was not formally abolished. The Cheka continued to be active in strike-breaking.

## 18–21 January

In Tashkent the War Commissar, Osipov, rebelled, shot a number of the leading members of the Turkestan Soviet government and seized large sums of money from the local bank before abandoning the city. Surviving communists took vengeance on those suspected of having supported Osipov, killing, according to Col. Bailey who was in the vicinity at the time, some 4,000 persons.

## 19–25 January

Bolshevik troops drove Ironside's US and Russian forces out of Shenkursk, 170 miles south of Archangel and the southernmost point of the allied advance on that front.

## 22 January

After consultation between the allied powers, an invitation was issued over President Wilson's signature to 'the various organised groups in Russia' to meet on the island of Prinkipo in the Sea of Marmara to see if a basis of agreement between them could be discovered. Kolchak, Denikin, Miller and Russian *émigré* leaders refused to meet Soviet representatives. The Soviets themselves sent a qualified acceptance on 4 February but Wilson had stipulated that the meeting should be preceded by a truce in Russia. It was clear by the end of February that the Soviets had no intention of accepting this condition.

## 23 January

Chaikovskii left Archangel to join the Russian Political Committee in Paris and in the hope of attending the Peace Conference there. Miller succeeded him as head of government in Archangel as well as commander of the local Russian forces.

## 24 January

The Red Army captured Orenburg from Dutov's forces but the advance of Kolchak's armies to the north of him enabled Dutov to return by the end of April to within twenty miles of the city.

Lenin and Trotsky on behalf of the Russian communist party and representatives of seven other communist parties invited the workers of the world to set up a new International and to use 'mass action' up to and including 'open armed conflict with the political power of capital' to destroy the institutions of bourgeois states and seize power in them.

## End of January

General Malleson was informed of the British decision to withdraw from Transcaspia and was asked to consider how much time would be needed.

## 1 February

General von der Goltz arrived at Libau in Latvia and took command of the remaining German troops there. (The terms of the armistice between the allies and the Germans permitted German troops to stay on temporarily in areas occupied by them to ensure an orderly transition of power. Many units of the German army in the Baltic area had melted away after the armistice but they had been partially replaced by volunteers interested in acquiring Baltic land who had formed themselves into an 'Iron Division'.) Von der Goltz's efforts to restore German domi-

nation of the Baltic states under the banner of anti-bolshevism were to cause the allies severe problems until December when the German government was finally persuaded to withdraw him.

## 4–6 February

The Red Army occupied Kiev which the Ukrainian Directory had evacuated having failed to obtain backing from the French forces in Odessa. The Directory were driven further into western Ukraine and Galicia.

## 8 February

In response to vigorous criticism of the Cheka, the communist party's Central Committee declared its support for the organisation.

## 9 February

The British navy landed further supplies of light arms for the Latvian army at Libau.

## 10–11 February

The regime reacted to Left SR denunciations of the Red Terror and demands for the abolition of the Cheka by arresting and imprisoning some 200 prominent Left SRs.

## 14 February

Following the withdrawal of the German army, Polish and Soviet troops clashed at Bereza Kartuska north-east of Brest-Litovsk, an encounter regarded by Norman Davies as the true beginning of the Polish–Soviet war, usually considered to have started in April 1920. According to Wandycz, unofficial Polish–Soviet contacts began about the middle of March and continued inter-mittently throughout the year (see also 11 October–15 December).

The Soviet Central Executive Committee issued a decree on the transition from the 'obsolete and transitory' system of individual land use to the collective system. It gave the Commissariat of Agriculture responsibility for the development and management of state and collective farms (*sovkhozy* and *kolkhozy*) whose different forms, constitutions, prerogatives and obligations it des-cribed. It also set out regulations for land settlement, the process of rationalising landholdings under the pre-revolutionary commune (*mir*) system. According to Male, the com-mune was born out of competition between households for the best land rather than any egalitarian concept. Its three principal functions were to arrange periodic redistributions of land according to the number and size of peasant households, to organ-ise crop rotation and to conduct local administration. The revolution ser-ved to strengthen the commune, which in practice handled most of the redistribution of expropriated land. Most of the land settlement work (which had begun early in the cen-tury) was concerned with consolidat-ing the intermingled landholdings of different communes and of individual peasants within the communes so as to avoid the loss of time involved in peasants cultivating anything up to fifty strips of land in different localit-ies. Some of the settlement work related to the division of larger com-munes and some to the transfer of households out of communes into enclosed farms. The work was con-ducted by a corps of specialists in the Commissariat of Agriculture. Ac-cording to Yaney in James R. Mil-lar's *The Soviet Rural Community*, their numbers increased from about 7,000 to about 17,000 in the decade 1919 to 1929. (Male's figures were somewhat lower.) In practice, state and collective farms were widely neglected in this period and tended to be staffed by the least effective peasants working poor land.

## 15 February

His Don Cossacks having suffered a number of local defeats, Krasnov resigned, leaving Denikin as the undisputed commander-in-chief of the Armed Forces of South Russia.

On the Murmansk front, May-nard's forces began an advance southwards from Soroka with a view to enlarging the area from which Russians could be recruited.

## 16 February

A note was received in Warsaw from the provisional revolutionary govern-ments of Soviet Lithuania and Soviet Byelorussia announcing the forma-tion of a joint Lithuanian–Byelorus-sian Soviet Republic (*Litbel*). The announcement heightened Polish apprehensions over bolshevik inten-tions towards Poland. Polish troops proceeded to occupy Brest-Litovsk, Bialystok and other towns. A *Litbel* government was formed in Vilna on 27 February. The two republics were officially separated on 31 July 1920.

## 18 February

The Ukrainian partisan leader, Gri-gor'ev, who had supported Skoro-padskii until August 1918 and then fought against him and the Germans under Petliura, agreed with reservations to ally himself with the sparse Red Army forces in the Ukraine under Antonov-Ovseenko's command. Grigor'ev had links with the Borotbists, a Ukrainian brand of Left SRs. He was also in touch with the Ukrainian anarchist, Makhno, who commanded another force of peasant insurgents based on Gulai Polye. Makhno had been collaborating with the Red Army against Denikin since December 1918.

## 24 February

With the help of the Northern Corps, the Estonians pushed the Red Army back beyond the ethnic frontiers of Estonia.

## 2–6 March

The First Congress of the Third (Communist) International (Comintern) in Moscow was attended by thirty-five delegates from nineteen parties and groups as full participants and by a further nineteen delegates from sixteen organisations with consultative votes. Most of the delegates were resident in Russia; only those from Germany, Austria, Norway, Sweden and Holland arrived from abroad. The congress adopted a set of theses by Lenin which underlined the necessity for 'dictatorship of the proletariat' and denounced 'bourgeois democracy' and the international Socialist Conference which had been held in Berne in February in an attempt to revive the pre-war Second (Socialist) International. An Executive Committee of the Comintern (IKKI) was elected to act on the organisation's behalf between congresses. Zinoviev became president of the committee and Radek (at the time in jail in Berlin) secretary.

Bukharin also played a prominent part in Comintern affairs from the beginning.

The statute of the Third International declared that the International had for its purpose the struggle by all available means, including armed force, for the overthrow of the international bourgeoisie and the creation of an international Soviet Republic as a transitional stage to the complete abolition of the state. Trotsky assured the delegates that the Red Army served not only to defend the Russian socialist republic but also as the Red Army of the Third International.

## 2–10 March

Grigor'ev's partisans drove the Odessa-based French and Greek forces out of Kherson.

## 4 March

The British War Cabinet decided to press the allies to agree to the withdrawal of allied forces from northern Russia. Generals Ironside and Maynard were warned that evacuation of northern Russia was likely during the summer.

## 5 March

An inter-allied committee was set up to supervise the Trans-Siberian railway. The American railway engineer, John F. Stevens (see late May/early June 1917), was appointed head of the committee's Technical Board. Stevens and the US Russian Railway Service Corps, who had withdrawn to Japan after the October/November revolution, returned to Harbin in February 1918 to work on the Chinese Eastern Railway. After the allied landings at Vladivostok in August 1918, they extended their operations to the Trans-Siberian railway, partly at least with a view to preventing the Japanese from gaining exclusive control over it.

## 8 March

William C. Bullitt, a US State Department official, arrived in Petrograd as leader of an unofficial delegation to Russia to ascertain the terms on which the Soviets might settle for peace. The mission had been despatched on 22 February with the prior knowledge of the British but not the French who were suspected of having sabotaged the Prinkipo invitation. After two days in Petrograd, the mission moved on to Moscow where it was received by Lenin.

## 10 March

The constitution of the Soviet Socialist Republic (SSR) of the Ukraine was adopted by the Third All-Ukrainian Congress of Soviets.

## 12 March

The Georgian Constituent Assembly, in which the Mensheviks had won an overwhelming majority in free elections, met for the first time. The menshevik government continued with its ambitious programme of nationalisation and land reform · hampered by rampant inflation and economic blockade imposed by Denikin as well as by the Soviets.

## 12–15 March

Grigor'ev occupied Nikolaev which the French had evacuated. The garrison contained a force of stranded German troops. Their arms were acquired by Grigor'ev who advanced on Odessa.

## 13 March

Kolchak launched his spring offensive westwards towards the Volga and captured Ufa between 14 and 16 March. The advance of troops under the command of the Czech General Gajda (he was a Captain in 1918) on the northern wing of Kolchak's forces may have taken some of the Red Army pressure off the precarious allied front south of Archangel. Although Kolchak's forces as a whole gained a lot of territory, they exposed themselves to a Red Army counter-attack. (In his report to the War Office dated 10 December 1919, General Knox gave 3 March as the date of the opening of the spring offensive.)

## 14 March

Bullitt received from Lenin a list of the minimum peace terms acceptable to the Soviet government provided they were put forward by the allies not later than 10 April. These included agreement that all existing governments on Russian territory should remain in control of the territories they occupied at the time of the armistice; in other words, the Soviets were, on the face of it, willing for the sake of peace to abandon (at least for the time being) Siberia, the Urals, the Caucasus, the Archangel and Murmansk areas, Finland, the Baltic states, some of Byelorussia and most of the Ukraine. Among other terms for an armistice deal were that the economic blockade of Russia should be lifted, that diplomatic relations should be restored, that allied troops should be withdrawn, that allied assistance to anti-Soviet governments should cease, that there should be a mutual, general amnesty for all political opponents, offenders and prisoners and that the Soviet and other governments on former Russian territory should recognise the financial obligations of the former Russian Empire.

By the time Bullitt returned from Russia at the end of March, President Wilson was more interested in a suggestion from Herbert Hoover that he should mount a relief operation for Russia (see 3 April). Lloyd George saw that Lenin's proposals (subsequently described by Churchill as 'fraudulent') would find no favour with conservative British or French opinion and did his best to dissociate himself from the mission. Lenin's terms were not submitted to the Peace Conference.

## 16 March

Dzerzhinskii was appointed Commissar of Internal Affairs while retaining his chairmanship of the Cheka. The effect of this dual appointment was to reduce friction between the two organisations and strengthen the Cheka's position.

## 18–23 March

The Russian communist party's Eighth Congress set up from within the Central Committee a Politburo of five members with power to take urgent decisions, an organisational bureau (Orgburo) of five members to conduct the organisational work of the party (including party appointments) and a Secretariat of the Central Committee consisting of a 'responsible secretary' (who was to be a member of the Orgburo) and five assistants with undefined responsibilities. Krestinskii was the first 'responsible secretary' and combined this post with membership of the Politburo and the Orgburo. Stalin was a member of the last two. The Politburo soon became the principal source of major policy decisions. Membership of the Central Committee was limited to nineteen with eight candidate members: the committee was to meet every two weeks.

According to the relevant resolution, the existence of the Ukraine, Latvia and Lithuania as separate republics did not imply that the Russian Communist Party (RKP(B)) should be reorganised as a federation of independent communist parties; there was to be a single centralised party, the RKP(B), whose decisions were binding on all branches of the party regardless of their national composition. The Central Committees of the Ukrainian, Latvian and Lithuanian parties were subordinate to the Central Committee of the RKP(B).

A new party programme was adopted. The programme reaffirmed the principle of self-determination of nations and the right of secession but qualified these rights by proposing a federal union of states as a transitional stage towards complete unity and by specifying that the question of who was the bearer of the will of a nation must be decided according to the historical stage of development of that nation.

The programme called for the consolidation of all economic activity in the country in accordance with 'one

# 1919 93

general state plan'. It referred favourably to the numerous 'bourgeois specialists' who were playing indispensable roles in the administration and economy.

While points 6 and 7 of the economic section of the programme envisaged state management of the trade unions, point 5 said that the unions must 'concentrate in their hands the entire administration of the whole public economy as a single economic unit' and thereby afford the opportunity of establishing 'a truly popular control over the results of production'. This point later provided the 'Workers' Opposition' with a text for their dispute with the party leadership (see 2 November 1920).

The programme called for free, universal and compulsory general and polytechnical education up to the age of 17.

*Note:*In practice, education in the 1920s was neither universal (see 17 December 1926) nor wholly free. In 1921/2, financial stringency obliged local Soviets to reintroduce school fees. They were abolished for primary, but not secondary, education early in 1927 (see Fitzpatrick, *Education and Social Mobility in the Soviet Union*). The school-leaving age was lowered to 15 in 1921.

The programme advocated state encouragement of agricultural co-operatives and a conciliatory policy towards the middle peasants which aimed at winning them over to socialist construction by ideological influence, not by means of suppression. The programme envisaged a major development of consumer co-operatives and the eventual abolition of money.

The party defined its goals as 'the achievement of decisive influence and complete leadership . . . in trade unions, co-operatives, agricultural communes, etc. . . . and complete domination in . . . the Soviets. The party should direct the activity of the Soviets but not replace them.' Party fractions subject to party discipline were to be set up in all Soviet organisations.

Lenin defended Trotsky's policy of building a conventionally disciplined, conscript Red Army with commanders drawn in large part from former Tsarist officers supervised politically by political commissars. The policy was challenged by the so-called Military Opposition in the party who objected to the use of Tsarist officers and wanted a democratised force using the tactics of partisan warfare.

A group known as the Democratic Centralists led by Sapronov and Osinskii complained that decisions were being taken by Lenin in consultation with only one or two of the colleagues immediately concerned, bypassing the Central Committee. Lenin argued that the civil war demanded the strictest centralism and severest discipline.

A reregistration (later to be called a cleansing or purge) of the party membership was to be conducted throughout the country to weed out unsuitable members. It was to be completed by 1 May and was to focus particularly on members who had joined after the October/November revolution. Categories considered unsuitable were those whose personal behaviour was unworthy (especially drunks and careerists), deserters and violators of party discipline, especially those who failed to attend party meetings or pay membership dues.

Registered party membership was given as 313,766.

Sverdlov, who had died on the eve of the congress, was succeeded as President of the Presidium of the Soviet Central Executive Committee and head of state by Kalinin. In Sverdlov's honour, Ekaterinburg was renamed Sverdlovsk on 7 November 1924.

Lenin, Kamenev, Trotsky, Stalin and Krestinskii were elected members of the Politburo. Zinoviev, Bukharin and Kalinin were elected candidate members.

## 19 March

Ludwig Martens delivered to the US State Department a letter dated 2 January 1919 and signed by Chicherin, appointing him as representative of the People's Commissariat of Foreign Affairs in the United States. An accompanying memorandum said that Martens was empowered by his government to negotiate for the opening of commercial relations with the United States. He was not recognised by the US government but opened a Russian Soviet Government Bureau in New York, which he ran until January 1921.

## 20 March

State control was imposed on hitherto autonomous co-operatives.

## 21 March

A communist-social democratic Republic of Workers', Peasants' and Soldiers' Soviets was set up in Hungary under the communist, Bela Kun. With the important exception of its agrarian policy, it based itself on the Soviet model; it aligned itself with Soviet Russia and lasted until 1 August.

## 24 March

Trotsky ordered that, in the event of retreat, the behaviour of party members in the armed forces must be rigorously checked by the army or divisional political department. At about the same time, an organisation known as *Tsentrokomdesertir* was set up with branches in the provinces to deal with the problem of desertion.

## 29 March

General Knox protested vigorously to Kolchak about the failure of his subordinates to agree to and implement any mobilisation plan for the spring or summer offensive.

## 1 April

A British War Office telegram was sent to Ironside, informing him that his force was to be relieved or evacuated altogether.

## 2 April

Threatened by the advance of Red troops and Grigor'ev's partisans on Odessa and by a bolshevik underground in the city and faced with continuing friction with Denikin's representatives, low morale among the French occupation forces and the difficulties of forming a coherent administration and supplying the local population with the necessities of life, the French commander at Odessa received orders from Paris to evacuate.

## 2–5 April

The last of General Malleson's British and Indian troops, which had to some extent been replaced by troops from Denikin's army to the north of the Caucasus, withdrew from Transcaspia leaving only a small naval base at Krasnovodsk which remained until June.

## 3 April

Prompted by Herbert Hoover, who was attracted by the idea of using food aid as a lever for securing moderation in bolshevik policies, the Norwegian explorer and philanthropist, Dr Fridtjof Nansen, proposed to' the allied Council of Four (the United States, Britain, France and Italy) that a neutral commission should be organised to carry out relief work in Russia.

## 3–6 April

French troops carried out their evacuation of Odessa which Grigor'ev's partisans occupied on 6 April.

## 3–10 April

Soviet troops entered the Crimea.

## 7 April

A Soviet Republic was proclaimed in Munich but it was never fully under communist control and lasted only until 1 May.

## 9 April

In consequence of a resolution at the party's Eighth Congress, a joint Soviet and Council of People's Commissars' decree established a People's Commissariat of State Control to supervise the working of the administration and root out inefficiency and corruption. Stalin was appointed commissar, a post which gave him unique insight into and influence over the administration (see also 7 February 1920).

## 11 April

A decree of the Soviet Central Executive Committee established forced labour camps organised by the Cheka and controlled by the Commissariat of Internal Affairs.

## 12 April

A decree, intended to reduce the scale of migration from the cities to the countryside where conditions were less severe, legally tied employees to their existing jobs.

## 17 April

A message was despatched to the Soviet government conveying allied agreement to Nansen's proposal of 3 April on condition that hostilities in Russia ceased and that distribution and transport of food and other aid was to be under the supervision of the Relief Commission. Nothing was said about the withdrawal of allied troops. In his reply, which reached Paris on 13 May, Chicherin agreed to meet Nansen but was not prepared to accept the allied conditions.

## 18 April

An order of the Revolutionary Military Council set up a political section which was converted by a further order of 26 May into the Political Administration of the Red Army (PUR) to administer the political commissars.

## 19 April

General Pilsudski's Polish forces drove the Red Army out of Vilna, the historic capital of Lithuania. The action evoked a strong Soviet protest. Control of the city became a running sore in Polish-Lithuanian relations.

## 21–28 April

Frunze, who had been given command of the whole of the southern sector including the First, Fourth, Fifth and Turkestan Red Armies, launched a counter-offensive against Kolchak, defeating his troops in the Buzuluk and Buguruslan regions to the east of the Volga. This marked the beginning of the end for Kolchak's forces which were devoid of any reserves to consolidate the gains they had made in the previous four months.

## 21 April and 27 May

The RSFSR and Afghanistan exchanged letters on reciprocal recognition.

## 23 April

The Bela Kun regime in Hungary having appealed to the Soviets for help, Antonov-Ovseenko was instructed to launch an attack on the Romanians in Bessarabia. With insufficient reliable troops at his disposal, Antonov persuaded Grigor'ev to undertake the attack.

## 24 April

The reregistration of communist party membership (see 18–23 March) was announced in *Pravda*. The purge, together with mass desertions

from the party by members anxious to avoid mobilisation for the civil war, caused a decline in membership to about 150,000 by August. Membership picked up again in response to a recruiting campaign in the autumn.

## 28 April

Precipitated by a French naval mutiny, French troops completed their evacuation of the Sevastopol' area, a Soviet having taken over control of the city on 19 April. The evacuation imposed a further severe strain on Denikin's relations with the French.

## 30 April

The Provisional Government of the Northern Region at Archangel, in conformity with the Russian Political Conference in Paris, recognised Kolchak as Supreme Ruler. Kolchak then appointed General Miller as governor-general of the northern region and commander-in-chief of the Russian forces there. The locally recruited Russian force in Archangel had reached a strength of 16,000.

Kolchak was informed that the allied troops would be withdrawn from north Russian before the following winter by which time it was hoped that the north Russian government and army would be able to hold their own.

## May

The fuel shortage was so acute that industry was estimated to be receiving only 10 per cent of its normal supplies.

## 1 and 3 May

The RSFSR and the Ukrainian Soviet Republic issued ultimata to the Romanians demanding the withdrawal of their troops from Bessarabia and Bukovina. Both ultimata were ignored.

## 1–21 May

Maynard's Murmansk-based forces, in order to strengthen their own position, to relieve pressure on Ironside's troops on the Archangel front and to help recruitment into the North Russian Army, pursued their southward advance until they reached the northern shore of Lake Onega.

## 3 May

In view of the vital importance to the communist party of the security and loyalty of the Red Army, the Cheka's Special Department (OO) was instructed to report once a week to the Orgburo through Stalin.

## 5 May

On Vatsetis' advice, Trotsky dismissed the commander of the eastern front, General Sergei S. Kamenev, whose determination to pursue Kolchak's forces east of the Urals led him to refuse to permit the diversion of troops to the south to meet the threat from Denikin. Kamenev's subordinates appealed to Lenin who interviewed Kamenev in Moscow and decided to reinstate him.

## 7–9 May

Grigor'ev abandoned any idea he may have had of attacking Romania, turned against the Soviet regime and issued a 'Universal' denouncing Rakovskii's bolshevik Ukrainian government, its commissars 'from the land where they crucified Christ', the Cheka and the agricultural communes. He told Antonov that he intended to seize Kiev, Poltava, Ekaterinoslav and Kharkov. Although the dispersal of Grigor'ev's followers in different directions enabled Antonov to contain the military threat they represented within a month or so, Adams considered that Grigor'ev's 'Universal' expressed the feelings of countless Ukrainian peasants: the rebellion was a significant factor in the virtual disintegration of the bolshevik administration in the Ukraine and the collapse of the front against Denikin.

## 13 May

From its Estonian base, General Iudenich's North-Western Russian Army (see 10 October 1918), which had achieved a strength of about 25,000, began an advance towards Petrograd. (After the armistice of 11 November 1918 the Northern Corps obtained the Estonian government's backing. At the end of April 1919 Iudenich arrived from Helsingfors and took command.)

## 14 May

A Council of People's Commissars decree established the State Publishing House, *Gosizdat*.

## 15–17 May

Grigor'ev's troops carried out a massive anti-semitic pogrom in Elizavetgrad.

## 19 May

Denikin launched his spring offensive. The 'Armed Forces of South Russia' were now over 50,000 strong and supplied with British equipment including tanks.

## 22–23 May

General von der Goltz's German, White Russian and Latvian volunteers, who had been largely instrumental in clearing Red forces out of southern Latvia, captured Riga.

The Red Army, driving into Transcaspia, captured Merv.

## 23 May

Makhno's partisans withdrew in the face of an attack by Denikin's cavalry and opened the way for Denikin's advance.

## 25 May

The Central Board of Universal Military Training (*Vsevobuch*) celebrated its first anniversary with a mass parade of sportsmen in Red Square reviewed by Lenin and Trotsky, the forerunner of many such parades.

## 26 May

An allied note to Kolchak signed by Clemenceau for France, Woodrow Wilson for the Unites States, Lloyd George for Britain, Orlando for Italy and Saionji for Japan declared that they sought to avoid interference in internal Russian affairs. They had intervened in Russia in order to assist those who wished to continue the struggle against Germany and to rescue the Czechoslovaks from annihilation. Since the armistice they had maintained troops in Russia. As

soon as the Peace Conference had assembled, they had invited representatives of all the warring governments in Russia to meet them to resolve Russia's problems. This proposal and an offer to relieve distress in Russia had been negated by the Soviet government's refusal to suspend hostilities. The object of allied policy was to restore peace in Russia by enabling the Russian people to resume control of their own affairs through a freely elected Constituent Assembly and to resolve disputes over Russia's borders through the League of Nations. The allies were convinced that it was impossible to achieve their ends by dealings with the Soviet government and were therefore disposed to assist Kolchak and his associates with munitions, supplies and food to establish themselves as the Government of All-Russia provided they gave the allies guarantees that their policy had the same objects as that of the allies. The conditions for continued allied aid to Kolchak were

1. that, on reaching Moscow, Kolchak would summon a freely elected Constituent Assembly or, if elections were impossible in the circumstances, the Constituent Assembly that was elected in 1917;
2. that local elections should be held in the area already under Kolchak's control;
3. that no special privileges of class or order should be revived in Russia, that the civil and religious liberty of all Russian citizens should be respected and that the regime the revolution had destroyed should not be reintroduced; the Constituent Assembly

should be left to decide on the question of land;

4. that the independence of Finland and Poland should be recognised;
5. that Kolchak's government should recognise the autonomy of Estonia, Latvia, Lithuania, the Caucasian and Transcaspian territories until settlement of their relations with Russia had been reached by agreement, if necessary, in consultation with 'the League of Nations; Kolchak's government should also recognise the existing relations between the allies and these territories;
6. that the right of the Peace Conference to determine the future of the Romanian part of Bessarabia should be recognised;
7. that as soon as a democratic government had been constituted, Russia should join the League of Nations and co-operate in the limitation of armaments;
8. that Kolchak should confirm his statement of 27 November 1918 on his government's acceptance of Russia's national debts.

The note stopped short of according allied recognition to Kolchak's government.

Kolchak's reply to this note dated 4 June was considered satisfactory by the allies who, on 12 June, confirmed by a further note that they would continue to support him.

## 26 May–10 June

About 8,000 British troops arrived in Archangel to relieve the troops who had wintered there. The British War Office had not yet abandoned hope of a link-up at Kotlas between British forces from Archangel and Kolchak's forces from Siberia. By the end of June the Russian army at Archangel had reached a strength of 22,000.

## 30 May

Makhno resigned his command in the Red Army.

## 31 May

Iudenich's advance, coupled with the discovery by the Cheka of an extensive sabotage and espionage network organised by the National Centre which was supplying the White armies with information on the Red Army and preparing the ground for insurrection in a number of cities, provoked a state of alarm in Petrograd. Lenin and Dzerzhinskii signed a proclamation opening with the words 'Death to Spies', an abbreviated version of which, *Smersh*, became the nickname for Soviet military counter-intelligence in the Second World War.

*Note:* The National Centre was based on the outlawed Kadet party.

## 1 June

A Soviet Central Executive Committee decree 'On the Unification of the Soviet Republics of Russia, the Ukraine, Latvia, Lithuania and Byelorussia for the Struggle against World Imperialism' deprived the non-Russian republics of their commissariats of war, national economy, railways, finance and labour: their functions were taken over by the relevant RSFSR commissariats.

## 2 June

Trotsky, who was at Kharkov, published a broadside against Makhno. A few days later, Grigor'ev met

Makhno and joined forces with him in a short-lived alliance.

## 9 June

The Red Army recovered Ufa from Kolchak's forces.

## 10 June

The British War Office suggested that some of the Czechoslovak troops should be encouraged to fight their way through to Archangel whence they could return home sooner than through Vladivostok. Kolchak rejected the idea because of the low state of the Czechoslovaks' morale; he urged that their evacuation through Vladivostok should be hastened.

## 10–13 June

Two forts guarding the approaches to Petrograd, Krasnaia Gorka and Seraia Loshad', switched their allegiance to General Iudenich but were recovered on 15–16 June by Soviet troops. A similar rising in Kronstadt was nipped in the bud and Iudenich was forced to retreat.

## 12–13 June

Denikin formally recognised Kolchak as Supreme Ruler of the Russian State and Supreme Commander-in-Chief of the Russian Armies.

## 17 June

A declaration signed by representatives of Azerbaijan, Estonia, Georgia, Latvia, the Mountain Republic in the North Caucasus, Byelorussia and the Ukraine sought recognition from the Paris Peace Conference of their independence from any pan-Russian government.

## 18 June

A British coastal motor boat torpedoed and sank the Soviet cruiser *Oleg* in Kronstadt roads.

## 18–20 June

The Ninth SR Conference in Moscow resolved to desist from armed struggle against the bolshevik government, to revert to political warfare and to seek to undermine the authority of Kolchak, Denikin and other anti-bolshevik leaders in the areas they controlled.

## 23 June

Von der Goltz's forces were defeated by the Estonian army and the Latvian Northern Corps. Under an armistice arranged by the allies, von der Goltz abandoned Riga on 5 July.

## 25 June

All citizens over 16 years old in Moscow and Petrograd were required to possess labour books which served as identity cards and entitled their bearers to a ration card and social security benefits.

## 25 June–1 July

Denikin captured Kharkov, Tsaritsyn and Ekaterinoslav and cleared the Crimea of bolshevik forces.

## 26 June

A Soviet note to Persia annulled all Persian debts to Tsarist Russia, renounced all public and private Russian concessions in Persia and handed over to the Persians all Russian properties on Persian territory including banks, railways and port installations.

## 28 June

The Versailles Peace Treaty was signed. It came into force on 10 January 1920.

## 30 June

The Siberian army to the south of him having crumbled, General Gajda's troops fell back, abandoning Perm' to the Red Army.

A decree said that any invention could be declared by the Supreme Council of National Economy to be state property. Royalties would be paid to the inventor.

## June–July

US, Canadian and French troops were withdrawn from north Russia.

## July

Kolchak recognised Iudenich as commander-in-chief of the North-Western Russian Army.

## 2 July

In the light of information on Kolchak's reverses, Ironside concluded that a junction with his forces at Kotlas was out of the question.

## 3 July

Against Trotsky's wishes and possibly at Stalin's instigation, the Central Committee confirmed the appointment of Sergei S. Kamenev as commander-in-chief of the Red Army in place of Vatsetis. Trotsky offered his resignation from the Politburo and War Commissariat but it was not accepted.

Denikin issued orders to his rapidly expanding army for a drive on Moscow.

## 4 July

The British Cabinet concluded that an undeclared state of war existed between Britain and Soviet Russia. This meant that British warships were authorised to engage Soviet warships when necessary.

## 8 July

Kolchak dismissed General Gajda and reorganised his Siberian armies.

## 11–15 July

Advancing along the Central Asian railway, the Red Army captured Ashkhabad.

## 14 July

The Red Army recaptured Ekaterinburg, the capital of the Ural territory, from Kolchak's forces.

## 20 July

A mutiny among Ironside's Russian troops left Onega in communist hands. They retained it until 10 September when General Miller recovered it.

## 23 July

A National Centre conspiracy was suppressed in Petrograd.

## 25–27 July

The Red Army reoccupied Cheliabinsk. Kolchak's retreat was becoming increasingly disorderly.

## 27 July

Grigor'ev was shot by Makhno or his followers. Unlike Makhno, Grigor'ev was prepared to have dealings with Denikin over forming a common front against the Bolsheviks.

General Miller's government in Archangel was given formal notification of the forthcoming British withdrawal and was offered the opportunity to evacuate up to 13,800 officers and civilians who were considered to be at risk from a communist take-over.

## 30 July

Denikin launched a new offensive on the Kharkov-Poltava front. His advance, together with Ukrainian peasant disenchantment with the bolshevik regime, facilitated a march on Kiev by Petliura's forces in western Ukraine which had been squeezed out of Galicia by the Poles in May.

## 1 August

Dissension between socialists and communists, the alienation from the government of the population including most of the industrial workers and a Romanian army advance towards Budapest brought about the collapse of Bela Kun's regime in Hungary.

## 5 August

Makhno issued his Order No. 1 listing his insurgents' enemies as the rich bourgeoisie, whether Russian, Ukrainian or Jewish, and those who upheld an unjust social order such as bolshevik commissars and the Cheka. (Unlike Grigor'ev, Makhno was not anti-semitic and his movement contained a number of Jews.) Shortly afterwards Makhno's insurgents briefly occupied Elizavetgrad.

The British War Office informed the British mission in Vladivostok that no further stores would be sent for Kolchak and that British training for his troops was to cease; it had been decided to concentrate support on Denikin and Iudenich.

## 8 August

The Polish army captured Minsk from the Red Army which fell back to the line of the Dvina and Berezina rivers.

## 10 August

Denikin's cavalry general, Mamontov, began a raid in the rear of the Red Army on the southern front which lasted until 19 September. From 18 to 21 August he held Tambov.

In order to cover the forthcoming evacuation of Archangel and to enable General Miller's north Russian forces to take up defensible positions, Ironside's forces south of Archangel attacked and dislocated the Red Army units facing them.

## 14 August

In the hope of gaining Estonian backing for an advance by Iudenich on Petrograd, a North-West Russian government for the provinces of Pskov, Novgorod and Petrograd was formed in the Estonian capital, Reval, on the local initiative of British and allied officers, subsequently repudiated by their governments.

## 18 August

A flotilla of British coastal motor boats torpedoed and put out of action two Soviet battleships and a submarine depot ship in Kronstadt harbour. The operation established British naval supremacy in the Baltic and virtually eliminated the potential Soviet naval threat to the independence of Finland and the Baltic states and also to the left flank of Iudenich's army as it advanced on Petrograd in October.

## 19 August

The allied Supreme Council decided in principle to invite Germany and the neutral powers to join with them in imposing measures amounting to a blockade of Soviet Russia. A blockade had originally been imposed under the umbrella of the allied blockade of Germany. After signature of the Versailles Treaty, the blockade of Soviet Russia continued informally while the Supreme Council discussed procedures and their legal implications under international law.

## 23–24 August

Denikin's forces occupied Odessa.

## 24–31 August

The Estonians, who had been largely instrumental in the capture of Pskov by Iudenich, quarrelled with him and abandoned the city which, soon afterwards, was retaken by the Red Army.

## 28–29 August

The Cheka caught the chairman of the National Centre in the act of receiving a courier from Denikin and found in his possession a list of members of his organisation and reports on the Red Army, ready for transmission to Denikin.

## 29 August

General Miller's north Russian army

carried out an offensive taking 1,000 prisoners. The force sent out from England to cover the evacuation of north Russia began to arrive at Murmansk.

## 30 August

The Red Army evacuated Kiev and Petliura's Ukrainian nationalist forces moved in with orders to avoid conflict with Denikin's troops approaching the city from the east.

## 31 August

A Soviet submarine sank a British destroyer in the Gulf of Finland.

A Soviet note to Estonia recognised her independence.

## 31 August–2 September

After an incident provoked by a Ukrainian nationalist officer, Denikin's troops occupied Kiev, driving Petliura's forces out of the city. Petliura's mission in Warsaw concluded an armistice with the Poles, with whom they had been negotiating an agreement since May and under whose influence Petliura increasingly fell.

## September

A special party conference discussed dissent in the party. Demands were made for freedom of discussion and workers' democracy. Control Commissions were set up by Zinoviev to deal with the problem. Their role was to be enhanced when freedom of discussion was curtailed by the party's Tenth Congress in March 1921.

Kolchak's Siberian army, now under the command of General Diterikhs, rallied and drove the Red

Army back about 100 miles to the Tobol river.

## 12 September

Ironside's force began its withdrawal from the line it had been holding south of Archangel.

## 13 September

Red Army troops pursuing the remnants of Kolchak's southern army gained control over the whole of the Tashkent railway and linked up with the Turkestan Red Army, restoring direct communications between Tashkent and Moscow which had been cut for nearly eighteen months. (They had been briefly restored from January to March 1918.)

## 14 September

Maynard launched a final offensive in the Lake Onega area before withdrawing to Murmansk.

## 18–19 September

In Moscow the Cheka rounded up about 1,000 mainly military supporters of the Kadet-backed National Centre who were allegedly planning a rising for mid-October.

## 20 September

Denikin's troops took Kursk.

## 23 September

The Soviet press named sixty-seven National Centre leaders who had been executed by the Cheka.

## 25 September

An anarchist and Left SR bomb attack on the communist party's Moscow committee headquarters led to savage reprisals against hostages. Dzerzhinskii ordered the Moscow Cheka to execute all Kadets, former gendarmes, aristocrats and other representatives of the Tsarist regime held in Moscow prisons and camps. Hostages were also shot in the provinces.

## 26 September

Makhno defeated a Denikin force at Peregonovka and thereafter advanced on the northern shore of the Sea of Azov, capturing Berdiansk, Aleksandrovsk, Nikopol', Mariupol' and other towns in the following four weeks but holding them for a week or two only.

## 27 September

The last British troops left Archangel. Some 6,500 Russians were also evacuated to the Baltic states and south Russia. Total British casualties in north Russia were 106 officers (41 killed) and 877 other ranks (286 killed). The British contingent reached a maximum strength of 18,400.

## 28 September

General Iudenich opened his second offensive against Petrograd. The resistance of the Seventh Red Army crumbled.

## 30 September

Denikin's troops took Voronezh.

## Early October

The Red Army attacked General Diterikhs' Siberian army and routed it.

## 2 October

The Central Committee of the Ukrainian Communist Party (KP (B)U) abolished itself, party members being transferred to the RKP (B). The KP(B)U was reconstituted in time for its fourth congress in March 1920 having absorbed the Borotbists. The new Ukrainian Central Committee was so hostile to Moscow that it had to be dissolved by the RKP (B) and replaced with a more compliant group.

## 5–8 October

The Second Komsomol Congress denounced the scouting movement for 'leaning towards the White Guards' and fostering a bourgeois outlook.

## 8 October–14 November

Attempts by a Russo-German force led by Bermondt-Avalov and backed by von der Goltz to recapture Riga and Libau were defeated by the Latvians assisted by British and French naval bombardment. Anxiety over Bermondt-Avalov's activities caused the Estonians to break off their participation in Iudenich's offensive.

## 11 October

Iudenich captured Yamburg.

## 11 October–15 December

A semi-official Polish–Soviet peace conference was held at Mikaszewicze. Although it failed to yield an armistice, it had the effect of stabilising the front for the time being.

## 12 October

The British evacuation of Murmansk was completed.

## 13 October

Iudenich took Luga.

## 14 October

Denikin's army took Orel, the northernmost point of its advance, 200-odd miles from Moscow. His forces had by this time reached their maximum strength of over 100,000.

## 16 October

Iudenich took Gatchina, 20 miles from Petrograd.

Trotsky left Moscow in his headquarters train to supervise the defence of Petrograd against Iudenich's forces.

## 19 October

In accordance with a decision taken by the British government originally on 6 March, British troops completed their withdrawal from the Caucasus, leaving only a small garrison in Batumi and a diplomatic mission which had arrived at the end of August.

## 20 October

Soviet troops reoccupied Orel and Denikin's army began a general retreat. His forces proved to be overextended and their headquarters at Taganrog and their lines of communication were threatened by partisan activity on the part of Chechen, Ingush, Daghestani, Georgian and, above all, Makhno's forces estimated at about 25,000 in number: all were antagonised by Denikin's determination to restore 'Great Russia'. Makhno's men occupied Ekatorinoslav intermittently from late October until 9 December.

## 21 October

Having taken Tsarskoe Selo, Iudenich's forces reached the Pulkovo
heights overlooking Petrograd.

Three Soviet destroyers were sunk
by allied mines in the Gulf of Finland
about fifty miles west of Petrograd.

## 22 October

Soviet troops launched a counter-
offensive against Iudenich, recover-
ing Tsarskoe Selo and Pavlovsk on
the following day.

## 24 October

Budennyi's Red cavalry recaptured
Voronezh from Denikin.

## 28 October

With the Red Army approaching
Petropavlovsk (which it occupied on
30 October), Kolchak set in hand the
transfer of his government from
Omsk to Irkutsk but decided that the
city of Omsk should be defended at
all costs. This decision, taken for political reasons, cost him the resignation of Diterikhs on 4 November.

## 1 November

The last British troops left Siberia;
only the military mission and a railway mission remained behind.

## 14 November

Having fallen back rapidly, Iudenich's forces evacuated Yamburg.
Iudenich resigned his command on
16 November. His troops crossed
into Estonia where they were disarmed and disbanded by the Estonians at the beginning of December,
the Red Army having agreed not to
enter Estonia.

## 15 November

The Red Army occupied Omsk
which had been abandoned on the
previous day, together with large
quantities of equipment, by the
remains of Kolchak's army.

## 17 November

The Red Army occupied Kursk. The
resistance of Denikin's army was
beginning to crumble.

General Gajda attempted a coup
in Vladivostok which was suppressed
by General Rozanov, the reactionary
governor of the city who escaped to
Japan in February 1920.

## 20 November

The British Cabinet decided that the
blockade of Soviet Russia should not
be renewed in the following spring
unless the situation changed drastically.

Chicherin broadcast a statement
welcoming Lloyd George's Guildhall
speech of 8 November which looked
forward to peace in Russia. Chicherin's statement held out hopes of close
economic connections between
Soviet Russia and Britain.

## 20–26 November

A Socialist Youth International
which had existed since before 1914
was reconstituted and held its first
conference in Berlin as the Communist Youth International under the
German communist, Willi Münzenberg, with eighteen 'delegates'
present.

## 22 November

The Chinese, having seized the
opportunity presented by Soviet

weakness during the civil war to displace Russian influence in Outer Mongolia, proclaimed the cancellation of Outer Mongolian autonomy and imposed a military administration on the country on 1 December.

## 25 November

A meeting took place in Copenhagen between Litvinov and a British Labour MP, James O'Grady, to discuss prisoner of war exchanges. This was the first formal, semi-official contact for over a year between the Soviets and any of the allied powers (see also 12 February 1920).

## December

The Commissariat of Justice issued a document on 'Leading Principles of the Criminal Law of the RSFSR'. It described crime as the consequence, not of the personal guilt of the individual, but of the class structure of society and treated the criminal law as a provisional expedient which would become superfluous when class divisions were dissolved.

## 2 December

Petliura's representative in Warsaw signed an agreement accepting Polish occupation of eastern Galicia. In return, the Poles recognised Ukrainian independence. The agreement widened the breach between Petliura's Ukrainian nationalists and their former Galician allies who were more anti-Polish than anti-Russian.

## 2–4 December

The party's Eighth Conference adopted new rules on the membership and organisation of the party.

Rule 50 demanded strict party discipline: resolutions of party centres were to be carried out rapidly and accurately. At the same time, freedom of discussion inside the party was to be permitted on all questions until a decision had been reached. Rules 60 to 66 governed the setting-up and functioning in every non-party organisation such as a Soviet or a trade union of communist party fractions subordinated to the party.

## 5–9 December

The Seventh All-Russian Congress of Soviets was held. Lenin defended the use of terror and the performance of the Cheka. The congress passed a resolution formally proposing to each and all of the allies the opening of immediate peace negotiations. It proclaimed the foundation of the Comintern as the greatest event in world history The congress was the first in over a year despite the stipulated six-month interval between congresses. The Soviet Central Executive Committee had also been inactive, decrees being issued by its presidium. The Mensheviks pointed out that the constitution was degenerating.

## 8 December

Denikin appointed Wrangel commander of the Volunteer Army. Wrangel advocated withdrawal into the Crimea but Denikin refused to abandon the Don Cossack country.

## 12 December

The Red Army reoccupied Kharkov.

## 16–17 December

The Red Army reoccupied Kiev.

## 17 December

Trotsky's theses on the militarisation of labour were published.

## 23 December

Kolchak, who was held up to the west of Nizhneudinsk, his eastward journey having been obstructed by the Czechoslovak forces who wished to make their own getaway, appointed the Cossack leader, Semenov, supreme commander in eastern Siberia and the Far East, an appointment which was unwelcome to the Americans and even more so to the Czechoslovaks since his undisciplined private army lay across their eastward line of escape.

## 24 December

A semi-clandestine group known as the Political Centre, composed of SRs, Mensheviks and perhaps some Bolsheviks, staged an anti-Kolchak revolt in Irkutsk and gained control over parts of the city.

Denikin renamed the Volunteer Army the Volunteer Corps and appointed Kutepov to command it in place of Wrangel.

## 28 December

Lenin stated that through the recognition of the independence of the Baltic states, 'we gain the trust . . . of the working masses of [these] states, . . . we detach them . . . from their native capitalists' and lead them towards a future, single, international Soviet republic.

## 30 December

The Red Army occupied Ekaterinoslav.

## 31 December

The Red Army reached Taiga and Tomsk, 500 miles east of Omsk.

# 1920

## 1 January

Soviet estimates of communist party membership give 431,400 rising to 611,978 in March.

## 3 January

The Red Army occupied Tsaritsyn.

## 3–5 January

The Poles, with Latvian co-operation, captured Dvinsk (Dünaburg, Daugavpils) from the Red Army.

## 5 January

The commander of Kolchak's forces in Irkutsk having abandoned the city for the east, the Political Centre assumed power.

## 6 January

From his train 300 miles north-west of Irkutsk, Kolchak announced his intention of resigning in favour of General Denikin.

## 8 January

General Graves announced that US troops were to be withdrawn from Siberia.

The Red Army occupied Krasnoiarsk where most of the remains of Kolchak's army surrendered. A small force continued south-eastwards towards Irkutsk on foot beside the railway track.

## 8–9 January

The Red Army took Rostov, Denikin's forces retreating south of the river Don.

## 9 January

After an unsuccessful attempt by the Fourteenth Red Army under Voroshilov to bring Makhno to heel and move him and his army to the Polish frontier, the Red Army declared him an outlaw and began a campaign to harass and deplete his forces, which met with some success.

## 10 January

Commanders of the victorious Third Red Army in the Urals obtained approval to change the army's name to 'The First Revolutionary Army of Labour' and to use it for economic tasks including the restoration of the transport system. The move heralded the largely unsuccessful attempt, inspired mainly by Trotsky, to use the army wherever possible for economic purposes and to apply military control and discipline to the entire civilian labour force.

## 11 January

Krasnoshchev, the local bolshevik leader, left Irkutsk with three representatives of the Political Centre in a Czechoslovak train to contact the Fifth Red Army which had its headquarters in Tomsk.

France, Britain and Italy granted *de facto* recognition to the independent Georgian and Azerbaijani governments. A similar decision on Armenia was deferred until 18 January because of the relevance of the Turkish peace settlement then under discussion.

## 12 January

US troops began their withdrawal from Vladivostok which was completed on 1 April. The Italian and French contingents had already been withdrawn. The Japanese, however, maintained their front west of Chita covering the junction of the Amur and Chinese Eastern railways and kept control of Vladivostok, Nikol'-sk, Khabarovsk and other centres.

## 14 January

Denikin gave *de facto* recognition to the independent Georgian and Azerbaijani governments.

## 15 January

Kolchak's train arrived at Glazkov, across the river Angara from Irkutsk. Czechoslovak officers, claiming to be acting on General Janin's orders, handed Kolchak over to forces of the Political Centre who imprisoned him in Irkutsk.

## 16 January

The British, French and Italian prime ministers agreed to permit trade with the supposedly independent All-Russian Central Union of Consumers' Co-operatives, *Tsentrosoiuz*, thereby in effect ending their blockade of Soviet Russia.

## 20–22 January

The commander of the Political Centre's forces having declared the situation to be beyond his control, the Political Centre handed over power to a bolshevik Revolutionary Committee.

An agreement reached at the same time by Krasnoshchekov with the Fifth Red Army in Tomsk and approved by Lenin in Moscow for the formation of an East Siberian buffer state based on the Political Centre in Irkutsk was thus overtaken by events. Krasnoshchekov moved to Verkhneudinsk where he arrived on 7 March.

## 21 January

An Extraordinary Investigating Commission, which had been appointed by the Political Centre and consisted of two SRs, one Menshevik and one Bolshevik with another Bolshevik as chairman, began the interrogation of Kolchak.

## 22 January

The Central Committee approved Trotsky's theses on the militarisation of the labour force and they were embodied in a decree a week later.

## 23 January

The Soviet government approved an agreement on trade signed in Paris on 20 January between *Tsentrosoiuz* (described by the leading Soviet

# 1920

111

propagandist Karl Radek on 9 July 1920 as a 'Trojan horse') and the allied Supreme Economic Council. (Although this agreement was not mentioned by Slusser and Triska, they listed a number of agreements between *Tsentrosoiuz* and European firms from March 1920 onwards.)

## 28 January

The Soviet government sent the Polish government a message following up a less specific peace proposal dated 22 December 1919. The stated aim of the message, which recognised without reservation the independence and sovereignty of Poland, was to prevent the war with Soviet Russia into which Poland 'was being drawn by the extreme imperialists among the allies'.

Chicherin addressed an appeal against intervention to the workers of the allied countries.

## 2 February

A revolt assisted by the Red Army overthrew the Khan of Khiva, an area to the south of the Aral Sea (see also 26 April).

A Soviet-Estonian peace treaty was signed, the Treaty of Dorpat (Tartu), under which Soviet Russia formally recognised the independence of Estonia and renounced voluntarily and for ever all rights of sovereignty possessed by Russia over the Estonia people and territory. Estonia agreed to establish diplomatic relations with the RSFSR.

A statement by the Soviet Central Executive Committee denied that they wished to introduce communism into Poland or other countries on the bayonets of the Red Army.

## 3–4 February

The Red Army attacked on the Dvina front south of Archangel.

## 4 February

A decree set up a special committee for establishing Soviet authority in the Caucasus. On 8 April a North Caucasian bureau of the RKP(B) was formed, its members including Ordzhonikidze, Kirov, Smil'ga and Mdivani.

## 5 February

The Red Army occupied Mariupol' and Taganrog on the coast of the Sea of Azov, dividing Denikin's forces. (Kenez in *Civil War in South Russia, 1919–1920* gave this date as 6 January.)

## 7 February

The Czechoslovaks signed an armistice with the Red Army at Kuitun which guaranteed the evacuation of the Czechoslovaks and their non-Russian allies provided that railway installations were not destroyed by them, that they did not interfere in the matter of Kolchak and others held by the Revolutionary Committee and that the state gold reserve was handed over on the departure of the last Czechoslovaks from Irkutsk.

With the remnants of Kolchak's army approaching Irkutsk in an attempt to rescue him, Kolchak was executed there by the Revolutionary Committee with the approval of the commander of the Fifth Red Army.

The Red Army entered Odessa.

The People's Commissariat of State Control (see 9 April 1919) was converted into the People's Commissariat of Workers' and Peasants' Inspection known as *Rabkrin*.

## 8 February

The remaining White forces abandoned the Irkutsk area for the east.

## 10 February

The capture of Krasnovodsk by the Red Army finally consolidated Soviet control of the Transcaspian area.

## 12 February

An Anglo-Soviet agreement on an exchange of prisoners was signed in Copenhagen by Litvinov and the Labour MP, O'Grady. The Germans signed a similar agreement with the Soviets in Berlin on 19 April followed by the French, Belgians, Italians and others.

## 19 February

The government of north Russia ordered the evacuation of Archangel which was occupied by Soviet troops on 21 February. General Miller, his staff and over 1,000 civilians got away by sea. Most of his troops surrendered to the Red Army but General Skobelev and about 1,500 men from Murmansk crossed into Finland. Kennan quoted estimates of 10,000 to 30,000 for the number of Russians subsequently shot by the regime for collaboration with the allies in north Russia.

## 20 February

Denikin's forces under Kutepov took Rostov but were able to hold it for only three days.

## 21 February

The Governmental Commission for the Electrification of Russia (GOELRO) was established under the chairmanship of the communist power engineer, Krzhizhanovskii.

## 25 February

The composition of a *Tsentrosoiuz* trade delegation was announced. Its members were Krasin, an engineer who had been deeply involved in the bolshevik party's pre-revolutionary underground activities, Litvinov, Nogin, Rozovskii and Khinchuk, only the last two being active members of the co-operative organisation. The delegation set out for Copenhagen and Stockholm in mid-March.

## 27 February

The War Office instructed the British military mission in Vladivostok to withdraw. Withdrawal was completed by mid-May.

## 28 February

An agreement was reached between the Japanese garrison at Nikolaevsk and a force of between 1,500 and 3,000 Russian partisans, Koreans and Chinese which had surrounded the town. The partisans' leader, Triapitsyn, was of mixed bolshevik and anarchist allegiance. The agreement provided for the disarming of all White Guards in the town and the transfer of the guard-posts to the partisans: the Japanese were allowed to keep their arms. Nikolaevsk was an important fishing-port in summer but in winter was cut off from the outside world. The town had been under Japanese occupation since September 1918. There were reported to be about 600 Japanese civilians and military in the town at the time.

## 1 March

The last trainload of Czechoslovaks left Irkutsk and the gold reserve was handed over to the Revolutionary Committee there.

## 5 March

The Polish army occupied the important rail junction of Mozyr, cutting the north–south rail link between two Soviet armies. Both Soviet and Polish forces were being rapidly reinforced by this time.

## 12–19 March ·

Fighting broke out in Nikolaevsk between the Japanese and the Russian partisans. Nish's account supported Russian versions according to which the Japanese attacked the partisans in breach of their agreement with them. The outnumbered Japanese were defeated: many of them were killed and 134 survivors were imprisoned.

## 17 March

The Red Army occupied Ekaterinodar, the capital of the Kuban, while Denikin's forces withdrew in disorder towards the Black Sea coast.

Lenin, concerned at the effects on industry of the fuel shortage, issued a directive to Ordzhonikidze, head of the RKP(B)'s North Caucasian bureau, saying 'It is extremely, extremely important for us to take Baku. Exert all efforts in this direction but . . . show yourself doubly diplomatic in your announcements and make as sure as possible that firm local Soviet authority has been pre-

pared. The same applies to Georgia but in this case I advise even greater circumspection.'

## 27 March

The Red Army occupied Novorossiisk, Denikin having evacuated most of his remaining forces, about 34,000 men, by sea to the Crimea.

A Polish proposal for peace talks at Borisov was received in Moscow but no agreement could be reached on the location or the conditions for the talks.

## 29 March–5 April

Lenin's report to the party's Ninth Congress emphasised the need for iron discipline to restore the shattered economy. His report evoked criticism from the Democratic Centralists for its tendencies towards 'vertical centralism' or rule by a small clique.

The Council of Workers' and Peasants' Defence (see 30 November 1918) became the Council of Labour and Defence (STO) and, in effect, a kind of economic general staff headed by the chairman of the Council of People's Commissars. Its members were normally the commissars of war, labour, transport, agriculture and supply together with the heads of the Supreme Council of National Economy, Workers' and Peasants' Inspection and the trade unions.

In his report on the economy, Trotsky developed his ideas on the mobilisation of the industrial proletariat, the liability to labour service, the use of military units for economic purposes and the general application of military discipline to economic life. Labour deserters were to be liable to enrolment in punishment working-gangs or imprisonment in concentration camps. Greater use was to be made of voluntary working holidays (*subbotniki*) which were obligatory for party members. Trotsky's report aroused criticism, largely from those who later joined the 'Workers' Opposition'.

The congress's resolution 'On the question of the trade unions and their organisation', based on a report by Bukharin, declared that 'the trade unions must be gradually converted into auxiliary organs of the proletarian state'. It rejected joint management bodies in industry composed of three or five persons and endorsed Lenin's demand for 'one-man management' which 'presupposes the selection of competent people' and 'even in cases where a specialist is in charge is a manifestation of the proletarian dictatorship'.

The congress adopted resolutions on the economy underlining the need for a unified economic plan. The basic problems were defined as

1. the improvement of transport and the shipment and creation of reserves of bread, fuel and raw material;
2. machine-building for transport and the production of fuel, raw material and bread;
3. machine-building for the production of articles of mass consumption; and
4. production of articles of mass consumption.

All this was to be based on the electrification of the country under GOELRO which was seen by Lenin as a means of binding the country together. (In November he told a Moscow party conference, 'Communism is Soviet power plus electrification of the whole country.' Foreign trade was to be subordinated to the requirements of the basic economic plan.

The congress decided to expand party organisation and propaganda amongst the peasantry. Such figures as there are suggest that the percentage of peasants in the party rose from 7.5 per cent in 1917 to 28.2 per cent in 1921 while that of workers fell from 60.2 per cent to 41 per cent in the same period. The white-collar and educated classes were greatly over-represented in the party in proportion to the population as a whole.

## 1 April

General Graves and the last contingent of US troops left Vladivostok.

## 4 April

Denikin resigned his command of the Armed Forces of South Russia and General Wrangel, having been informed of a British ultimatum to Denikin to give up the struggle or face a total withdrawal of British support, took over as his successor.

## 4–5 April

After the conclusion of negotiations between the Japanese and the local Russian authorities in Vladivostok over new conditions for the Japanese occupation, fighting broke out in the city. On 5 April Japanese troops also opened fire in Nikol'sk-Ussuriisk and Khabarovsk, killing large numbers of civilians. Norton interpreted these incidents as a concerted effort by the Japanese military to extend their control over the Maritime Province by the deliberate use of terror. Unterberger mentioned accounts from eye-witnesses who saw no evidence of Russian provocation of the Japanese in Vladivostok.

## 6 April

With a view to re-establishing Russian and, subsequently, Soviet control over the whole of the former Russian territories in the Far East while avoiding a direct confrontation with the Japanese and, at the same time, exploiting conflicts of interest between them and the Americans, the Soviet government indirectly sponsored a constituent convention of the peoples of the Transbaikal territory at Verkhneudinsk which proclaimed an 'independent' democratic Far Eastern Republic (DVR). Krasnoshchekov became President and Minister of Foreign Affairs. The republic addressed a declaration of independence to all the governments of the world claiming that it embraced Transbaikalia, the Amur district, the Maritime Province, Sakhalin, Kamchatka and the zone of the Chinese Eastern railway in Manchuria. Its authority was accepted by the anti-White but non-Bolshevik government of the Amur district on 25 May and also by a similar government in Vladivostok between 10 November 1920 and 26 May 1921 when it was deposed by the Japanese.

## 21 April

The Poles, who had feared Denikin's Great Russian ambitions and had contemplated his defeat by the Red Army without regret, signed a secret treaty with Petliura's representative in Warsaw, recognising Ukrainian independence under Petliura. This agreement was followed by a military agreement on 24 April. The latter provided for Polish command of Ukrainian forces west of the Dnieper, Ukrainian supplies for the Polish army and Polish arms for the Ukrainians.

## 25 April

The Poles launched what was subsequently described by the French General Weygand as a 'preventive offensive' on the western Ukraine and advanced rapidly on Kiev. By Wandycz's account, Pilsudski was activated by anti-Russian rather than anti-bolshevik sentiment in his aim to restore Poland as a major power in eastern Europe secured by a federation of independent states bordering Russia from Finland through the Baltic states to the Caucasus. On 26 April Pilsudski declared that Polish forces would withdraw from Ukrainian territory when a Ukrainian government had been established. The following day, Petliura issued a proclamation on national liberation from Muscovite bolshevik domination.

## 26 April

The British Prime Minister, Lloyd George, secured the allied Supreme Economic Council's assent to discussing with a Soviet trade delegation 'general' (i.e. political as well as commercial) questions arising out of the resumption of trade with Soviet Russia.

The first All-Khorezm People's Kurultai (congress) abolished the Khanate of Khiva and established a Khorezm People's Soviet (but not socialist) Republic which signed an alliance with the RSFSR on 13 September. It took until October 1923 for the central government, with the help of the Red Army and high-level delegates from Moscow including Ordzhonikidze, to convert the republic into a Soviet Socialist Republic (SSR) eligible for membership of the USSR.

## 27 April

The Red Army entered Azerbaijan, occupied Baku on 28 April, removed the Musavat government and proclaimed a Soviet republic: it met little resistance since the Azerbaijanis were fighting the Armenians over Karabakh.

## 2 May

General Brusilov and a number of other former senior officers of the Tsarist army volunteered their services to the Soviet government for the war against Poland.

## 2–3 May

An attempt was made at a bolshevik coup in Tiflis in the expectation that the Red Army would advance into Georgia. The coup failed largely because the advance was delayed by Armenian and Georgian resistance and by the Polish campaign in the Ukraine.

## 6–8 May

Polish forces occupied Kiev and thereafter took up defensive positions along the Dnieper river to the north of the city.

## 7 May

The RSFSR signed a peace treaty with the menshevik government of Georgia, recognising the independence and autonomy of the Georgian state and undertaking to refrain from interference in its internal affairs. In a secret supplement, Georgia recognised the right to free existence and activity of all communist organisations on its territory.

## 14 May

The Soviet government recognised the Far Eastern Republic which, in practice, it controlled.

## 15 May

The Red Army's western front under Tukhachevskii's command launched a pre-emptive attack on the Polish forces in Byelorussia which were threatening a drive on Mogilev.

An unofficial trade agreement was signed between Krasin's trade delegation and fifteen Swedish firms which broke new ground in that part payment for Swedish agricultural and railway equipment was accepted in Soviet gold.

## 18 May

Soviet forces carried out a surprise landing at Enzeli on the Persian coast, driving out the small British and Indian garrison and taking over the Caspian fleet of eighteen small warships which the British had created in 1918 and had handed over to Denikin in August 1919. Soviet troops advanced to Resht early in June and were instrumental in establishing a Soviet regime in the surrounding Persian province of Ghilan which lasted until October 1921.

## 20 May

Persia and the RSFSR exchanged notes on sending a Persian diplomatic mission to Moscow.

## 25–27 May

Threatened by the approach of a Japanese relief force, the Russian partisans in control of Nikolaevsk, having given the Russian and Chinese inhabitants two days to leave, burnt the town down and massacred the 134 Japanese prisoners there (see 12–15 March). The Japanese retaliated in the next few weeks by occupying northern Sakhalin and Nikolaevsk and strengthening their hold over the coast of the Maritime Province. The partisan leader, Triapitsyn, was captured, tried and executed at the end of July by partisan forces of the northern Maritime Province.

## 31 May

Krasin, who had arrived in London a few days earlier as head of a Soviet trade delegation to negotiate the resumption of Anglo-Soviet trade, had a meeting with Lloyd George, the first occasion on which a Soviet emissary had been officially received by the head of the government of a great power.

## June

The North Caucasian bureau of the RKP(B) sponsored an unsuccessful rising by 20,000 Ossetians against the Georgian government.

## 2 June

Chicherin responded positively to a note from Kemal Atatürk proposing the establishment of diplomatic relations between Soviet Russia and Kemalist Turkey.

## 5–7 June

After unsuccessful probing attacks on Polish positions near Kiev from 27 May to 2 June, Budennyi's Red cavalry and other units of the south-western front under Egorov's overall command, broke through and seized Berdichev and Zhitomir behind the Polish lines to the west of Kiev.

## 6–7 June

Wrangel, having rebuilt an effective army about 40,000 strong out of the remains of Denikin's forces, broke out of the Crimea and, despite the withdrawal of British support, occupied the whole of the North Tauride province before the end of the month.

## 8–10 June

Lenin's 'Left-wing communism, an infantile disorder' was published.

## 10–12 June

Egorov's forces recovered Kiev which the Poles had evacuated. The Polish army, while escaping from threatened encirclement, was obliged to fall back to the south of the Pripet marshes.

## 11 June

The People's Commissariat of Trade and Industry was converted into the People's Commissariat of Foreign Trade (*Vneshtorg*) headed by Krasin.

## 15 June

An International Council of Trade and Industrial Unions (*Mezhsovprof*) was set up under a provisional committee consisting of Lozovskii, Tomskii and the British communist J. T. Murphy with a view to founding a Red International of Labour Unions.

It issued its first manifesto on 1 August during the Second Comintern Congress demanding that the 'yellow' International Federation of Trade Unions in Amsterdam be smashed.

## 27 June

The British military mission in south Russia, which had already been reduced from about 2,000 to 625 officers and men, was evacuated, leaving behind a team of four officers as observers. Shortly afterwards, the French withdrew their much smaller military mission.

## 1 July

Wrangel despatched an emissary to Makhno with proposals for joint operations against the communists. Makhno rejected the approach and, on 22 July, killed the emissary. In the following two months, Makhno suggested joint actions against Wrangel to Moscow and Kharkov. (Dates as in Palij: other sources give 18 June and 9 July, probably quoting the old style versions.)

The conclusion of the Second All-Russian Congress on Food Supply was that requisitioning of surplus agricultural production was the only practicable method of solving the food supply problem. The peasants reacted by reducing the acreage cultivated.

## 4 July

The western front armies under Tukhachevskii, who claimed to have 160,000 men under his command, took the offensive against the Polish forces in Byelorussia.

## 7–9 July

The last remaining British troops on greater Russian territory left Batumi, handing the port over to the Georgians.

## 8 July

The US State Department announced the raising of the embargo on trade with Soviet Russia but declared that recognition of the Soviet regime was neither granted nor implied.

## 10 July

On the Galician front, Budennyi's cavalry reached Rovno (Rowne).

## 11 July

Tukhachevskii's armies recovered Minsk from the Poles.

## 12 July

A Soviet–Lithuanian peace treaty was signed in Moscow. It recognised Lithuanian independence and Vilna as Lithuanian. The treaty provided for the establishment of diplomatic and consular relations on ratification. Acts of ratification were exchanged in Moscow on 14 October.

## 14 July

Tukhachevskii's troops occupied Vilna, the Lithuanian army collaborating with the Red Army against the Poles.

## 16 or 17 July

The Japanese signed an agreement with the Far Eastern Republic at Gongotta. On the understanding that the republic was not communist and that the Soviet army would be excluded from its territory, the Japanese agreed to the cessation of hostilities and the withdrawal of their troops from Transbaikalia. This was carried out between 17 and 26 August.

## 17 July

The Politburo decided to carry the war into Polish territory. Lenin was the chief protagonist of this course, his sights being set as much on linking up with a potentially revolutionary Germany and destroying the Versailles Treaty as with provoking revolution in Poland. Trotsky opposed the extension of the war on the grounds that there was no reason to expect a communist insurrection in Poland without which the Red Army could not hope for success. Stalin is thought to have agreed at first with Trotsky but to have switched his support to Lenin.

## 19 July to 7 August

The Second Congress of the Comintern was attended by 217 delegates from forty-one countries. Zinoviev spoke of the need to convert the Comintern from a propaganda organisation into a disciplined and centralised fighting organ of the international proletariat. It was envisaged that the Comintern would become a single communist party, its branches being the communist parties in different countries; as one organisation, they would continue the struggle until Soviet Russia had become a link in a federation of Soviet republics of the whole world. The congress adopted twenty-one conditions of admission to the Comintern inspired largely by Lenin and designed to keep out all but fully

committed communists. The conditions demanded centralisation, conformity, discipline, legal and illegal agitation in the countryside, the trade unions and the armed forces and the creation of illegal organisations alongside legal parties everywhere. Support was to be given to any Soviet republic struggling against counter-revolutionary forces. A ban on Freemasonry was not included in the twenty-one conditions only because it was covered by a separate resolution. A congress resolution on national and colonial questions called on all communist parties to give practical aid to revolutionary liberation movements in colonial territories in Asia and Africa. 'Bourgeois democratic' national liberation movements were to be supported in so far as they were genuinely directed against imperialist domination.

## 20 July

Lord Curzon, the British Foreign Secretary, sent Chicherin a telegram repeating a warning conveyed on 11 July that if the Soviet advance into Poland continued despite a Polish request for an armistice, the British government in conjunction with their allies would give Poland 'the assistance and support they have promised in that event' (which meant in practice arms supplies) and that the negotiations for a resumption of trade between Soviet Russia and the British Empire could not usefully be pursued.

## 22 July

Partly as a result of pressure from Lloyd George, the Poles sought an armistice with the Soviets. Contact between the two sides was broken off after meetings between 31 July and 2 August.

## 30 July

In the expectation that the Red Army's entry into Poland would provoke a revolutionary situation, a Provisional Polish Revolutionary Committee headed by Marchlevskii, Dzerzhinskii, Unshlikht and Felix Kon who with others had formed a Polish Committee on 4 July, established itself on Polish territory at Bialystok. A similar Revolutionary Committee had been set up in Galicia on 8 July. Neither committee achieved any notable successes.

## 30 July–2 August

A conference of communist women was held. It led to the formation of an International Women's Secretariat which functioned in Moscow and Berlin and survived until 1926 without making much international impact, partly because of disagreements over tactics.

## August

A Joint Central Transport Committee (*Tsektran*) was set up by the Central Committee with Trotsky as chairman to deal with the chaotic transport situation. The centralised control it implied was unpopular and Zinoviev used its unpopularity to undermine Trotsky at the party's Tenth Congress in March 1921.

## 1 August

The Red Army took Brest-Litovsk and continued its advance towards Warsaw.

## 4 August

Kamenev, who had arrived in London as chairman of the Soviet delegation (which had been upgraded from a trade delegation to a 'special peace delegation'), had the first of a series of meetings with Lloyd George. Lloyd George informed him that, in view of the Soviet advance into ethnic Polish territory, the British government and their allies were in honour bound to assist the Poles and had already taken steps to ensure that arms were delivered to them through Danzig. Furthermore, he had arranged that the British fleet should sail to the Baltic with a view to reimposing the blockade of Soviet Russia.

## 6 August

Kamenev and Lloyd George had a lengthy discussion on the terms for a truce between Soviet Russia and Poland.

## 8–9 August

An Anglo-French conference at Hythe (Lympne) discussed possible allied measures to protect Polish independence. Millerand, the French Prime Minister, expressed the view that the Soviets were using their negotiations with the British to gain time while the Red Army overran Poland: he recommended that the British should break off negotiations and send Kamenev and Krasin back to Russia. Lloyd George thought the British Cabinet would not accept this because of the importance of Soviet raw materials and the effect a resumption of trade would have in bringing about the disintegration of bolshevism. An Anglo-French declaration urged the Poles to do their utmost to conclude an armistice with the Soviets and spelt out the nature and conditions of Franco-British support for Poland if the Soviets insisted on terms infringing Polish independence.

## 10 August

Kamenev sent Lloyd George a note setting out Soviet conditions for an armistice with Poland. In outline these were that the Polish army should be reduced to 50,000 men within a month, that arms in excess of the requirements of this army and the civil militia should be handed over to Soviet Russia and the Ukraine, that these arms should not be replaced from abroad, that Poland's war industry should be dismantled and that the armistice line should not be further east than the 'Curzon Line', a more or less ethnic frontier drawn up by the British Foreign Office.

Curzon warned the Poles that the British would not take hostile action against Soviet Russia if the Poles refused to accept in substance the Soviet conditions for an armistice. The French government regarded the terms as leaving Poland defenceless.

The treaty of Sèvres was signed under which Armenia was given formal recognition by the Turkish government in Constantinople and by the principal allied powers. (At this time, British, French and Italian forces were occupying Constantinople.) The Kemalists refused to accept the treaty and opened an offensive against Armenia (see 30 October).

The Armenian government signed an agreement with Soviet representatives in Tiflis, under which the Soviets recognised the independence and sovereignty of the Armenian republic while Armenia accepted the provisional occupation by the Red Army of two areas in dispute between Armenia and Azerbaijan.

## 11 August

In sharp contrast with the British, the French government recognised Wrangel's government of south Russia.

A Soviet–Latvian peace treaty was signed at Riga. The Soviets recognised Latvian independence and the Letts agreed to establish diplomatic relations with the Soviet government.

## 12–15 August

An initially successful Soviet attack on the Polish defences immediately to the east of Warsaw was eventually repulsed.

## 14 August

A force of 7,000 of Wrangel's troops landed successfully on the Kuban coast of the Sea of Azov. The main force reached Timoshevskaia, about half-way to Ekaterinodar. Smaller contingents landed near Novorossiisk and on the Taman peninsula. Superior Red Army forces pushed them all back to the coast which they evacuated between 1 and 7 September.

## 14–17 August

Polish troops under General Sikorski's command attacked Tukhachevskii's force to the north of Warsaw.

## 16 August

Polish forces moving northwards

from south-east of Warsaw broke through the gap between Tukhachevskii's forces, which were aiming to outflank the Warsaw defences from the north-west, and Egorov's forces (including Budennyi's cavalry) which were approaching L'vov to the south. Following Trotsky's example, many commentators have held Stalin (Egorov's principal political commissar) responsible for the failure to divert Egorov's forces northwards from the L'vov area in time to counter the threat to Tukhachevskii's extended communications. Norman Davies, however, found Stalin's 'guilt' in this respect not proven. Tukhachevskii was obliged to withdraw rapidly eastwards losing the bulk of one army and substantial elements of four others.

## 16–20 August

The Supreme Revolutionary Tribunal, chaired by the deputy chairman of the Cheka, heard the case of the Tactical Centre, a secret political front formed in February 1919 to bring together the leaders of the Council of Men in Public Life (SOD), the National Centre and the Union for the Regeneration of Russia (SVR). The SOD was made up of industrialists and landowners. The SVR, led by Professor S. P. Melgunov, contained left-wing Kadets, Populist Socialists, SRs and right-wing Mensheviks. The four leading figures had their death sentences immediately commuted to ten years' imprisonment and they were amnestied in 1921.

## 17 August

Polish–Soviet armistice talks reopened in Minsk. The Soviets were pre-pared to recognise the independence of Poland and to accept the 'Curzon line' as the Polish frontier. At the same time they made other demands which would have facilitated a communist take-over in Poland (see 21 August). The negotiations broke down on 30 August and were resumed at Polish suggestion in Riga on 21 September.

## 17–26 August

Japanese troops withdrew from eastern Transbaikalia and along the Chinese Eastern railway as far as Harbin.

## 19 August

Starving peasants in Tambov province rebelled against food requisitioning. The revolt spread through most of the province and parts of Saratov and Penza provinces. It enabled Aleksandr Stepanovich Antonov, an outlaw with an SR and Left SR background who had broken with the Bolsheviks in August 1918, to build up a combat force of between 20,000 and 40,000 men by February 1921. His control of the area lasted until the summer of 1921 (see 27 April 1921). This was the most spectacular of several hundred anti-Soviet revolts which had been occurring in different parts of the country since 1918.

The Poles recaptured Brest-Litovsk from the Red Army.

## 21 August

*The Times*, quoting Kamenev's delegation, published the terms for an armistice which the Soviets said they had handed to the Poles at Minsk on 19 August. These differed from the terms given to Lloyd George on 10 August, particularly with regard to the proposed workers' civil militia, the organisation of which was to be settled in the eventual peace treaty.

## 23 August

The Poles recaptured Bialystok.

## 26 August

The Kirghiz Autonomous SSR was formed. It was renamed the Kazakh ASSR in 1925 and became a union-republic on 5 December 1936. A new Kirghiz ASSR was formed on 1 February 1926: it too became a union-republic on 5 December 1936.

## 30 August–1 September

Budennyi narrowly escaped complete encirclement near Zamosc on the Galician front and was obliged to retreat hastily eastwards.

## 30 August–2 September

The Red Army acting notionally in support of a Bukharan revolutionary force, attacked and captured the city of Bukhara. The Emir escaped into the mountains to the east. A Bukharan People's Soviet (but not socialist) Republic was proclaimed on 8 October. The new 'Young Bukharan' government was more of a Muslim reformist than a socialist government. It signed a treaty of alliance with the RSFSR on 4 March 1921. With help from the Red Army and guidance from Rudzutak in 1923, Bukhara became a Soviet Socialist Republic from 19 September until 27 October 1924 when it was absorbed into the USSR.

## September

The agitation and propaganda section of the Central Committee (*Agitprop*) was set up.

## 2 September

The Congress of Peoples of the East, intended to stimulate anti-imperialist revolutionary movements in Asia, opened in Baku. It was attended by nearly 2,000 Turks, Persians, Armenians, Indians, Chinese and the various nationalities of Soviet Russia. Zinoviev, president of the Comintern's Executive Committee, Karl Radek, the prominent communist propagandist, and Bela Kun, the Hungarian communist leader, played conspicuous parts. British imperialism in Asia and Africa was the principal target but French and US imperialism were also condemned.

## 10 September

Lloyd George accused Kamenev of breaching the conditions under which the Soviet delegation had been accepted in Britain by arranging a subsidy of £75,000 for the *Daily Herald*, by dealing in precious stones, by co-operating with the Council of Action, which was threatening a general strike against any possible British intervention in support of Poland, and by deliberately misleading the British government over the proposed Soviet peace terms for Poland (see 21 August). Kamenev was told that, if he had not been due to return to Moscow for consultations on the following day, he would have been expelled. In speaking thus to Kamenev, Lloyd George was careful not to implicate Krasin or other members of the

Soviet delegation still in London or to prejudice to any greater extent the negotiations for a trade agreement.

*Note*: The Council of Action was a widely based labour movement which arose on 9 August out of the communist-inspired 'Hands off Russia' campaign dating from February 1919.

## 20–27 September

A battle between Pilsudski's and Tukhachevskii's forces on the River Niemen ended in a Polish victory and a general Polish advance.

## 21 September

Polish–Soviet peace talks were renewed in Riga.

## 22–25 September

The party's Ninth Conference adopted a resolution 'On present tasks of party construction'. This included a decision to establish a Control Commission of the most experienced and impartial party members elected by the Central Committee to receive and examine all manner of complaints against the party from members and non-members. When necessary it was to hold joint sessions with the Central Committee and refer questions to the party congress. Dzerzhinskii, Muranov and Preobrazhenskii were nominated as temporary members although, to ensure impartiality, it was specified that members of the Central Committee were not eligible to serve on the Control Commission. McNeal and Gregor commented that, although the formation of the Control Commission was a con-

cession to the members of the party opposition (the 'Workers' Opposition' emerged as a group for the first time at the conference), the commission was soon to be used against them.

## 30 September

The Azerbaijani SSR signed a series of treaties with the RSFSR, under which the RSFSR took over the functions of the local organisations concerned with war, supplies, finance, transport, communications, internal economy and foreign trade, Azerbaijan being left with its own Commissariat of Foreign Affairs.

## October

The All-Russian Co-operative Society (*Arcos*) was registered in London as a Soviet trading company and within three months placed orders to a value of £2 million.

Sponsored initially by a group of poets who had broken away from *Proletkul't* (see 1 December), the All-Russian Association of Proletarian Writers (VAPP), few of whose members were themselves of proletarian origin, was founded to organise 'proletarian' literature throughout the country. The association developed a degree of discipline and intolerance comparable to that of the party and it attracted support from some party leaders including Kamenev and Radek.

The purchasing power of the ruble was estimated by a Soviet source quoted by Zaleski in *Planning for Economic Growth in the Soviet Union 1918–1932* as having fallen to 1 per cent of its level in October 1917.

## 2–10 October

The Third Komsomol Congress passed a resolution on physical education whose aims were given as training young people for work and preparing them for the military defence of Soviet power. During the month the 'First Central Asian Olympics' were held in Tashkent. Sport was regarded by the regime as an important means of integrating the national minorities into the Soviet state.

## 8–9 October

One of Pilsudski's Polish divisions, having staged a 'mutiny' on his secret orders, occupied Vilna which had been recognised as Lithuanian by the Soviets and provisionally by the western allies, subject to League of Nations approval.

## 8–15 October

Wrangel's forces crossed the Dnieper in the hope of linking up with Polish and Ukrainian forces but were unable to hold their bridgeheads. (Dates given in old style in Wrangel's memoirs as 25 September and 2 October.)

## 10–15 October

Makhno negotiated military and political agreements with the Red Army in Kharkov in which he undertook to collaborate in the campaign against Wrangel in return for concessions including the release of anarchists from Soviet jails.

## 12 October

A Soviet–Polish armistice was signed at Riga, providing for a cease-fire on 18 October. The frontiers agreed upon incorporated territory inhabited by some 3 million Byelorussians and Ukrainians into Poland: a comparable number of Poles remained in Soviet territory. The frontier lasted until the beginning of the Second World War. Signature of the armistice released Soviet forces for the final assault on Wrangel.

## 14 October

A Soviet-Finnish peace treaty was signed at Dorpat (Tartu), under which Finland agreed to establish diplomatic relations with the Soviet government and the latter confirmed its recognition of Finnish independence.

## 20–21 October

Semenov was driven out of Chita by partisan auxiliaries of the Far Eastern Republic of which Chita became the capital on 22 October. Semenov retreated into Manchuria in November. Meanwhile, one of his most savage officers, Baron Ungern-Sternberg, who was interested in forming a Buddhist empire embracing Mongolia and Tibet with himself as its temporal ruler, had made his way with his followers into Outer Mongolia in August and attacked the capital Urga in October. He was repulsed by the Chinese forces there.

## 28 October

Red Army forces under Frunze's command began their final offensive against Wrangel in the North Tauride province.

Britain, France, Italy and Japan in effect recognised Bessarabian union with Romania. The province remained a bone of contention between the Soviets and the Romanians.

## 30 October

Turkish troops occupied Kars, the principal fortress in Armenian territory, and went on to take Aleksandropol' on 6–7 November.

## 2 November

At the Fifth All-Russian Trade Union Conference, party disagreements over the role of the trade unions came out into the open. Trotsky uncompromisingly advocated the appointment from above of trade union leaders and argued that the unions should form part of the machinery for 'militarising' the economy. Lenin supported the trade union leader, Tomskii, in attacking *Tsektran*, of which Trotsky was chairman, and criticised Trotsky for antagonising the communist unionists. Zinoviev supported Lenin and misrepresented himself as the champion of inner-party democracy in order to pursue his personal campaign against Trotsky. Stalin was active behind the scenes on behalf of Lenin and Zinoviev. The 'Workers' Opposition', led by Shliapnikov and Alexandra Kollontai, demanded that the unions should control industry and, without in any way challenging the party's monopoly of power, used the issue to express pent-up dissatisfaction with the party bureaucracy, the privileged position of the commissars, the suppression of discussion and initiative and the corruption of ideology by the use of bourgeois principles of management.

## 2–3 November

Heavily outnumbered by the Red Army, Wrangel's forces retreated into the Crimea.

## 7 November

With the civil war drawing to its close, an amnesty decree issued by the Soviet Central Executive Committee led to an easing of Cheka pressure on the population. Arrested specialists, if needed by the regime, had their cases reviewed even if they were of bourgeois origin. Workers and poor peasants who had offended tended to be let off more lightly.

## 7–11 November

The Red Army successfully penetrated Wrangel's defences on the Perekop isthmus leading into the Crimea. Supplemented by an outflanking move across the Sivash shallows, the attack obliged Wrangel to order the evacuation of the Crimea on 11 November, the order being published on 12 November.

## 10 November

In a note to the Peking government, the Soviet government (who were engaged in forming a 'Red' Mongolian government on Soviet territory) said that they were preparing to drive Ungern-Sternberg out of Outer Mongolia at the request of the Chinese authorities in Urga. On 31 December the Peking government disavowed this alleged request.

## 13–16 November

Having placed his followers under French protection, Wrangel evacuated the Crimea, taking into emigration with him 146,693 soldiers and civilians. He also took with him a cruiser, several destroyers and dozens of other ships from the former Black Sea fleet which had been surrendered to the Germans in the Crimea in June 1918. These ships were subsequently handed over to the French and were impounded at Bizerta.

## 18 November

A decree legalised free abortion provided it was carried out by a doctor in a Soviet hospital. The decree described abortion as an unavoidable evil in existing circumstances and made it clear that legalisation had been introduced only as a means of protecting the health of women.

The British government decided to reopen the trade talks with Krasin's Soviet trade delegation which had been suspended during the Soviet–Polish war. Formal talks began on 1 December.

## 23 November

A decree of the Council of People's Commissars noted that Europe and the United States needed raw materials and had capital to spare and pointed out that the economic recovery of Russia could be speeded up many times by bringing in foreign firms to develop the country's natural resources. Carr observed that, in addition to the economic motive, Lenin was interested in concessions to foreign firms partly as a means of promoting rivalries between the capitalist powers, e.g. the United States and Japan, but more especially as a means of establishing a place for Soviet Russia in the world economy. (See also Lenin's report on con-

cessions to the communist fraction at the Eighth All-Russian Congress of Soviets, 22–30 December 1920, quoted in Eudin and Fisher.)

## 29 November

The Supreme Council of National Economy issued a decree nationalising small industrial enterprises employing more than five workers with mechanical power or more than ten workers without mechanical power.

A few Armenian Bolsheviks crossed into Armenia from Azerbaijan, proclaimed Armenia to be a Soviet republic and appealed for Red Army intervention.

The Red Army opened a drive against Makhno, who was outlawed again on 26 November, arresting as many of his followers as it could and hounding the rest throughout the length and breadth of the Ukraine.

## 30 November

According to Fleming's account, the last troopships carrying Czechoslovaks left Vladivostok.

## 1 December

A party circular on the Proletarian Cultural and Educational Organisation (*Proletkul't*) declared that it was party policy that the organisation should function as a subordinate body within the Commissariat of Education although the organisation's autonomy in the field of artistic creativity was assured. At the same time decadent and non-Marxist trends were condemned. *Proletkul't* dated back to before the October/November revolution. Its leading spirit was A. A. Bogdanov (a pseudonym of A. A. Malinovskii) who believed that literature and the arts should serve to mobilise and educate the proletarian masses but that they should do so independently of organisations concerned with politics and economics. Although *Proletkul't* received state help with its various publications during the civil war, its pretensions to independence and Lenin's view that Bogdanovism was heretical brought it into conflict with the party leadership and it was wound up in 1923.

## 2 December

The Armenian Dashnaks signed a treaty with the RSFSR. The treaty declared Armenia to be an independent socialist republic, granted liberal terms to the defeated Dashnaks and provided for the handover of power to a Provisional Military Revolutionary Committee consisting of five members appointed by the communist party and two by the Dashnak party upon agreement with the communist party. When this committee took over on 6 December (the Red Army having arrived in Erevan), it ignored the treaty, arrested the leading Dashnaks and on 21 December decreed all laws of the Soviet Russian government to be in force in Soviet Armenia on which it imposed a harsh regime of repression and 'war communism'.

## 16 December

Georgia's application to join the League of Nations was rejected although she was admitted to the League's technical sub-committees.

## 20 December

Probable date of the formation of the Foreign Department of the Cheka, known later as the INO. The Cheka had run agent operations abroad before this date, the earliest quoted by Leggett being in late January 1918.

## 22–30 December

The Eighth All-Russian Congress of Soviets decreed the formation of 'sowing committees' in every province, county and township. The purpose of the committees was to compel the peasants to plant as much acreage as the state required. The communist economist, Osinskii, advocated the militarisation of agricultural labour. The congress was the last to admit, though without voting rights, delegates from the menshevik and SR parties and other minor groups.

At a public session in Moscow's Bolshoi Theatre, Lenin and Trotsky publicly defended their differing views on the role of the trade unions.

## 24 December

The party Central Committee decided to allow free discussion of the trade union issue in the period before its Tenth Congress in the following March. As a result, eight 'platforms' or programmes were put forward by individuals and groups. Of these, the important ones were the Platform of Ten put forward by Lenin and nine supporters in the Central Committee, Trotsky's platform and that of the 'Workers' Opposition' led by Shliapnikov and Alexandra Kollontai. Trotsky argued that, since private employers had been virtually abolished, trade unions were no longer necessary to protect workers' interests. He suggested that they should become part of the state machine for running industry. Lenin, disagreeing openly with Trotsky, said that trade unions should become 'schools of communism' to educate the workers and also to protect their interests against the bureaucracy. The 'Workers' Opposition', basing themselves on the party programme (see 18–23 March 1919) contended that the trade unions should themselves take over responsibility for management of the economy.

## 25 December

*Pravda* firmly rejected any idea of free trade being tolerated in Soviet Russia.

## 28 December

The Ukrainian SSR and the RSFSR signed a 'Workers'–Peasants' Treaty of Alliance' in Moscow unifying their commissariats for war, the economy, foreign trade, finance, labour, communications and posts and telegraphs.

# 1921

## 1 January

Soviet figures for party membership give 576,000 or 585,000 for January and 732,521 for March.

## 11 January

The Marx–Engels Institute was founded in Moscow as the central research body on the works of Marx and Engels.

## 16 January

Byelorussia signed a treaty with the RSFSR on similar lines to the Ukrainian model of 28 December 1920.

## 22 January

Although the main civil war campaigns had ended, there was still an acute food shortage. A cut of one-third was ordered in the bread ration in Moscow, Petrograd and elsewhere. In western Siberia a peasant rising during the month mobilised over 50,000 peasants.

## 25 January

The Economic Administration of the Cheka was set up. In addition to tackling bribery, corruption, economic espionage and sabotage, it attempted to supervise the economic performance of industrial and commercial enterprises.

*Pravda* published the theses of the 'Workers' Opposition' led by Shliapnikov and Alexandra Kollontai which aimed to give the trade unions the major say in economic management.

## 26 January

The allied Supreme Council extended *de jure* recognition to Estonia and Latvia. Recognition of Lithuania was postponed until December 1922 because of the dispute with Poland over Vilna.

## 27 January

An Allied Conference in Paris accorded Georgia *de jure* recognition as an independent sovereign state.

## February

Twelve young writers of bourgeois origin, including Vsevolod Ivanov and Konstantin Fedin, founded a group known as the 'Serapion brothers', modelling themselves on classic western and Russian literature. Despite their declarations in favour of artistic freedom and political non-alignment (Serapion was a hermit character from E. T. A. Hoffmann), they were in general sympathetic to the revolution and their work began to be published by party-controlled literary-political journals and by the State Publishing House (*Gosizdat*). Writers such as the 'Serapion brothers', Pil'niak and others were described later by Trotsky as 'artistic fellow-travellers of the revolution'.

## 1–3 February

Ungern-Sternberg carried out his second attack on Urga. Mongolian resentment against the Chinese military having deepened since his first attack, Ungern-Sternberg succeeded in driving the Chinese out of Urga and established himself there as 'military adviser' to and virtual dictator of an Outer Mongolian government set up on 21 March under Bogdo Gegen, the Hutukhtu or Living Buddha of Urga.

## 11 February

In *Pravda*, a Siberian peasant argued that it would benefit the state to impose a fixed tax on grain production leaving the peasant free to dispose of any surplus. The subject was discussed at a meeting of the Central Committee presided over by Lenin on 24–25 February.

A decree of the Council of People's Commissars set up the Institute of Red Professors for training teachers for higher educational institutions. The rector from 1921 to 1932 was the Marxist historian, Pokrovskii.

## 11–12 February

A rising of the Armenian and Russian population of the Borchali and Lori districts, at that time under Georgian control, was almost certainly engineered by the Soviets as their first move against the Georgian menshevik government.

## 12 February

In a leading article headed 'Alarm', *Pravda* announced that sixty-four large factories in Petrograd, including the Putilov works, had closed for lack of fuel.

Elections having been held in January, the Constituent Assembly of the Far Eastern Republic met in Chita with a peasant majority.

## 16–20 February

Troops of the new Armenian Red Army and Soviet troops from Azerbaijan began a combined drive on Tiflis, the Georgian capital.

## 17 February

The Soviet government set up a Central Commission for Famine Relief to deal with the consequences of the drought of 1920.

Two communists signed an article in *Pravda* repeating the idea of a fixed tax on grain production and rejecting as ineffective attempts to coerce peasants into cultivating their land.

## 17–19 February

Armenian Dashnaks rebelled against Soviet rule, seized Erevan and other areas and held out until April.

## 21 February

The Red Army occupied Dushanbe, the main town of eastern Bukhara, forcing the Emir to flee into Afghanistan.

## 22 February

A State General Planning Commission (Gosplan) was set up to work out 'a single, general, state economic plan and methods and means of implementing it'. Its members were appointed by the Council of Labour and Defence (STO). Its first chairman was Krzhizhanovskii, formerly chairman of GOELRO, who served until 1923 and again from 1925 to 1930.

The Angora Turkish government sent the Georgian government an ultimatum demanding the return to them of Artvin, Ardahan and Batumi which had been ceded to them by the Treaty of Brest-Litovsk (3 March 1918). The Georgians agreed, specifying a temporary Turkish occupation of Batumi.

## 22–28 February

A strike wave in Petrograd was provoked by fuel and food shortages and the government's attempts to prevent illicit food-collecting expeditions into the countryside. There was some evidence of menshevik and SR exploitation of the strikes which seem to have been spontaneous in origin. The Petrograd committee of the communist party broke the strikes by declaring a state of emergency, arresting known Mensheviks and SRs, shipping food into the city and relaxing the rules on food-collection.

## 25 February

Tiflis fell to the Red Army and a Georgian SSR was proclaimed there. The Georgian menshevik government withdrew towards Batumi which was occupied by the Turks on 11 March.

## 26 February

A Soviet–Persian treaty of friendship was signed in Moscow, which gave the Soviet government the right to move troops into Persia if a third party should attempt to usurp power there by armed intervention or seek to use Persian territory as a base for operations against Russia.

## 27 February

A fact-finding delegation from Kronstadt made contact with the Petrograd strikers. Kronstadt, the naval base on the ice-bound island of Kotlin, had a tradition of revolutionary radicalism tinged with anarchism. It provided crucial support to the Bolsheviks during the October/November revolution.

## 28 February

Reacting to the Petrograd strikes and to the government's harsh, repressive policies, sailors of the Baltic fleet passed a resolution on board the battleship *Petropavlovsk*. The resolution's more important demands were:

- •• re-election of the existing unrepresentative Soviets by secret ballot;
- •• freedom of speech for workers, peasants, anarchists and left socialists;
- •• freedom of assembly for trade unions and peasant organisations;
- •• the convocation of a non-party conference of workers, soldiers and sailors of Petrograd and Kronstadt;
- •• the release of political prisoners belonging to socialist parties or workers' or peasants' movements;
- •• the abolition of political depart-

ments which gave a single party the privilege of using state funds to propagate its ideas;

●● the abolition of the food-requisitioning detachments on trains or roads;

●● the equalisation of all rations except for workers in unhealthy trades;

●● the abolition of communist fighting detachments in military units and communist factory guards;

●● the right of peasants to do as they saw fit with their land and to possess cattle but not to employ hired labour;

●● the right of individual small-scale manufacture without the hiring of labour; and

●● widespread publication of the contents of the resolution.

The Afghans, led by the progressive, nationalist Emir Amanullah, signed a treaty of friendship with the RSFSR in Moscow, followed the next day, also in Moscow, by a treaty of friendship with Kemalist Turkey. The Soviet–Afghan treaty provided for the opening of five Soviet consulates in the Afghan provinces: this conflicted with an undertaking previously given to the British by the Afghan foreign minister. The Soviets agreed to pay the Afghans an annual subsidy allegedly of 1 million rubles in gold or silver. The agreement led to an increase in the Soviet presence in Afghanistan. In his lectures 'On the Foundations of Leninism' (see 26 April–18 May 1924), Stalin referred to the Emir's anti-imperialist struggle as objectively revolutionary despite his monarchism. By 1926 the Afghan air force of twelve aircraft was staffed almost entirely by Russians. Other Russians were engaged in road-building and telecommunications.

## 1 March

A public meeting was held in Kronstadt. A tactless performance by Kalinin who addressed the meeting failed to prevent it from passing almost unanimously the *Petropavlovsk* resolution of the previous day.

## 1–3 March

The so-called First Congress of the Mongolian People's Party was held under the leadership of Sukhe-Bator at Kiakhta on the frontier with Siberia. Sukhe-Bator and Choibalsan were the leaders of two revolutionary groups which emerged at the beginning of 1920 and were brought together by a Comintern delegate in the spring of that year. The congress decided to form a Mongolian People's Government and a national army to free Outer Mongolia from Chinese and White Russian rule.

## 2 March

Foreshadowing the introduction of the New Economic Policy (NEP) at the Tenth Congress of the party, Lenin told the Moscow Soviet that there was much to be said for taxation as a substitute for grain requisitioning.

At a meeting in Kronstadt to prepare for new elections to the local Soviet, the delegates were so incensed by the speeches of the bolshevik commissars of the Baltic fleet and the battleship squadron and the chairman of the Kronstadt Soviet that they decided to arrest all three of them. The presidium of the meeting formed itself into the nucleus of a

Provisional Revolutionary Committee which was expanded on 4 March to fifteen members. The committee rapidly established its authority throughout the island. It also distributed copies of the *Petropavlovsk* resolution at Oranienbaum and other towns in the Petrograd province. The naval air squadron at Oranienbaum endorsed the resolution.

## 2–3 March

During the night a force of 250 Kronstadters tried to reach Oranienbaum across the ice but were repelled by machine-gun fire.

## 3 March

The Provisional Revolutionary Committee in Kronstadt produced the first issue of their newspaper, *Izvestiia of the Provisional Revolutionary Committee of Sailors, Red Army men and workers of Kronstadt*.

In the early hours an armoured train arrived at Oranienbaum and the disaffected elements in the naval air squadron were arrested. In the afternoon forty-five of them were shot.

## 4 March

The Petrograd Soviet declared the Kronstadt movement counter-revolutionary and demanded its immediate surrender. The Petrograd authorities began taking hostages among the families of the Kronstadters.

Military, political and economic agreements with the RSFSR affirmed the complete independence and autonomy of the Soviet Republic of Bukhara.

## 5 March

Trotsky issued an ultimatum to the Kronstadt rebels who were denounced in government statements as being in the grip of White Guardists.

## 7–8 March

The Kronstadt *Izvestiia* attacked Trotsky as 'the dictator of Soviet Russia who cares little about what is to become of the labouring masses provided that power remains in the hands of the communist party'. The paper expressed its disillusionment with the results of the October/November revolution and denounced the Cheka, the horror of whose torture chambers 'far exceeded the police rule of the Tsarist regime'. The paper called for a third revolution in favour of freely elected Soviets and free associations of workers, peasants and the working intelligentsia.

## 8 March

The first Soviet infantry attack across the ice on Kronstadt, which had been preceded by an artillery barrage on 7 March, was beaten off. Bolshevik casualties were estimated at 500 killed and 2,000 wounded.

## 8–16 March

At the party's Tenth Congress, in response to the Kronstadt rising, to the debate on the role of trade unions and to the emergence in the party of different groups with different platforms, Lenin made it clear that opposition within the party would be crushed. But it was not until the last day of the congress when many delegates had left that he introduced resolutions 'On party unity' and 'On the syndicalist and anarchist deviation in our party'. The first of these decreed the immediate dissolution of all groups with platforms, prohibited all manifestations of factionalism and demanded expulsion from the party for non-compliance. This applied even to members of the Central Committee and Control Commission if agreed by a two-thirds majority at a joint plenary session of the two bodies. The second resolution condemned the views of the 'Workers' Opposition', represented by about fifty delegates at the congress, as inconsistent with membership of the party. The subordination of the unions to the party ('the only body capable of unifying, teaching and organising a vanguard of the proletariat and of the entire mass of working people') was reaffirmed.

A further congress resolution 'On the role and tasks of trade unions' described their most important role as acting as 'schools of communism'. This role would be impeded by the over-rapid conversion of the unions into state institutions: the task was to win them over to the state in fact while leaving them open to membership by non-party as well as party workers. 'The selection of the executive personnel of the trade union movement should be made . . . under the directing control of the party but . . . the trade unions . . . are the one place . . . where the selection of leaders should be done by the organised masses themselves.'

Lenin maintained that a reactionary coalition of enemies of the Soviet state from White Guards to anarchists lay behind the Kronstadt rebellion.

The Central Committee was enlarged from nineteen to twenty-five members and was required to meet every two months instead of every two weeks as laid down by the Eighth Congress in 1919. The Orgburo was enlarged from five to seven members. The three members of the Secretariat, who had in fact behaved moderately in office, were denounced for their dictatorial methods and were replaced in the name of inner-party democracy by Molotov and two others close to Stalin. The staff of the Secretariat had already grown from thirty in 1919 to 602.

The Control Commission became the Central Control Commission, provision being made for the establishment of local control commissions. All members of the Central Control Commission and some members of local control commissions were to be freed from all other work.

Towards the end of the congress, on 15 March, thus avoiding a major debate, Lenin announced the adoption of the first measure of the New Economic Policy (NEP), the replacement of grain requisitions by a less onerous and progressive tax in kind, a sharp break with the policies of 'war communism'.

*Note on 'War Communism' and NEP:* According mainly to Chamberlin, the characteristic policies of 'war communism' were:

1. the attack on private ownership, not only of the means of production, distribution and exchange, but also of large private houses, libraries, jewellery and other objects of value;
2. the attempt to impose state control over the labour of every citizen and over all production, agricultural as well as industrial;
3. centralisation of control over the economy in the hands of a few

hastily improvised state organisations;

4. a state monopoly of distribution exercised through the Supply Commissariat;
5. the attempt to abolish the monetary system;
6. the rationing of basic goods; and
7. an egalitarian wages policy in industry.

Chamberlin gave three main causes for the failure of 'war communism': the civil war, the allied blockade and the defects of the system. Of these, he considered the second the least important. 'War communism' had brought the economy to the brink of collapse. Unemployment, food and fuel shortages and the quest for land had induced roughly half the industrial proletariat to leave the cities for the countryside. The sharp decline in industrial production entailed a shortage of manufactured goods to exchange for the peasants' food production, hence the use of coercion to obtain grain. The peasants reacted to coercion by reducing production to roughly half the 1913 level. The black market probably supplied more food to the cities than the official distribution system.

Chamberlin gave the cornerstone of NEP as the substitution of a tax in kind for food requisitioning and its other characteristics as: the abolition of labour armies and compulsory labour; a rapid spread of private retail trade; a more limited toleration of private enterprise in small-scale industry, construction, etc. while the 'commanding heights' of the economy remained in state hands; and the restoration of a currency and taxation system. By 1924 the tax on grain had been fully converted into a money tax. (See R. W. Davies in *The Development of the Soviet Budgetary System* for details of the revival and partial decentralisation of the budgetary system in 1921–2.)

NEP brought some immediate signs of economic revival but it was not until the summer of 1922 that industrial employment, which had fallen sharply in the post-revolutionary years, began to rise steadily towards the pre-war level which it surpassed in 1928. At the same time, given rural over-population, the number of registered unemployed also rose consistently (apart from a break in 1924/5) until it peaked at 1.74 million in April 1929.

Along with the economic measures of NEP went an intensified effort to break out of Soviet Russia's diplomatic isolation, to neutralise the influence of the Russian *émigrés*, to prevent the formation of an anti-Soviet coalition among the western powers and to enlist, in a carefully controlled manner, the aid of western capital in reconstructing the Soviet economy. Internally, the introduction of NEP was accompanied by a severe tightening of party discipline and by a renewed attack on the Mensheviks who had for long been advocating many of the NEP policies. In April Lenin wrote, 'The place for the Mensheviks and the SRs is in prison.' While the Mensheviks had been virtually excluded from the Soviets, they enjoyed increasing working-class support as disillusionment with bolshevism intensified. In the first quarter of 1921, about 2,000 Mensheviks were arrested including the whole of the party's central committee: the party's organisation never recovered.

Carr described the essence of NEP

as 'the use of [capitalist forms] for the eventual advancement of socialism' (*Socialism in One Country*, vol. I, p. 53).

## 9–16 March

The Kronstadt *Izvestiia* demanded 'all power to the Soviet and not to the parties'. (Although the Kronstadt rebels imprisoned some 300 or 20 per cent of the local communists, they did not maltreat them and did not demand that the communist party should be excluded from the Soviets. Many of the island's communists joined the rebels.) The paper complained that Russian workers had been transformed from slaves of the capitalists into slaves of the state and that the peasants, instead of freedom to till their liberated land, had received bullets and bayonets in exchange for their bread. The paper indignantly denied the government's assertions about White Guardist inspiration of the rebellion.

*Note:* The Kronstadters rejected a suggestion from the SRs that they should call for restoration of the Constituent Assembly and voted by a large majority for Soviet power. While there were similarities between the Kronstadt programme and the programme of the 'Workers' Opposition', members of the latter group were among the delegates to the Tenth Congress who fought against Kronstadt (see 17–18 March) having been persuaded that the only alternative to Lenin was counter-revolution. Avrich's detailed study of the Kronstadt rising concluded that, although a rising in Kronstadt was forecast in Russian *émigré* publications and although various *émigré* groups sought unsuccessfully to organise support for the rebels once the rising had begun, there was no evidence that the rising was other than spontaneous in its origin and in the course which it took.

## 13 March

A provisional Mongolian People's Government was formed with Sukhe-Bator as commander-in-chief. The government invoked Soviet aid to establish itself in Outer Mongolia.

## 16 March

An Anglo-Soviet trade agreement (entailing *de facto* but not *de jure* recognition of the Soviet government) was signed in London. Two prior conditions were included in the text: that each side should refrain from propaganda activities against the other – in particular that the Soviets should not encourage action against British interests in India or Afghanistan in return for a reciprocal British undertaking in relation to those independent countries which had previously formed part of the Russian Empire – and that all citizens of either country at that time in the other should be free to return to their home country if they wished. In addition the Soviet government recognised 'in principle' its obligation to pay compensation to 'private persons who have supplied goods or services to Russia for which they have not been paid', the details of payment of these and other debts to be worked out in a future formal peace treaty.

A treaty of friendship and fraternity was signed in Moscow between the Soviets and the Kemalist Turkish government, based on common hostility to the occupation of a large part of Anatolia by the Greek army and the control exercised over the Black Sea straits by the western allies. The treaty implicitly accorded Turkish recognition to the Soviet government. Under its terms each party agreed not to accept any treaties or agreements which might be imposed on the other against its will. (The Treaty of Sèvres was deemed to be an example.) The Turks conceded Batumi to Georgia, subject to freedom from duty of goods in transit to or from Turkey. Both parties recognised the right of the peoples of the East to freedom and independence. The treaty envisaged a special conference of the Black Sea littoral states to draw up an international statute governing access through the straits. The treaty was followed by closely related treaties between the Turkish government and the Soviet governments of Georgia, Armenia and Azerbaijan signed at Kars on 13 October 1921 and between the Turkish government and the Ukraine signed at Angora on 2 January 1922.

## 17–18 March

Preceded by an artillery barrage on 16 March, a Red Army force of about 50,000 led by Tukhachevskii and including a strong contingent of Cheka troops and some 300 delegates to the Tenth Congress of the party stormed Kotlin island across the ice before dawn camouflaged in white clothing. According to Avrich the morale of the troops had been sharply improved by the congress resolution on the replacement of food requisitioning by a fixed tax in kind. By the early hours of 18 March the resistance of the 15,000-odd defenders of Kronstadt, sapped by

shortages of food, sleep and ammunition and by the lack of support from the mainland, had been broken but it was not until late afternoon that mopping-up was completed.

During the evening of 17 March, eleven members of Kronstadt's Provisional Revolutionary Committee escaped across the ice to Finland. They were followed by about 8,000 others. Of the defenders who were captured, many were either shot or imprisoned in the Northern Camps of Special Designation in the White Sea area which were already being used by the Cheka to house opponents of the regime, particularly those who had fought for the 'Whites' in the civil war. Some of those who took refuge in Finland later responded to a Soviet offer of amnesty and returned to the USSR. They were imprisoned. Total Soviet casualties in the fighting were estimated at roughly 10,000.

## 17–19 March

Fighting in Batumi between the Turks and the Georgians (who signed an armistice with the Soviets at Kutaisi on 18 March) ended with the expulsion of the Turks from Batumi and its occupation by the Red Army which finally extinguished Transcaucasian independence. The menshevik Georgian government and the British diplomatic mission which had been accredited to it left Batumi by sea.

## 18 March

The final Soviet peace treaty with Poland, including agreement to resume diplomatic relations, was signed at Riga.

## 21 March

Following the resolution of the Tenth Congress of the party on 15 March, a decree of the Soviet Central Executive Committee, published on 23 March, replaced the system of requisitions of peasants' products with a fixed tax in kind. The tax was to be smaller in scale than previous requisitions, progressive in incidence and levied on individual households, not villages or other communities. The peasants were to be free to dispose of their surplus production as they chose, whether in exchange for machinery and articles of consumption provided by the state from home-produced stocks or imports or through co-operatives or local markets.

## 22 March

Lenin, Trotsky, Zinoviev, Stalin and Kamenev were elected full members of the Politburo. Molotov, Kalinin and Bukharin were elected candidate members.

The Far Eastern Republic formally protested to the US government over the continuing Japanese occupation of Vladivostok.

## 11 April

A new constitution for the Turkestan Autonomous SSR within the RSFSR was approved by the Soviet Central Executive Committee.

## 14 April

Dzerzhinskii was appointed People's Commissar of Communications in addition to his responsibility for internal affairs and the Cheka.

## 17 April

The Far Eastern Republic adopted a constitution which preserved 'bourgeois democratic' forms. A new permanent government was elected with Krasnoshchekov at its head. Ostensibly it remained independent of Moscow but two well-known Soviet generals, Bliukher and Uborevich, served as successive commanders-in-chief of the republic's armed forces. The republic opened an international campaign against the Japanese occupation of former Russian territory in the Far East.

## 21 April

A Communist University of Toilers of the East was established to give training in political work in their own languages to natives of eastern countries within and outside the RSFSR. The university was based in Moscow with branches in Turkestan, Baku and Irkutsk. It offered courses of up to five years in length.

## 27 April

Tukhachevskii took command of the Red Army forces in Tambov province which were reinforced and stiffened with Cheka troops. A drive was launched against Antonov's forces which were reduced from an estimated 20,000 men in early April to about 1,200 in mid-July. Antonov fled and was killed by the GPU (the successor to the Cheka) on 24 June 1922.

## Spring

As a consequnce of the Red Army's invasion of Georgia, Daghestan, which had proved itself a thorn in the Soviets' flesh in 1918 and 1920 and in

Denikin's in 1919, was finally sub-
dued by the Red Army at the cost of
over 5,000 soldiers killed.

## May–June

In the first issue of the journal
*Pechat' i Revolutsiia*, Lunacharskii,
the Commissar for Education, wrote
that the party in no way shrank from
the necessity of applying censorship,
even to *belles-lettres*.

## 6 May

A provisional Soviet–German agreement was signed allowing for the
attachment of trade representatives
to the delegations in the two countries concerned with prisoners of
war. The agreement entailed
German recognition of the Soviet
trade representatives as the only representatives of the Russian state in
Germany and the withdrawal of the
informal German recognition of
White Russian organisations in
Berlin.

## 17 May

The decree nationalising small-scale
industry was revoked.

## 21 May

The Georgian SSR signed a treaty
with the RSFSR following the pattern of the Ukrainian and Byelorussian treaties of 20 December 1920
and 16 January 1921.

In Urga, Ungern-Sternberg proclaimed the Grand Duke Michael
'All-Russian Emperor' and
announced his intention of liquidating all commissars, communists and
Jews in Mongolia. Anticipating a
move by the Mongolian People's
Government, he launched an attack

on Soviet Transbaikalian territory
and was defeated by the Red Army
near Kiakhta on 6 June.

## 26–28 May

The communist party's Tenth Conference recognised that NEP would
last for a prolonged period spanning
a number of years and set about
explaining to party organisations the
principles underlying the policy
(which was regarded by some as a
betrayal of the revolution).

## 13 June

A decree prohibited the religious
instruction of groups of persons
under 18 years of age.

## 22 June–12 July

The Third Comintern Congress was
attended by 509 delegates from forty-
eight countries. The failure of a communist insurrection in Germany in
March coupled with the Kronstadt
rising and the introduction of NEP
forced the congress to recognise that
the tempo of international revolution
had slowed down. Emphasis was laid
on winning exclusive control over the
proletariat by the creation of mass
communist parties rather than ideologically pure sects. Joint actions
with other left-wing parties were
envisaged. At the same time greater
discipline and centralisation were
imposed with the accent on illegal
activity. The Executive Committee
(IKKI) was enlarged and an inner
bureau of seven members was set up
with particular responsibility for
illegal action. In order to attract the
masses, the Comintern and *Mezhsovprof* issued invitations for the
founding of a Red International of

Labour Unions, the Profintern. The Communist Youth International (see 20–26 November 1919) was brought under tighter Comintern control and its headquarters were transferred from Germany to Moscow. A Communist Women's International also held a conference simultaneously with the Third Comintern Congress but does not appear to have developed.

The Red Sport International (Sportintern) was formed as an affiliate of the Comintern and as a rival to the social-democratic Workers' Sport International (WSI) based in Lucerne. The Sportintern attracted members from Czechoslovakia, Finland, France, Germany, Hungary, Italy, Sweden and, later, Belgium, Estonia, Norway, Uruguay and the United States. The Sportintern's aggressively revolutionary tactics (in December 1925 Zinoviev described the sporting organisations of Czechoslovakia, Germany and other countries as 'the future cells of a Red Guard') caused a breach in its relations with the WSI in 1927. Although Sportintern is said to have survived until 1942 (Riordan, p. 363), it seems to have had no major international achievements to its credit.

The Mongolian People's Party was recognised as a sympathising party of the Comintern and its two delegates were given consultative status.

## 26 June

Severe drought coming on top of the loss of agricultural production resulting from world war, revolution, civil war, food-requisitioning and the breakdown of the transport system, brought on an acute crisis in food supplies. *Pravda* admitted that about 25 million people were facing famine. Even so, grain-requisitioning continued in the Volga region, one of the areas worst affected by the drought.

## 27 June

The Red Army entered Outer Mongolia. Rokossovskii was among the Red Army officers engaged in the operation.

## 30 June

*Pravda* announced that a purge of the party membership would begin on 1 August. Up to the beginning of 1922, 136,386 members, one-fifth of the total, were reported to have been expelled. Rigby in *Communist Party Membership* pointed out that Kronstadt had shown the danger of the party becoming 'isolated from the masses'. The revival of elements of capitalism under NEP intensified the dangers. A primary purpose of the purge and of party recruitment policy was therefore to increase the proportion of workers in the party and to eliminate 'petty bourgeois' influences.

## July

A group of Russian *émigrés* in Prague published a collection of essays known as *Smena Vekh* (*Change of Landmarks* or *Signposts*) arguing the need for reconciliation between the *émigrés* and the Soviet regime. Further publications of this movement appeared in Paris and Berlin. *Smena Vekh* welcomed the appearance of the Eurasian movement which had begun by publishing in Sofia a collection of essays entitled 'The Way Out to the East – a Declaration of the Eurasians' on the theme that Russia was not only European but also Asian. (See also 20 February 1918.) In *New Lies for Old*, Golitsyn stated that both the *Smena Vekh* and the Eurasian movements were used for their own purposes by the OGPU.

## 3–19 July

According to the GSE, the founding congress of the Profintern was attended by 380 delegates from forty-two countries. After vigorous discussion, close linkage between Profintern and Comintern was established. The IFTU in Amsterdam was condemned but communists were instructed to remain in its affiliates in order to gain control over them.

## 4 July

The Soviet government protested to the Polish government about Savinkov's anti-Soviet activities. During the Soviet–Polish war, Savinkov had become chairman of the *émigré* Russian Political Committee in Warsaw and had helped to raise a Russian people's army which fought under Polish command. In January 1921 he had revived his defunct SZRiS (see 6 July 1918) as the People's Union for Defence of the Motherland and Freedom (NSZRiS). This was successfully penetrated by the Cheka provocateur known as Selianinov or Operput. In August 1921 the Soviet press reported the arrest of forty-four Savinkov agents. Operput himself was among those arrested. On 7 October the Poles agreed with the Soviets that they would expel Savinkov and his principal lieutenants who were obliged to leave Poland before the end of the month.

## 5 July

A decree regulated the leasing of enterprises owned by the Supreme Council of National Economy. By October 1923 nearly 6,000 enterprises employing on average sixteen workers had been leased, in some cases to their former owners. Many were in the food-processing industry or hides and skins.

## 6–7 July

Acting in the name of the Mongolian People's Government, the Red Army, assisted by Mongolian and Far East Republican troops, captured Urga. A few days later, a new government was formed with Sukhe-Bator as Minister of War. Ungern-Sternberg, whose forces rebelled against him, fell into Soviet hands in Mongolia on 21 August and was executed in Novonikolaevsk on 15 September. The Living Buddha changed sides and was allowed by the Red government to retain his spiritual primacy while forfeiting his temporal authority. The government asked Moscow not to withdraw its troops for the time being, a request to which the Soviet government agreed on 10 August. Between them, Soviet advisers, Red Army troops, Comintern agents and russified Mongols converted Mongolia in the course of the next few years into the first Soviet satellite state, the pro-Chinese Prime Minister, Lama Bodo, having been executed on 7 August 1922 (Rupen's date – other sources give 10 April). Fourteen other leading Mongolian personalities were arrested and shot with him. Systematic purges were instituted, a particularly severe one being carried out in 1924. Hammond described the communist take-over of Outer Mongolia as an isolated success for the Comintern during its existence and as a pattern for the later communist take-overs in Poland, East Germany, Bulgaria, Romania, Hungary and North Korea.

## 7 July

Individuals were authorised 'freely to undertake handicraft production and also to organise small-scale industrial enterprises' employing not more than ten to twenty workers.

## 13 July

Gorky issued an appeal, published in the press on 23 July, to 'all honest European and American people' for prompt food and medical aid to the Russian people.

## 21 July

The Soviet Central Executive Committee set up an All-Russian Committee for Famine Relief (VKPG) under communist leadership but with support from non-communist members of the intelligentsia in order to attract foreign support.

## 25 July

Gorky announced that the Soviet government would accept the offer of famine relief sent to him on 23 July by Herbert Hoover on behalf of the American Relief Administration (ARA). This developed into the biggest of the relief operations in Russia.

## 7 August

The poet, Alexander Blok, died. While active in bringing literature and theatre to the masses and becoming the first president of the Petrograd branch of the All-Russian Union of Soviet Poets, he wrote little poetry after 1918 and sank into a state of depression and acute mental anguish before his death.

## 9 August

A Council of People's Commissars' 'instruction', the first important NEP measure dealing with large-scale industry, called for the concentration into 'unions', soon to be known as 'trusts', of a number of the more efficient enterprises in a given branch of industry. While remaining state property, the 'trusts' were to have a degree of independence from state administration and were to operate on principles of economic accounting known as *khozraschet* (see 10 April 1923). By the end of the year fifteen major 'trusts' had been set up. By the end of August 1922 the number had grown to 421, including fifty each in the textile, metallurgical and food industries, forty in leather, thirty-five in chemicals and twenty in the electrical industry. By 1923 they employed 75 per cent of workers in nationalised industry.

## 20 August

Litvinov signed an agreement in Riga with the ARA for the provision of massive supplies of food.

## 27 August

The first group of ARA representatives arrived in Moscow. On 1 September an ARA team left for the Volga area where the relief work was initially concentrated. The first ARA kitchen was opened in Petrograd on

7 September. In October and November the ARA extended its operations to Tsaritsyn, Orenburg, Ufa, Astrakhan and the Kirghiz and Bashkir republics. By 1 December 568,000 people were receiving rations at about 3,000 feeding points in 191 towns and villages from Petrograd to Astrakhan. Operations were later extended into southern and western Ukraine.

For fear of political 'contamination', the Cheka arrested and imprisoned the non-communist members of the All-Russian Committee for Famine Relief.

At about this time, the Cheka formed a counter-espionage department (KRO) to deal with the threat of espionage and subversion arising from increasing contacts between Soviet Russia and the West.

Dr Fridtjof Nansen, High Commissioner of the Geneva Conference for Aid to the Famine Victims in Russia, signed an agreement on famine relief credits with the Soviet government on behalf of the Red Cross and other relief organisations. (On 24 August, Nansen had been appointed League of Nations High Commissioner to deal with the problem of Russian refugees.)

## 28 August

Makhno and eighty-three surviving followers finally gave up the struggle against the Red Army and crossed the River Dniester into Romania. Makhno died in Paris on 27 July 1934.

## 1 September

*Petrogradskaia Pravda* announced that sixty-one participants in a Petrograd conspiracy had been shot by decision of the Cheka. The leader, Professor of Geography Tagantsev, was head of the Petrograd Fighting Organisation (PBO) which had been planning an armed uprising in Petrograd. It included a wide political spectrum from Kadet to Left SR. Among those shot was Gumilev, the Acmeist poet and former husband of the poetess, Anna Akhmatova.

## 2 September

A preliminary Soviet–Norwegian agreement for the resumption of trade was signed at Christiania (Oslo).

## 7 September

A British note to the Soviet government protesting about Soviet propaganda to the East evoked a negative reply on 27 September which claimed that the Comintern could no more be identified with the Soviet government than the Second International could be with the Belgian or British governments.

## 12 September

The International Workers' Aid Society (MRP) was founded in Berlin by Willi Münzenberg. It was intended both as a communist front organisation (it spawned many others) and, in competition with the ARA, to bring famine relief and, later, industrial and technical help to the Russians. Its British branch was known as Workers' International Relief. At about the same time the Friends of Soviet Russia was founded in the United States with similar aims. In France several literary figures including Anatole France, Henri Barbusse and Romain Rolland, set up a pro-Soviet group known as *Clarté*. The MRP's headquarters moved from Berlin to Paris in 1933 and it was wound up in 1935.

## 30 September

The RSFSR signed a treaty of union with the Armenian SSR on the lines of other existing treaties with SSRs (see 21 May).

## 28 October

Dr Armand Hammer, who had already arranged a shipment of US grain to the famine-stricken Ural area in return for furs and other goods there, signed a concession agreement to operate an asbestos mine in the Urals. He claimed that this was the first US concession which actually came into being in Soviet Russia. In a 1981 article Gillette attributed the fact that Lenin granted Hammer an interview in part to Hammer's father's financing of the US communist party and in part to Lenin's desire to have an American concessionaire to play off against the Europeans. Gillette also described the help given to Hammer by Ludwig Martens, the former Soviet representative in the United States, and by Boris Reinstein, the Comintern official in charge of relations with the United States.

## 5 November

A treaty was signed in Moscow between the RSFSR and the Mongolian People's Republic in which each side recognised the other as the sole legal authority in its territory, thus implicitly denying Chinese sovereignty over Outer Mongolia. Despite this treaty, the Sino-Soviet agreement of 31 May 1924 recognised Outer Mongolia as part of China. The Tannu Tuva (formerly Urianghai) area, the north-western part of Mongolia, was set up as a separate state. On 22 July 1925, it signed a treaty of friendship with the USSR and on 24 November 1926, a People's Republic of Tannu Tuva was proclaimed. It was annexed by the USSR on 13 October 1944 and became an Autonomous Region of the RSFSR although it was still nominally subject to Chinese sovereignty.

## 10 November

The Young Turk leader, Enver Pasha, whose schemes for overthrowing Kemal Atatürk in Turkey the Soviet government refused to support, arrived in eastern Bukhara, proclaimed himself 'commander-in-chief of all the armed forces of Islam' and added strength and a degree of cohesion to the *Basmachi* movement as an anti-Soviet force. According to Agabekov, Enver Pasha had agreed with Lenin after the Congress of Peoples of the East in September 1920 that he would attempt to pacify Turkestan, unify the *Basmachis* and lead them into India by way of Afghanistan. The Soviet treaty with Kemalist Turkey of 16 March may have been a factor in Enver Pasha's change of allegiance.

## 22 November

A Soviet waterways official, Iakushev, was arrested by the Cheka, confessed to being a member of an underground monarchist organisation and agreed to work with the Cheka. This was the beginning of one of the best-known Cheka/OGPU

provocation and deception operations which undermined the effectiveness of the Russian *émigrés* as an
external opposition force and aimed
to influence western attitudes to the
communist regime (see Geoffrey
Bailey, Leggett and sources quoted
by him, and Golitsyn).

## 25 November

Estonia and the Ukrainian SSR
signed a treaty in Moscow on their
future relations.

## 26 November

The Finnish government appealed
unsuccessfully to the League of
Nations against the alleged failure of
the Soviet government to carry out
its obligations under the Treaty of
Dorpat of 14 October 1920 in
relation to East Karelia where an
insurrection had broken out in
October. The Soviets refused to
allow a League of Nations investigation on the spot. The insurrection
was not finally extinguished until 17
February 1922. On 6 March 1922 the
'Karelian Workers' Commune' proclaimed the lifting of the state of
siege.

## December

The Ninth All-Russian Congress of
Soviets formalised the practice which
had obtained since 1918 of holding
congresses annually instead of quar-
terly as originally intended.

The Executive Committee of the
Comintern issued twenty-five theses
on the 'United Workers' Front',
endorsing united front tactics which
the German communist party was
already using. Communist parties
were urged to work with other parties in pursuit of common objectives
while preserving their own independence of organisation and doctrine
and their right of criticism.

## 7 December

A provisional RSFSR-Austrian
agreement on future relations was
signed in Vienna: it was extended to
cover the whole of the USSR on 8
September 1923. It provided for delegations concerned with prisoners of
war to be combined with trade delegations and to be regarded as the
sole representatives of the Russian
state in Austria.

## 10 December

A decree returned to their original
owners small enterprises which,
though theoretically nationalised,
had not in practice been taken over
by the state.

## 15 December

A decree deprived all Russian refugees and *émigrés* of their nationality.
This affected a total of about 1.5
million persons throughout Europe.

## 19–22 December

At the party's Eleventh Conference,
the resolution 'On the current tasks
of the party in connection with the
restoration of the economy' signified
the conference's approval of NEP,
whose features were seen as: the formation of an internal market as a
result of the abolition of requisitions;
the development of exchange based
on money; the limitation of paper
money issues and the restoration of
a gold-based currency. The basic task
was defined as the strengthening of
large-scale, state-controlled industry

in accordance with a general state plan while at the same time developing ties between industry and the internal market.

## 21 December

Japanese-backed White Russian forces captured Khabarovsk and held it until driven out by General Bliukher on 14 February 1922.

## 26 December

Provisional economic and political agreements were signed between Italy and the RSFSR and the Ukrainian SSR providing for the resumption of trade and including a mutual undertaking to abstain from engaging in propaganda against one another.

## 29 December

According to Eudin and Fisher, Stalin became People's Commissar of Workers' and Peasants' Inspection (*Rabkrin*).

## 30 December

Following a congressional appropriation of $20 million for Russian relief, an additional agreement was signed in London between Krasin and the ARA permitting relief to be extended to adults as well as children. The ARA also agreed to purchase and ship food supplies and seed to the value of $10 million in gold provided by the Soviet government. A further agreement was signed with the Ukrainian government on 1 February 1922.

## 31 December

By the end of the year, Soviet trade delegations had been established in Finland, Estonia, Latvia, Lithuania, Poland, Sweden, Norway, Germany, Czechoslovakia, Austria, Italy, Great Britain, Turkey (Angora and Constantinople) and Persia.

# 1922

## 1 January

Party membership was given as 410,430 full members and 117,924 candidate members. This was the first year in which candidate members were shown separately. The figures, and those for successive years below, are from Rigby quoting *Partiinaia zhizn'*, no. 19, October 1967. Up to 1932, figures from other Soviet sources varied by up to 9 per cent from those in *Partiinaia zhizn'*.

## 6 January

A resolution was adopted at an allied conference in Cannes that Soviet Russia, once having accepted conditions relating to the recognition of debt and abstinence from aggression and hostile propaganda, should be invited on an equal footing to a general economic and financial conference in Genoa. The Soviet government's informal acceptance was conveyed in a telegram from Chicherin on 8 January.

## 23–30 January

The First Congress of Toilers of the Far East met in Moscow after a preliminary meeting in Irkutsk where the Comintern had established a Far Eastern secretariat including Profintern representatives in the spring of 1921. Korea sent fifty-two delegates, China thirty-seven, Japan seventy-three, Mongolia fourteen, India and Indonesia smaller delegations.

## 6 February

The Soviet Central Executive Committee passed a decree abolishing the Cheka and replacing it with the State Political Administration (GPU) with Dzerzhinskii as chairman. The GPU was made responsible for the suppression of counter-revolutionary activity, counter-espionage, the protection of railways, waterways and frontiers and the 'fulfilment of any special assignments for the maintenance of revolutionary order'. Purely criminal matters were to be dealt with by the courts. Restrictions on the GPU's powers of detention and punishment proved to be short-lived. Its incorporation into the People's Commissariat of Internal Affairs (NKVD) gave it an official standing which the Cheka, as an 'Extraordinary Commission', lacked.

*Note:* Leggett estimated the total number of deaths for which the Cheka was responsible in its four-year existence at 280,000 of which roughly half were executions and half deaths in the course of repressive actions. Leggett's study showed that, in addition to its repressive role, the

148

Cheka functioned as an intelligence and security service using the techniques of provocation and deception which it had inherited largely from the Tsarist political police system. The Cheka was also used by the government in tackling a wide variety of immediate political, social and economic as well as military problems such as the threat from nearly 2 million *émigrés* in Europe, the near breakdown of the railway system, the control of typhus, fire-fighting, fuel shortages, labour conscription and the rescue of waifs and strays.

## 17 February

A treaty of economic alliance was signed between the RSFSR and the Far Eastern Republic.

## 23 February

A decree ordered that articles containing gold, silver and precious stones owned by the churches should be handed over to the Commissariat of Finance for sale abroad for the benefit of the hunger-stricken population. Resistance by the churches led to disorders followed by the arrest of the Patriarch Tikhon, Mgr Constantin Budkiewicz, Dean of the Roman Catholic clergy in Petrograd, and a number of other Catholic churchmen.

## 12 March

The Transcaucasian Socialist Federation of Soviet Republics (SFSR) was formed from the Soviet republics of Armenia, Georgia and Azerbaijan.

## 23 March

A Council of People's Commissars' decree recognised the reintroduction of fees at all levels of the educational system which had in practice been spreading since the autumn of 1921 primarily for reasons of financial stringency. By October the number of primary schools had dropped from a high point of about 80,000 schools with over 6 million pupils early in 1921 to 49,000 schools with 3.7 million pupils. The pre-war figure was 73,000 schools with 4.9 million pupils.

## 27 March–2 April

At the party's Eleventh Congress, Lenin, who for health reasons attended only the opening and closing sessions, described NEP as a retreat which, like a military retreat, required a tightening of discipline. But the retreat was at an end and it was time to regroup and resume the advance. For that to be possible, the vanguard must be better educated and must go forward together with the peasantry.

A resolution 'On the strengthening and the new tasks of the party' laid particular stress on the recruitment of more workers into the party: it also instructed party organisations, while giving overall direction to the work of the economic agencies, to refrain from interfering in their day-to-day work or attempting to take over their responsibilities. Entry into the party was made more difficult for office workers and other employees.

Twenty-two party critics of the party's policy, including Shliapnikov and Kollontai of the 'Workers' Opposition', who had appealed unsuccessfully to the Executive Committee of the Comintern for support, were accused of factionalism but the congress refused to ratify a recommendation that they should be expelled from the party. They were warned that expulsion would follow any further anti-party activities on their part and two other less prominent figures were expelled. Miasnikov, founder and leader of the 'Workers' Group', who was involved in the appeal to the Comintern, had been expelled from the party before the congress.

A resolution on trade unions acknowledged that, as participants in state power, they could not refuse to engage in coercive measures.

The congress received a report on the purge of the party membership ordered by the Tenth Congress: of 650,000 (sic) members, 24 per cent had been expelled, reducing total membership to just below 500,000.

A report on the work of the party's control commissions, which had in practice been used to enforce party discipline, proved highly contentious and led to demands for their abolition

## 29 March

*Izvestiia* reprinted a letter to *Krasnaia Gazeta* from a group of priests who rejected the Patriarchate and denounced Tikhon for his resistance to the seizure of church treasures. This was the beginning of the Living Church (later known as the 'synodal') movement.

## 3 April

The new Central Committee of twenty-seven members and nineteen candidates elected Stalin as General Secretary of the communist party with Molotov and Kuibyshev as his two assistants. Stalin was the only Soviet leader to be simultaneously a member of the Central Committee, the Politburo, the Orgburo and the Secretariat.

The Politburo consisted of Lenin, Kamenev, Trotsky, Stalin, Zinoviev, Rykov and Tomskii. Bukharin, Molotov and Kalinin were elected candidate members.

Rosenfeldt pointed out that Stalin, probably in common with other leaders, already had a personal secretariat. According to Rosenfeldt's necessarily tentative analysis, Stalin gradually developed a secret apparatus associated with Tovstukha from 1921 to 1930 and with Poskrebyshev from 1932 onwards which gave him exclusive control over the flow of the most sensitive secret information, particularly that concerning other individuals including party leaders. Rosenfeldt speculated that it was this inner 'government' which enabled Stalin to carry on running the country while the party and administration including the security service were drastically purged in the late 1930s.

## 10 April–19 May

The Genoa Conference was attended by thirty-four states, the Soviet delegation being led by Chicherin acting under detailed instructions from Lenin. Chicherin's opening speech held out prospects of a significant Soviet contribution to world economic recovery. He also called for a general reduction in armaments and a world peace conference. No agreements were reached with the Soviet delegation on the questions of debts or compensation for foreign property confiscated or nationalised after the revolution. The problem was referred to a further conference at The Hague.

*Note:* Secret contacts between the Germans and Soviets on German help with the reconstruction of the Soviet armaments industry had been taking place for the past year or more. Drafts of a Soviet–German political treaty had also been discussed in Berlin immediately before the conference.

## 16 April

In the early hours of Easter Sunday morning, the Soviet delegation to the Genoa Conference invited the German delegation to a meeting in Rapallo at which a Soviet–German treaty was negotiated in the course of the day and signed in the evening. The treaty provided for the resumption of diplomatic and consular relations. Reparations were mutually renounced and the Germans agreed to forgo compensation for losses incurred by German nationals in Russia as a result of the revolution provided that claims by other states' nationals were not satisfied. The effect of the treaty was to ensure that Germany would not join with the western allies in an anti-bolshevik coalition. It marked the end of Soviet Russia's diplomatic isolation as far as the great powers were concerned and provided the basis for a special relationship between the Soviets and Germans which survived until the advent of Hitler. While the Genoa Conference did not result in immediate general western recognition of the Soviet government, the Soviet delegation was accepted at the conference as an equal negotiating partner. The Soviets gained experience in promoting and exploiting differences of interest not only between the Germans and the western allies

but between the allies themselves by playing on their different attitudes to disarmament, economic concessions and Russian debt repayment.

## 26 April–6 May

Fifty-four Orthodox priests and laymen were tried on charges of counter-revolutionary activities. Five were executed.

## May

Enver Pasha, who had imposed a degree of unity on the *Basmachi* movement, sent an ultimatum to Moscow demanding Soviet evacuation of Khiva, Bukhara and Turkestan.

## 13 May

An article in *Izvestiia* paraphrased a manifesto from the Moscow journal *The Living Church* accusing the existing church leaders of a conspiracy against the authorities and appealing to the government to hold a synod to condemn the bishops and restore order in church affairs. The article was sceptical about the need for the Living Church movement, which enjoyed government favour, because a victory of socialism on all fronts would involve the unmasking to the peasantry of all priests as counter-revolutionaries.

## 26 May

After several months of declining health, Lenin suffered his first stroke.

The Soviet Central Executive Committee adopted a new criminal code for the RSFSR which came into effect on 1 June. The code was designed to defend the 'workers' and peasants' government' and the revolutionary legal order from those who would destroy it and from 'socially dangerous elements'. It distinguished crimes against the state, for which minimum penalties were laid down, from crimes against the individual, for which maximum penalties were prescribed. The death penalty, by shooting, was reserved for crimes against the state. In dealing with a 'socially dangerous act' not specified in the code, the courts were to apply 'by analogy' the article of the code dealing with the 'socially dangerous act' which most closely resembled the act in question in character and importance. The code established the crime of 'hooliganism' defined as a 'mischievous action accompanied by a clear disrespect toward society'. It was one of the commonest offences. Particularly serious or persistent offenders were liable to deprivation of liberty for up to two years.

At the same time the People's Commissariat of Justice produced a draft decree establishing public procurators whose task was not only to investigate crimes and decide whether prosecutions should take place but also to ensure centralised control over and uniformity in judicial and administrative decisions by annulling or amending any that were contrary to the law. The procuracy was responsible to the People's Commissariat of Justice, its members being appointed by the party.

## June

The Red Army defeated Enver Pasha near Baisun and drove him back into eastern Bukhara.

## 5 and 6 June

Provisional Soviet–Czechoslovak and Ukrainian–Czechoslovak treaties of friendship and commerce were signed in Prague which included undertakings by each side to observe neutrality in the event of conflict between one of them and a third power.

## 6 June

A Chief Administration for Literary and Publishing Affairs (which came to be known as *Glavlit*) was established to bring together all forms of censorship of domestic and imported publishable material. Censorship had been conducted since the revolution partly by the Commissariat of Education, partly by the State Publishing House, *Gosizdat* and separately by the military.

## 8 June–25 July

The first political show trial was held. It involved thirty-four leading SRs accused of plotting the attempt on Lenin's life, assassinating Volodarskii and Uritskii, collaborating with Denikin and planning the overthrow of the Soviet government. The three judges were all communists of long standing. The defendants fell into two groups: those whom the government had held prisoner since February and those who had been persuaded to collaborate with the regime. The first group were defended by the Belgian socialist, Vandervelde, until he withdrew in protest at the manner in which the trial was being conducted. The second group, who were used to incriminate the first, were 'defended' by Bukharin. Fourteen of the first group were sentenced to death and, although their sentences were commuted or suspended, they were not reliably heard of again. In *Let History Judge*, Roy Medvedev gave the names of nine defendants on whose behalf the tribunal petitioned the presidium of the Soviet Central Executive Committee requesting that they should be excused from any form of punishment.

## 26 June–20 July

Following on from the Genoa Conference, the lower-level Hague Conference discussed Soviet debts and compensation for nationalisation and confiscation of foreign-owned private property without reaching solutions.

## 30 June

The US State Department withdrew recognition from Bakhmet'ev, the ambassador in Washington of the Provisional Russian Government of 1917. B. Shvirski, who had arrived in Washington in 1921 to represent the Far Eastern Republic, acted as an unofficial Moscow representative in Washington.

## 3 July

Nansen convened an international conference in Geneva as a result of which thirty-four governments had, by the end of 1923, agreed to adopt and accept a standard identity card for Russian refugees, the 'Nansen passport'.

## 29 July

A secret preliminary agreement on Soviet–German military collaboration is reported to have been signed in Berlin and is listed in Slusser and Triska. Other less reliable dates for secret military agreements are given by other sources. Contacts between the German and Soviet armies and armaments industries certainly went back at least to 1921 and military collaboration undoubtedly continued until the early 1930s although information on it is incomplete and opinions vary on its importance to either side. The collaboration provided the Germans with opportunities to circumvent some of the restrictions on rearmament imposed upon them by the Versailles Treaty. The Soviets were hungry for foreign advice and expertise in building up their armed forces and the predominant foreign influence on them at least until 1933 and probably later was German. The two sides shared a common hostility to Poland. The original agreement envisaged the manufacture by the German firm Junkers of aircraft and aircraft engines at Fili near Moscow, but in fact engines appear to have been supplied from Germany and the whole project collapsed in 1927 apparently for financial reasons. A German air-training base was established at Lipetsk probably in 1924. The Seatons quoted a figure of 130 German fighter pilots and 80 air observers trained there between 1925 and 1933 together with a few navy fliers. Carsten gave the numbers as about 120 fighter pilots and about 100 observers. The trainees were sent to the USSR in civilian clothes under false names. The Seatons maintained that training courses for Red Army personnel at Lipetsk were restricted to ground staff. Carsten mentioned a shipment to Germany of 300,000 shells manufactured at Zlatoust, Tula and Leningrad. Carr mentioned a tank factory at Kazan. Erickson denied its existence but referred to a Krupps concession for heavy tractors which were of military significance. A German tank-training school was opened at Kama (near Kazan) between 1926 and 1928. A joint facility for producing poison-gas near Samara appears to have been unsuccessful but there are references to a gas-warfare training school known as 'Tomka' near Saratov and an artillery school near Voronezh. The Soviets received rent for the German bases and shared in the training and testing programmes which were carried out in them. There were significant exchanges of visits between German and Soviet officers, some of which are mentioned below. Erickson estimated that not less than 120 senior Soviet officers received some German training. It seems likely that the testing of equipment, training and the acquisition of military advice and technical information for their own production facilities were the most valuable aspects of the relationship from the point of view of the Soviet military.

## August

The Dutch Indonesian communist Maring (a pseudonym for Sneevliet), a representative of the Comintern who had had talks with Dr Sun Yat-sen in the summer of 1921, reached agreement with him that members of the nascent Chinese communist party should be allowed to join the Kuomintang on an individual basis. Maring apparently secured the agreement of the Chinese communist party to the adoption of this form of united front tactics. He also reported to Moscow that Sun Yat-sen, disil-

lusioned with the Washington Conference of 1921–2, was thinking of seeking Soviet assistance.

The destruction of the Greek army in Anatolia and the acquisition of control over the Black Sea straits by the Kemalist Turkish government removed the underpinning from the Soviet–Turkish alliance expressed in the treaty of 16 March 1921.

At the height of its relief work in August, the ARA had overcome the problems of official (mainly Cheka) obstruction and chaotic transport conditions sufficiently well to be feeding almost 10.5 million persons daily, 40 per cent of them children and 60 per cent adults. With the new harvest, the numbers particularly of adults fell away sharply. Medical aid was an important additional aspect of the ARA's work.

## 4 August

Enver Pasha was killed by a Red cavalry patrol near the Afghan frontier. Chamberlin considered that, with his death, the civil war proper came to an end though turbulence continued for many years, especially in Central Asia. The strength of the Red Army, which was 4,400,000 in March 1921, was gradually reduced to 560,000 by the end of 1923.

In Olcutt's opinion, the *Basmachi* continued to represent a direct threat to Soviet rule in their area at least until 1924. Although it was officially stated that the *Basmachi* had been cleared from Tadzhikistan in October 1925, they re-formed under their leader, Ibrahim Bek, in Afghanistan and, using that country as a base, continued to operate in Tadzhikistan (see also June 1930).

## 4–7 August

The party's Twelfth Conference adopted a new version of the party rules of 4 December 1919. It also passed a resolution on anti-Soviet parties and tendencies. While warning that the *Smena Vekh* movement shared with the Mensheviks and SRs the hope that economic concessions would be followed by political concessions in the direction of bourgeois democracy, it described the movement as playing an objectively progressive role. The party was to take advantage of every group formerly hostile to the Soviet power which showed the slightest desire to assist the working-class and peasantry in restoring the economy and raising the cultural level of the population.

## 12 August

Ioffe arrived in Peking at the outset of a mission to the Far East which lasted a year. His negotiations with the weak Peking government focused mainly on the establishment of diplomatic relations, Outer Mongolia and the Chinese Eastern railway and were inconclusive, Chinese apprehensions having been aroused by Soviet activities in Outer Mongolia and by Soviet repudiation of an offer, signed by Karakhan on 25 July 1919, to return the Chinese Eastern railway to China free of any compensation whatever.

## 13 August

*Izvestiia* announced that Metropolitan Veniamin of Petrograd and three other priests had been executed for counter-revolutionary offences.

## 23 August

The organ of the Polish bureau of the Russian communist party published an appeal on behalf of the victims of 'bourgeois terror' in Poland. This was the origin of the International Organisation for Aid to Revolutionaries (MOPR) also known as *Rote Hilfe* or International Red Aid, officially founded, according to the GSE, late in 1922 by the Fourth Comintern Congress (see 5 November) at the urging of the Society of Old Bolsheviks. It developed into an international communist front organisation taking up the cause of 'victims of repression'. In late 1937 its headquarters moved from Moscow to Paris. Its worldwide activities ceased on the outbreak of the Second World War although the Moscow section remained active among foreign residents up to 1947.

## 4 September

A conference opened at Changchun in Manchuria between the Japanese and a Soviet delegation led by Ioffe together with a delegation from the Far Eastern Republic. Although the conference broke down, leaving unresolved the questions of northern Sakhalin and Japanese fishing rights, the Japanese, disunited at home over intervention and under pressure from the United States and the Far Eastern Republic to abandon it, began to withdraw from the Maritime Province.

## 12 September

A decree abolished the All-Russian Committee for Famine Relief and established a Committee for the

Struggle against the Consequences of the Famine.

## 27 September

Japanese troops evacuated Nikolaevsk.

## 2 October

Lenin returned to Moscow after convalescence from his stroke in May. He did regular part-time work until December.

## 11 October

A decree authorised the issue of the 'chervonets' which was intended originally as a unit of value for the transactions of the State Bank (Gosbank) but developed gradually into a gold-backed currency and an alternative to the depreciated ruble which it replaced in March 1924 at a rate of 50,000 million rubles for one 'chervonets'.

## 11–19 October

The Fifth Congress of the Komsomol, which claimed a membership of 250,000, adopted a resolution condemning laxity in sexual morals and excessive indulgence in tobacco and alcohol. It also launched the Young Pioneers' for 10 to 14-year-olds with an initial enrolment of 4,000 members. (The GSE gives the date of foundation of the Pioneers as 19 May 1922.) By March 1926 the organisation had 1.5 million members and the Little Octobrists had been formed for children under ten. By December 1939 the Young Pioneers were claiming a membership of 13 million.

## 25–31 October

The last Japanese troops were withdrawn from Vladivostok, the Far Eastern Republic immediately taking over control. A consequence of the final Japanese withdrawal was the winding-up on 24 October of the Inter-Allied Committee which had been set up on 5 March 1919 by the allied powers involved in the intervention to supervise the Siberian railway system. The committee's Technical Board under its president, John F. Stevens, was abolished on 1 November.

## 31 October

The Soviet Central Executive Committee approved a statute which revived the professional status of the judiciary and subordinated it to the Soviet Central Executive Committee which was responsible for appointing the president of the Supreme Court and his two deputies. The draft civil, agrarian and labour codes were also approved. Under the civil code of 11 November 1922, civil rights were protected by law except where they were exercised in a sense contrary to the economic and social purposes for which they had been granted by the state. Private ownership of land and the means of production in nationalised industries were excluded. But enterprises might be leased to individuals for up to six years. The right of inheritance by legal and testamentary succession for estates of less than 10,000 rubles and other possessions defined by the decree of 27 April 1918 was codified.

The agrarian code, by laying down rules for the redistribution of land and the holding of meetings within the commune system, tacitly recognised the continuation of that system. The code gave the peasants considerable freedom of choice over the system of land holding they adopted including the choice of leaving or remaining in the commune (see 14 February 1919).

The labour code which came into force on 15 November to some extent restored the contract between employer and worker as the basis of employment and gave the employer the right to dismiss the employed. The working day was not to exceed eight hours or seven in those undertakings which had gone over to the seven-hour day. An uninterrupted weekly rest period of forty-two hours. was laid down including Sunday or any other day of the week according to the national and denominational composition of the work-force in each locality. Wages were to be fixed by collective and individual contracts of work at a level not less than the minimum prescribed by the state for the class of work in question. Workers who failed to meet the standards of output agreed between management and trade unions faced reductions in wages or, in persistent cases, dismissal. The code covered conciliation boards and arbitration courts for settling disputes and investigating complaints and it included regulations on industrial safety, social security benefits and the rights and duties of trade unions.

## 5 November–5 December

Attendance at the Fourth Comintern Congress was variously reported as 394 or 408 delegates from fifty-eight or sixty-two countries. The keynote of the congress was the long-haul approach to world revolution in place

of precipitate action. Lenin argued that the parties must be prepared for retreat as well as offence and dwelt on the need for study to develop effective revolutionary work. Support by the workers of the world for Soviet power was stressed. The primacy of the Executive Committee, the predominance of Soviet influence and the necessity for strict discipline were all reaffirmed together with the right of the Comintern to 'interfere' in the affairs of the national sections (i.e. parties). Heavy emphasis was placed on the anti-imperialist liberation struggle in the East. United front tactics were endorsed. The congress adopted a set of theses on the racial question in the United States and relations were subsequently established with black organisations there.

The Second Profintern Congress, which followed on immediately from the Comintern congress, called for organisation of the transport workers of the Pacific basin and the creation of port bureaux which would serve as links between the revolutionary seamen of the whole world. A conference of transport workers, including Chinese and Indonesians, was held at the same time as the congress.

## 6 November

Count Ulrich Brockdorff-Rantzau presented his credentials as German ambassador in Moscow.

## 14 November

The Far Eastern Republic, which had fulfilled its task of restoring Russian control over the whole of the Far Eastern territory of the former Russian Empire except northern Sakhalin, voted itself out of existence and applied for union with the RSFSR. On the following day the Soviet Central Executive Committee issued a decree on the unification of the RSFSR and the Far Eastern Republic.

## 4 December

Chicherin led the Soviet delegation to that part of the Lausanne Conference which discussed the question of the Black Sea straits. The western allies proposed that the straits should be open in peace and in war to a limited number of warships of powers not at war with Turkey. The Soviets proposed that the straits should be closed to all warships (except those of Turkey) at all times: in other words, they were prepared to forgo naval access to the Mediterranean for the sake of denying naval access to the Black Sea to non-littoral states. The Turks sided with the western allies and drafted a convention jointly with them. The draft was rejected on 1 February 1923 by Chicherin who claimed that the Turks had acted under *force majeure* (see also 14 August 1923).

## 16 December

Lenin suffered his second stroke.

## 23 December

A letter from Lenin's wife, Krupskaia, to Kamenev (mentioned in Khrushchev's 'secret speech' of February 1956) complained of Stalin's rude behaviour towards her concerning a note to Trotsky dictated to her by Lenin. The note, which Krupskaia said had been dictated with the doctor's permission, asked Trotsky to press for consolidation of the foreign trade monopoly at the forthcoming party congress, an issue on which Stalin had disagreed with Lenin. Stalin, who on 18 December had been given responsibility by the Central Committee for overseeing Lenin's medical treatment, had abused Krupskaia for violating doctor's orders.

## 23–26 December

Lenin, with the forthcoming Twelfth Congress of the party in view, dictated his 'testament' in which he said that Stalin had concentrated enormous power in his hands and that he was not sure whether he always knew how to use that power with sufficient caution. Of Trotsky, he said he was the most able man in the Central Committee but too much attracted by the purely administrative side of affairs. Lenin said that a split in the party might result from the differences between these two leaders and advocated enlargement of the Central Committee as a means of preventing it. The fact that Zinoviev and Kamenev had opposed the October/November revolution, though not accidental, and that Trotsky had not been a member of the bolshevik party before August 1917 should not be held against them. Of the two ablest younger men, Bukharin was the most valuable theoretician and the favourite of the whole party but his views could only with the greatest doubt be regarded as fully Marxist and he had never fully learned and understood the dialectic. Piatakov was too much concerned with administration to be relied on regarding a serious political question.

## 23–27 December

The Tenth All-Russian Congress of Soviets passed a resolution sponsored by Stalin in favour of creating a Union of Soviet Socialist Republics (USSR).

## 30 December

The delegates of the RSFSR, the Ukrainian and Byelorussian SSRs and the Transcaucasian SFSR constituted themselves as the First Congress of Soviets of the USSR and approved the formation of the Union of Soviet Socialist Republics with the RSFSR as one of its constituent republics. The new union was hailed as a decisive step towards the unification of the toilers of all countries into a World Soviet Socialist Republic. A new Soviet Central Executive Committee of the USSR was then elected.

## 30–31 December

Lenin dictated his memorandum on the national question in which he condemned Russian nationalism and chauvinism and criticised Stalin, Ordzhonikidze and Dzerzhinskii for their insensitive handling of the problem of Georgian nationalism.

## Winter 1922–1923

The scale of economic concessions actually granted to foreign companies proved to be small, Germany taking first place in both concessions and mixed companies and increasing its share of the Soviet Union's external trade at the expense of the British and others. According to Soviet figures quoted by Nove, the sixty-eight concessions which existed in 1928 accounted for only 0.6 per cent of industrial output.

The Committee for the Struggle against the Consequences of the Famine published figures showing that 1 million people had died, 1.5 million had emigrated and 2 million children had been left homeless as a result of famine in 1921–2.

On the other hand, the harvest of 1922 was relatively successful permitting the resumption of grain exports from Russia on a modest scale in 1923 for the first time since the revolution.

# 1923

## 1 January

Party membership was given as 381,400 with 117,700 candidate members.

## 4 January

Lenin added a postscript to his 'testament' of 25 December 1922 saying that Stalin was too rough, an insupportable fault in a general secretary, and proposing that the party should remove him from that position. In Tucker's view, Lenin's actions and reported remarks make it plain that he was definitely intending to 'explode a bomb' under Stalin at the congress in order to get him removed from the secretary-generalship.

## 10 January

The presidium of the new USSR Soviet Central Executive Committee appointed a commission to draw up the constitution of the USSR.

## 25 January and 4 March

*Pravda* published two articles by Lenin advocating an increase in the membership of the Central Committee to fifty or even 100 by the inclusion, for the most part, of workers and peasants. The second article, 'Better Less, but Better', said that the lack of elementary education

was the most serious problem facing Russia. The articles underlined the importance of the intended functions of the Commissariat of Workers' and Peasants' Inspection (*Rabkrin*) but contained biting criticism of its performance: Stalin had recently resigned after three years at its head. Lenin suggested that a new Central Control Commission (also composed of workers and peasants) should be fused with an enlarged and reformed *Rabkrin*. As far as the economy was concerned, his principal aim was to preserve at all costs the unity between workers and peasants.

## 26 January

After a series of meetings, Ioffe and Dr Sun Yat-sen announced that they had reached agreement that conditions for communism and sovietism did not exist in China but that China could count on Soviet support in solving what Ioffe regarded as China's most pressing problems, the achievement of total national unification and independence.

## February

Ioffe left China for six months in Japan where he had inconclusive discussions on the Japanese occupation of Sakhalin, Japanese fishing rights,

Soviet debts and possible compensation payments.

## 9 February

A Chief Committee for the Control over Repertoire (*Glavrepertkom*) was set up in connection with *Glavlit* to censor plays, films, circuses, concerts, records, variety shows and all other forms of public entertainment.

## 5 March

Lenin dictated letters to Trotsky and Stalin. The letter to Trotsky enclosed the notes on the national question which he had dictated ten weeks previously and urged him to undertake the defence of the Georgian deviationists at the Central Committee meeting preceding the party's Twelfth Congress. Trotsky referred Lenin's letter to the Politburo which decided that the notes on the national question should not be published as a congress document but should be read to members of delegations in closed session. The letter to Stalin was delivered to him by Lenin's secretary on 7 March. It demanded an apology for his rude behaviour towards Krupskaia and threatened to break off relations with him (see Khrushchev's 'secret speech' of February 1956). Stalin there and then dictated an apology.

## 6 March

Lenin sent a telegram to the Georgian party leaders, Mdivani and Makharadze, supporting them against Ordzhonikidze, Stalin and Dzerzhinskii.

## 7–9 March

Lenin's health deteriorated and he suffered his third stroke which further paralysed him and affected his speech.

## 26 March

At the climax of a wave of persecution of the Catholic church, the Catholic Archbishop of Mogilev, John Cieplak, was sentenced to ten years' imprisonment, later commuted to banishment from the country for life, and Mgr Budkiewicz was sentenced to death. He was executed on 31 March despite protests from the Vatican and the British government.

## 31 March

The Lenin Institute was founded to collect and publish Lenin's works. Kamenev was made director of it.

## 10 April

A decree defined and regulated the status of the industrial 'trusts' (see 9 August 1921). It described them as 'state industrial enterprises to which the state accords independence in the conduct of their operations . . . and which operate on principles of commercial accounting with the object of earning a profit', i.e. on the system known as *khozraschet*. The decree emphasised the importance of the profit-making element and laid down rules for calculating profits and distributing them between the 'trust' itself and expenditure on welfare and bonus payments to its management and work force.

## 17–25 April

At the Twelfth Congress of the party, Zinoviev delivered the Central Committee report in Lenin's absence:

Stalin delivered the report on organisation.

The resolution on the Central Committee report laid special emphasis on developing the 'union of the working class and the peasantry' while restating that the dictatorship of the working class could only be assured by the dictatorship of its vanguard, the communist party. The resolution urged the party to struggle against Great Russian chauvinism. It instructed the Central Committee to give high priority to the work of the records and assignments section (*Uchraspred*) so as to ensure that the party exerted real leadership in all areas of the economy and administration.

A resolution on tax policy in the countryside envisaged replacing part of the tax in kind on the peasantry by consolidated, monetary taxation.

Following the lines of Lenin's suggestion, the party's Central Committee was enlarged to forty members with fifteen to twenty candidates and the Central Control Commission to fifty members. It was laid down that the Commissar for Workers' and Peasants' Inspection (*Rabkrin*) should be appointed by the party's Central Committee, if possible, from among the members of the presidium of the party's Central Control Commission, members of which were also to be appointed to other people's commissariats. The Central Control Commission, acting in co-operation with the GPU, was thus in a position to exercise supervision over the whole of the administration. While on paper the congress went some way towards carrying out Lenin's proposal that *Rabkrin* should be fused with the Central Control Commission, the practical consequence

was arguably a strengthening of Stalin's control over the apparatus through the Secretariat largely because enlargement of the Central Committee and Central Control Commission made it more difficult for them to meet frequently. Joint meetings of the presidium of the Central Control Commission and the board of *Rabkrin* were to be held twice a month.

Stalin described the trade unions, co-operatives, leagues of youth, women's conferences, schools, the press and the army as the seven 'transmission belts' between the party and the working class: the percentage of communists among the leaders of all these organisations was increasing rapidly.

The national question was debated at length with special reference to Georgia. With Lenin out of action, Stalin and his fellow believers in centralisation easily won the day, Stalin having allegedly packed the congress with his own supporters. Trotsky remained silent on the question. Bukharin, however, openly criticised Stalin and Zinoviev and drew attention to Lenin's warnings on Great Russian chauvinism.

The congress set out various guidelines for the conduct of anti-religious propaganda and said that it was essential to work out methods of liquidating the medieval prejudices linked with religion and preserved among 30 million Muslims in the Soviet Union. Anti-Islamic work was, however, carried out with great caution in this period.

A prominent issue at the congress was the relationship of the peasantry to the proletariat and the importance of agriculture as the foundation of the Soviet economy. Zinoviev and

Trotsky dismissed the arguments of the 'Workers' Truth' and 'Workers' Group' movements which had been reflecting discontent over the rise in unemployment, the fall in real wages in industry, the growth in the influence of the managerial class, the decline in the importance of the trade unions and the relative enrichment of the peasantry at the expense of the proletariat, all of which accompanied the early years of NEP.

Trotsky argued that NEP was not helping heavy industry which could only be revived within the framework of a planned economy and which alone could provide a solid foundation for the dictatorship of the proletariat.

The congress marked the emergence of a triumvirate of Stalin, Zinoviev and Kamenev in the absence of Lenin's leadership. The three shared a common hostility to Trotsky which took the form of circulating rumours and anonymous pamphlets undermining his reputation.

## 23 April

A provisional Soviet–Danish agreement on economic relations was signed in Moscow providing for an exchange of trade delegations.

## 26 April

Lenin, Kamenev, Trotsky, Stalin, Zinoviev, Rykov and Tomskii were re-elected to membership of the Politburo. Bukharin, Molotov, Rudzutak and Kalinin were elected candidate members.

## May

Miasnikov, leader of the 'Workers' Group' was arrested by the GPU which was becoming increasingly involved in internal party affairs (see also 8 October).

## 2 May

The British government addressed a memorandum known as the 'Curzon ultimatum' (Lord Curzon was Foreign Secretary) to the Soviet government threatening to abrogate the Anglo-Soviet trade agreement of 16 March 1921 and break off relations if the Soviet government did not desist from flagrant violations of its undertaking to refrain from hostile propaganda and subversive activities. The note was delivered on 8 May.

## 10 May

Vorovskii, the Soviet observer at the reconvened Lausanne conference, was assassinated in Lausanne by a Russian *émigré* of Swiss descent named Conradi who was later acquitted of murder. The assassination had an adverse effect on Soviet–Swiss relations and provided a reason or pretext for Soviet refusal to attend international conferences on Swiss territory until the dispute was ended by an exchange of notes on 14 April 1927, shortly before the World Economic Conference in Geneva.

## 13 May

Litvinov's reply to the 'Curzon ultimatum' was received. It was conciliatory but included the usual denial that the Soviet government could in any way be identified with the Comintern.

## 20 May

A decree introduced a 'single agricultural tax' which could be paid partly in cash and partly in kind.

## 27 May

A decree allowed religious organisations to call conventions and elect executive boards only with the permission of the Soviet authorities. This was used to discriminate in favour of the Living Church which, with two other groups which had split off from it, held a holy synod in May. The synod declared the Patriarch Tikhon deposed, the Patriarchate abolished and the Soviet power recognised as the force which was leading the world to fraternity, equality and peace.

## 30 May

*Pravda* noted that anti-religious work was becoming one of the main branches of communist propaganda.

## 13 and 18 June

After the Soviets, in a note dated 4 June, had reaffirmed their undertaking to abstain from hostile propaganda and had made concessions on other outstanding issues, British and Soviet notes closed the correspondence.

## 15 June

The ARA signed an agreement with the Soviet government liquidating its operations in Russia. The number of persons fed daily by the ARA, which had dropped to below the million mark at the end of 1922, rose again to 3 million in 1923, the great majority of them children suffering from malnutrition rather than famine. Sufficient stocks of food were left behind to see them through

to the next harvest. The end of the operation was celebrated with much goodwill but the arrests of Soviet collaborators with the ARA, which had hampered its operations in the early stages, became much more widespread when its work was over.

## 18 June

A Central Committee circular explained that financial restraints prevented the maintenance of a large standing army and urged the party to help in the creation of territorial units.

## 24 June

The *Dynamo* sports club was founded by Dzerzhinskii. Membership was restricted initially to members of the GPU. The club expanded rapidly both in Moscow and the provinces.

## 26 June

The Patriarch Tikhon confessed to anti-Soviet acts, expressed his repentance, declared that he had severed all connections with monarchists and counter-revolutionary elements and denied that he was any longer an enemy of the Soviet government. He was released and resumed his patriarchal functions. Some of the Living Church leaders returned to the Patriarchate: others formed a Holy Synod of the Russian Orthodox Church.

## Summer

The All-Russian Association of Proletarian Writers (VAPP) started publishing a journal *Na Postu (On Guard)* reacting against the revival of ideologically suspect 'fellow-travel-

ling' literature that had accompanied
NEP.

## July–September

A wave of strikes affected heavy
industry in particular. Deutscher
(*The Prophet Unarmed*) described
the strikes as a largely spontaneous
manifestation of discontent but
claimed that the 'Workers' Truth'
group and Miasnikov's followers
including N. Kuznetsov in the 'Workers' Group' were involved in the
agitation.

## 6 July

The Constitution of the USSR was
adopted by the All-Union Soviet
Central Executive Committee and
came into force immediately. (It was
formally confirmed by the second
All-Union Congress of Soviets on 31
January 1924). Sovereign authority
was transferred to the new All-Union
Congress of Soviets, the All-Russian
Congress of Soviets remaining as the
supreme organ of the RSFSR.
Between sessions of the congress
(which were held each year initially,
then every two years from 1925 and
less frequently in the 1930s) its authority was delegated to the All-Union
Central Executive Committee
(VTsIK). This was divided into two
chambers – the Council of the Union,
consisting of members elected by the
All-Union Congress from representatives of the constituent republics in
proportion to their populations, and
the Council of Nationalities consisting of five delegates from each union-
republic or autonomous republic and
one from each autonomous region.
More often than not, the two chambers sat together. In the intervals
between meetings of the All-Union

Central Executive Committee (which
had over 500 members), its Presidium exercised its authority. The
Presidium consisted of the seven
members each of the presidium of
the Council of the Union and the
Council of Nationalities plus seven
others elected jointly by the two
councils.

The Council of People's Commissars of the RSFSR (which had
developed legislative as well as
executive functions) became the
Council of People's Commissars of
the USSR, the RSFSR, like the other
republics, retaining a subordinate
Council of People's Commissars.
Foreign affairs, defence, foreign
trade, communications and posts and
telegraphs were reserved to all-
Union commissariats. The Supreme
Council of National Economy and
the all-Union commissariats of
labour, food, finance and workers'
and peasants' inspection each had
subordinate counterparts in the
republics. The Commissariat for
Nationalities was wound up. The
GPU became the OGPU (United –
sometimes rendered as 'Federal' –
State Political Administration). It
was removed from the Commissariat
of Internal Affairs and attached to
the All-Union Council of People's
Commissars, its republican organs
working (nominally) to republican
councils of people's commissars. The
commissariats of internal affairs, justice, education, health and social
welfare were organised at republican
level with no all-Union counterpart
although the establishment of the
basic principles on which these commissariats worked was reserved to
the Union. A Supreme Court was
attached to the All-Union Central
Executive Committee 'to strengthen

revolutionary legality and co-ordi-
nate the efforts of the republics in the
struggle against counter-revolution'.
In other words, the all-Union authorities were given jurisdiction over
the principles of court organisation
and procedure and of civil and criminal legislation.

Neither the party's monopoly of
power nor even its existence was
acknowledged in the constitution
although it was the party that provided the centralising force which
held an otherwise unworkable system
together and governed its practice.

Adoption of the USSR constitution entailed revision of the constitutions of the RSFSR and the other
constituent republics, a process
which continued until 1927 and is
described in Carr, *Socialism in One
Country*, vol. ii.

## 14 July

Dr Armand Hammer's Allied American Corporation, representing a
number of US exporters including
the Ford Motor Company, signed a
concession contract with the Soviets
providing for the supply of machinery, automobiles and tractors against
Soviet exports mainly of furs to a
minimum overall annual value of
$2.4 million. Actual turnover up to
1925 was $12.5 million after which
the Soviets diverted the trade to their
own trading agencies, *Arcos* and
*Amtorg*. Hammer then obtained a
concession for a pencil factory which
he operated until 1930.

## 23 July

Finland and Poland established
diplomatic relations with the USSR.

## 2 August

Karakhan left Moscow to take up his
appointment as diplomatic representative in Peking where he arrived on
2 September.

## 8 August

A decree set out the conditions of
service in territorial military units.

## 14 August

The USSR signed the Lausanne Convention on the Black Sea straits
under protest in Constantinople. The
convention had been signed on 24
July by the United Kingdom, France,
Italy, Japan, Bulgaria, Greece,
Romania, Turkey and the Kingdom
of the Serbs, Croats and Slovenes.
Although the Soviets did not ratify
the convention, they subsequently
provided information to the Turkish
government on Soviet naval forces in
the Black Sea.

## 25 August–29 November

Dr Sun Yat-sen's chief-of-staff,
Chiang Kai-shek, who was by his
own account an advocate at this time
of co-operation between the Kuomintang and the Soviets, visited the
USSR on Dr Sun's instructions to
study the Soviet political and military
system. Again by his own account,
Chiang returned from the USSR
having lost his illusions about the disinterestedness of Soviet aims in
China and apprehensive about the
possible long-term consequences of
collaboration. Nevertheless, Soviet
influence on Dr Sun and the Kuomintang in Canton steadily increased.

## September

The Central Committee set up a subcommittee chaired by Dzerzhinskii to look into the internal party situation. N. Kuznetsov, who had succeeded Miasnikov as leader of the 'Workers' Group', and twenty other members of it were arrested. Kuznetsov was detained for a few months, nine of the others were expelled from the party and the rest were reprimanded.

## 18 September

The Council of People's Commissars appointed Dzerzhinskii chairman of the OGPU.

## 23 September

An unsuccessful Comintern-backed armed uprising took place in Bulgaria.

## 6 October

Mikhail Borodin, who had emigrated to the United States after the 1905 revolution and who had been active on behalf of the Comintern in Scandinavia, Mexico, Spain, Britain, Germany and elsewhere, arrived in Canton as the Politburo's adviser and mentor to Sun Yat-sen. He had been introduced to the Kuomintang by Karakhan but was not subordinate to him. A number of Red Army commanders joined Borodin's mission with a view to developing the Kuomintang into a fighting force as well as an anti-imperialist, revolutionary party capable of exploiting the surge in labour and peasant unrest in China. The most senior of the military advisers was Bliukher (alias Galin or Galen) who arrived in October 1924.

## 8 October

Trotsky addressed a letter to the Central Committee, asserting that discontent among the workers and peasants was attributable to mistakes in the party's economic policy. He underlined the necessity for central planning to revive heavy industry and drew attention to the 'scissors crisis', i.e. the disparity between agricultural prices (well below the 1913 level) and industrial prices (well above that level) which reached its maximum extent at the beginning of October. Trotsky said that the unhealthy internal state of the party could lead to its degeneration. He complained at the 'packing' of meetings, the stifling of debate and the appointment 'from above' by the Orgburo and the Secretariat of conformist party officials. The immediate cause of Trotsky's action was a proposal from Dzerzhinskii that party members should be obliged to help maintain party discipline by disclosing to the OGPU any information on the existence of factions or groups in the party.

## 10 October

Three communists joined the government in Saxony. A few days later, two more entered the Thuringian government. According to Ruth Fischer's account, this was intended as the first stage in what proved to be an ill-judged Comintern-planned uprising wished on a divided and unconvinced German party leadership. In Saxony and Thuringia, the uprising failed to take off and the two provinces were soon occupied by government troops. Owing to poor communications, an uprising in Hamburg went ahead on 22–23 October despite the fiasco in Saxony. The Hamburg communists succeeded in taking several police stations and capturing some rifles. Street fighting continued for three days before the communists called it off. The net result of the uprising was the banning of the German communist party. The failure in Germany, despite the favourable conditions arising from hyper-inflation, political instability and labour unrest, put an end to the optimistic brand of post-revolutionary internationalism: the failure became a factor in the power struggle in the Soviet party and in the subsequent adoption of 'socialism in one country'.

## 10–16 October

The First International Peasant Conference in Moscow founded a Peasants' International as an auxiliary organisation of the Comintern. It remained in being, largely as a propaganda organisation, at least until the end of 1926 but its only solid achievement seems to have been the setting-up of an International Agrarian Institute in Moscow which continued into the 1930s.

## 15 October

Forty-six prominent party members, including Preobrazhenskii, Antonov-Ovseenko, Piatakov, Muralov and Osinskii, addressed a declaration to the Politburo (known as the 'Platform of the 46') on economic policy and the internal situation in the party. Its complaints were closely in line with Trotsky's letter of 8 October. Trotsky, however, presumably to avoid accusations of factionalism, did not associate himself with the forty-six of whom he would have been the natural leader.

## 27 October

A joint resolution of the Central Committee, the Central Control Commission and other party organisations described Trotsky's letter of 8 October as a profound political error and condemned the 'Platform of the 46' as factional. Nevertheless, a debate on the issues involved was conducted in *Pravda* during November.

## 15 November

The Presidium of the Soviet Central Executive Committee decreed that the chairman and deputy chairman of the OGPU should be *ex officio* members of the Council of People's Commissars with a consultative vote.

## 21 November

Nogin, head of the Soviet textile trust, arrived in New York with the intention of buying $1.5 million worth of cotton. As a result, a US company, the All-Russian Textile Syndicate, was set up in New York with a loan of $2 million from the Chase National Bank. The syndicate shipped $39 million worth of cotton to the USSR up to 30 September 1924.

## 27 November

The menshevik *Sotsialisticheskii Vestnik* in Paris quoted a circular from the propaganda section of the Central Committee recommending the withdrawal from libraries of out-of-date, harmful or counter-revolutionary books and also of material of Soviet origin on matters on which Soviet policy had changed.

## 5 December

A resolution on 'The New Course' drafted jointly by Trotsky, Stalin and Kamenev was approved at a joint session of the Politburo and the presidium of the Central Control Commission. While it paid lip-service to some of Trotsky's points, the main apparent purpose of the resolution from the point of view of Kamenev and Stalin was to drive a wedge between Trotsky (who enjoyed considerable support in the army and the youth movement) and the rest of the internal opposition by binding him formally to their side of the argument.

## 8 December

Trotsky wrote a letter to the party on 'The New Course' (published on 11 December) giving his interpretation of the resolution of 5 December and describing the danger of the bureaucratic 'old guard' of the party stifling all criticism and frustrating the younger generation, thereby promoting inefficiency in the economy.

## 15 December

Writing in *Pravda*, Stalin ended a general attack on opposition in the party with criticism of Trotsky's remarks about the degeneration of the 'old guard' and accused him of being 'in a bloc with the Democratic Centralists and with a section of the "Left" communists'. Zinoviev followed up on the same day with a reference to Trotskyism as a definite tendency in the Russian workers' movement.

## 28 December

*Izvestiia* reported that 1,000 'socially dangerous persons' had been arrested and expelled from Moscow in OGPU raids on places of entertainment frequented by prosperous traders and speculators and that these arrests had caused dismay among the 'parasites'.

## 28–29 December

Two articles in *Pravda* by Trotsky on 'The New Course' were accompanied by unsigned material by Bukharin accusing Trotsky of factionalism and departures from Leninism but opposing demands for his expulsion from the leadership of the party.

# 1924

## 1 January

Owing to purges and reviews of membership, party strength was down to 350,000 and 122,000 candidate members.

## 7 January

The Presidium of the Central Control Commission ruled that, as the organ of the party's Central Committee, *Pravda* was obliged to carry the Central Committee's line. Thenceforward, *Pravda* ceased to give space to opposition platforms and arguments.

## 16–18 January

At the party's Thirteenth Conference, a resolution introduced by Stalin accused Trotsky (who was absent for health reasons) of leading the whole 'opposition bloc' and hinted at the possibility of his expulsion from the Central Committee by confirming the Tenth Congress's prohibition of factional groupings and by publishing its provision for the expulsion of Central Committee members who 'tolerated factionalism'. The resolution was approved by the conference on 18 January by an overwhelming majority.

The conference took decisions on currency reform, wage rates (to give workers some compensation for loss of real wages consequent on the currency reform) and the reinforcement of price controls.

## 20 January

Of 165 delegates to the First Kuomintang Conference in Canton, about twenty-four (Jacobs' figures) were said to have been communists. In the anti-imperialism of its manifesto and in its organisational statutes, the party followed the Russian communist model fairly closely. But the social and agrarian clauses of its manifesto have been described as neither lucid nor particularly revolutionary. It was accepted that members of the Chinese communist party could join the Kuomintang as individuals. Three of the twenty-four full members and six of the candidate members of the Kuomintang's new Central Executive Committee were communists.

## 21 January

Lenin died.

## 26 January

The Second All-Union Congress of Soviets decided to preserve Lenin's body in a mausoleum, to change the name of Petrograd to Leningrad and to publish Lenin's works.

## 31 January

The Central Committee approved a decision of the Thirteenth Conference to launch a party recruiting-drive (the 'Lenin enrolment') exclusively among 'workers on the bench'. This opened a period of steady expansion of the party contrasting with Lenin's policy of concentrating on the quality rather than the quantity of the party membership.

## 1 February

A British note of this date, delivered in Moscow on the following day, informed the Soviet government that the British government recognised the USSR as 'the *de jure* rulers of those territories of the old Russian Empire which acknowledge their authority'. The note also raised the following subjects: treaties signed with Russia before the revolution; the restoration of Russian credit in London; the claims of the governments and individuals of one party against the other; and subversive propaganda. It suggested that representatives should be sent to London to discuss the basis for a treaty to settle all outstanding matters. The Soviet reply dated 8 February accepted all these points for discussion.

## 2 February

Rykov, who had become chairman of the Council of People's Commissars of both the USSR and the RSFSR, was succeeded as chairman of the Supreme Council of National Economy by Dzerzhinskii. Dzerzhinskii shed the Commissariat of Communications but retained the chairmanship of the OGPU.

## 7 February

A Soviet–Italian treaty of commerce and navigation was signed in Rome, establishing normal diplomatic and consular relations. Mussolini despatched a note to the Soviet government conveying the Italian government's *de jure* recognition. The following governments also exchanged notes with the USSR establishing diplomatic relations: Norway (15 February/10 March), Austria (25/29 February), Greece (8 March), the free city of Danzig (13 March), Sweden (15/18 March and a commercial agreement), Canada (24 March), Denmark (18 June), Albania (4 July/4 September), Mexico (4 August) and Hejaz (6 August).

## 14–25 February

Although not a member of the League of Nations, the USSR was invited to the Rome Conference of Naval Experts on the limitation of naval armaments. The Soviet delegate, Admiral Berens, reopened the controversy over the Black Sea straits, which had arisen at Lausanne (see 4 December 1922), and by demanding an unreasonably high tonnage for Soviet capital ships, ensured the failure of the conference.

## 7 March

The last of a series of decrees issued in the previous five weeks established a new gold-backed ruble, the 'chervonets'. The value of 1 million rubles at this point was calculated at 0.00002 of one pre-war ruble (Zaleski quoting Serge N. Prokopovicz, *Histoire Economique de l'URSS*, Paris, 1952). The quest for a stable currency formed an essential part of NEP and brought the Soviet economy more into line with its prospective trading partners in the capitalist world. The introduction of orthodox financial regulation of the economy enhanced the importance of the Commissariat of Finance and the State Bank at the expense of the Supreme Council of National Economy and the Commissariat of Supply. The functions of the Supreme Council of National Economy were confined to the management of industry for the revival of which Dzerzhinskii sought large sums of money. The Commissariat of Supply was absorbed in May into a new Commissariat of Internal Trade whose primary responsibility was price control.

## 11 March

Frunze was appointed Trotsky's deputy and effective head of the army. He had been one of the main exponents of 'Unitary Military Doctrine' propounded at the party's Tenth Congress in March 1921, the application to military doctrine of Marxist principles and the imperatives of world socialist revolution. Frunze believed in an idealised form of partisan warfare, offensive rather than defensive, a war of manoeuvre rather than position and in sharp contrast with the more traditional views of the former Tsarist 'military specialists'. The argument gave Stalin and Zinoviev further opportunities to undermine Trotsky on account of his use of 'military specialists' which, though vigorously defended by him, had always been regarded as controversial. Voroshilov replaced Trotsky's friend Muralov as commander of the politically vital Moscow Military District and Bubnov replaced another friend of Trotsky, Antonov-Ovseenko, as head of the political administration of the army (PUR).

## 14 March

A Sino-Soviet treaty on the re-establishment of relations was signed by Karakhan and a Chinese delegate but the Peking government refused to ratify it.

## 23 March–2 April

A conference in Vienna to discuss the resumption of normal Soviet–Romanian relations broke down over Romanian refusal to discuss Bessarabia.

## April

Bukharin, while retaining the editorship of *Pravda*, became editor of the Central Committee's fortnightly journal *Bol'shevik* which, according to Souvarine, was produced especially to combat Trotsky and his supporters.

## 1 April

Frunze was appointed chief of a reorganised staff which in due course developed into the Soviet General Staff. In the summer, Tukhachevskii and Shaposhnikov were appointed as his two deputies. Frunze described the task of the new staff as being 'to raise itself above the point of view of the nation-state . . . to help the proletariat of [other countries] to victory over their internal class enemy'. Frunze's reforms extended to the air force and the navy with heavy emphasis on modernisation and the appointment of young, communist commanders.

# 14 April

An Anglo-Soviet conference opened in London to discuss the terms of a treaty.

The Soviet negotiating team included the trade union leader, Tomskii, who took up contact with members of the British Trade Union Congress. A relationship between British and Soviet trade unions had existed since the anti-intervention 'Hands off Russia' campaign starting early in 1919. The campaign was intensified during the Soviet–Polish war.

# 25 April

The Soviet press said that the task of the State General Planning commission (Gosplan) was to establish a general perspective plan of the economic activity of the USSR for a number of years (five or ten). Tsiurupa had recently taken over as president of Gosplan, combining the job until 1925 with that of deputy president of the Council of People's Commissars. The needs of economic planning were one of the main motives behind the enlargement and rationalisation of the units of local government ('regionalisation') on lines laid down by the party's Twelfth Congress in April 1923. The new subdivision was based on the region (*oblast* or *krai*), the department (*okrug*) and the district (*raion*). The process of reorganisation was pronounced complete at the Sixteenth Congress of the party in June–July 1930.

# 26 April–18 May

*Pravda* published Stalin's lectures to the Sverdlov Communist University 'On the Foundations of Leninism'. The lectures described Leninism as a development of Marxism arising from and taking into account the growth of imperialism since Marx's time: Leninism had established itself in opposition to the 'opportunism' of the Second (socialist) International. Without mentioning Trotsky, the lectures condemned the theory of permanent revolution for its underestimation of the role of the peasantry. The lectures argued that since the definitive triumph of socialism in one country could not be secured without the combined efforts of the proletariat in several advanced countries, the victorious revolution in one country had the essential task of supporting the revolution in other countries. The dictatorship of the proletariat, described as 'the point of departure' of Leninism, was the essential condition for achieving and consolidating the revolution and guaranteeing the transition from capitalism to communism. In the struggle against imperialism, the dictatorship of the proletariat should make use of genuinely anti-imperialist national movements abroad. The party was not just the vanguard but the 'organised detachment' of the proletariat: its unity and iron discipline alone enabled it to act as the instrument of the dictatorship of the proletariat. The lectures ended with an appeal for a combination of Russian revolutionary 'sweep' with American efficiency.

Tucker saw the work as an effort by Stalin to establish himself as Lenin's ideological successor and at the same time to provide the post-revolutionary majority of the party's members with a popular, dogmatic guide to the theory and practice of Leninism.

## 8–9 May

The press section of the Central Committee held a conference on literature at which the 'fellow-travellers' (see February 1921), who had been supported by Lenin, Trotsky and Bukharin among others, were attacked by supporters of the VAPP – *Na Postu* line (see October 1920 and Summer 1923), mainly aspiring young writers who demanded that the party should give its exclusive support to ideologically committed 'proletarian' writers. The conference resolution dated 19 May confirmed the party's benevolent attitude to the 'fellow-travellers' and, while not unsympathetic to the youthful *Na Postu* group, rejected the claim of any one literary group to speak in the name of the party. Bukharin was an enthusiastic advocate of 'proletarian culture' but believed that it should establish its pre-eminence through competition with other movements and the more movements the better.

## 20 May

A detailed decree encouraged the formation and functioning of co-operatives as an ideologically preferable alternative to the system of private trade which NEP had encouraged. Lack of credit proved to be a limiting factor in the growth of co-operatives but the situation was improved by a further decree of 31 March 1925.

## 21 May

According to Tucker's account, the Central Committee discussed Lenin's hitherto secret 'testament' dictated on 23–25 December 1922 and 4 January 1923 which had been given to the committee by Krupskaia on 18 May. Krupskaia having protested against a proposal by Kamenev to withhold the 'testament' from the congress, it was decided that it should be read aloud to the delegation caucuses of the major party organisations but not made part of the congress's public proceedings. Zinoviev, supported by Kamenev, argued against carrying out Lenin's proposal that Stalin should be removed from the post of General Secretary and this was agreed. Trotsky, who had recently returned from convalescence in the Caucasus, remained silent.

## 23–31 May

The party held its Thirteenth Congress, sometimes known as the 'Bolshevisation Congress'. As a result of the 'Lenin enrolment', the party claimed a membership of 600,000 (including candidates) to which another 112,000 recruits were added by the end of May. For the first time, over half the members were workers (by social origin but not by current occupation). Molotov spoke of the need to make it easier for peasants to join the party. Carr considered that the 'Lenin enrolment' entailed a change in the attitude towards party membership from something which imposed extra obligations to something which provided extra privileges. The lower level of education of the membership necessitated a drive for party education and even greater centralised control.

Zinoviev, who delivered the Central Committee's report, held Trotsky responsible for factionalism in the party and called on him to admit his mistakes and recant. Trotsky responded with a speech in which, alluding to the English expression 'my country right or wrong', he said, 'When the party passes a decision which one or another of us finds unjust, he says "just or unjust, this is my party and I shall bear the consequences of its decisions to the end".' The final congress resolution on the Central Committee report reaffirmed the thirteenth conference's verdict on the 'petty bourgeois deviation' of the opposition. Trotsky was re-elected to the Central Committee by a narrow margin. Radek, who was blamed for the failure of the German rising of October 1923, was dropped from the Central Committee.

The congress enlarged the Central Committee to fifty-three members and thirty-four candidates.

A resolution, mainly on the press, while endorsing the resolution of 19 May that no one literary trend or group should be allowed to speak in the name of the party, emphasised the importance of 'regulating questions of literary criticism' and advocated material support for proletarian and peasant writers.

The congress decided that the closing of churches, synagogues, mosques and other places of worship should cease. This applied until 1928.

## 31 May

A new Sino-Soviet agreement was signed by Karakhan and Dr Wellington Koo, Foreign Minister of the Peking government. The agreement restored normal diplomatic relations between the Soviet and Peking governments. All treaties between China and the Tsarist government were annulled. The signatories agreed to abstain from hostile propaganda or armed subversion against one another. The agreement provided for the redemarcation of their common frontier. The USSR renounced certain extra-territorial rights in China. The Soviets also recognised Outer Mongolia as an 'integral part' of China and undertook to withdraw Soviet troops after negotiating a time limit. Chicherin, however, told the Soviet Central Executive Committee in March 1925, 'We recognise the Mongolian People's Republic as part of the Chinese Republic but we also recognise its autonomy in so far-reaching a sense that we consider it not only as independent of China in its internal life but as capable of pursuing its foreign policy independently.'

A separate agreement was signed on joint Soviet–Chinese management of the Chinese Eastern railway (see also 20 September). The Chinese undertook to desist from employing White Russians in the Chinese army and police.

## 2 June

Kamenev, Trotsky, Stalin, Zinoviev, Rykov, Tomskii and Bukharin (who had replaced Lenin) were elected to the Politburo. Molotov, Kalinin, Frunze, Dzerzhinskii, Rudzutak and Sokol'nikov were elected candidate members.

## 16 June

Sun Yat-sen opened a new Military Academy at Whampoa near Canton. Chiang Kai-shek was appointed commandant with the Soviet General

Bliukher as his chief of staff. The academy was funded by the Soviets and used Soviet methods. Chou En-lai, already an avowed communist, was employed in its political department. According to Chiang Kai-shek, the Chinese army received 3,000 tons of Soviet military equipment during 1924.

## 17 June–8 July

The Fifth Comintern Congress was held in Moscow. Attendance was variously reported as 406 or 510 delegates from forty or fifty-two different parties. The congress was held against the background of the failure of the uprising in Germany in October 1923, the growth of fascism in Italy and Germany (which provoked much discussion of united front tactics) and the disputes in the Russian communist party. Both fascism and social-democracy were denounced as 'bourgeois movements'. The keynote of the congress was the 'bolshevisation' of the European parties which meant in practice an effort to enforce strict discipline in the maintenance of party unity and centralised control under the direction of the Comintern. The effort continued throughout 1925 encountering difficulties notably in the German party in which the disagreements in the Soviet leadership were reflected.

The congress discussed how the Comintern should react to a British-inspired IFTU resolution to continue consultations on securing the inclusion of the USSR in the international trade union movement. The matter was referred to the Comintern's Executive Committee.

Trotsky, who was greeted with applause at the opening of the congress, and Radek, who was associated with the German failure and was also identified with internal opposition, were both dropped from the Executive Committee although Trotsky remained a candidate member. Stalin was elected a full member of the committee for the first time. Rykov and Kamenev, both People's Commissars of the USSR and therefore members of the Soviet government in the fullest sense, were also elected to the committee together with Zinoviev (its president) and Bukharin.

## 18 June

A provisional Soviet–Danish commercial agreement was signed.

## 24 June

A decree set up a committee to coordinate the activities and credit policy of the rapidly increasing number of banks concerned with different aspects of economic development.

A conference of transport workers from China, Indonesia and the Philippines was held in Canton under Profintern auspices.

## 1 July

The formation was announced of the Soviet trading organisation in New York, *Amtorg*, under the chairmanship of Khurgin (Hoorgin). This superseded *Arcos America* which had been established early in the year as a branch of *Arcos*, London. For *Amtorg*'s espionage activities, see *The New KGB* by Corson and Crowley.

## 8 July

The Third Profintern Congress opened. The congress endorsed a French proposal to work towards a world congress of IFTU and Profintern affiliates.

## 16 July

The teaching of religion in churches was prohibited.

## 30 July

Six members of the Soviet legation in Warsaw were expelled by the Poles for propaganda and espionage activities.

## August

Preobrazhenskii published a paper on 'The Fundamental Law of Socialist Accumulation' which might be considered the opening shot of the party's left wing in the 'Industrialisation Debate'. The debate lasted until 1928 (see Gregory and Stuart for a concise account). Preobrazhenskii favoured a sharp rise in investment in heavy industry to increase the USSR's industrial capacity. He argued that this could be financed without inflation only by a cut in consumption and an increase in forced savings procured by state trading monopolies buying cheap and selling dear. Since the effective demand of the peasantry had been increased by the revolution in that the level of taxation in 1924 was a lesser burden than the pre-revolutionary exactions of the landlords and the state, the terms of trade should be turned against the peasantry who, together with workers in the private sector, should bear the major part of the cost of rapid industrialisation.

Shanin, representing the opposite pole in the debate, argued that agriculture should be given priority over industry. The short-term return on a given amount of capital would be higher in agriculture than in industry. Peasants had a higher propensity to save than workers: their exportable surplus would pay for the import of capital goods for industry.

Bukharin called for a balanced development of agriculture and industry which he considered interdependent. The productivity of workers depended on agriculture producing a marketable surplus. The peasantry needed an incentive to increase and sell their production: the terms of trade should be turned in their favour. In the short term, agricultural exports would pay for the import of capital goods for industry. In the longer term, the aim should be a socialist system in one country independent of the capitalist states. Meanwhile, the market relations established by NEP and the worker–peasant alliance should be preserved even if this entailed a process of growing into socialism at a snail's pace.

The economist, Varga, published *Outlines of the Agrarian Question* maintaining that, under NEP conditions, individual peasant enterprise was more efficient than large-scale collective cultivation which should be left for a later stage in the building of socialism.

## 8 August

General and commercial Anglo-Soviet treaties, which had been under negotiation in London since 14 April and which envisaged a British government-backed loan to the

Soviet Union, were signed in London. They were not ratified owing to the change-over from a Labour to a Conservative government after the elections of 29 October.

## 27–28 August

An attempt at a general insurrection in Georgia misfired. The rising was finally quelled after about three weeks by Red Army troops who, according to Lang, killed between 7,000 and 10,000 prisoners and hostages in reprisal. Suny gave a figure of 4,000. Souvarine mentioned indications that the mistiming of the outbreak was the result of provocation by the OGPU which was well informed on the local situation. According to Suny, one of the organisers of the rebellion was arrested by the OGPU on 6 August.

## 27–29 August

Savinkov, who had been running an anti-Soviet resistance movement from Prague since his expulsion from Poland and had entered Russia within the previous two weeks, was tried by the Military Collegium of the USSR Supreme Court. He confessed to anti-Soviet activities and was sentenced to death, later commuted to ten years' imprisonment. He was reported to have committed suicide in jail on 7 May 1925. A Soviet account of the case published in the 1960s claimed that Savinkov's arrest was the result of a complex provocation and deception operation known as *Sindicat–2* but the correct interpretation of the Savinkov trial is still a matter for conjecture.

## 4 September

Tomskii addressed the annual British Trade Union Congress at Hull. He advocated unity between the IFTU and the Profintern and argued that the British unions could contribute to that end. The congress agreed enthusiastically. Tomskii also urged the congress to accept a Soviet invitation of 20 July to send a delegation to the USSR.

## 18 September

Signature of a Soviet–Hungarian trade agreement accompanied the restoration of diplomatic relations.

## 20 September

Since the Peking government did not effectively control Manchuria, a separate agreement was signed between the Soviet government and Marshal Chang Tso-lin, the military governor of Manchuria, covering the operation of the Chinese Eastern railway under joint Chinese and Russian management. The terms followed closely those of the agreement signed in Peking on 31 May except that they included reversion of the railway to Chinese ownership sixty years after its completion. The railway was to be run as a purely commercial enterprise, was not to be used for political purposes and the Chinese were to have an equal share in its management. These terms were not observed in practice, giving rise from the outset to friction which was to become a factor in the rupture of Sino-Soviet relations in 1929.

## 24 September

Bukhara and Khorezm announced their wish to unite with part of Turkestan to form two new Uzbek and Turkmen Soviet Socialist Republics. These republics, 'national in form, socialist in essence', were established and admitted into the USSR on 27 October. The Turkestan Autonomous SSR was abolished at the same time.

## 26 September

While allowing parents to give their own children religious instruction, the presence of more than three children from other families was prohibited. (Timasheff gives 1 September for this decree.)

## 9 October

The British Foreign Office received a copy of a letter allegedly written by Zinoviev in his Comintern capacity to the British communist party urging it to carry out subversive work in the British armed forces. The precise origin of the letter and its authenticity have not been established but its publication on 25 October is often considered to have contributed to the Labour Party's defeat at the general election on 29 October. (Natalie Grant questioned this in her 1967 article.) The letter was the subject of a British protest dated 24 October to the Soviet government. Ruth Fischer, who was a member of the presidium of the Comintern's Executive Committee and close to Zinoviev, claimed (p. 463) to have been told by him that he suspected, but could not prove, that the letter was an OGPU forgery. The implication was that Stalin arranged the forgery to undermine Zinoviev's position by highlighting the Comintern as the chief obstacle to closer Anglo-Soviet relations.

## 11 October

In order to strengthen the party in the rural areas and counteract the apathy and hostility of the peasantry in general and the growth in the influence of the kulaks in particular, Zinoviev launched a campaign to 'revitalise the Soviets'. It aimed to attract non-party peasants into the village Soviets while strengthening the communist fractions within them. The responsibilities of local Soviets for elementary education, health and local administration were defined more clearly. The campaign continued until 1926 without much apparent effect.

## 28 October

The French government of M. Herriot gave *de jure* recognition to the Soviet government.

## November

The Living Buddha of Urga having died, the first Great People's Khural proclaimed Mongolia a people's republic and ratified its first constitution.

## 2 November

An unsigned article in *Pravda* attributed to Bukharin condemned Trotsky's *Lessons of October* which, though not published until 6 November, was available to the party in October. In it Trotsky had argued that revolutionary leaders were to be judged by their ability to recognise and take advantage of a transient revolutionary situation. By implication this was a justification of his own role in the October/November revolution and an attack in particular on Zinoviev who had voted against the insurrection on 10/23 October 1917 and whose attempt to promote revolution in Germany in October 1923 had misfired. In short, Tucker saw *Lessons of October* as Trotsky's reply to the underground efforts of the Zinoviev–Kamenev–Stalin triumvirate to undermine him which had been in operation since April 1923. The dispute now came out into the open and became known as the 'Literary Discussion'.

## 7 November

Pestkovskii presented his credentials as the first Soviet minister to Mexico and the only Soviet diplomatic representative in Latin America in the 1920s.

## 11 November

A ten-member British trade union delegation arrived in Moscow for a month's goodwill visit to the USSR. The delegation agreed to the formation of an Anglo-Soviet joint trade union council (known as the Anglo-Russian Committee) to promote trade union unity. The British unions being the most powerful individual component of the IFTU, the Soviets sought to use the committee as an intermediary in persuading the IFTU to agree to a conference with the Soviet unions to discuss unity without preconditions. Despite British efforts, the IFTU insisted that an application by the Soviet unions for IFTU membership should precede any such conference. The British delegation's visit was followed by a number of similar visits by trade union delegations from other European countries.

## 18–26 November

In speeches and articles, Kamenev accused Trotsky of acting as an agent of Menshevism before 1917. Kamenev quoted disparaging comments made by Lenin about Trotsky and rejected Trotsky's theory of permanent revolution. He accused Trotsky of neglecting the peasantry, condemned his denunciations of other party leaders, his exaggeration of his own role and his underestimation of the role of the party and of Lenin within it. He criticised his 'errors' over Brest-Litovsk, the role of trade unions and the importance of economic planning. Stalin supported Kamenev and in order to diminish Trotsky's reputation, introduced a falsified version of the insurrection of October/November 1917, the organisation of which was attributed to a 'military revolutionary centre' consisting of Sverdlov, Stalin, Dzerzhinskii, Bubnov and Uritskii. Stalin also unearthed some scathing remarks about Lenin made by Trotsky in 1913. A press campaign ensued, blaming Trotsky and Trotskyism for causing dissension in the party.

## 1 December

An armed communist rising in Reval (Tallinn), carried out by some 200 activists widely believed to be under Comintern direction, was put down by the Estonian government with considerable bloodshed on both sides. Ruth Fischer suggested that the coup was launched by Zinoviev himself in order to boost his waning prestige and that its failure was used against him by Stalin.

## 3 December

*Pravda* published a resolution of the

Revolutionary Military Council stabilising the combined strength of the
Red Army and the Red Fleet at
562,000 regulars serving for two
years plus 250,000 territorials serving
for short periods each year for five
years. The ceiling for the regular
forces remained in being until 1934.

## 12 December

In an article in *Pravda* (followed by
an article in *Bol'shevik* of 15 January
1925 written on the instructions of
the Central Committee), Bukharin
denounced Preobrazhenskii's paper
published in August as the economic
foundation of Trotskyism and a con-
tradiction of the Leninist view expressed in NEP that socialism could only
be built in alliance with the peasantry
who must be given the right conditions in which to increase
production.

## 20 December

In an article entitled 'October and
Comrade Trotsky's Theory of Permanent Revolution' published in
*Pravda* and *Izvestiia*, Stalin emphasised the concept of 'socialism in one
country' as the antithesis to the
theory of permanent revolution.
'Socialism in one country' rejected
the notion that socialism could not
be built in a backward economy in
the absence of proletarian revolution
in other major capitalist states. At
the same time, it did not imply the
abandonment of world revolution
(see 26 April–18 May). In later years
it came increasingly to be identified
with the USSR's drive for industrialisation under state. ownership in a
planned economy (which Trotsky
had been advocating). In that it
implied Russian self-reliance in
building a new economic and social
system in a hostile environment, the
slogan could be used to appeal to
Russian national sentiment and to
boost bolshevik self-confidence: it
enabled Stalin and his supporters to
taunt their opponents like Trotsky
and, later, Zinoviev with pessimism
and faint-heartedness. Tucker and
others have argued that striking these
chords was a significant factor in
Stalin's victory over Trotsky.

# 1925

## 1 January

Party membership was given as 440,365 plus 361,439 candidate members. Less than 10 per cent of members were working peasants.

## 15 January

Trotsky addressed a letter to the Central Committee denying that there was any such thing as Trotskyism or that he had tried to revise Leninism. He wrote that he was ready to do any work whatever assigned to him by the Central Committee in any or no position but that the 'interests of the work' demanded that he be freed immediately from his duties as president of the Revolutionary Military Council.

## 17–20 January

On the first day of a joint meeting of the Central Committee and Central Control Commission, it was unanimously decided to accept Trotsky's resignation from the presidency of the Revolutionary Military Council. The meeting postponed until the next party congress consideration of his future employment by the party.

The meeting more than restored cuts which had been made in the budget for heavy industry in the previous November.

In the context of a debate on defence expenditure, Stalin told the meeting on 19 January that the preconditions for war were ripening though war itself might still be some years away. The revolutionary forces in the West might overthrow the bourgeoisie here or there but it would be difficult for them to hold their ground. The question of the strength and readiness of the Red Army would inevitably arise in the event of complications in the countries surrounding the USSR. This did not mean that in any such situation the USSR was bound to intervene actively against anybody. The banner of peace remained the banner of the USSR. But if war began, the USSR would not sit with folded arms. It would have to take action: but it would be the last power to do so and would throw its decisive weight on the scales, the weight that could tilt the balance. The army, chemical defence and aviation must all be prepared for all contingencies.

## 20 January

Karakhan signed a treaty with the Japanese in Peking which, in addition to providing for the renewal of diplomatic relations and including a no-propaganda clause, restored to the Soviet Union by 15 May the last bit of territory occupied by the allies, the northern part of Sakhalin Island. Japanese companies gained concessions for the exploitation of northern Sakhalin's oil and coal. A Soviet apology for the Nikolaevsk incident was annexed to the agreement. The withdrawal of Japanese troops from northern Sakhalin was completed on 4 April.

## 21 January

A second 'Lenin enrolment' was launched on the anniversary of Lenin's death. It brought in a further 300,000 candidates.

## 26 January

The presidium of the Soviet Central Executive Committee announced the appointment of Frunze to succeed Trotsky as People's Commissar for War and president of the Revolutionary Military Council.

## 7 February

The USSR League of the Godless was founded as a successor to the Society of Friends of the newspaper *Bezbozhnik (Godless)*. The League was intended to raise the level of sophistication of anti-religious work and to form cells of atheists in factories, shops, villages, Red Army units and so on.

## 6 March

Karakhan notified the Peking government that Soviet troops had completed the withdrawal from the Mongolian People's Republic which they had begun in 1922. By 1925 the communist regime there had been consolidated and there was no serious external military threat. There is

some doubt whether all Soviet troops were in fact withdrawn. In any case Soviet advisers continued to be employed in key positions including the Mongolian secret police. All postal and telegraphic communications between Mongolia and the outside world, including China, passed through Soviet territory.

The Central Committee adopted a resolution on one-man control in the Red Army. The role of political commissars was to be radically changed. Commanders who were party members were to be responsible for party political leadership: other commanders were to be responsible for operational, training, administrative and economic functions while the commissar remained responsible for party-political work and morale.

## 7 March

A budget commission headed by Kuibyshev and attached to the Soviet Central Executive Committee was set up to supervise the budget. The new budgetary system, which had been firmly established by 1924, retained many features of the pre-war system but with a higher proportion of revenue from direct and, to an increasing extent, progressive taxation (R.W. Davis in *The Development of the Soviet Budgetary System*). The year 1924–5 was the first in which the budget covered the whole territory of the USSR. It was revised upwards several times, reflecting the rapid economic recovery stimulated by NEP and in the end showed a small surplus of revenue over expenditure (Carr in *Socialism in One Country*, vol.I, pp.458–64).

## 12 March

Sun Yat-sen died. His death led to increased factionalism in the Kuomintang and even greater opportunities for Borodin to exert influence. The Comintern maintained its support for the united front with the Kuomintang.

## 22 March

In an article on 'The International Situation and the Tasks of the Communist Parties', Stalin wrote that the capitalist countries had succeeded in extricating themselves from the postwar crisis, the revolutionary advance in Germany and Central Europe having for the time being come to an end. Nevertheless, contradictions in the capitalist world were deepening and the strength of national liberation movements in the Middle and Far East was growing as were the strength of the USSR itself and the struggle for unity of the English trade union movement supported by the Soviet Union against the Amsterdam International.

## 7 April

Patriarch Tikhon died.

## 16 April

The Politburo decided to relax restrictions on the hiring of labour and the leasing of land.

A bomb detonated in Sofia cathedral during the funeral of an assassinated Bulgarian military-political figure, killed over 100 prominent Bulgarians. The outrage led to a reign of terror in Bulgaria. Those ultimately responsible were not clearly identified. The Soviets indignantly denied responsibility. Ruth Fischer, quoting contemporary rumours in the Comintern and other not very strong evidence, surmised that the OGPU was responsible and claimed that Stalin was quick to make use of the scandal further to weaken Zinoviev's standing. At the Reichstag Fire Trial in December 1933, Dimitrov, the Bulgarian communist and Comintern leader, denied that the Bulgarian communist party had organised the outrage for which he held the Bulgarian police responsible. But in his report to the Fifth Congress of the Bulgarian communist party in December 1948, he attributed it to the Bulgarian communist party's military organisation which, he claimed, was pursuing a left-wing deviation at the time.

## 17 April

In a speech to a mass party meeting in Moscow, Bukharin spoke in favour of removing restrictions on the growth of well-to-do and kulak farms. He saw this as a means of expanding not only the agricultural sector but the economy as a whole by providing the capital necessary for industrialisation. He argued that light consumer-goods industry should be developed first and thereafter heavy industry with market forces providing the necessary impetus. The building of socialism would continue if only at a snail's pace. Bukharin's speech included the phrase 'to all the peasants we say "enrich yourselves".' In private, Stalin dissociated himself at the time from this slogan but he nevertheless continued to rely on Bukharin's support against the 'left' opposition of Zinoviev, Kamenev and others until 1928. Bukharin had an influential group of talented young followers, particularly in the Institute of Red Professors which had been founded in 1921 and provided three-year courses in philosophy, history and economics for graduates intended eventually to replace non-party academics. Its graduates permeated the party press and also state economic institutions such as Gosplan.

## 27–29 April

The party's Fourteenth Conference, in the interests of increasing agricultural production, agreed to reduce the tax burden on the peasantry and endorsed the Politburo's decision to relax restrictions on the hiring of labour and the leasing of land. Larin, however, attacked Bukharin for his speech of 17 April and looked forward to the expropriation of the kulaks in fifteen to twenty years' time.

A conference resolution was redrafted after the conference was over to include various measures aimed at increasing the number of peasants in the party. These were put into effect immediately except in the Leningrad province which was under Zinoviev's control.

## 30 April

The Central Committee adopted a resolution which in effect favoured the growth of relatively large individual land holdings in the hands of efficient peasants while at the same time drawing attention to the problem of rural over-population. The resolution encouraged the formation of co-operatives which also tended to favour the better-off rather than the poor peasants. The resolution paid lip-service to state and collective farms. Bukharin's advocacy of co-operatives which would 'grow into' socialism was to be used against him in 1929.

An agreement was signed in Moscow between Piatakov, president of the Chief Concessions Committee, and the British Lena Goldfields Company which had US financial backing. The agreement provided for the company to mine gold, silver, copper, lead and zinc for thirty years in the area of Siberia which the company had exploited before the revolution. The company's engineers took possession of the properties on 1 October.

## May

Trotsky, having returned to Moscow after a period of ill health, was appointed president of the Chief Concessions Committee, president of the Chief Administration of the Electrical Industry (*Glavelektro*) and president of the Scientific and Technical Council. He withdrew from the last of these at his own request in January 1926.

## 13–20 May

At the Third All-Union Congress of Soviets, Kalinin stated that the most democratic organ in the countryside was not the rural Soviet but the traditional assembly (*skhod*) of heads of households in a commune (*mir*): the replacement of the *skhod* by the Soviet should, he said, be approached very cautiously (see 14 March 1927).

## 9 June

In an address to the students of Sverdlov University, which was not published until 1947, Stalin spoke of the need for Soviet domestic policies to be based on the assumption that the USSR would remain an Isolated socialist society for the next twenty years. He contrasted the nationalist view of foreign policy, which would have the USSR co-operate with the great powers in working out spheres of influence, with the revolutionary internationalist view which saw the USSR as a part of the world revolutionary movement and therefore obliged to support the emancipation of China or of Germany, Persia, Turkey or Afghanistan even at the risk of quarrels with other countries.

## 12 June

W. Averell Harriman and associates signed a concession agreement to mine the manganese ore deposits at Chiaturi in the Caucasus and to provide facilities to ship the ore from Poti. The concession, the most important to be concluded with a US company, was to have lasted for twenty years. Like other concessions, it was wound up as the NEP period came to an end from 1928 onwards.

## 16 June

The USSR reratified the Geneva and Hague conventions on the treatment of sick and wounded soldiers and seamen in wartime.

## 25 June

The Supreme Council of National Economy approved a major investment plan to revive industry in Leningrad and raise production above the pre-war level.

## 1 July

*Izvestiia* published a Central Committee resolution dated 18 June on literature which, while admitting that proletarian writers did not yet have hegemony, pledged the party's support to them in earning their historic right to that hegemony. Peasant writers also had the party's unconditional support. Meanwhile the party was enjoined to tolerate the 'fellow-travellers' while seeking to win them over to communism and combating any revival of bourgeois ideology. For the time being, the party was not to bind itself to any one tendency or to attempt to dictate form or style; it was to allow free competition between groups and repudiate incompetent administrative interference in literary matters.

## 13 July

A party resolution declared that physical culture should be considered not only as a way of improving public health and preparation for military training but as part of character-building and as a means of drawing workers and peasants into the activities of party, Soviet and trade union organisations. During the NEP period there was rivalry between the unions and Komsomol for control over sport and differing views on its purposes, the 'hygienists' and the 'proletarians' in particular opposing competitive sport on ideological grounds. In practice the difficulty of providing facilities militated against sport being treated as a high priority.

## 14 August

The All-Union Central Executive Committee issued a decree (further amplified on 27 April 1926) on espionage and the collection and transmission of economic information which was not open to publication. Penalties for the former included death by shooting and, for the latter, imprisonment for up to three years. The decree underlined the fact that offences against the state were outside the scope of ordinary criminal law and were dealt with centrally under the aegis of the OGPU.

## 20 August

Gosplan published its control figures for the national economy for the year 1925–6. The control figures were non-binding estimates. Their compilation marked an important stage in the development on a national scale for the whole of the USSR of the concept of planning which had hitherto been carried on for individual sectors of the economy and for different regions of the Union. The figures were hailed by Trotsky but were treated with scepticism, hostility or indifference by many of the party leaders who had not yet accepted the view that the decision to revive heavy industry entailed the development of a planned economy.

## September

The Russian Academy of Sciences celebrated its 200th anniversary in Leningrad. The regime had recognised it in July as 'the supreme scientific institution of the USSR'. Zinoviev addressed the international gathering which attended the celebrations. Up to 1927 the academy remained unreformed: not one academician was a communist party member.
*Note*: The academy has always included, for example, lawyers, historians and economists as well as natural scientists.

## 1 September

The Sun Yat-sen University of Toilers of China opened in Moscow. It was intended to attract in particular young members of the Kuomintang. Its first president was Radek.

## 4 September

Kamenev drew attention to the fact that co-operatives were helping mainly the better-off peasants and called for limits to be set to the enrichment of the latter in order to give more help to the middle and poor peasants.

## 5 September

Zinoviev, Kamenev, Sokol'nikov and Krupskaia signed an unpublished document known as the 'platform of the four'. It almost certainly dealt with the question of internal party democracy, the four signatories being united principally by their common concern over Stalin's growing power and their desire to force a debate on the controversial issues facing the party.

## 12 September

Stalin rejected a draft article by Zinoviev indirectly attacking Bukharin's encouragement of the rich peasants and calling for greater equality. In a book published slightly later, Zinoviev reverted to the danger that NEP would allow the bourgeoisie and the kulaks to undermine the dictatorship of the proletariat and argued that class struggle in the countryside should continue.(Bukharin had been asserting that progress towards socialism would mean an easing of class conflict.) Zinoviev's book emphasised the impossibility of building socialism in a single, isolated, backward economy and, by underlining Lenin's internationalism, implicitly criticised Stalin's identification with socialism in one country.

## 17 September

Following the annual British Congress of Trade Unions at Scarborough which Tomskii attended, the Anglo-Russian Committee held its first meeting. Calhoun cited evidence that the Soviet leadership saw the committee as a means of promoting revolution in Britain as well as trade union unity and as providing a deterrent against British aggressiveness towards the USSR.

## 18 September

A decree stated that all citizens aged from 21 to 40 were liable for military service (with pre-military training from 19 to 21) either for two years in the regular army or for eight to twelve months spread over five years or for not more than six months in all without enrolment. Citizens without political rights were to be enrolled for non-combatant service. This decree governed the shape of the Red Army for nearly ten years.

## 30 September

Chicherin arrived in Berlin after visiting Warsaw and publicly underlined Soviet hostility to the League of Nations. He questioned the benefits Germany would reap from membership. (The League voted to admit Germany on 8 September 1926.)

Chicherin was reported to have received an oral assurance from the Germans that they were not abandoning their friendship with the USSR. On 2 October Chicherin alluded to the 'innumerable proofs' that Britain was pursuing a policy of encirclement of the USSR which entailed separating Germany from the USSR.

## 12 October

Four days before the initialling of the Locarno security pact, denounced by the Soviets as an attempt by the British to form an anti-Soviet coalition of European powers including France and Germany, a Soviet–German commercial treaty was signed in Moscow. It declared that the treaty of Rapallo would continue to be regarded as the foundation for regulating Soviet–German relations and looked forward to the restoration of pre-war levels of trade between the two countries. The agreement was accompanied by the grant of short-term credit to the Soviet government to allow it to make immediate purchases of German equipment.

## 31 October

Dzerzhinskii published an order of the Supreme Council of National Economy calling on all economic organs to put an end to the rise in retail prices. At the same time he issued an instruction to the OGPU to enforce the order by action against speculators. These measures failed to restrain the rise in prices.

Frunze died and was succeeded as War Commissar by an old associate of Stalin, Voroshilov, with a Zinoviev supporter, Lashevich, as his deputy. Rumours that Frunze's death on the operating table was a medical murder ordered by Stalin formed the basis for a story by Pil'niak, *The Tale of the Inextinguishable Moon*, published in 1926.

## 7 November

Stalin's article in *Pravda* on the anniversary of the revolution took precedence over Zinoviev's. It drew a parallel between 1917 and 1925: 1917 had seen the transition from bourgeois to proletarian power. In 1925 'Leninist hardness' was needed to secure a revolutionary transition from NEP to a socialist economy. Tucker, in *Stalin as Revolutionary*, contrasted this outlook with the gradualist approach of Bukharin with whom Stalin was in tactical alliance against the left opposition.

Zinoviev, whose power base was in Leningrad, appeared on the same platform as Zalutskii whose dismissal as secretary of the Leningrad provincial party committee had been demanded by the Central Control Commission and reluctantly agreed to by the Leningrad committee. This triggered off an outburst of polemics both in the press and behind the scenes between Leningrad on the one hand and Moscow and the central party machine on the other. Since September 1924 the Moscow committee had been in the hands of Uglanov who was formerly in Leningrad and who seems to have been appointed to Moscow to clean out Trotskyite influence there. He has sometimes been referred to as a Stalinist but Cohen pointed out that he consistently supported Bukharin when his path diverged from Stalin's; a factor in this loyalty was Moscow's

local economic interest in the development of light rather than heavy industry.

## 14 November

Writing in *Pravda*, Bukharin withdrew his phrase 'enrich yourselves' and substituted the line that the party should promote the prosperity of the countryside in general.

## 15 November

Metropolitan Vvedenskii, the head of the Living Church, denounced Metropolitan Peter of Krutitskii, who was acting as patriarch in succession to Tikhon, for having counter-revolutionary connections.

Shapiro's *Soviet Treaty Series* gave the text of a Soviet–Norwegian treaty of commerce and navigation signed in Moscow on this date. Slusser and Triska listed the date as 15 December.

## 18 November

The People's Commissariats of Internal and Foreign Trade were amalgamated into a single People's Commissariat for Trade.

## 25 November

*Pravda* published Kamenev's economic report to the forthcoming party congress; the report dwelt mainly on the planned expansion of industry.

## 17 December

Two days after the League of Nations awarded Mosul (which was claimed by Turkey) to Iraq, a three-year Soviet–Turkish treaty of friendship and neutrality was signed in Paris. Each side agreed to observe neutrality in the event of the other being involved in hostilities with a third power. Each side also agreed not to participate in any alliance, agreement or action, including financial or economic action, hostile to the other initiated by one or more other powers. The treaty with Turkey was described by *Izvestiia* of 24 December as an 'anti-Locarno act'. It may also have been intended by the Soviets to keep Turkey out of the League of Nations.

## 18–31 December

At the party's Fourteenth Congress, the 'Industrialisation Congress', Stalin for the first time presented the Central Committee's report. Zinoviev, however, was granted the right to deliver a co-report in which he criticised in particular the party's policy towards the peasantry and Bukharin's exposition of it. Kamenev delivered an attack on Stalin, rejecting the idea of leadership of the party by an individual and deploring the secretariat's responsibility for both policy and organisation. Stalin's reply was to the effect that the party wanted unity and would achieve it with Kamenev and Zinoviev if they so wished or without them if they did not. The party, he said, could not be led on any basis other than a collective one. The resolution on Stalin's report was carried by 559 votes to 65.

On international relations, the resolution, following the lines of Stalin's report, said that a period of peaceful coexistence between the USSR and the partially stabilised capitalist states had begun despite the sharpening contradictions between the latter. Economic ties with foreign countries benefited construction in the USSR:

at the same time, the USSR had to remain economically independent. The Central Committee should

1. promote the alliance between the workers of the USSR, the European workers and the oppressed colonial peoples;
2. conduct a foreign policy of peace;
3. convert the USSR from an importer into a producer of machinery so that it retained its independence in conditions of capitalist encirclement;
4. build up economic reserves against all contingencies;
5. strengthen the Soviet armed forces.

In the countryside the party and the poor peasants should consolidate their alliance with the mass of middle peasants in order to win them over to socialist construction and to isolate the kulaks. Deviationists who sought to frustrate the party's present line in the village threatened the party's whole effort to build socialism. The resolution confirmed the Fourteenth Conference's decisions on the leasing of land and the hiring of labour. Voluntary co-operatives were to be built up and village Soviets revived.

Kalinin introduced an appeal to all members of the Leningrad party organisation protesting against their delegation's behaviour in putting forward its own co-reporter (Zinoviev) and issuing a declaration over the signature of Kamenev and others. Thirty-eight delegates contested the appeal which was the opening shot in an attack on the Leningrad-based 'New Opposition'.

The endorsement by the congress of the policy of intensive industrialisation on the basis of socialism and national self-sufficiency coincided with growing recognition of the failure of the concessions policy to attract any significant volume of foreign capital on terms acceptable to the regime. Carr in *Socialism in One Country*, vol. I, p. 455 gave the following figures on concessions:

|           | proposals received | agreements concluded |
|-----------|--------------------|----------------------|
| 1921–22   | 338                | 18                   |
| 1923      | 607                | 44                   |
| 1924      | 311                | 26                   |
| 1925      |                    |                      |
| Jan-April | 30                 | 3                    |

Germany had 24 per cent of the agreements (including the large Mologales timber concession), followed by Britain, the United States and France.

At the congress the party changed its name to the All-Union Communist Party (Bolsheviks) (AUCP(B) or VKP(B)).

The Central Committee was enlarged to sixty-three members and forty-three candidates, the Control Commission to 163 and the Politburo to nine.

Zinoviev retained the presidency of the Comintern but Bukharin became the dominant figure in it. Zinoviev also retained his party posts but most of his associates in the Central Committee lost their footings and a new editor was appointed by the Central Committee to the Leningrad party newspaper on 29 December. Zinoviev was effectively muzzled.

## 25 December

Metropolitan Peter of Krutitskii was arrested and in 1926 exiled to Siberia. He was succeeded in effect by Metropolitan Sergei of Nizhny Novgorod who had had earlier associations with the Living Church.

The poet, Esenin, who as a young man of peasant origin and SR sympathies had at first welcomed the revolution and had later suffered disillusionment, committed suicide. He had been married briefly to Isadora Duncan.

# 1926

At communist instigation, a Turcological conference in Baku in 1926 gave its blessing to the idea, pre-revolutionary in origin, of Latinising the alphabets of the eastern nationalities of the USSR. From a communist point of view, the advantages of Latinisation were that by replacing Arabic script, it would serve to undermine the influence of Islam; that it would promote cultural and economic collaboration between the different peoples of the USSR; and that a change of alphabet would provide a useful opportunity for weeding out unsuitable books in the minority languages. Use of the universal Latin alphabet was considered more consistent with proletarian internationalism than use of the Slavic Cyrillic alphabet. An All-Union Central Committee for the New Turkic Alphabet was set up in Baku in 1927. In 1930 it moved to Moscow and became the All-Union Central Committee for the New Alphabet attached to the Central Executive Committee of the USSR. The Latinisation campaign continued into the mid-1930s but from 1937 onwards the Latin alphabet was replaced by slightly modified Cyrillic.

## 1 January

Party membership was given as 639,652 with 440,162 candidate members.

Bukharin, Voroshilov, Zinoviev, Kalinin, Molotov, Rykov, Stalin, Tomskii and Trotsky were elected members of the Politburo. Kamenev, on demotion, joined Rudzutak, Dzerzhinskii, Petrovskii and Uglanov as a candidate member. Kamenev was dismissed from the chairmanship of the Council of Labour and Defence, the chairmanship of the Moscow Soviet and the deputy chairmanship of the Council of People's Commissars. He was, however, made People's Commissar for Trade.

## 5 January

A high-powered Central Committee delegation led by Molotov arrived in Leningrad to report to the Leningrad workers on the Fourteenth Congress and in effect to restore the Central Committee's authority there. Zinoviev was removed from the chairmanship of the Leningrad Soviet. In February he was succeeded as first secretary of the Leningrad party organisation by Kirov.

## 21 January

The Chinese military authorities arrested the Soviet manager of the Chinese Eastern railway who had refused to transport Manchurian troops without prepayment of their fares. A vigorous protest by Karakhan secured the manager's release.

## 25 January

Stalin completed 'Concerning Questions of Leninism', published as a pamphlet on 6 February and in *Bol'-shevik* no. 3 on 15 February. In it he enlarged on 'The Foundations of Leninism' (see 26 April–18 May 1924) and developed the concept of socialism in one country, condemning Zinoviev who was described as 'hopelessly infected with scepticism' over the victory of socialist construction in the USSR.

## 15 February

A decree removed the upper limit of 10,000 rubles to the value of an estate which might be inherited.

## 16/19 February

The USSR was the first state to exchange notes recognising King Abdul Aziz Ibn Saud who had captured Jedda on 22 December 1925 and had assumed the titles of King of Hejaz and Sultan of Nejd and Associated Territories.

## 17 February–15 March

The sixth (enlarged) meeting of the Executive Committee of the Comintern took place. The presence of numerous delegates from the East, including the Chinese communist party, the Kuomintang and the Mongolian People's Revolutionary Party, illustrated the growing importance of the Far East in Soviet policy. The meeting declared that the Kuomintang government in Canton was the vanguard of the liberation struggle of the Chinese people.

The meeting expressed its support for the Anglo-Russian Committee on trade union unity.

## 10 March

The First All-Union Congress of Planning Organs met in Moscow. Krzhizhanovskii, who served as chairman of Gosplan from 1925 to 1930, divided its work into three parts – a general plan for the national economy, a perspective five-year plan and annual operational plans with a corresponding system of control figures. Gosplan was in the course of preparing control figures for a perspective plan for the coming five years. Strumilin, the Gosplan economist concerned with this plan, described the fundamental task as 'the industrialisation of the economy on the basis of electrification . . . with annual reinforcement of its socialistic outposts at the expense of . . . the elements of a private economy'.

## 11–22 March

The Seventh Komsomol Congress, at which members of the opposition were allowed to speak, confirmed the organisation's loyalty to the party leadership. The opposition was roundly condemned. The Komsomol claimed 1.75 million members.

## 20 March

In the absence of Borodin and Bliukher from Canton, Chiang Kai-shek, who was emerging as the leading figure in the Kuomintang, arrested a number of prominent communists and for a few hours confined the

Soviet advisers to their quarters. At Chiang's request some of the Soviet advisers were later withdrawn. Both sides subsequently played down the importance of the coup: nevertheless, when Borodin returned to Canton on 29 April, he found his wings clipped though Bliukher for the time being retained his position as Chiang's principal military adviser. As the price of their continuing relationship with Chiang, the Soviet advisers had no option but to go along with his northern expedition intended to reunite China. Some of them had sought at least to delay the expedition. It was finally launched in July. The idea that the Chinese communist party should seek to re-establish its independence, advocated by Trotsky and by some members of the Chinese party's Central Committee, was squashed by the Comintern. The party remained for the time being subordinate to the Kuomintang.

## 6–9 April

At a Central Committee meeting largely devoted to economic policy, Trotsky participated actively in the debate for the first time in nearly two years and there were signs of a reconciliation between him and Zinoviev and Kamenev.

## 24 April

The question of German entry into the League of Nations having been postponed by the League in March, a five-year Soviet–German neutrality and non-aggression treaty was signed in Berlin. It invoked the Rapallo treaty as the basis of relations between the two countries. It provided that if either side were attacked by one or more third powers the

other would observe neutrality and it ruled out participation of either party in a coalition of third powers seeking to impose an economic or financial boycott of the other. From a Soviet point of view, the treaty could be seen as an effort to forestall a European anti-Soviet coalition which the Locarno pact and German entry into the League of Nations seemed to threaten. The treaties with Germany and Turkey (see 17 December 1925) were the forerunners of a series of neutrality and non-aggression pacts signed by the USSR with bordering states which gave the USSR some guarantee that use could not be made of their territories by the 'capitalist' powers for an attack on the USSR, at least without some warning being given.

## 25 April

As part of a campaign for economy in the bureaucracy and with a view to finding the resources necessary for industrialisation, the party leadership called for severe cuts in the staffs of the people's commissariats and other state organisations.

## 7–10 May

The British Trade Union Congress refused to accept a sum of £26,427 sent by the All-Russian Central Council of Trade Unions in support of the British general strike declared on 3 May which the government held to be illegal. The transfer of a second sum of £200,000 was blocked by a London bank on the instructions of the Home Secretary, Sir William Joynson-Hicks. Further sums from the Soviet trade unions and co-operatives were however received by the Miners' Federation, whose legal strike continued after the general strike collapsed on 12 May. Quoting British trade union sources, Calhoun gave a total figure of £1,233,788 for the Soviet contribution to the miners' strike, more than twice as much as they received from other British unions and the IFTU together. The question of relations with the British union leaders became an issue between the leadership and the opposition in the Russian communist party, Trotsky arguing that Soviet collaboration with reformist British union leaders was a betrayal of the British communist party and of revolutionary internationalism in general and a natural consequence of 'socialism in one country'.

## 12–15 May

The Polish communist party lent its support to Pilsudski's seizure of power in Poland. The Polish commission of the Comintern resolved on 15 May that this was an error, a view endorsed by the German communist leader Thälmann in *Pravda* on 30 May and by Bukharin on 9 June. The issue split the Polish party and represented another setback for united front tactics.

## 2–18 June

A German naval mission made a tour of inspection of Soviet ships and naval installations and held talks with Soviet naval commanders. The Soviet side evinced a strong desire for German help, in particular over submarines. The Germans supplied plans of First World War U-boats to the Soviets. Muklevich, who played a leading role in the re-equipment of the Soviet navy, did so with the benefit of German advice even though the German naval department was more reserved than the German army in its dealings with the Soviets and less dependent on Soviet help in providing facilities for training and equipment-testing.

## 6 June

Lashevich, Deputy People's Commissar for War and a Zinoviev supporter, addressed a meeting of the party opposition in a forest near Moscow.

## 10 June

Metropolitan Sergei, the acting head of the Patriarchate who had been imprisoned in the early part of the year, announced the formal registration of the church with the Commissariat of Internal Affairs, proclaimed the church's loyalty to the Soviet government and disavowed anti-Soviet activities on the part of *émigré* priests.

## 12 June

The presidium of the party Control Commission severely reprimanded Lashevich and the organiser of the meeting of 6 June and threatened them with expulsion from the party if they did not desist from opposition activity.

## 22/24 June

Iceland and the USSR exchanged notes on recognition.

## 9 July

A decree prohibited the export of *chervontsy*. This act 'formally sealed the abandonment of the short-lived attempt to maintain a Soviet currency based on gold and linked by its gold parity to the international monetary system' (Carr, *Socialism in One Country*, vol. I, p. 488). The decision was taken in the wake of a severe bout of inflation during the previous nine months and was in part a reflection of the determination to press ahead with industrialisation and a planned economy largely independent of the capitalist world.

## 14–23 July

A joint session of the Central Committee and the Central Control Commission met to deal with the question of the opposition. After several months of improving relations, Trotsky had buried the hatchet with Zinoviev and Kamenev. Together with Krupskaia and nine other Central Committee members, they had signed a 'declaration of the thirteen' members of the 'united opposition' dealing mainly with suppression of opposition within the party and the need for accelerated, planned industrialisation financed by higher taxation of the richer peasants and increased exports of grain to pay for imports of machinery. The declaration also raised the sensitive question of increases in industrial wages. The joint session's resolution on 'the affair of Lashevich and others and on party unity' claimed that the united opposition had resorted to illegal, conspiratorial methods and that the threads of the conspiracy led to Zinoviev, a member of whose Comintern apparatus had arranged the meeting in the woods on 6 June. The resolution refused the opposition's demands, expelled Zinoviev from the Politburo and deprived Lashevich of his post as Deputy

Commissar for War and his candidate membership of the Central Committee. Rudzutak replaced Zinoviev in the Politburo. Ordzhonikidze, Andreev, Kirov, Mikoyan, Kaganovich and Chubar' were added to the candidate membership of the Politburo.

## 20 July

Dzerzhinskii died. According to Deutscher his death occurred immediately after he had delivered an impassioned attack on the opposition at the joint session of the Central Committee and Central Control Commission. He was succeeded as chairman of the OGPU by Menzhinskii (much of the day-to-day business being conducted by his deputy, Iagoda) and as president of the Supreme Council of National Economy by Kuibyshev, an associate of Stalin.

## 14 August

A decree removed Kamenev from the post of Commissar for Trade and appointed Mikoyan in his place.

## 16 August

Following a campaign for higher labour productivity and lower absenteeism, which reached a climax in June and July, a declaration signed by Rykov, Stalin and Kuibyshev condemned measures which had harmed the welfare of the workers. The following day, steps were taken to introduce an all-round increase in industrial wages. The attempt to keep increases in productivity ahead of wage increases failed in 1926/7 but was more successful in 1927/8.

## 21/22 August

Uruguay and the USSR exchanged notes regarding *de jure* recognition but diplomatic missions were not exchanged until March–May 1934.

## 31 August

A three-year Soviet–Afghan neutrality and non-aggression pact was signed.

## 11 September

Karakhan was withdrawn from Peking at the request of the Peking government in part as a consequence of Sino-Soviet friction during the year over the Chinese Eastern railway.

## 28 September

A five-year Soviet–Lithuanian non-aggression treaty was signed in Moscow. It reaffirmed in effect that Vilna belonged to Lithuania although it was under Polish control at the time. The dispute with Poland over Vilna provided the Lithuanians with a motive for being the first of the Baltic states to sign a pact of this kind with the USSR.

## 16 October

Having been denounced by the party for addressing party meetings at factories in several cities during the preceding weeks, Zinoviev, Kamenev, Trotsky, Piatakov and two other opposition leaders signed a declaration accepting Stalin's demands that they should unconditionally obey party decisions, renounce factional activities and disavow their supporters in the all-union and foreign communist parties.

## 18 October

*The New York Times* published Lenin's 'testament' (see 23–26 December 1922).

## 23 October

A resolution of a joint plenum of the Central Committee and the Central Control Commission issued a severe warning to Trotsky, Zinoviev, Kamenev, Piatakov, Sokol'nikov, Smil'ga and other oppositionists for breaches of party discipline. The resolution 'found it impossible' that Zinoviev should continue to work in the Comintern.

## 25–26 October

At a meeting of the Politburo, Trotsky referred to Stalin as 'the gravedigger of the revolution'. He and Kamenev were deprived of their membership and candidate membership of the Politburo.

## 26 October–3 November

The opening of the party's Fifteenth Conference coincided with the publication of Stalin's theses on the opposition. The theses noted that despite the opposition's declaration of 16 October, it had not renounced its errors of principle – its social-democratic deviation – and intended to go on cultivating a spirit of pessimism and capitulation in the party: a determined ideological struggle against the opposition's errors was therefore necessary. Stalin, followed by Bukharin, denounced the opposition in speeches on 1 and 3 November and revealed that Krupskaia had severed her connection with it. Trotsky, making his last speech to a party audience, was heard in silence,

Kamenev was interrupted and Zinoviev heckled. The opposition leaders having consultative votes only, the conference unanimously adopted a resolution based on Stalin's theses.

The party leadership, including Bukharin, resolved to catch up and surpass the levels of industrial development of the leading capitalist countries in a 'relatively minimal historical period'. Socialist industrialisation, Stalin argued, could only be achieved through improvement in the material situation of the vast labouring masses including the peasantry.

To help raise finance for industrialisation, the conference promoted the issue to the public of 'industrialisation loans' at low rates of interest paid partly or wholly in lottery prizes.

Ordzhonikidze succeeded Kuibyshev as president of the Central Control Commission and therefore ceased to be a candidate member of the Politburo.

## 12–13 November

Communist-led disturbances occurred at a number of points in western and central Java and in Sumatra, lasting until 17 November. They were followed by similar disturbances in western Sumatra in January 1927 lasting about ten days. A third outbreak planned for 17–18 July 1927 was forestalled by police action. The official Dutch report traced the disturbance back to the Fifth Comintern Congress and the transport workers' congress in Canton (see 24 June 1924).

## 19 November

The Soviet Central Executive Committee approved the Code of Laws on Marriage and Divorce, the Family and Guardianship. Among the new elements in this family code were the recognition of the rights of women in *de facto* as well as in registered marriages and the substitution of the Registrar's Office for the courts as the recipient and arbiter in the first instance of petitions for divorce. The marriageable age for women was raised from 16 to 18 (the same as men) though certain exceptions were allowed. The right of one spouse in need and unable to work to receive alimony from the other expired after not more than one year from the dissolution of the marriage.

## 22 November

A new RSFSR criminal code was introduced taking into account the Fundamental Principles of Criminal Legislation enacted in October 1924. The code provided that persons who had committed 'socially dangerous acts' (crimes) or who represented a danger because of their connection with a 'criminal environment' or because of their past activity would be liable to 'measures of social defence of a judicial-correctional, medical or medico-educational character'. It also stated that the bases and limits of criminal responsibility for a 'socially dangerous act' not provided for in the code should be determined by applying the article of the code which provided for the crimes most similar to it. A 'socially dangerous act' was defined as 'any act or omission that is directed against the Soviet system or that violates the legal order established by the worker–peasant power during the period of transition to the communist system'. The code made a sharp distinction between political and all other sorts of crime and provided heavier penalties for the former. The purpose of 'measures of social defence' was to prevent repetition of crimes by those who had committed them, to influence other 'unstable' members of society and to adjust those who had been guilty to the conditions of life in the working-people's state. 'Measures of social defence' were not to involve the infliction of physical harm or degradation and were not to be applied for the purpose of retribution or chastisement.

Article 58 on counter-revolutionary crimes (a translation of which is included as Appendix G in Conquest's *The Great Terror*) defined as counter-revolutionary any act designed to overthrow, undermine or weaken the authority of the government of the USSR, its external security or its basic economic, political and national achievements. It made treason, including espionage, betrayal of military or state secrets, desertion to the enemy or flight abroad, punishable by death by shooting and confiscation of all property. In the event of flight abroad by a member of the armed forces, the adult members of his family, if they in any way assisted or if they knew of the act and failed to report it to the authorities, were to be punished by deprivation of liberty for five to ten years and confiscation of all property. Armed insurrection entailed death by shooting or declaration as an enemy of the labouring masses, confiscation of property, loss of citizenship and permanent banishment. In extenuating circumstances, sentence might be reduced to three years' deprivation of liberty and confiscation of all or

part of property. Similar penalties were prescribed for, for example, the maintenance of relations for counter-revolutionary purposes with representatives of foreign states or organisations under the influence of the international bourgeoisie; attempts to influence foreign states towards hostile acts against the USSR; the undermining of state industry, transport, trade, monetary exchange and credit systems and the co-operatives; terrorist acts; sabotage of means of transport and communication and state property; anti-Soviet propaganda in times of mass unrest, martial law and war or involving the religious or national prejudices of the masses; and serious cases of non-fulfilment or careless execution of duties to the state. Lesser penalties were prescribed for other forms of anti-Soviet propaganda, failure to report counter-revolutionary crime and less serious forms of counter-revolutionary sabotage.

## 22 November–16 December

The seventh meeting of the enlarged Executive Committee of the Comintern accepted Zinoviev's letter of resignation as president. Despite Stalin's objections, Zinoviev, Trotsky and Kamenev all spoke at the meeting but the committee endorsed the resolution of the party's Fifteenth Conference condemning the opposition. Bukharin became general secretary of the Executive Committee and effective head of the organisation, the office of president having been abolished.

## 24 November

Krasin died. He had arrived in

London from Paris at the end of September to take over as chargé d'affaires from Rakovskii who replaced him in Paris. Krasin's death was used as an occasion for renewed pressure on the British government, particularly from the Association of British Creditors of Russia, to break off relations with the USSR.

## 26 November

A circular from the All-Union Soviet Central Executive Committee to the republics urged them to liquidate the political influence of the kulaks by stepping up class war in the countryside.

The Central Committee resolved to give the Dneprostroi project and construction of the Turksib railway priority over the Svir–Neva project near Leningrad and the Volga–Don canal, work on which was restricted to completing the survey and port works at Azov. Dneprostroi involved the construction of a large dam, a 500-megawatt hydroelectric power station, irrigation works and the building of new factories to use the electric power. The purpose of the Turksib (or Semirech'e) railway was to link Frunze in cotton-producing Turkestan with Semipalatinsk in grain and timber-producing Siberia. The northern and southern sections of the railway were joined on 25 April 1930, over a year earlier than planned.

## 3 and 6 December

*The Manchester Guardian* published apparently well-informed articles from Berlin on secret Soviet–German military collaboration mainly concerning the Junkers débâcle (see 29 July 1922).

## 17 December

A census gave the population of the USSR as 147,027,915. Of these 26.3 million lived in towns and 120.7 million in rural areas. Great Russians numbered 77.8 million, Ukrainians 31.2 million, Byelorussians 4.7 million, the Turkic peoples in different areas 14.9 million, Georgians 1.8 million and Armenians 1.15 million. The RSFSR had 92.7 per cent of the land area and 68.7 per of the population, the Ukraine 2 per cent of the area and 19.7 per cent of the population. The overall rate of literacy in the population aged 9 or over was 51 per cent, 67 per cent among men and 37 per cent among women. According to Rigby, in *Communist Party Membership*, only 2.4 per cent of party members were illiterate at this time. Fitzpatrick (*Education and Social Mobility*, chapter 8, footnote 69) quoted Lunacharskii as saying that 60.5 per cent of Russian children of primary school age were in school in 1926 and Krupskaia as giving a figure of 50 per cent in 1928: another source gave 55 per cent for 1929.

## 27 December

On the initiative of VAPP (see 8–9 May 1924), now dominated by a group including Averbakh who had accepted the terms of the Central Committee resolution published on 1 July 1925, a Federation of Organisations of Soviet Writers (FOSP) was formed out of VAPP, the mainly 'fellow-travelling' Union of Writers, the All-Union Society of Peasant Writers and other groups. VAPP soon began to dominate the FOSP with increasing support from the Central Committee.

## 30 December

A Central Committee resolution said that the collectivisation movement was emerging from the crisis in which it had found itself during the early years of NEP. The number of collective farms was increasing and was linked to the growing use of tractors. But the resolution considered that compulsory organisation of collective farms would damage and delay development of the movement.

# 1927

## January

Kamenev lost his post as director of the Lenin Institute and, like several other opposition leaders, was given an overseas post, as representative in Rome.

## 1 January

Party membership was given as 786,288 with 426,217 candidate members.

## 10 January

The party carried out a census and reregistration of its membership. Although the statistics need to be treated with reserve, the census gave a breakdown of the composition of the party membership by social origin as 55.7 per cent workers, 19.0 per cent peasants and 25.3 per cent white-collar workers and others. By current occupation, the membership consisted of 30 per cent (or 343,000) factory and transport workers, 1.5 per cent farm labourers, 8.4 per cent (or 100,000) peasants working their own farms, 42.8 per cent (or nearly half a million) employees in offices of government, party organisations, trade unions, etc. and 18.8 per cent 'others'. A substantial proportion of recruits had thus abandoned their former occupations to become party or government workers. Largely in response to the census, the party renewed the drive to proletarianise its membership.

## 23 January

The Society for Assistance to the Defence Industry, Aviation and Chemical Defence, *Osoaviakhim*, was formed from the amalgamation of *OSO*, the Society for the Promotion of Defence, formerly the Military Scientific Society, and *Aviakhim*. *Aviakhim* arose out of the amalgamation in May 1925 of ODVF, the Society of Friends of the Red Air Fleet (founded in March 1923) and *Dobrokhim*, the Society for Chemical Defence. These two were successors to the Central Board of Universal Military Training, *Vsevobuch*, which was dissolved in 1923. In October *Osoaviakhim* claimed nearly 3 million members.

## 7–12 February

A session of the Central Committee was devoted to adjusting prices and reducing industrial costs so as to provide additional resources for developing state industry. Measures were also taken to reduce the role of private capital, especially in trade. The session marked the beginning of the end of NEP. By 1929 private retail trade had been reduced to 13 per cent of the total from 42.3 per cent in 1925–6.

## 10–15 February

The League against Imperialism was founded at a conference in Brussels. It grew out of various societies which had sprung up in protest against foreign intervention in China. Münzenberg was the moving spirit and the conference had the support of the MRP (see 12 September 1921) and probably the Comintern, but the communist hand was sufficiently well concealed for the conference to attract support from figures such as Nehru and Einstein. By the end of 1929 the League had lost the support of most of its leading non-communist members and faded out of existence.

## 15 February

An editorial in *Pravda* gave an account of two members of the opposition, Nikolaeva and Bakaev, who had confessed their errors and thrown in their lot with the majority.

## 19 February and 7 March

Chiang Kai-shek, now based in Nanchang, made two speeches in which, while professing continuing friendship with the USSR, he attacked the Chinese communists and some of the Soviet advisers including Borodin who was with the radical left wing of the Kuomintang in Wuhan (the Hankow–Hanyang–Wuchang complex). Wuhan had fallen to left Kuomintang forces in October 1926. Chiang continued to make use of Bliukher as military adviser.

On 12 November 1926 the Soviet Commissariat for Foreign Affairs had sent a telegram to the Soviet representative in Peking stating that Borodin was to take his orders direct from Moscow and that the Far Eastern Bureau [of the Comintern] was to be informed that all its policy decisions on Kuomintang and military political work were to be agreed with Borodin. The contents of this telegram were revealed by the British Prime Minister, Baldwin, in the House of Commons on 24 May 1927. Baldwin added that both Litvinov in Moscow and the Soviet chargé d'affaires in London had specifically denied any official Soviet connection with Borodin.

## 22 February

On the eve of the ninth anniversary of the Red Army, its Political Administration (PUR) published theses on the need to make serious defence preparations. Voroshilov followed up with a report to the Fourth All-Union Congress of Soviets in April stressing the need to build up an efficient regular army with adequate reserves, to create the capacity to mobilise the economy and to prepare the workers and peasants psychologically for national defence. The Executive Committee of the Comintern adopted a resolution on the Comintern's tasks in the struggle against war and the danger of war.

## 23 February

The British government protested to the Soviet government about further breaches of its undertaking to abstain from hostile propaganda.

## 28 February

The Soviet ship *Pamyat' Lenina* was

seized by a local Chinese warlord backed by Russian *émigrés* while sailing up the Yangtze river to Wuhan. The crew, together with Borodin's wife and three Soviet couriers, were imprisoned despite energetic Soviet protests to the Peking government. Early in May the ship's captain, Borodin's wife and the three couriers were moved to Peking and were committed for trial but were released on 11–12 July.

## 8 March

International Women's Day was used to launch a campaign, repeated on the same day in 1928 and 1929, in favour of the emancipation of women and the discarding of the veil in the Muslim areas of the USSR. Though it encountered stiff resistance and cost many lives, especially in Uzbekistan, the campaign probably served its long-term purpose of weakening the influence of the Islamic leadership.

## 11 March

A Soviet–Turkish treaty of commerce and navigation was signed in Ankara.

## 14 March

A decree attempted unsuccessfully to strengthen the village Soviets at the expense of the traditional commune (*mir*) run by its gathering of heads of households (*skhod*). In 1917 less than 50 per cent of the land was owned communally through the *mir*. By 1927 this figure had risen to about 95 per cent in the RSFSR largely because the redistribution of land consequent on the revolution was handled in practice through the *mir*. Male quoted a Soviet estimate of the

number of communes in the mid-1920s as 319,000, outnumbering the village Soviets by anything up to five to one.

## 21–22 March

With Kuomintang forces in the outskirts of Shanghai, the communists and the General Labour Union called a general strike and insurrection. By the evening of 22 March the resistance of the police and the Shantung soldiery from the north had been broken and the city, apart from the International Settlement and the French Concession, was in the workers' hands. The Kuomintang troops deliberately delayed their entry into the city until the fighting was over. This and other evidence available to the Comintern representatives on the spot was either suppressed or ignored and the Comintern and the international communist press hailed the events in Shanghai as a victory for the revolutionary forces under Chiang Kai-shek's leadership.

## 26 March

Chiang Kai-shek arrived in Shanghai.

## 31 March

When the danger of a counter-stroke against the insurrection in Shanghai had become apparent, the Comintern instructed the Shanghai communists not to engage in an open struggle but to hide their arms, many of which had been acquired during the events of 21–22 March.

In a letter to the Politburo and the Central Committee, Trotsky opened a campaign of criticism of their handling of events in China, arguing that the Chinese communists should be instructed to break with the Kuomintang, establish their independence and form workers' and peasants' Soviets.

## 1 April

The Council of Labour and Defence (STO) decided to build a tractor factory at Stalingrad. The production of farm machinery was seen as a means of encouraging the collectivisation of agriculture.

## 6 April

Chinese police raided Soviet buildings in Peking including the military attaché's office, seizing papers and detaining twenty-two Soviet officials and forty or more Chinese communists. Twenty of the Chinese were later executed. On 10 April the Soviet chargé d'affaires and his diplomatic staff left Peking. The Chinese chargé d'affaires and consular staff remained in the USSR. Publication of documents captured by the Chinese, which the Soviets repudiated as forgeries, was reported to have had a considerable effect in hardening Chinese attitudes against the Soviets.

## 12 April

In the early hours, Chiang Kai-shek's troops in Shanghai, assisted by underworld gangs, attacked the headquarters of workers' organisations throughout the city, disarming, capturing or killing the occupants. The General Workers Union was still able to call a general strike for 13 April but this was made the occasion for further repressive action by Chiang's forces against the now defenceless demonstrators. The General Workers Union was subsequently 'reorganised'. A round-up of communists and union leaders followed in other southern cities, notably in Canton on 15–16 April.

## 14 April

An exchange of notes between the Soviet and Swiss governments terminated the dispute between them which had arisen from the assassination of Vorovskii on 10 May 1923. The Soviet economic boycott of Switzerland was formally lifted on 4 May removing the last obstacle of Soviet attendance at international meetings in Switzerland.

On the day before the opening of the Fourth All-Union Congress of Soviets, *Pravda* announced the completion of elections to the Soviets which were still supposed to be held annually. The Soviet Central Executive Committee said that the political purpose the election campaign was intended to serve was to cement the alliance between the workers and the poor and middle peasants and to liquidate the influence of the kulaks on the peasant masses.

The congress resolution spoke of the need for voluntary collectivisation of agriculture on a large scale to increase agricultural production and thus enable industrialisation to proceed.

## 15 April

The Soviet consul-general in the Hejaz conveyed his government's congratulations to King Abdul Aziz Ibn Saud on his proclamation as King of the Nejd and associated territories.

## 21 April

In theses for propagandists on 'Questions of the Chinese Revolution', Stalin denounced Chiang Kai-shek and the right wing of the Kuomintang for selling out to imperialism and turning against the Chinese workers. Stalin repudiated the Soviet opposition's suggestion that the Chinese communist party should leave the Kuomintang and form Soviets of workers' and peasants' deputies: the party was directed to remain in the Kuomintang and work with the left wing in Wuhan which would become the 'organ of a revolutionary-democratic dictatorship of the proletariat and peasantry'. The aim should be to eliminate the Rights from the Kuomintang. While 'fighting in the same ranks as the revolutionary Kuomintangists', the Chinese communist party should 'more than ever preserve its independence to ensure proletarian hegemony in the bourgeois-democratic revolution'.

## 4 May

A strong Soviet delegation under Osinskii attended the World Economic Conference in Geneva which lasted for three weeks. A large part of the conference was devoted to discussing the removal of trade barriers. From a western point of view, the autarchically-minded Soviet delegates contributed little that was constructive and the bitterness of their attacks on non-communist labour delegates to the conference was noted. Osinskii claimed on 2 June that, from the Soviet point of view, the conference had been useful, particularly for enlarging the Soviets' circle of contacts in western business and industrial circles and informing these contacts of the true state of the Soviet economy.

## 9 May

Zinoviev publicly accused *Pravda* of boycotting opposition views and was denounced for so doing in the next few days by the Moscow and Leningrad party committees.

## 12 May

British police raided Soviet House, the premises of *Arcos* and the Soviet Trade Delegation in London, finding a number of documents referring to the Comintern and propaganda, trade union and espionage activities.

## 13 May

Consequent on the decline in the number of former Tsarist officers in the armed forces and the increasing numbers of party members among senior commanders, the War Commissar, Voroshilov, issued a circular attempting to make a further adjustment in the vexed relationship between military commanders and their political commissars and assistants (*politruks*) in favour of the commanders. The downgrading of the status of the political commissars encountered some resistance in the party. For a detailed discussion of this topic, see Erickson, *The Soviet High Command*.

## 18–30 May

The eighth enlarged Executive Committee meeting of the Comintern demanded the expulsion of Trotsky and Zinoviev from the Central Committee. In his speech Stalin maintained, 'The Wuhan Kuomintang must be supported and the communists must participate in this Kuomintang and in its revolutionary government provided that the leading role of the proletariat and its party is ensured both inside and outside the Kuomintang.' The Wuhan government, however, was already moving to the right in reaction to widespread worker and peasant disturbances.

## 19–26 May

A pan-Pacific trade union conference was held in Hankow. It established a secretariat which survived for about two years, encouraging communist trade union activity in the Far East.

## 24 May

In the House of Commons the British Prime Minister, Baldwin, described the evidence that espionage was being conducted from Soviet House. He said that this evidence had formed the basis for the warrant for the police search of the premises on 12 May. Together with the evidence obtained during the raid, it proved that both military espionage and subversive activities throughout the British Empire and North and South America were directed and carried out from Soviet House and that both *Arcos* and the Soviet Trade Delegation had been involved. Baldwin announced the decision to cancel the Anglo-Soviet trade agreement and break off diplomatic relations with the Soviet Union: some *Arcos* staff were to be allowed to remain for genuine commercial purposes. A Foreign Office note to this effect dated 26 May was delivered on the following day.

The breach, coming on top of the raids on Soviet premises in Peking and London and followed by the Voikov assassination in Warsaw on 7 June, was used by the Soviet government as evidence of an imminent imperialist war against the Soviet Union. While denying that, at least as far as the British were concerned, there was any basis for this war scare (which persisted through 1928 into 1929) and describing how it was used by the Soviets for internal and external political purposes, Carr (*Foundations of a Planned Economy*, vol. III, part I) contended that there was some genuine fear of war amongst the Soviet leadership at this time. A flare-up in the Polish–Lithuanian dispute towards the end of the year may have contributed to this fear.

## 25–26 May

Eighty-four leading members of the opposition, later supported by others, signed a declaration criticising the leadership for its domestic and Comintern failures and demanding publicity for the opposition platform.

## 1 June

The party appealed for special support for the Red Army and 'worker–peasant defence'. The week beginning 10 July was declared 'defence week'.

## 2 June

A declaration by fourteen leading oppositionists quoted by Roy Medvedev in *Let History Judge* (p. 54) stated that owing to Russia's economic backwardness, a transition to a truly socialist organisation of production in the USSR was impossible without aid from more advanced countries consequent on a socialist revolution in them.

A Soviet–Latvian commercial treaty was signed in Moscow.

## 7 June

A young *émigré* member of the Russian Orthodox church, named Boris Kowerda, assassinated Voikov, the Soviet representative in Warsaw. The assassin's self-declared motive was revenge for the Soviet regime's misdeeds, not least, according to his mother, the closure of his former church at Samara and its conversion into a dance-hall. His act was used by the regime to discredit the church. The assassination further complicated Polish–Soviet relations which were already tense.

A new charter for the Academy of Sciences was adopted giving the Council of People's Commissars power to approve the academy's work plans which at the time did not exist. Membership was increased from forty-five to seventy and in April 1928 to eighty-five, 'social organisations' being given the right to nominate members. Academicians were required to 'assist socialist construction of the USSR' and could be removed if they harmed the interests of the USSR. The academy retained an appreciable degree of freedom but increasing pressure was brought to bear on it to accept an influx of communist members (see 12 January 1929). A decree directly subordinating the academy to the Council of People's Commissars followed on 18 June.

## 8 June

A Council of People's Commissars decree strengthened the role of Gosplan and called for the creation of a 'united, all-union plan which . . . would facilitate the maximum development of economic regions on the basis of their specialisation and the maximum utilisation of their resources for the industrialisation of the country.'

The Council of People's Commissars resolved that, while it would 'note' the parts of Gosplan's control figures which related to general economic prospects, it would in future recommend to the commissariats of the USSR and the republics 'for fulfilment' the parts containing the 'numerical ceilings and main directives'.

## 9 June

Twenty individuals were summarily executed by the OGPU as an 'answer' to the Voikov assassination and as a warning to opponents of the regime. Four of them were accused of espionage on behalf of the British. Similar charges were brought against a number of other persons arrested and imprisoned or executed in the summer and autumn.

## 10–12 June

General Feng Yu-hsiang, who had built up a substantial army in north-west China with Soviet backing (according to Jacobs, the Soviets saw him in 1925–6 as a possible alternative to Chiang Kai-shek), met leaders of the left Kuomintang from Wuhan in Chengchow, Honan province. The Wuhan government had hopes of allying themselves with Feng against Chiang Kai-shek and his government in Nanking. Feng's price for co-operation, however, was a break with

Borodin and the Chinese communist party.

## 20–21 June

Generals Feng Yu-hsiang and Chiang Kai-shek met at Hsuchow, Honan province, and reached agreement based on common opposition to the northern war-lord, General Chang Tso-lin, and reconciliation between Chiang and a Wuhan government purged of Soviet advisers and communists. Feng sent a telegram to Wuhan, demanding the removal of Borodin and advising the government leaders under threat of military action either to join forces with Chiang Kai-shek or to go abroad. By the end of the month the Wuhan government was taking repressive action against trade union organisations.

## 24 June

Zinoviev and Trotsky appeared before the presidium of the Central Control Commission which considered their failure to respect the undertaking given by them on 16 October 1926 to renounce factional activities and referred the matter to the meeting beginning on 29 July.

## 14 July

The Executive Committee of the Comintern announced that the Wuhan government had become a counter-revolutionary force and that continued support for it by the Chinese communist party would be disastrous. Nevertheless, the communists were instructed to remain in the Kuomintang, demanding that its leaders be changed and at the same time fighting against the opportunism

of their own communist leaders (including the general secretary, Ch'en Tu-hsiu) who were accused of errors and violations of Comintern discipline.

## 15 July

The Kuomintang political council ordered all communist members of the Kuomintang to renounce their communist party membership or face extreme penalties.

## 18 July

Martial law was proclaimed in Hankow (Wuhan): communists, trade unionists and leaders of peasant associations were rounded up with much brutality and the government was reconstructed without communists. The communist leader, Ch'en Tu-hsiu, resigned and was formally deposed on 7 August: other leaders, including Mao Tse-tung, fled. Borodin finally left Hankow on 27 July on his way back to the USSR via Mongolia. General Bliukher left in August by the same route. Chiang Kai-shek retained his high regard for Bliukher and, by his own account, asked Stalin more than once to send him back to China as military adviser.

## 27 July

The title 'Hero of Labour' was introduced as one of various means adopted to improve labour discipline and productivity.

## 29 July

Metropolitan Sergei issued a letter to be read in all Orthodox churches aligning the church more closely with the regime than his letter of 10 June

1926 and threatening to withdraw recognition from *émigré* priests who failed to give a written undertaking of total loyalty to the Soviet government. An interview with Sergei was published in *Izvestiia* on 19 August.

## 29 July–9 August

A joint plenum of the Central Committee and the Central Control Commission considered a motion to expel Trotsky and Zinoviev from the Central Committee. The plenum at first approved their expulsion but later reached a compromise under which they once more declared their loyalty to the Central Committee and were let off with a warning.

## 27 August

A decree was issued governing the Soviet diplomatic and consular service.

## 30 August

The Council of People's Commissars ordered a cut of 20 per cent in administrative costs in the financial year 1927/8 in order to provide funds for industrialisation.

## 6 September

The opposition demanded of the Politburo and the Central Committee that a platform signed by thirteen of its leaders, 'The Real Situation in Russia', should be printed and circulated in advance of the party congress due to open on 1 December.

## 8 September

A joint meeting of the Politburo and the Central Control Commission prohibited publication and circulation of the opposition platform.

The British Trade Union Congress voted to dissolve the Anglo-Russian Committee on trade union unity.

## 12–13 September

The OGPU seized a duplicating-machine which was being used to run off copies of the opposition's platform. Preobrazhenskii and two other opposition leaders who accepted responsibility for the machine were expelled from the party and one of them was arrested.

## 26 September

A revised statute of village Soviets was issued which contained a clause on the observance of laws on the separation of church and state. This led to an intensification of anti-religious propaganda, particularly in the countryside, and an effort to identify religion with the kulaks. The Komsomol participated actively in the campaign whose targets included the sects, especially the Baptists.

## 27–28 September

Trotsky appeared before the Executive Committee of the Comintern, which decided to expel him.

## 28 September

The Moscow party expelled fourteen members who had been involved with the illicit duplication of the opposition platform.

## 1 October

A three-year Soviet–Persian non-aggression and neutrality treaty was signed in Moscow together with a trade agreement and customs and fisheries conventions. The USSR agreed to return to Persia the port of Pahlevi (formerly Enzeli), which it had occupied since 18 May 1920, in return for a Persian undertaking to keep the port in good condition and not to employ foreigners in it for twenty-five years.

## 7 October

The French government demanded the recall of Rakovskii, the Soviet envoy in Paris, on the grounds that on 8 August in Moscow he had signed a declaration by the party opposition which included an appeal to all honest proletarians in the capitalist countries to work for the defeat of their governments and a call for the desertion to the Red Army of all foreign soldiers who objected to helping the slave-masters of their own countries. In a note dated 12 October the Soviets reluctantly agreed to recall Rakovskii. Since early in 1925 intermittent, inconclusive Franco-Soviet negotiations had been in progress over Soviet demands for French credits and French demands for settlement of Russian debts to French individuals and the state. The recall of Rakovskii offered a sop to the considerable body of French opinion calling on the government to follow the British example and break off relations with the USSR in protest against Soviet subversion and espionage in France and its overseas possessions.

## 11 October

*Pravda* printed declarations by six party members from Leningrad, Moscow and Sverdlovsk who had renounced the opposition. *Pravda* also claimed that twenty-five members of the Georgian party had defected from the opposition.

## 12 October

Bukharin announced that it was possible to begin a 'forced offensive against the *kulak*' and to 'limit his exploiting tendencies' by measures such as higher taxation.

## 15 October

Partly with an eye to undercutting the opposition, a draft manifesto for the tenth anniversary of the revolution submitted to the party fraction of the Soviet Central Executive Committee announced the introduction over the next few years of the seven-hour day without reduction in earnings. This was later approved by the Central Committee and was used to ease the introduction where possible of three-shift working intended to maximise production from existing machinery.

## 21–23 October

Trotsky having privately circulated his 'letter to *Istpart*' (the bureau of party history) describing Stalin's record in early 1917 (see 12/25 March 1917), condemning his falsified version of the October/November insurrection (see 18–26 November 1924) and highlighting the rift between Lenin and Stalin in 1923–4 culminating in Lenin's 'testament', a joint session of the Central Committee and Central Control Commission decided to expel Trotsky and Zinoviev from the Central Committee and submitted the question of factional activity to the Fifteenth Congress of the party.

## 6–7 November

In an article on 'The International Character of the October Revolution', Stalin wrote that the revolution had ushered in the era of proletarian revolutions in the imperialist countries and of colonial revolutions in the oppressed countries. Having thus sown the seeds of revolution both in the centre and in the rear of imperialism, the October revolution had jeopardised the existence of world capitalism as a whole. It had also created a base and centre for the world revolutionary movement which it had never before possessed. The era of the stability of capitalism had passed. The October revolution had cast social democracy into the camp of the defenders of capitalism against the first proletarian dictatorship in the world. It was impossible to put an end to capitalism without putting an end to social democracy in the labour movement.

## 7 November

On the tenth anniversary of the revolution, the party launched the 'October enrolment', once more laying heavy stress on recruitment of workers and imposing certain restrictions on the entry of peasants.

Trotsky and Zinoviev attempted unsuccessfully to demonstrate publicly during the celebrations that the opposition enjoyed mass support in Moscow and Leningrad.

## 9–13 November

In celebration of the tenth anniversary of the revolution, about 950 delegates from forty-three countries attended a World Congress of Friends of the Soviet Union in Moscow.

The congress's resolution praised the Soviet government as the builder of socialism and the only government which represented the workers and the oppressed of all nations. It denounced the warlike preparations of the imperialist powers. The delegates were invited to form societies or committees of Friends of the Soviet Union on return to their native countries and a number of them did so.

## 15 November

*Pravda* announced a joint Central Committee and Central Control Commission decision to expel Trotsky and Zinoviev from the party for inciting counter-revolutionary demonstrations and to remove Kamenev, Rakovskii, Smil'ga and two other opposition leaders from the Central Committee and Muralov and five others from the Central Control Commission.

## 15–19 November

A number of Orthodox bishops loyal to the late Patriarch Tikhon and hostile to Metropolitan Sergei met in Moscow and issued a manifesto. Most of them ended up in exile.

## 19 November

At the funeral of Ioffe, who had committed suicide three days earlier, Trotsky made his last public appearance in the Soviet Union.

## 30 November

Litvinov led the Soviet delegation to a meeting in Geneva of the League of Nations Preparatory Commission for the Disarmament Conference and proposed the complete abolition of all land, naval and air forces. The proposal did not find favour with the commission. Litvinov followed up with slightly less extreme proposals in March and April 1928.

## 2–19 December

The party's Fifteenth Congress, the so-called Collectivisation Congress, met against the background of widespread, though by now passive, opposition and an estimated decline of 50 per cent in November and December in relation to the previous year in the grain collection effort by the state grain-collecting organisations.

The congress's resolution on the opposition endorsed the expulsion of Trotsky and Zinoviev from the party and of others from the Central Committee and Central Control Commission as well as the expulsion of Ruth Fischer, Boris Souvarine and others from the Comintern. The resolution expelled from the party a further seventy-five members of the Trotskyite opposition, including Kamenev, Piatakov, Radek, Rakovskii, Smil'ga, Lashevich and Zalutskii. It also expelled twenty-three members of Sapronov's group of Democratic Centralists and instructed the Central Committee and Central Control Commission to purge the party of all clearly incorrigible elements of the Trotskyite opposition.

Before the end of the congress, Zinoviev and Kamenev recanted but their expulsion was not revoked and they were put on probation for six months.

Stalin's report on the work of the Central Committee and the congress resolutions based on it said that the period of coexistence was giving way to a period of imperialist attacks and preparations for intervention against the USSR. The party's task was to safeguard socialist construction by strengthening the armed forces, accumulating economic reserves and delaying the outbreak of war which in the long run was inevitable.

Stalin claimed that, although in 1926/7 both industrial and agricultural production had surpassed the pre-war level, the rate of agricultural development was unsatisfactory. The primary task was the collective cultivation of land through the intensification and mechanisation of agriculture on a basis of co-operation with the peasants.

Referring to the need for Soviet economic independence, Stalin illustrated the increase in the share of total industrial production of the heavy, producer-goods industries. This emphasis on heavy industry was to be maintained throughout the rest of his lifetime.

He mentioned five internal shortcomings which needed to be overcome: unemployment, the housing crisis, anti-Semitism, a slackening of the anti-religious struggle and the frightful cultural backwardness of the people, including illiteracy.

Reporting on the party's work in the countryside, Molotov called for a campaign to strengthen the village Soviets at the expense of the *skhod* (see 14 March). He said that the campaign should be energetic but not drastic or peremptory. (There had been differences of opinion in the party on whether the *mir* was a conservative or a socialising influence but it was coming to be seen increasingly as an obstacle to collectivisation.) Molotov's slogan of the moment was 'forward to a large-scale collectivisation of agriculture'. There were also references to more systematic restrictions on the kulaks and private property owners.

A last-minute amendment to the congress's resolution on farm policy called for the amalgamation of small individual farms into large-scale collectives farms.

The congress devoted seven of its twenty-nine sessions to consideration of draft five-year plans drawn up by Gosplan and the Supreme Council of National Economy. General directives, but not detailed figures, were approved. The Central Committee was instructed to continue its policy of socialist industrialisation.

Bukharin's report on the Comintern was criticised for glossing over dangerous rightist errors in foreign communist parties.

The interval between party congresses was extended from one to two years and the Central Committee was enlarged to seventy-one members and fifty candidates.

The new Politburo consisted of Stalin, Kuibyshev, Molotov, Rudzutak, Voroshilov, Bukharin, Kalinin, Rykov and Tomskii. The candidate members were Petrovskii, Uglanov, Andreev, Kirov, Mikoyan, Kaganovich, Chubar' and Kosior.

## 11–13 December

The Comintern having switched its Chinese line from alliance with the Kuomintang to direct insurrectionary action by the Chinese communist party, a communist rising took place in Canton. Its timing may well have been deliberately chosen to coincide with the Fifteenth Congress of the Russian party. The Chinese party succeeded in establishing a commune in Canton which lasted for three days. It was then violently suppressed, the Soviet vice-consul and four other members of the consular staff being killed.

## 15 December

The Shanghai commissioner for foreign affairs of the Nanking government handed the Soviet consul in Shanghai a note withdrawing recognition from the Soviet consuls in various provinces. Chicherin replied the following day with a denial that the Soviet government had ever recognised the Nanking government: the consuls had been appointed under the treaty with the Peking government of 31 May 1924. Nevertheless, it was reported that Soviet consular staffs in Canton, Shanghai, Nanking, Chinkiang and Hankow were withdrawn. On the other hand, consular relations between the USSR and Sinkiang (see 31 October 1931) survived the breach.

## 31 December

Trotsky, Zinoviev, Kamenev, Rakovskii and others were expelled from the Soviet Central Executive Committee.

# 1928

## 1 January

Party membership was given as 914,307 with 391,547 candidate members.

## 3 January

According to a German press report, thirty prominent leaders of the opposition were informed by the OGPU of the decision to deport them from Moscow. Many were offered work of a humble nature in remote parts of the Soviet Union. Trotsky, who refused to accept a summons to the OGPU offices, was later told that he would be deported under the article of the criminal code dealing with counter-revolutionary activities.

## 15 January–6 February

Stalin visited the Urals and Siberia where the grain collection effort was particularly far short of the previous year's figure despite a good harvest. He supervised the reintroduction of coercive measures reminiscent of 'war communism' to compel the peasants to part with their grain. Other leaders including Mikoyan, Kaganovich, Zhdanov, Shvernik, Postyshev, Kosior and Andreev visited other areas.

## 17 January

Trotsky was surreptitiously removed from Moscow by train, his ultimate destination being Alma-Ata. His departure had been delayed by twenty-four hours because a crowd had gathered at the station on the previous evening in the hope of seeing him off. Other opposition figures were subsequently exiled: Rakovskii was sent, initially, to Astrakhan, Radek to Tomsk and then Tobol'sk and many others to Siberia. Zinoviev and Kamenev were sent to Kaluga but their exile does not seem to have been strictly enforced and, in July, Kamenev, who had been readmitted to the party, was reported to be living in Moscow.

## 23 January

After two years of contention, the USSR signed a fisheries convention with Japan. Traditionally, most of the fishing off the Russian Far Eastern coast and the associated canning industry had been in Japanese hands. With the advent of the first five-year plan, the Soviets were determined to build up their own share of the industry, dispensing with Japanese labour and edging the Japanese out of more and more fishing grounds. Feelings ran high even after the convention

215

was signed and incidents were frequent.

## 27 January

*Pravda* published a letter from Zinoviev and Kamenev dissociating themselves from Trotsky.

## 9–25 February

The ninth plenary session of the Executive Committee of the Comintern adopted a resolution outlining a new long-term strategy for the Chinese communist party, the details of which were worked out at the Sixth Congress of the Chinese party held in Moscow from 18 June to 11 July. The main elements of the strategy were the seizure by the party of remote areas of the Chinese countryside and the gradual extension of these areas by guerrilla warfare. At the same time the Kuomintang regime in the cities was to be undermined through political subversion. It was the strategy successfully developed by Mao Tse-tung over the next twenty years (see Richard C. Thornton's contribution in *The Comintern: Historical highlights*, edited by Drachkovitch and Lazitch).

## 17 February

*Pravda* announced the replacement of Aleksandr P. Smirnov as RSFSR Commissar for Agriculture by Kubiak. The change coincided with a reversion to methods of forcible grain collection during the first three months of 1928, whose impact fell on the middle peasants at least as much as on the kulaks. As a result collections for these months exceeded those for the corresponding period of 1927.

## 23 February

The tenth anniversary of the Red Army was marked by emphasis on the importance of the development of heavy industry as the basis of military power.

## 29 February

*Pravda* published a letter from Piatakov dissociating himself from the opposition and petitioning for readmission to the party.

## 2 March

A decree of the Council of People's Commissars instructed Gosplan to study the organisation of the new large-scale agricultural enterprises.

## 11 March

*Pravda* announced that a counter-revolutionary organisation had been carrying out sabotage in the mines of the Shakhty district of the Don basin. Fifty-five mainly technical staff had been arrested including five German engineers, two of whom were soon released. French finance and Polish counter-espionage were allegedly involved. The trial opened on 18 May and lasted for six weeks. Some of the defendants' 'confessions' were plainly forced. Five defendants were executed: many others, including one German, were imprisoned. The trial was used to demonstrate the hostility of the bourgeoisie, domestic and foreign, to socialist construction and to make 'international capitalism' the scapegoat for negligence and mismanagement in industry which had led to explosions and other serious accidents. Stalin publicly pinned the blame for the sabotage on 'international capital' working through 'bourgeois specialists'. Cohen suggested that Stalin also used it to undermine Bukharin, an advocate of civil peace, Rykov, a 'patron' of non-communist technical specialists, and Tomskii, the trade union leader. Fitzpatrick in *Cultural Revolution* considered that the trial gave a powerful impulse to what she and others have called the cultural revolution of the 1928–31 period, a wave of radical proletarianism which, even if triggered 'from above', was at least partly a revolution 'from below' on the part of young communists. Among its manifestations were campaigns against 'bourgeois' academics, artistic and literary figures, engineers and technicians and a demand for the replacement of the latter by 'Red specialists'. The campaign led to the workers' educational drive launched by the plenum of 4–12 July.

## 17 March–3 April

The Fourth Profintern Congress was attended by 421 delegates from forty-seven countries. It was marked by a thinly veiled struggle between Tomskii's 'rightists' who favoured united front tactics for the achievement of immediate goals and 'leftists' like the Stalinist Lozovskii who saw the social democrats as their most dangerous enemies. Profintern's probably exaggerated figures claimed that its affiliated unions numbered 13,862,000 members of whom 10,248,800 were Russians, 2,800,000 Chinese, 525,000 French (CGTU) and 196,000 Czechoslovaks (MOS). In addition Profintern claimed over 3 million members among trade unions with affiliations elsewhere or without formal relations on account of police repression.

## 21 March

A decree severely restricted purchases of foreign currency for travel or for remittance abroad and banned absolutely the export of Soviet bank notes or coins.

## 28 March

The Presidium of the Soviet Central Executive Committee assigned free land in the Birobidzhan district on the Amur river in the Far Eastern region for mass settlement by Jewish workers. Although Birobidzhan became an autonomous region in 1934, the attempt to set up a 'Jewish national administrative-territorial unit' was not a success.

## April

At an All-Union Congress of Proletarian Writers, the All-Russian Association of Proletarian Writers (VAPP) became the Russian Association of Proletarian Writers (RAPP) and part of an All-Union Organisation of APPs (VOAPP) embracing the Ukrainian, Siberian and other republics. The RAPP was much the most important member of the VOAPP which is often loosely referred to as the RAPP. Lunacharskii and other party and government leaders lent their support to the organisation. Brown identified Tolstoy and Plekhanov as the fundamental influences on the ideas of the RAPP leadership in its attempts to promote the application of dialectical materialism to the realistic portrayal of life and the individual human psyche, including the darker sides of both: they saw honesty on this last point as the factor distinguishing literature from propaganda. Sholokhov was a member of RAPP and *The Quiet Don* was regarded as a good example of the RAPP, method. Averbakh and others wrote much on the necessity for cultural revolution without which the political and economic revolution would fail, 'cultural' being understood in a broad sense to include, for example, literacy and personal hygiene.

## 5 April

The USSR ratified its adherence with reservations on 2 December 1927 to the Geneva Protocol of 17 June 1925 which prohibited the use of poison gas and bacteriological methods of warfare.

## 30 April

A joint Soviet Central Executive Committee and Council of People's Commissars' decree in effect subordinated the state budget to the economic plan. The Supreme Council of National Economy and Gosplan increased their influence over the next two years at the expense of the traditionally conservative, anti-inflationary Commissariat of Finance. Whereas it had originally been envisaged that further industrialisation would be financed largely out of the growing profits stemming from increased productivity of existing industry, the failure of productivity to grow at the rate expected reduced the potential value of this source. Instead the budget became the principal source of finance for industrialisation. Heavier taxation of the private sector and the better-off peasants was imposed in 1928 but this led to a decline in the proportion of revenue received from direct taxation. Indirect taxes and state loans

to individuals compensated to some extent. But recourse to deficit financing resulted in inflation, acute shortages of goods and the introduction of rationing.

## 3 May

In the course of a tour of the Middle East and Europe, King Amanullah of Afghanistan arrived in Moscow for a goodwill visit to the USSR. According to Fraser-Tytler, he acquired a quantity of munitions including thirteen aeroplanes from the Soviets. On his return to Afghanistan, his attempt to introduce sweeping westernising reforms provoked widespread rebellion which culminated in his abdication and flight on 14 January 1929 to Kandahar and later to Italy.

## 5–16 May

At the Eighth Komsomol Congress, Bukharin pointed out the important role of the Komsomol in collectivisation because the Komsomol had 49,000 rural cells as against 18,000 rural party cells; hence in many villages the Komsomol would be the party's main instrument for collectivisation and anti-religious work. By this time the Komsomol claimed 1,960,000 members. Throughout the NEP period it had inveighed against smoking, drinking, hooliganism and sexual promiscuity.

## 15 May

A Central Committee circular advocated contract buying as a means of promoting increased agricultural production and of encouraging the poor and middle peasants to join producer co-operatives. Before the revolution, sugar factories had contracted in advance with beet growers to buy their crops at a given price. The practice spread to cotton-growing in 1923 and to crops such as flax, sunflowers, soya beans, tobacco and potatoes in 1926–7. The grain collection crisis in early 1928 led to its introduction into the grain market. As a means of inducing the peasantry to increase sowings it does not appear to have been successful.

## 28 May

Gorky, whose links were with the 'fellow-travelling' rather than the 'proletarian' writers of the RAPP (see April), arrived in Moscow after seven years of voluntary exile to be welcomed by Bukharin, Lunacharskii and other leading regime figures.

## 3 June

A Central Committee appeal to party members deplored laxity in discipline and the occurrence of scandals: it demanded increased self-criticism.

## 22 June

The Central Control Commission decided to readmit to the party Zinoviev, Kamenev and nearly forty other former members of the opposition who had unequivocally recanted. In the six months following the Fifteenth Congress in December 1927, 2,270 party members had been expelled for opposition activity and 3,098 had recanted.

## 30 June

Total grain collections for the year at 10,382,000 tons were 200,000 tons less than in 1926–7. The decline in grain collections led to an intensifi-

cation of forcible measures and consequently to widespread discontent which threatened to affect the (largely peasant) army. Bread shortages led to the reintroduction of bread cards, initially in the Ural area. In the third quarter of the year, 250,000 tons of grain were imported. Even so, according to Lewin, reserves stood at a dangerously low level. In *The Harvest of Sorrow* (pp. 88–9), Conquest, quoting Karcz, claimed that the grain figures on which the regime relied were inaccurate and that the grain shortage at the beginning of 1928 was less acute than Stalin believed and quite insufficient to justify the emergency measures which he introduced and which destroyed the peasants' confidence in the market and hence their incentive to produce. Karcz's estimates of grain marketings are not however universally accepted and it is doubtful if there is sufficient evidence for a definite conclusion to be reached.

## 4–12 July

A Central Committee plenum partially exposed the division which had been developing since April between the Stalinists and the Bukharinist 'Right' over the pace and methods of collectivisation and industrialisation. While Stalin was talking of intensified class struggle which inevitably grew sharper during the advance towards socialism and advocating an attack on 'capitalist elements' in the countryside to compel them to accept low agricultural and high industrial prices to finance industrialisation, Bukharin's supporters spoke of a gradual approach to collectivisation and industrialisation which would not disrupt the worker–peasant alliance or the market relations established by NEP. While the resolutions of the meeting reflected the 'rightist' position in that they announced an increase in grain prices and the termination of the extraordinary grain collection measures (which, according to Rykov, bore more heavily on the middle and poor peasants than on the kulaks), Stalin had begun to use his hold over the party organisation to undermine Bukharin. His line appears to have been more in harmony than Bukharin's with the party's latent impatience with NEP and the survival of the kulak.

In a speech on the draft programme of the Comintern on 5 July, Stalin quoted Lenin in support of the view that the USSR existed to do everything possible for the development and triumph of the proletarian revolution in other countries. In return the international proletariat was obliged to support the USSR against its internal and external foes, to engage in the war against a war to strangle the proletarian dictatorship in the USSR and to campaign for the crossing-over of the imperialist armies to the side of the USSR in the event of an attack on it.

The plenum ordered a special mobilisation of 1,000 communists to study engineering, the beginning of a major drive to give workers higher technical education. In Fitzpatrick's view this was intended not only to meet the immediate needs of the first five-year plan but also to provide the party with a new generation of technically qualified party leaders. The group was to benefit from rapid promotion as a result of the purges of the late 1930s. Fitzpatrick estimated the number of students involved in this drive, the majority of them

adults, at over 150,000. According to Bailes, only 138 Soviet engineers in industry in early 1928 were communist party members. The quality of the technical education provided dropped dramatically in the course of the first five-year plan. The selection by social origin of candidates for higher education, introduced in 1928, was not abandoned until 29 December 1935.

## 11 July

Bukharin had a confidential meeting with Kamenev who had been readmitted to the party together with Zinoviev. Bukharin described the struggle going on behind the scenes over Stalin's extremist policies which he said would lead to a catastrophic blood-bath: he spoke of the support he had received from Rykov, Tomskii, Uglanov and Iagoda. Bukharin's attempt to enlist Kamenev's support was unsuccessful: Kamenev apparently already regarded Bukharin as a doomed man.

## 17 July–1 September

The Sixth Comintern Congress was attended by 532 or 575 delegates representing fifty-eight parties. Most of the Latin American countries were represented, many of them for the first time. There was a swing away from united front tactics in favour of independent action by communist parties which were encouraged to denounce social democrats as 'social fascists' and as the primary obstacle in the way of the 'dictatorship of the proletariat'. This swing followed naturally from the growing influence of the Stalinist view that the advanced capitalist countries were on the brink of major upheavals which the communist parties should be poised to exploit. In contrast, Bukharin's school of thought argued that western capitalism had reached a new stability on the basis of advanced technology: while revolutions were still inevitable, they were more likely to result from external contradictions leading to war than from internal crises. The congress endorsed the resolutions of the party's Fifteenth Congress and of the Comintern's Executive Committee expelling the 'Left' opposition from the party and the Comintern. A new programme, drafted by Bukharin, was adopted but was seldom invoked. Behind the scenes at the congress, Stalinists took the opportunity to undermine Bukharin's position by hinting to foreign delegates that he no longer enjoyed the full confidence of the party. While the congress was in session, there were shake-ups in the staff of *Pravda* and the party's theoretical journal *Bol'shevik* where Stalin's influence was increased at Bukharin's expense. A similar process occurred in Bukharin's stronghold, the Institute of Red Professors. According to Jules Humbert-Droz, a close collaborator of Bukharin in the Comintern, Bukharin, while officially retaining his position, never returned to the Comintern offices after the congress.

## 31 July

A decree established a State Arctic Committee to draft a programme of work to be carried out in the Arctic during the first five-year plan. Systematic Soviet exploration of the Arctic had begun in 1919 – even before the allied evacuation of north Russia – with a view to opening up the area economically. A special

Committee of the North Sea Route (*Komseveroput'*) was set up in 1920.

## 19 August–17 September

General von Blomberg, head of the German *Truppenamt* (the nearest approach to a general staff allowed under the Versailles Treaty), spent a month in the USSR visiting the air-training and test-flying base at Lipetsk, the Kama tank training school near Kazan, the 'Tomka' gas warfare training school and an artillery establishment near Voronezh where German units experimented with the combined use of aircraft and ground artillery and in the use of gas shells. In conversation with Blomberg, Voroshilov laid particular stress on the importance of chemical warfare. Blomberg met all the main Soviet military leaders and attended manoeuvres near Kiev. His report strongly recommended that Soviet–German military collaboration should continue. Annual visits to the USSR by the head of the *Truppenamt* were in fact made up to and including 1932.

## 27 August

In Kazakhstan it was decided that 700 families owning the largest herds or occupying positions of privilege should be expropriated and their herds distributed to poor peasants and land-workers in existing or newly established collectives. The expropriations were carried out between September and November by commissions under the chairmanship of the local Soviet Executive Committee and containing representatives of the Council of People's Commissars, the OGPU, the Commissariat for Agriculture and the peasants' and agricultural workers' unions with the local procurator in attendance. The expropriations served as a model for the much more extensive expropriations elsewhere in 1930. The effects of forced settlement and collectivisation in 1930 were particularly severe in Kazakhstan, costing, according to Conquest's estimate, roughly a million lives.

## 29 August

The USSR adhered to the Kellogg Pact which had been signed in Paris on 27 August by fifteen states which bound themselves to renounce war as an instrument of national policy.

## 5 September

*Pravda* admitted that grain collections in the two previous months were below expectations.

## 18 September

*Pravda* referred specifically to the existence of right-wing attitudes in the Comintern and the Soviet party itself.

## 30 September

*Pravda* published Bukharin's *Notes of an Economist*, regarded as a manifesto of the right wing of the party. The notes argued for the development of agriculture and restraint in the pace of industrialisation. There was increasing polarisation in the leadership between Bukharinists who believed that conciliation of the peasantry was the only way of guaranteeing grain supplies, and Stalinists who believed that grain for the expanding and industrialising cities could be procured at reasonable prices in the long run only by fighting kulak influence and by collectivising production. Bukharin's views on the pace of industrialisation were a reaction against speeches by Kuibyshev and Stalin and the increasingly ambitious figures for the rate of industrialisation included in successive drafts of the five-year plan produced by Gosplan and the Supreme Council of National Economy.

## 19 October

In a speech to the Moscow party committee, Stalin emphasised the rightist danger from those who denied the need for an offensive against capitalist elements in the countryside or who demanded a contraction of industry: he called for an urgent and relentless struggle against 'rightist opportunism' in the party. In the two or three preceding weeks, the position of Uglanov, who controlled the Moscow party organisation and had consistently thrown its weight behind Bukharin, had been undermined through his subordinates.

## 20 October

An editorial in *Pravda* stated explicitly that the struggle against the 'right danger' was the most important task for the coming period. Publicity was given to acts of violence by kulaks.

## 21 October

Over a hundred Trotskyite oppositionists were arrested in Leningrad, Kharkov and Moscow.

## 1 November

A ten-year treaty of friendship and commerce between the USSR and the Yemen was signed at Sana'a. The USSR recognised the independence and sovereignty of the government of the Yemen and its king. The parties to the treaty regarded official relations as established between them. (Date as in GSE and Slusser and Triska. Shapiro and the RIIA's *Documents on International Affairs* (1929, p. 274) give 12 November. Connolly gave a translation of an abbreviated Arabic text of the treaty dated 17 Jumad al Awal which she placed in July 1928). On 28 January 1939 the treaty was extended to 25 June 1949 although the Soviet legation in the Yemen is said to have been closed in 1938.

## 7 November

Slogans such as 'down with the kulak' and 'down with the NEPmen' (private traders, artisans and small-scale entrepreneurs who had prospered under NEP and who were now being eliminated by punitive taxation, sanctions and, in many cases, prosecution) were adopted as official slogans for the anniversary of the revolution. A year earlier, the left opposition had been condemned for using the same slogans. A Central Committee resolution deplored the small membership of collective farms and complained at the presence of rightist and near-kulak influences in rural party organisations in which proletarian elements were extremely weak. There was a marked decline in grain collections in November and December and it became clear that there had been a crop failure in the central and south-east regions. Free market prices for grain increasingly outstripped prices paid by the official grain-collecting agencies.

## 9–15 November

Following stormy arguments between Stalin and Bukharin in the Politburo, Bukharin, Tomskii and Rykov submitted their resignations. Rykov seems to have withdrawn his promptly since only the other two were criticised in the resolution of 9 February 1929 for refusing to comply with repeated Politburo demands for the withdrawal of their resignations.

## 19 November

At a Central Committee meeting Stalin spoke of the need for the USSR to catch up with and surpass the advanced capitalist countries by which it was encircled; otherwise it would be 'forced to the wall'. The Central Committee approved a figure for capital investment in industry for 1928/9, which was slightly reduced at Bukharin's insistence but none the less 25 per cent higher than the figure for 1927/8. The decision tacitly accepted that the shortage of goods would continue. Agricultural growth was to be secured by the additional tools and machinery which industrialisation would provide. The decision represented a victory for the viewpoint of the Supreme Council of National Economy headed by the Stalinist, Kuibyshev, over that of Gosplan where Bukharin's influence was still strong. A resolution, drafted by Bukharin in an attempt to rid himself of the 'rightist' label which had been pinned on him, affirmed that 'right deviationism' was the main danger to the party. Another resolution ordered a purge of the party membership.

## 27 November

The secretary of the Moscow party

organisation, Uglanov, and his deputy were replaced by Molotov and Bauman. Many other Bukharinists were purged at the same time.

## 10–24 December

At the Eighth Congress of Soviet Trade Unions Kuibyshev, the chairman of the Supreme Council of National Economy, declared that there was no alternative to the rapid development of heavy industry. The congress approved his line. This represented a defeat for Tomskii and led to his withdrawal as the active head of the All-Union Central Council of Trade Unions although he was not officially removed from this post until 1 June 1929. He reaffirmed his resignation from the Politburo.

## 16 December

An OGPU representative called on Trotsky in Alma-Ata and formally demanded an undertaking from him that he would abstain from political activity. Trotsky refused to comply.

## 19 December

At a meeting of the Executive Committee of the Comintern, Stalin denounced the craven opportunism of Humbert-Droz and another Bukharin supporter, the Italian Angelo Tasca (Serra). This opened the way to a purge of Bukharin supporters in other parties, notably the German, which continued through 1929. While retaining his posts in the Comintern and *Pravda* until April 1929, Bukharin ceased to be active in either body though he launched occasional attacks in *Pravda* on Stalinist policies without mentioning Stalin by name.

## 28 December

The Central Committee resolved that greater use should be made of mass literature as an instrument for mobilising the masses for fundamental political and economic tasks and for educating them in the achievements of science and technology, in the propagation of Leninism and in the rejection of bourgeois influences. Publishing houses were obliged to increase the percentage of mass books in their publishing plans, drawing into the work qualified communists and other specialists through the writers' organisations. Special emphasis was to be placed on easily read Marxist-Leninist histories of the revolutionary movement, on literature on production and popular science and on *belles-lettres* directed against bourgeois influences.

# 1929

## 1 January

Party membership was given as 1,090,508 with 444,854 candidate members. Village Soviets covering an average of eight 'inhabited points' were said to number 72,163 but many of them did not meet regularly.

## 2 January

A decree obliged all production undertakings to convert to the seven-hour day by 1 October 1933.

## 12 January

Elections were held to fill forty-two vacancies at the Academy of Sciences. Bukharin, Krzhizhanovskii and three other communists were elected. Another three communists sponsored by the party were rejected. But faced with the alternative of dissolution and probable loss of employment by its members, the academy agreed that the names of these three should be resubmitted and on 13 February they were elected by large majorities. Prominent among the academicians resisting communist encroachment in the academy was the world-famous physiologist, Pavlov. A purge of the academy's employees began in July. In April 1934 the academy moved from Leningrad to Moscow and in 1936 it absorbed the Communist Academy, founded in 1918 to study the history, theory and practice of socialism (see also 13 July).

## 16 January

An attempt to promote voluntary collectivisation of agriculture was launched with an article in the Central Committee journal entitled 'Organise a *kolkhoz* or leave the party'.

## 18 January

Acting on a Politburo decision taken against opposition from Bukharin, Rykov and Tomskii, a special OGPU conference resolved to banish Trotsky from Soviet territory. He left Alma-Ata on 22 January for Odessa where he embarked for Constantinople on 10 February.

## 20 January

As the opening shot in a major campaign, *Pravda* published an article on 'socialist emulation' as the correct way of appealing to the workers for increased production in the building of socialism.

*Pravda* also published an article by Lenin's widow, Krupskaia, restating Lenin's view that coercion should play no part in economic relations with the middle peasantry.

## 21 January

Bukharin delivered a speech on the fifth anniversary of Lenin's death giving an account of Lenin's last directives. As summarised by Cohen, these were as follows:

> The revolution's future depends on a firm collaborative alliance with the peasantry; party policy must centre now on 'peaceful, organisational, "cultural" work', on conciliating peasant interests, not on a 'third revolution'; capital accumulation and industrialisation must proceed on the 'healthy base' of expanding market relations, with prospering peasant farmers joining into market-oriented co-operatives (which were not collective farms), and on a rational utilisation of resources combined with a relentless cutback in unproductive and bureaucratic expenditure. The watchwords of Lenin's 'testament' were caution, conciliation, civil peace, education and efficiency. Its central directive was preventing a 'split' with the peasantry, for this would mean 'the destruction of the Soviet Republic'.

The title of Bukharin's speech, 'Lenin's Political Testament', would have reminded those in the know of Lenin's view of Stalin's unsuitability for the post of General Secretary.

## 25 January

A Soviet–German convention was signed providing for annual meetings of a conciliation commission to deal with disputes of all kinds between the two countries, particularly differences of opinion of the interpretation of treaties between them.

## 30 January

An underground Trotskyite pamphlet gave an account of Bukharin's secret meeting with Kamenev on 11 July 1928. In consequence Stalin convened a joint session of the Politburo and the Presidium of the Central Control Commission at which he attacked Bukharin for his factionalism. Bukharin responded with vigorous criticism of Stalin's agricultural and industrial policies and, without naming Stalin, protested against the demand for unconditional submission to the decisions of an individual leader rather than a collective organ. He justified his meeting with Kamenev on the grounds that the situation in the party was abnormal.

## 7 February

Bukharin rejected a proposal that, in return for a withdrawal of the censure motion against him, he should admit his errors, retract his statement of 30 January and return to his posts.

## 9 February

Rykov read to a joint meeting of the Politburo and the Presidium of the Central Control Commission a statement drafted by Bukharin and signed by himself and Tomskii affirming Bukharin's declaration of 30 January. The session passed a resolution condemning Bukharin's meeting with Kamenev as a factional move directed at changing the economic policies of the Central Committee and the composition of the Politburo. It described Rykov's and Tomskii's concealment of their knowledge of the meeting as impermissible. It criticised Bukharin for his refusal to work at *Pravda* or in the Comintern, for his publication of 'Notes of an Economist' without the Central Committee's permission, and for his resignation prior to the November plenum and his repeated refusal to withdraw it. It declared his complaints against the Central Committee groundless and advised him to renounce his rightist views on domestic and Comintern matters. It refused to accept his and Tomskii's resignations and enjoined them both to carry out loyally all Central Committee and Comintern decisions. No publicity was given to the dispute at the time.

A pact accepting as valid between themselves the obligations of the Kellogg Pact on the renunciation of war (see 29 August 1928) was signed in Moscow by the USSR, Poland, Latvia, Estonia and Romania. The inclusion of Romania was noteworthy in that diplomatic relations had not been established with the USSR which had an outstanding claim against Romania over Bessarabia. Lithuania, Turkey, Persia and the free city of Danzig adhered to the pact later.

## 21 February

The Moscow Soviet issued a decree on bread rationing. A similar decree had already been issued in Leningrad in November 1928. Odessa, Kiev and Kharkov had reintroduced bread cards in 1928. Preferential treatment was given to workers in certain industries. Individuals disqualified from voting received no ration books. The system came into effect in Moscow on 17 March. Rationing was later extended to sugar, tea, meat, soap, dairy products, potatoes and textiles. Rationing applied only to the socialised sector. Supplies were also available at greatly inflated prices in the 'unorganised' private sector. Communal feeding in canteens helped to alleviate hardship.

A Central Committee appeal was issued to all party organisations to strengthen labour discipline.

## 23 February–6 March

The Moscow provincial party conference attacked right deviationists without publicly naming Bukharin, Rykov and Tomskii.

## March

The *Basmachi* leader, Ibrahim Bek, crossed the Soviet frontier from Afghanistan with 600 supporters.

## 9 March

*Pravda* blamed kulak elements and bad organisational work in the countryside for the failure of the 1928/9 grain collection effort. At about this time the 'Ural-Siberian method' of grain collection, a combination of coercive measures aimed at raising village quotas (see 15 January –6 February 1928), was applied nationwide. Instances of kulaks being sent into exile began to occur on a small scale.

## 9–10 March

An anti-fascist congress was held in Berlin in which Barbusse and Münzenberg appear to have been the moving spirits. Soviet support was muted and this was the last important example for the next four years or so of communist co-operation with the radical Left (see 3–19 July).

## 23 March

A decree of the Council of People's Commissars of the RSFSR said that forced labour should be one of the fundamental 'measures of social defence' and called for efforts to make forced-labour institutions economically productive. The foundation was thus laid for the later development of labour camps under OGPU direction. Dallin and Nicolaevsky gave an estimate of 30,000 prisoners in concentration camps in 1928.

## 25 March

British exports to the USSR having suffered as a result of the breach in relations, a British trade delegation of eighty-eight businessmen representing 230 firms left London for the USSR. In his speech of welcome on 5 April, Piatakov, the president of Gosbank, said that large-scale British participation in Russian economic development would be possible only if diplomatic relations were restored.

## April

King Amanullah of Afghanistan having abdicated on 14 January and fled to Kandahar, an invasion force of between 800 and 1,200 Red Army soldiers dressed as Afghans and nominally led by Ghulam Nabi, Amanullah's ambassador to Moscow, crossed into Afghanistan in support of Amanullah. According to Agabekov, the expedition was withdrawn after heavy fighting partly because the Soviets heard that Amanullah had fled from Kandahar to India and partly because of adverse international reaction to the Soviet incursion.

## 8 April

A decree prohibited virtually all forms of financial, social, educational or recreational activity by the churches, restricting them in practice to the holding of religious services. This bore particularly hard on sects such as Baptists and Evangelical Christians who in the early 1920s had grown rapidly and enjoyed a degree of official favour partly because of their successful communal farms. Severe harassment of the sects continued until the Second World War.

## 15 April

The Politburo, having rejected Rykov's and Bukharin's suggestions on maintaining a balance between industry and agriculture more favourable to the latter, voted to endorse the most ambitious variant of Gosplan's five-year plan, the variant backed by the Supreme Council of National Economy, and submitted the plan to the Central Committee for approval and transmission to the Sixteenth Conference. Bukharin, Rykov and Tomskii abstained from voting on this decision.

## 16–23 April

The Central Committee met jointly with the Central Control Commission and accepted the five-year plan.

Stalin sought the meeting's approval of the Politburo-Control Commission resolution censuring Bukharin. He dragged up Bukharin's disagreements with Lenin, castigated his theoretical mistakes and accused him of having conspired with Left SRs who were planning to imprison Lenin and carry out a coup at the time of the Brest-Litovsk Treaty. Bukharin, whose supporters at the meeting numbered about a dozen out of over 300, counter-attacked with criticisms of Stalin's rudeness and argued that it was Stalin who had deviated from the party line by adopting 'extraordinary measures' against the peasantry which were incompatible with NEP: this Bukharin described as nothing less than a capitulation to Trotskyism. The Central Committee decided, without publicising the fact at the time, to endorse the resolution of 9 February. It accused Bukharin of seeking to reduce the pace of industrialisation, develop the kulak economy, undermine the grain collection effort and deny the sharpening of the class struggle in the country. The meeting resolved

1. to condemn the views of the Bukharin group as incompatible with the general line of the party and to bind them to carry out party decisions;
2. to condemn the meeting with Kamenev;
3. to condemn Bukharin's and Tomskii's policy of resignation as a violation of party discipline;
4. to remove Bukharin and Tomskii from their posts in *Pravda*, the Comintern and the All-Union Central Council of Trade Unions (AUCCTU);
5. to warn them that violations of resolutions would lead to their removal from the Politburo.

The fourth of these resolutions was not implemented until after the Sixteenth Conference. On 1 June the executive committee of the AUCCTU was reorganised: the post of president was abolished and replaced by a presidium of five to which Shvernik was elected, becoming its most prominent member. Molotov succeeded Bukharin in the Comintern. Rykov remained president of the Council of People's Commissars until December. All three retained their membership of the Politburo for the time being.

Cohen argued that Stalin's victory over Bukharin was not attributable solely to Stalin's control over the party machine: the militancy of Stalin's approach to industrialisation and socialised agriculture (long-term objectives which Bukharin shared) and the doctrine that the party could achieve anything given the will to do it proved more attractive to the ambitious higher-level party leaders than the cautious Bukharinist approach which was vulnerable to accusations of pessimism and of favouring the better-off sections of society. Other party leaders who were not necessarily wholly committed to Stalin and the younger party activists saw less clearly than Bukharin how Stalinist policies would lead to virtual civil war, a police state, a despotic bureaucracy, economic chaos, the destruction of international working-class solidarity and the weakening of the security of the Soviet Union in the face of its enemies consequent on the disaffection of the peasantry. Like Trotsky before him, Bukharin had been inhibited by loyalty to the party and fear of the counter-revolution from fighting his corner publicly.

## 23–29 April

Discussion of the five-year plan took up five of the twelve sessions of the party's Sixteenth Conference which gave the most ambitious version of the plan its approval.

A conference resolution called for a broad network of state and co-operative Machine Tractor Stations (MTS) as a means of promoting collectivisation and increasing agricultural productivity. The first MTS had been developed in 1928 in the Shevchenko state farm (*sovkhoz*) in the Ukraine. At this time only 2.8 per cent of the motive power in Soviet agriculture was mechanical. The conference approved a plan to collectivise 17.5 per cent of farm land during the five-year period. Many speakers advocated comprehensive collectivisation of whole villages.

The conference unanimously approved a purge (or verification) of the party membership, which had been set in motion by the Central Committee on 19 November 1928 and which lasted until May 1930. It resulted in the expulsion of about 170,000 party members or 11 per cent of the total. Of these, about 37,000 were reinstated on appeal. Evidence quoted by Getty suggested that the large majority were expelled for drunkenness, sexual misconduct, criminality, careerism, passiveness and violations of party discipline. Connections with opposition groups inside the party seem to have been a relatively minor factor. The stated purpose of the purge was to strengthen the proletarian core of the party to give it the homogeneity, unity and Leninist tenacity in needed to fulfil the tasks that lay ahead.

According to Carr in *Foundations* of a Planned Economy the party purge was accompanied by a purge of government officials, 51,000 of whom were dismissed before the Sixteenth Congress of the party in June 1930, neutralising the influence of Rykov and other 'rightists'. The majority of trade union officials were also changed. Carr observed that the purge, while perhaps increasing efficiency, had the effect of removing those with sufficient initiative and courage to challenge the party line and led to a rigid and uncritical obedience to orders from above.

During the conference thirty-eight Trotskyites renounced their support of the opposition platform, condemned Trotsky's statements in the foreign press and sought readmission to the party. A further thirty-odd names of seceders from the opposition were published on 17 May.

## 29 April

Uglanov, who had consistently supported Bukharin, was replaced as a candidate member of the Politburo by Bauman. Uglanov was also removed from the Secretariat.

## 14–18 May

A resolution of the Fourteenth RSFSR Congress of Soviets pressed for the completion of the system of village Soviet budgets by the financial year 1932/3 in order to achieve subordination of the traditional village commune or *mir* to the local Soviet. Lack of finance had been one of the main weaknesses of the village Soviets.

## 17 May

Estonia signed a treaty of commerce with the Soviet Union.

## 20 May

A plan was due to be completed for the use on the land of up to 20,000 junior commanders and men to be released specially from the Red Army to help with the collectivisation programme.

## 20–28 May

The Fifth All-Union Congress of Soviets approved the 1,700-page five-year plan of National Economic Construction for the Years October 1928/9 to October 1932/3 and appealed to all concerned to carry it out. Under the plan national income was to increase by 103 per cent, total investment by 228 per cent, industrial production by 180 per cent and agricultural production by 55 per cent. An annual rate of production of 10 million tons of pig-iron and 75 million tons of coal was to be reached by the end of the plan. Labour productivity was to go up by 110 per cent and nominal wages by 47 per cent. Production costs were to fall by 35 per cent and retail prices of industrial goods by 23 per cent.

Also during May the Congresses of Soviets of the RSFSR and the Ukraine approved the plans for their respective republics.

Rassweiler quoted an estimate of about 1,500 for the number of new industrial projects started under the first five-year plan.

To illustrate the scale of overall Soviet industrial expansion, Hough and Fainsod quoted official Soviet statistics from *Narodnoe khoziaistvo SSSR 1922–72*, Moscow, Statistika, 1972. These showed that between 1928 and 1940 – roughly the period of the first three five-year plans – Soviet oil production increased from 11.6 million tons to 31.3 million tons, coal from 35.5 million tons to 165.9 million tons, steel from 4.3 million tons to 18.3 million tons, electricity from 5,000 million kWh to 48,300 million kWh and cotton cloth from 2,700 million square metres to 4,000 million square metres. Light industry expanded much more slowly.

According to Gregory and Stuart's figures, the share of agriculture in the net national product measured in 1937 prices fell from 49 per cent in 1928 to 29 per cent in 1940 while in the same period the share of industry rose from 28 per cent to 45 per cent and that of services from 23 per cent to 26 per cent. In the manufacturing sector the net product share of heavy manufacturing in 1928 prices rose from 31 per cent in 1928 to 63 per cent in 1937, while the share of light manufacturing fell from 68 per cent to 36 per cent. Gross industrial capital stock in 1937 prices rose from 34,800 million rubles in 1928 to 119,000 million in 1937 and 170,000 million in 1940. Annual growth rates over the period 1928 to 1937 were: for Gross National Product in 1937 prices 4.8 per cent, for the non-agricultural labour force 8.7 per cent, for the agricultural labour force a negative rate of 2.5 per cent, for industrial production in 1937 prices a positive rate of 11.3 per cent, for agricultural production 1.1 per cent, for household consumption 0.8 per cent, for government administration and defence 15.6 per cent and for gross capital investment 14.4 per cent. In 1937 the prices of consumer goods in state and co-operative stores were seven times and the average realised prices of farm products were 5.39 times the 1928 levels.

The official Soviet index of industrial production showed an increase of 852 per cent in 1940 over the 1928 level. As against this, Nutter quoted eight different western indices of Soviet industrial production calculated on widely differing bases. The equivalent figures they gave for 1940 (1928 = 100) were: Colin Clark (based on a rather small sample of industries) 339; Jasny 330; Hodgman (based on large-scale industry) 430; Shimkin-Leedy (including military production) 294; Seton (based on fuel, steel and electricity) 462; Kaplan-Moorsteen 263, Nutter and the National Bureau of Economic Research, civilian production 267, total production 312.

While expressing reservations about the basis of both Tsarist and Soviet indices, Nutter concluded that the annual average industrial growth rate over the period 1870 to 1913 was higher than that for the period 1913 to 1955 but lower than that for 1928 to 1955 (the period of the five-year plans). The growth rate for 1928 to 1955 was roughly equivalent to the rate of the period 1880 to 1900.

Nutter estimated that industrial output in 1920 was less than one-fifth of its 1916 level which was about 12 per cent higher than the 1913 level. There seems to be general agreement between western and Soviet sources that the 1913 level of output was regained between 1925 and 1927 though Nutter pointed out that there had been a deterioration in the quality especially of consumer goods since the pre-war period. Gregory and Stuart referred to evidence that Soviet national income and industrial capacity in 1928 were both still below the pre-war level owing to the low rate of investment under NEP.

Nutter claimed that the growth rate declined between 1928 and 1940 for every industrial group except agricultural machinery. This group did relatively well during the first five-year plan but less well in the second. The growth rate for this group was lower in the period 1928 to 1955 than it was in the period 1913 to 1928.

Nutter described the output targets set for the first and second five-year plans as rather poor forecasts. The total value added achieved by all listed products was no more than 77 per cent of the planned value. Jasny asserted that many of the target figures in the first five-year plan were determined by political pressure rather than economic argument and were completely unrealistic. He described the plan in the form eventually adopted as a perversion of real economic planning: its primary real purpose was propagandistic.

Jasny argued that, while a major industrial revolution was achieved in a relatively short time, the five-year plans served to mask very uneven growth rates in the Soviet economy as a whole, two periods in particular – the period of collectivisation and the early stages of industrialisation from 1930 to 1932 and the period of the purges and their aftermath from 1937 to 1940 – being periods of stagnation and, to some extent, decline in growth. Nutter's findings broadly supported Jasny; he added that war preparations may have been a factor, though an unquantifiable one, in the stagnation of the period 1937 to 1940 in which the output of chemicals, construction materials, machinery, equipment and consumer durables actually declined. Such increase as there was in aggregate industrial production in 1937 to 1940 was largely if not wholly attributable to the Soviet acquisition of the Baltic states and parts of Poland and Romania in 1939. On the other hand, according to R. W. Davies in *Soviet Investment for Planned Industrialisation*, investment increased at an unprecedented rate between 1929 and 1931 when some of the giant five-year plan projects were under construction.

Zaleski pointed out that the plan provided only for cautious measures in the agricultural field. The fact that Stalin was to go for wholesale socialisation of agriculture in 1929–30 was one of the indications that, although the plan was given the force of law, it was overridden at will by the authorities and was not really taken seriously by them. He deduced from this and from his detailed studies of the inconsistencies in the plans themselves (some of which are mentioned below) that, by creating the myth that *ad hoc* government measures had a rational, scientific and scholarly basis, the plans served their real purpose which was to induce the population to collaborate in a drive that entailed severe austerity for them. According to Jasny's calculations, the industrialisation drive led to a cut in the level of real wages. These did not regain their 1928 level until 1958. Peasants' per capita real incomes were even slower to recover.

## 27 May

The Chinese searched the Soviet consulates at Harbin and three other places on the Chinese Eastern railway to obtain evidence relating to violations by the Soviets of their undertakings in the treaties of 31 May and 20 September 1924 to abstain from hostile propaganda and acts of violence. The Chinese arrested about fifty Soviet citizens (see also 10 July).

## June

Bukharin was appointed director of the scientific and technological department of the Supreme Council of National Economy.

## 3 June

A Central Committee resolution summed up the results of the elections to the Soviets which, having been postponed from January 1928, had been going on since January 1929. The resolution admitted that party work had been weak among the poor peasants and agricultural labourers and that some Soviet organisations had been in league with the 'kulak top stratum'. Carr described the election campaign as a final attempt by the regime to undermine the resistance of the peasantry from within; its failure led to the naked coercion of 'revolution from above' beginning at the end of the year.

## 5 June

A decree launched Machine Tractor Stations on a large scale, some 2,500 being established between 1929 and 1932.

## 10 June

As part of an anti-religious campaign which had been in progress since 1928 and which continued into 1930, especially in the countryside, and was extended for the first time systematically to Islam as well as Christianity, the League of the Godless (now the Militant Godless) held its Second (and last) All-Union Congress on the Countering of Religion. The congress was addressed by Lunacharskii, Bukharin and Kalinin. The league's journal claimed that 1,440 churches were closed in 1929. Synagogues were closed in parallel as were many of the Buddhist monasteries in the Buriat-Mongolian and Kalmuk Autonomous SSRs and the Tuvinian People's Republic.

## 11 June

A convention on commerce and navigation was concluded between the USSR and Greece.

## 26 June

The Central Committee ordered an enlargement and improvement in graduate studies. (See DeWitt's *Education and Professional Employment in the USSR* for details of the expansion of higher education in the early 1930s to meet the needs of the five-year plans.)

## 28 June

A decree allowed village Soviets to assign grain delivery quotas to separate households as they wished and to punish failures to meet the quotas.

## 30 June

According to official statistics, state grain collections for 1928/9 reached only 8.3 million tons, 2 million tons below the previous year's total. Private trade in grain had increased its share of the grain market from 12 per cent in the previous year to 23 per cent. Much of the privately traded grain did not reach the large cities. There was general peasant hostility towards the party and the cities. The

rise in free market food prices threatened the wage structure of industry. *Pravda* of 13 June quoted Mikoyan as having admitted to the unsatisfactory results of the grain collection. The recurrence of these crises was an important factor in the decision taken, probably in October, in favour of forcible collectivisation. In June, collectivisation was still considered in the party as a voluntary process which would be spread over a number of years and would be accompanied by mechanisation. The majority of collective farms in existence at this time were small (a few families cultivating thirty or forty hectares) and not truly socialised.

## 3–19 July

At the tenth plenary meeting of the Comintern's Executive Committee, Molotov, who presided, identified Bukharin as a 'right deviationist'. The committee approved the party Central Committee's decision to remove Bukharin from the Presidium of the executive committee and debar him from further participation in Comintern affairs.

The swing away from united front tactics, begun at the Sixth Congress in July–September 1928, was carried much further. The stabilisation of capitalism was declared to be at an end and revolutionary situations in the West imminent. Communist parties were instructed to purge their moderates, cut their ties with social democratic parties, denounce social democrats as 'social fascists' and form rival trade unions. The consequences of this line were to be particularly marked in Germany where splits in the communist party and the labour movement as a whole were to facilitate Hitler's rise to power.

## 10 July

Radek, Smil'ga and Preobrazhenskii signed a declaration that they had broken ideologically and organisationally with Trotsky and requested readmission to the party. Over 150 other members of the opposition followed suit, their names being published on 21 and 28 July.

Acting allegedly on information obtained in the Harbin raid (see 27 May), the Chinese took over the telegraphic installations on the Chinese Eastern railway and charged various Soviet railway officials with complicity in Soviet propaganda and political intrigue. On the following day they suspended the Soviet general manager and other Soviet officials, most of whom left for Moscow. The Chinese then attempted to take over the whole railway. The Soviet trade delegation in Manchuria was closed.

## 11 July

A Council of People's Commissars decree (quoted by Solomon) introduced the idea that prisons and labour colonies should become self-supporting as soon as possible. It called on the OGPU to establish a number of timber camps in remote regions housing prisoners taken from prisons run by the Commissariat of the Interior. About 64,000 prisoners were so transferred in the autumn. The primary task of the camps was not the rehabilitation of the inmates but the earning of foreign exchange to finance industrialisation.

## 13 July

*Pravda* reported that the Communist

Academy (founded in 1918 for the study of the history, theory and practice of socialism) had been designated as the national centre for research and graduate teaching. It later came to include the institutes of the Russian Association of Social Science Institutes and the Institute of Red Professors. In 1936 the Communist Academy was absorbed by the Academy of Sciences.

## 15 July

The British government informed the Soviet government of its willingness to resume diplomatic relations and invited a Soviet representative to London to discuss procedure.

## 15 July–15 August

A delegation of ninety American bankers, industrialists and businessmen visited the USSR. Despite the absence of diplomatic relations, the United States was beginning to challenge Germany as the USSR's biggest supplier. A number of American engineers were working in the Soviet Union.

## 17 July

As a result of the dispute over the Chinese Eastern railway, the Soviet government recalled its remaining diplomatic, consular, commercial and railway staff from China and demanded the recall of Chinese officials in the USSR, thus breaking off what had remained of diplomatic and consular relations with China since 6 April 1927. The breach was formally confirmed on 16 August. Rail traffic between the Trans-Siberian and Chinese Eastern railways was suspended. Soviet–Sinkiang consular relations were not interrupted.

## 18 July

Using French diplomatic channels to the Soviets, the US government drew the attention of the Soviet and Chinese governments to their obligations under the Kellogg Pact (see 29 August 1928). This was the first occasion on which the Kellogg Pact was invoked.

## 29 July

A Central Committee resolution called for maximum efforts by the party to ensure the success of the grain collection programme under Mikoyan's direction. The programme called for a 34 per cent increase in the quantity to be collected without any increase in the general level of prices paid to the peasant. The effort entailed pressure on the kulak and an attempt to improve the supply of manufactured goods to the countryside.

## 6 August

A Special Far Eastern Red Army was established in the eastern part of the Siberian Military District under General Bliukher's command with its headquarters in Khabarovsk.

## 16 August

The first of a series of raids over the Manchurian border was carried out by the Special Far Eastern Army with a view to bringing pressure to bear on the Chinese to agree to the restoration of the Soviet position on the Chinese Eastern railway. Talks on the subject proceeded intermit-

tently either directly or through intermediaries.

## 21 and 24 August

Opening a campaign which lasted for the rest of the year, *Pravda* publicly attacked moderation in general and Bukharin in particular, describing him as the chief leader of right deviationism.

## 22 August

A declaration by Rakovskii and others written from Saratov and calling for party democracy was supported by 500 members of the opposition. As a result Rakovskii was moved to Barnaul. The Trotskyite opposition was broken up partly by the physical isolation of its leaders in various remote parts of the country: it was also undermined by the regime's adoption of some of the main planks of its policy – rapid industrialisation at the expense of the well-to-do peasantry.

## 7 September

The Central Committee resolved that one-man management should apply in every industrial undertaking.

## 9 September

In the face of widespread peasant hoarding and resistance to the grain collection effort, a decree of the RSFSR instructed local committees to fix quotas to be met by the better-off peasants as well as kulaks. The decree was followed by a stepped-up campaign against the kulaks which seems to have had very limited success in mobilising the middle and poor peasants against them. Male thought that pressure from the regime may have tended to increase peasant solidarity rather than exacerbate whatever tensions there may have been between rich and poor. But the campaign did lead to more grain being collected than in 1928.

## 13 September

*Izvestiia* reported the resignation of Lunacharskii as Commissar of Education of the RSFSR. Other leading members of the commissariat resigned in the same month. According to Roy Medvedev in *On Stalin and Stalinism*, the resignations were in protest against the regime's proposals for vocational education. Fitzpatrick in *Education and Social Mobility* considered that contributory factors were the handing over to the Supreme Council of National Economy of a number of technical training establishments and the leadership's failure to halt the purging of students on account of their social origin.

Bubnov was appointed as the new Commissar of Education.

## 18 September

Ordzhonikidze, the head of Workers' and Peasants' Inspection (*Rabkrin*) which played an influential role together with the OGPU in securing party unity behind the drive for rapid industrialisation and collectivisation, said that years of work would be needed to organise the 25 million peasant economies round the tractor and the collective farm.

With active official encouragement and relatively mild but gradually increasing administrative pressure, the overall percentage of households collectivised had risen from about 3.9

per cent on 1 June to 7.5 per cent on 1 October, the figure being considerably higher in the main grain-producing areas (see R. W. Davies's *Collectivisation of Soviet Agriculture* for detailed figures). The majority of the collective farms were of the simplest type in which only the land and heavy implements were held in common. Plans for further collectivisation were becoming increasingly ambitious and the time-scale progressively shortened.

## 24 September

A decree introduced the continuous five-day working week: with certain exceptions, undertakings were to remain in continuous production with workers working for four days followed by one day's rest, rest days being taken by different workers on different days according to timetables worked out by management in agreement with factory committees or their equivalents. Apart from its economic implications, the decree militated against regular weekly religious observance.

## 28 September

A Central Committee resolution (not published until 1931) said that the main task of social insurance was to promote further increases in the productivity of labour on the basis of the industrialisation plan. This signalled the whittling away of many of the generous social insurance provisions of the early 1920s, especially those of the labour code (see 31 October 1922).

## 3 October

A protocol on the procedure to be

adopted on the settlement of questions outstanding on the resumption of Anglo-Soviet diplomatic relations was signed in London.

## 12 October

The Soviet Far Eastern Army launched an attack on north-eastern Manchuria to the south of Khabarovsk. The operation continued until early November when the Soviet troops withdrew having first occupied the town of Fukdin and destroyed the Manchurian units defending it.

## 7 November

Stalin's manifesto on 'The Year of the Great Breakthrough' was published. It spoke of the decisive offensive of socialism against the capitalist elements in town and countryside and laid heavy emphasis on accelerated collectivisation.

## 10–17 November

A Central Committee plenum expelled Bukharin from the Politburo and gave Rykov and Tomskii a severe warning of the consequences of any renewed struggle against the party line. (The relevant resolution was first published in 1932.) On 15 November Molotov spoke in terms of collectivising millions of peasant households by March 1930 and of treating the kulak as a most cunning and undefeated enemy.

The plenum decided to establish an All-Union Commissariat of Agriculture.

The resolution on the control figures for the economy in 1929/30 drew attention to the failure of industry to supply tractors, farm machinery and fertilisers on the scale necessary for collectivisation.

R. W. Davies contended that the resolutions of the plenum reflected but did not fully express a decision reached by the party leadership probably in October to launch a crash programme of forced collectivisation. Factors behind this decision were the progress of more or less voluntary collectivisation during the summer, the successful use of coercion in the 1929 grain collection programme and the belief that radical action was needed if declining agricultural production was not to act as a brake on rapid industrialisation.

Karcz argued in 1967 that the decision was based on faulty statistics on grain production and was a consequence of gross errors in pricing policy: by lowering government prices for grain and allowing prices of animal products to rise, the government had encouraged the peasants to move out of grain into animal products.

## 11 November

The Politburo accepted the resignation of Chicherin, whose health was failing, as Commissar for Foreign Affairs.

## 17–27 November

Three divisions of the Soviet Far Eastern Army entered north-western Manchuria occupying the towns of Manchouli and Chalainor. In heavy fighting with Manchurian troops, the Soviets suffered numerous casualties attributable in part to poor communications and co-ordination between their infantry, tanks and artillery.

## 26 November

*Pravda* published recantations by Rykov, Tomskii and Bukharin admitting that their views had been mistaken and that the party and its Central Committee had been proved right.

## 30 November

In response to the fighting in Manchuria, the US government again reminded the Soviet and Chinese governments of their obligations under the Kellogg Pact with support from some forty other signatories of the pact.

## 4 December

*Pravda* recognised that the Russian Association of Proletarian Writers (RAPP) followed a line in literature close to the party line and called for a consolidation of literary forces round RAPP. RAPP was in fact given the leading role in harnessing literature to the needs of the five-year plan. Writers were expected to become 'shock workers' in 'artistic brigades' engaging in socialist emulation and collective effort to produce factual literature on the five-year plan. While RAPP was dogmatic, intolerant of non-conformity and widely regarded as acting on behalf of the party, its leaders were insufficiently diligent in carrying out these instructions which ran counter to their philosophy (see April 1928). The RAPP leaders found themselves up against increasing internal opposition in their organisation in 1931 and it was wound up on 23 April 1932. Gorky on the other hand played his part for the state by sponsoring a collective history of the civil war and some of

the 'fellow-travellers' like Pil'niak were recruited to write a *History of Factories and Plants* including a volume on the building of the Stalin White Sea–Baltic canal, largely with prison labour. In fact, from the party's point of view, the 'fellow-travellers' proved to be at least as useful as the 'proletarians' as propagandists for the five-year plan.

## 5 December

The Siberian party committee was the first to solve the question of whether kulaks should be admitted to the collective farms by deciding to exile them *en masse*. The OGPU and its troops were extensively used to round up kulaks, suppress local rebellions and force the peasants into collectives.

The newly formed Tadzhik SSR joined the USSR.

## 7 December

The Soviet Central Executive Committee formally approved the setting up of an All-Union Commissariat of Agriculture. (Republican commissariats of agriculture had hitherto enjoyed a considerable degree of autonomy.) Iakovlev, an ardent exponent of industrialisation and higher agricultural production, was appointed commissar.

## 16 December

As the culmination of numerous difficulties placed in the way of the Lena Goldfields Company, the OGPU raided the company's Moscow offices and arrested a number of its employees. When approached by the British ambassador, Litvinov claimed to be ignorant of the affair. In February 1930 the State Bank prevented the company from paying wages. On 18 April 1930 the trial opened of a number of Lena employees charged with espionage and counter-revolutionary activities. With one exception the employees pleaded guilty and were given prison sentences. The company ordered non-Russian employees to leave the country. On 5 May 1930 the Soviet government claimed that, by its actions, the company had dissolved the concession agreement. Argument over the company's assets continued until November 1934.

## 17 December

The Soviet–Turkish treaty of friendship and neutrality of 17 December 1925 was extended for two years with an additional clause binding the parties not to negotiate a political agreement with a neighbouring state without consulting the other or to conclude such an agreement without the other's consent.

## 20 December

Sokol'nikov presented his credentials as ambassador in London on the restoration of Anglo-Soviet diplomatic relations which had been under negotiation since 17 July. Mutual undertakings to abstain from hostile propaganda were exchanged, the undertaking extending to Canada, Australia, New Zealand, South Africa, the Irish Free State, Newfoundland and India.

## 21 December

Stalin's fiftieth birthday was celebrated with calls for party unity and massive homage to his leadership,

the beginning of the cult of Stalin's personality.

## 22 December

Following the incursions by the Red Army into north-eastern and north-western Manchuria in October and November, a protocol was signed at Khabarovsk under which the status quo ante was restored on the Chinese Eastern railway under newly appointed Soviet and Chinese managers. Both sides agreed to release those who had been imprisoned in connection with the dispute. The Chinese undertook to disarm and deport White Guard detachments from Manchuria and both sides agreed to withdraw troops from the frontier. Provision was made for the reopening of Chinese consulates in the Soviet Far East and Soviet consulates in Manchuria. A Sino-Soviet conference was arranged for January 1930 to settle outstanding questions. This did not meet until 11 October 1930 and then proceeded in desultory fashion with the Soviet side insisting on implementation of the Khabarovsk agreement and the Chinese resisting pressure to ratify it. The conference died altogether as a result of the Japanese action in Manchuria on 18 September 1931. In Tang's opinion, the Soviets, no less than their Tsarist predecessors, sought to use the Chinese Eastern railway in the period 1923–31 as a means of achieving political and economic preponderance in northern Manchuria.

## 27 December

In a speech to the First All-Union Conference of Marxist Agrarians, Stalin said that the party had gone over from a policy of limiting the exploiting tendencies of the kulaks to a policy of eliminating them as a class: it was wrong to admit them to collective farms because they were the sworn enemies of them. Stalin extolled the benefits that collectivisation could bring even without mechanisation.

In fact the supply of tractors during the next four years reached little over half the planned figures, 4.5 million horsepower at the end of 1934 instead of 8 million. In 1930 the additional tractor-power made available to the collectives failed even to compensate for the loss of slaughtered animal-power.

# 1930

## 1 January

Party membership was given as 1,184,651 with 493,259 candidate members.

The first issue of the British *Daily Worker* contained an inflammatory message from the Comintern, which was widely regarded as inconsistent with the Soviet undertaking to refrain from hostile propaganda. The British Foreign Secretary raised the subject with the Soviet ambassador in London and received the usual reply that the Soviet government was not responsible for and could not control the Comintern.

## 5 January

The Politburo approved a Central Committee resolution accepting that the socialised sown area in the spring of 1930 should exceed 30 million hectares or about a quarter of the total. Furthermore, instead of 17.5 per cent of farmlands being collectivised as in the five-year plan, the more important grain areas such as the Lower and Central Volga and North Caucasus should, in the main, be completely collectivised by the autumn of 1930 (or the spring of 1931 at the latest) and other grain areas by the autumn of 1931 (or the spring of 1932 at the latest). The resolution warned the party against collectivisation 'from above' by decree. It instructed the Commissariat of Agriculture to draw up a model charter for the *artel* type of collective farm bearing in mind the inadmissibility of allowing kulaks to join collective farms.

## 7 January

A decree directed that all land reform projects in the individual sector should be abandoned and that all efforts should be concentrated on collectivisation. This decree put an end to the work of the agricultural specialists who had been working for the Commissariat of Agriculture during the 1920s on the rationalisation of landholdings under the communal system (see 14 February 1919). These specialists had formed an important administrative link between central government and the villages. They were stripped of their authority by an order of 18 January. Their disappearance was one of the factors behind the use of the military and the '25,000-ers' (see 1 February) to enforce collectivisation and to compel the peasants to sow the fields (see Yaney's contribution to Millar's *The Soviet Rural Community*).

## 26 January

General Kutepov, who had fought with Denikin and Wrangel in south

Russia and after Wrangel's death on 26 April 1928 had succeeded him as leader of the Russian Armed Services' Union (ROVS), was kidnapped in Paris and was not seen again. There was strong circumstantial evidence of Soviet involvement in his disappearance.

## 29 January

Mexico broke off diplomatic relations with the USSR. The arrest in Mexico of large numbers of anarchists and communists had led to demonstrations against the Mexican embassies in Rio de Janeiro and Buenos Aires and against the Mexican president-elect during a visit to Detroit. The Mexicans also complained about Soviet propaganda in Mexico.

## 1 February

A decree of the Soviet Central Executive Committee gave local Soviets the power to apply 'all necessary measures' in the struggle against the kulaks including banishment and total confiscation of their property.

R. W. Davies considered the decree to be a pale reflection of an unpublished Central Committee resolution of 30 January which divided kulaks into three categories:

1. Counter-revolutionaries not exceeding 63,000 in number to be named by the OGPU, whose property was to be confiscated and who were to be sentenced to death or imprisonment, their families being exiled.
2. 150,000 households of exploiters or active opponents of collectivisation, lists of whom were to be compiled by local authorities and who were to be allowed to retain some possessions while being exiled to remote areas.
3. Other kulaks numbering probably about 850,000 who were to be resettled on land outside the collective farms.

In practice, 'de-kulakisation' had already begun under local auspices in 1929 and was intensified in January 1930: in February it developed into a reign of terror.

On 16 August 1942 Stalin told Churchill that 10 million peasants had been 'dealt with' during collectivisation. In *On Stalin and Stalinism*, 1979, Roy Medvedev, quoting the Soviet journal *Voprosy istorii KPSS*, no. 5, 1975, stated that 115,000 kulak families were deported to remote areas in 1930 and 265,000 in 1931. On the basis of six to seven members for each family, this gave a total of about 2.5 million persons. Deportations continued in 1932 and a number of families were resettled in other districts in their own region. Medvedev thought there was reason to believe that these statistics were understated. In *The Harvest of Sorrow*, p.306, Conquest gave an overall estimate of 6.5 million peasant deaths between 1930 and 1937 as a result of 'de-kulakisation'. Rosefielde's estimate was 5.8 million deaths due to collectivisation between 1929 and 1932. Wheatcroft, however, argued in 1985 that there was no demographic evidence of more than a total of 6 million 'excess deaths' in the USSR between 1926 and 1939, of which perhaps 3 or 4 million were attributable to the famine of 1932–4 (see End

December 1939 for further comment on Soviet mortality statistics).

Davies estimated that about 250,000 (Conquest put the figure at 100,000) volunteer and conscripted agents of the authorities (including Red Army men, party workers and 25,000 politically experienced industrial workers – the '25,000-ers') were despatched from the towns to the countryside to help cajole or bully 25 million peasant households into changing their way of life. Male quoted a Soviet figure of 72,402 men in 10,422 brigades sent out from the cities in 1929–30 to repair and service agricultural equipment and to conduct propaganda in favour of collectivisation. Hostility to these collectivisation brigades, the persecution of the kulaks, the collectivisation of animals, the anti-religious campaign and the growth in size of collectives to embrace more than one village may all have contributed to the marked stiffening of peasant resistance to collectivisation in February.

For a detailed account of what forced collectivisation and 'dekulakisation' meant at the local official level, see chapter 12 of Fainsod's *Smolensk under Soviet Rule*, based on those parts of the Smolensk communist party archives which were captured by the German army in 1941 and by the US army in 1945.

## 8 February

Pope Pius XI launched a protest against religious persecution in the USSR which was supported by the Lutheran church in Germany and the Church of England.

## 10 February

A provisional agreement was reached between the Soviet government and the state-subsidised armaments firm Rheinmetall which covered German help in the manufacture of arms for the Red Army. The agreement was not ratified by Rheinmetall but there is evidence that they signed a modified agreement with the Soviets in July.

## 13 February

A decree set out regulations on pensions and social security benefits. The basic principles of Soviet social insurance policy had been laid down in the labour code (see 31 October 1922).

## 15 February and 15 May

Central Committee resolutions called for an increase in metal production. In R. W. Davies' *Soviet Investment for Planned Industrialisation*, Tatjana Kirstein stated that between 17 January 1929 and 15 February 1930 the planned capacity of the Magnitogorsk metallurgical plant was raised from the original 650,000 tons to 2,500,000 tons of pig-iron per annum, partly to make the plant comparable in scale to that in Gary, Indiana.

## 2 March

*Pravda* published Stalin's article 'Dizzy with Success: Problems of the *Kolkhoz* Movement'. It called for a restoration of the voluntary principle in collectivisation, condemned the wholesale socialisation of cattle, small livestock and poultry and the removal of bells from the village churches and criticised those whose dizziness with success had led them to try to solve all the problems of socialist construction 'in two ticks'. It was presumably written in response to peasant resistance to collectivisation and reflected official concern at Politburo level over the potential threat to the spring sowing campaign and the situation generally. During the following two months the line was developed that local officials, not the Central Committee, were to blame for the excesses of the collectivisation campaign. Kosior, the Ukrainian leader and Politburo member, is said to have objected to this line.

*Pravda* indicated that peasants were to be allowed to leave the collective farms although in practice economic restraints were imposed on their doing so. Those that remained in the collectives were to be allowed to keep a cow, sheep, pigs and implements to work private plots of land. *Izvestiia* published model regulations of association for collective farms of this type known as *artels*.

## 7 March

In the course of a Soviet naval visit to Germany, 'Flagman' (the revolutionary substitute for 'Admiral') V. M. Orlov, who like Muklevich was a key figure in the revival of the Soviet navy, was allowed to inspect the first of the German 'pocket battleships'. An exchange visit by senior German naval officers to the USSR took place in July. Thereafter Soviet–German naval exchanges seem to have declined through reluctance on the German side to compromise themselves in the eyes of other navies in the absence of compensating divi-

dends from their liaison with the Soviets.

Bukharin published an article in *Pravda* on the Jesuits which was in fact a thinly veiled condemnation of Stalin's forced collectivisation policy. He published no further political articles in *Pravda* or *Izvestiia* for the next three years but he continued to write on the planning of scientific research and development, including in his articles a good deal of implicit criticism of Soviet economic planning. He became an influential member of the Commissariat of Heavy Industry under Ordzhonikidze in 1932.

## 9 March–20 April

A series of trials of about forty-five alleged members of an underground Union for the Liberation of the Ukraine (SVU) began in Kharkov. The defendants were members of the intelligentsia including priests of the Ukrainian Autocephalous Orthodox Church. The apparent object of the trials was to decapitate nationalism in the Ukraine where resistance to collectivisation was particularly strong.

## 14 March

A Central Committee resolution following the general lines of Stalin's 'Dizzy with Success' condemned distortions of the party line on collectivisation and demanded the correction of errors over 'de-kulakisation'. The collectivisation drive had peaked with about 15 million households (c. 60 per cent) at least nominally collectivised as compared with under 2 million on 1 October 1929 and about 5 million on 1 January 1930. By 1 April the number of collectivised households had dropped to under 10 million and from May to the end of the year remained at or below 6 million. A total of 70,000 families in five regions who had been 'de-kulakised' were rehabilitated.

## 2 April

Agitation in Britain over religious persecution in the USSR culminated in a speech by the Archbishop of Canterbury in the House of Lords. In the opinion of the British ambassador in Moscow, the depth of foreign feeling on this subject did have some moderating effect on the Soviet authorities.

## 3 April

The All-Union Physical Culture Council attached to the Soviet Central Executive Committee, described by Riordan as a virtual ministry of sport, was established. Thenceforward sporting clubs were based on place of work or on cultural and educational establishments. From 1935 onwards clubs tended to be grouped into trade union sports societies following the lines of *Spartak* which represented members of producers' co-operatives. The largest and most successful clubs with the best facilities were those run by the security services (*Dynamo*) and the army (TsDKA). In 1930 'production gymnastics' intended to improve productivity began to be introduced.

## 5 April

Bauman, an enthusiastic advocate of rapid collectivisation, was dismissed as secretary of the Moscow party committee.

## 7 April

A new decree was issued on corrective labour camps under OGPU control. Up to 1928 labour camps had been concentrated in the White Sea area. The new decree marked the transition to the large-scale use of prison labour under the five-year plans. *GULag* (the Chief Administration of Camps) came into being under OGPU auspices. By 1930 the camp population had risen sharply from the figure of 30,000 in 1928 given by Dallin and Nicolaevsky. The great majority of prisoners were peasants, NEPmen and other 'socially dangerous elements' including priests, returned *émigrés*, Ukrainian separatists and victims of reprisals for the murder of Voikov in Warsaw.

## 14 April

Mayakovsky, the 'bard' or as he put it, the 'drumbeater' of the revolution, having joined the Russian Association of Proletarian Writers (RAPP) in February, committed suicide. His suicide is attributed by the Small Soviet Encyclopaedia (vol. v, 1949) in part to persecution by RAPP officials. Victor Serge wrote that 'having become the most requested rhymester of hack journalism . . . , he felt he was going to the dogs'. Brown and Struve both regarded the incompatibility between Mayakovsky's individualism and the prevailing atmosphere of collectivism as a likely factor in his suicide.

## 16 April

A temporary Anglo-Soviet commercial agreement was signed in London.

# 1 May

The Turksib railway officially opened. It opened for normal traffic on 1 January 1931.

# 23 May

The Soviet Central Executive Committee approved a new charter for the Academy of Sciences binding it to 'fulfil the needs of the socialist reconstruction of the country' and further reducing the possibilities of resistance by the old guard to the election of communist candidates.

# June

Soviet forces penetrated forty miles into Afghan territory in an effort to capture the *Basmachi* leader, Ibrahim Bek, or to induce the Afghans to take action against him. This the Afghans were in no position to do until April 1931 when he was driven back into the USSR.

# 25 June

Despite the confusion over collectivisation, the total of autumn and spring sowings for the 1930 harvest was above that for 1929: the collective farms achieved the target of over 30 million sown hectares set for them by the resolution of 5 January.

# 26 June–13 July

At the party's Sixteenth Congress which had been postponed from April, Stalin, in his political report of the Central Committee, described France as the most aggressive and militarist of all the aggressive and militarist countries of the world which were tending towards adventurist assaults on the USSR, a tend-

ency strengthened by the world economic crisis. (Deutscher quoted this to illustrate Stalin's slowness to appreciate the threat of Nazism which Stalin continued to bracket with German social democracy.)

Stalin attributed the world economic crisis to over-production: only in the USSR was there a rapid upswing of large-scale industry.

He claimed that the resistance of the kulak had been broken and that the grain crisis had in the main been solved. Its final solution was first in the order of problems in agriculture and would only be achieved through large-scale, mechanised, collectivised agriculture. Industrial crops such as cotton, sugar-beet, flax and oil crops were performing well but livestock production was falling.

He said that collectivisation and industrialisation had laid the foundations for a radical improvement in the material and cultural conditions of the workers and peasants. The literacy rate had risen to 62.6 per cent of the population. Universal compulsory elementary education was essential. The reconstruction of industry and agriculture demanded new technically trained cadres.

He maintained that the Soviet Union's difficulties arose out of progress and growth on the one hand and the internal and external resistance of wreckers and class enemies on the other. The Sixteenth Congress was the congress of the sweeping offensive of socialism on all fronts, not the 'growing into socialism' of Bukharin. The offensive had already been crowned with success and must be pursued to the end in uncompromising struggle with deviations of right or left.

In the course of the congress it was

admitted that mistakes had been made, for example, in arousing peasant resentment through the enforced closing of churches. But emphasis was laid on the renewal of the drive for comprehensive collectivisation after the harvest had been gathered in and of continued struggle against the kulaks. Difficulties in selling raw materials to the depressed economies of the West and a deterioration in the terms of trade from the Soviet point of view reinforced the strategic and political arguments for the goal set before the congress by Ordzhonikidze of converting the USSR from an importer of machinery into an independent economic unit.

In the section on industrialisation, the resolution on the Central Committee report called for the rapid creation of the new coal and metallurgical complex of the Urals–Kuznetsk Basin Combine, which had been talked about at least since 1918. Work had started on it in 1929.

The resolution on the report of the Central Control Commission and the Commissariat of Workers' and Peasants' Inspection (*Rabkrin*) noted that tens of thousands of unsuitable and corrupt persons and other elements of a hostile class character had been expelled in the purge of the Soviet apparatus. The purge was to be extended to all branches of management in the administration, the Soviets and the economy including the co-operatives and collective farms. The resolution dwelt at length on the importance of the Central Control Commission's and *Rabkrin*'s tasks in fighting bureaucratism and supervising compliance with party directives in all branches of the economy.

Bubnov, the Commissar for Education, protested about the state of the country's schools. Referring to the decision taken in 1921 to make education compulsory from the age of 7, he said it had been necessary to repeat the decision in 1930; in the meanwhile very little had been achieved.

The resolution on the fulfilment of the five-year plan called for a major expansion of factory apprenticeship schools and the training and retraining of workers.

Rykov, Tomskii and Uglanov admitted their past errors and expressed their support for the party line. Together with Bukharin (who was ill), they were re-elected to the Central Committee consisting of seventy-one members and thirty-five candidates. Rykov remained in the Politburo along with Voroshilov, Kaganovich, Kalinin, Kirov, Kosior, Kuibyshev, Molotov, Rudzutak and Stalin. Mikoyan, Chubar', Petrovskii, Syrtsov and Andreev were elected candidate members.

## 30 June

Despite peasant resistance, administrative chaos and arbitrariness in the fixing of quotas, the centralised grain collection effort for the agricultural year July 1929 to June 1930 yielded 14.9 million tons, exceeding the target of 13.9 million tons. However, the proportion of food grains was lower than in 1928/9, and within this category the actual quantity of wheat collected declined while that of rye more than doubled. Collections from the socialised sector (state and collective farms, especially the former) were below target, the over-fulfilment of the plan being due to additional collections from individual peasants.

# 1930

249

## July

Despite the absence of diplomatic relations between the United States and the USSR, the number of American specialists employed in the USSR had risen to over 600. In terms of technical contracts with the USSR, the Americans were second only to the Germans.

## 21 July

Litvinov was officially appointed to succeed Chicherin as Commissar for Foreign Affairs.

## 25 July

In view of adverse publicity in the West about the use of forced labour in the USSR, particularly in the lumber industry, a ban on Soviet imports was imposed by the US Treasury. It was not supported by the State Department and was lifted after a week.

## 30 July

A decree (one of several on the subject in 1930) abolished the *mir* (or commune) in areas of wholesale collectivisation, its functions being taken over by the collective farms and village Soviets.

## August

A group of bacteriologists were tried in secret for having allegedly organised an epidemic among horses.

## 2 August

A Soviet–Italian credit agreement was concluded. The agreement was accompanied by a marked improvement in the tone of Soviet press comment on Italy.

## 26 August

An arbitration court decided that the USSR should pay £13 million in compensation to the Lena Goldfields Company whose concession in the USSR had been cancelled in 1929. The USSR refused to comply. A direct agreement for the payment of £3 million in instalments was reached on 4 November 1934.

## 2 September

As part of a major overhaul of the taxation system, a decree paved the way for the introduction of a turnover tax on 1 October. This provided additional revenue for industrialisation and mopped up some of the surplus purchasing power held by the population. Mass lottery loans were promoted. Heavily discriminatory taxation was imposed on those peasants classified as kulaks.

## 3 September

*Izvestiia* reported the arrest of nine 'agricultural specialists' and others. The list of those named included three of the most important agricultural economists of the 1920s as well as Groman, an economic planner, and Sukhanov, the journalist. They were tried with others on 1–9 March 1931.

*Pravda* said that at least 50 per cent of all peasant households would be collectivised by the end of 1930/31.

## 6 September

A decree ordered the permanent settlement of all nomads in the RSFSR.

## 25 September

Forty-eight 'counter-revolutionaries' in the food industry, charged with sabotaging supplies to the 'working people, were shot by the OGPU.

## 9 October

In view of the shortage of labour in all branches of state industry, a decree discontinued the payment of unemployment benefit, implying that unemployment itself had been abolished. In fact according to Schwarz, over a million had been registered as unemployed in April and there were still many hundreds of thousands of workers listed as unemployed in October. Labour exchanges were instructed to ensure that all unemployed were directed into work not necessarily in their own trade.

Zaleski, quoting a Soviet source, stated in his first volume that, between 1 August 1929 and 1 November 1930, the number of registered unemployed fell from 1,298,000 to 240,000 largely owing to the initiation of vast construction projects but that the restriction and final elimination of unemployment benefit was also partly responsible.

## 29 October

Protests were made in the British Parliament about Soviet propaganda activities. The Soviets responded as usual by dissociating the Comintern from the Soviet government.

## 14 November

While the purge of employees of the Academy of Sciences continued, an academician was for the first time arrested and exiled. His case was followed by three others in the next three months. As the academy was brought under closer party control, the numbers of staff and students and the scope of their activities were all greatly expanded.

## 20 November

Bukharin published a further recantation in *Pravda*.

## 24 November

Litvinov met the Italian Foreign Minister, Count Grandi, in Milan. The meeting was followed in December by a Soviet naval mission to Italy.

Limited Soviet–Italian naval collaboration resulted in the transfer of a 2,900-ton destroyer to the Soviet navy, the *Tashkent*.

## 25 November–7 December

Eight experts belonging to the 'Industrial Party' including Professor Ramzin, at least four of them officials of Gosplan or the Supreme Council of National Economy, were tried for conspiring with *émigrés*, prominent French and British citizens and 2,000 of their fellow engineers to undermine Soviet industry. The five death sentences pronounced were all commuted to imprisonment. Some of the defendants were restored to their posts after a few years. The British government protested against the allegations of British involvement in conspiracy against the Soviet government.

Victor Serge, who regarded the accusations of sabotage by technicians at this and many other trials as in general a monstrous slander dictated by the need to find scapegoats for the regime's economic failures, described the 'Industrial Party' as a police invention sanctioned by the Politburo. Serge assessed Ramzin as an *agent provocateur* and wrote that having confessed to plotting military intervention against the USSR with British and French representatives Ramzin 'was pardoned, continued his scientific work in mild captivity and was rehabilitated at the beginning of 1936'. Ramzin won a Stalin prize in 1943 and retained his professorship until his death in 1947.

Zaleski argued that Stalin, seeking to pursue new objectives through new methods, found it necessary not only to replace the old planners (Krzhizhanovskii was dismissed from the chairmanship of Gosplan in December) but to discredit and punish them in order to strengthen discipline. He interpreted the lightness of the sentences as an indication that the government could not justify its case against the defendants.

Bailes thought that the evidence against the defendants did not stand up to scrutiny. The defendants shared the common outlook of the old generation of specialists, opposed to Stalinist leadership as expressed in the five-year plan and in the changes in higher education; the defendants represented a technocratic threat to the Marxist-Leninist monopoly and may also have had links with Bukharin and the 'right' opposition. Bailes quoted estimates of the number of engineers arrested in the period 1928 to 1931 of between 2,000 and 7,000.

## 1 December

*Pravda* announced that Lominadze (first secretary of the Transcaucasian regional committee of the AUCP (B)) and Syrtsov (a candidate member of the Politburo who had been removed from the chairmanship of the RSFSR Council of People's Commissars on 3 November) had been expelled from the Central Committee and that Shatskin (a Komsomol leader close to Lominadze) had been expelled from the Central Control Commission for having formed a 'left-right bloc' against the party line. Syrtsov, who had been a strong supporter of collectivisation in 1929, had more recently warned against excessive collectivisation especially if the supply of tractors and machinery was inadequate: he had also been sceptical about the programme for reviving livestock production and about the tractor factory at Stalingrad which he described as a 'Potemkin village'. He believed in the necessity for honest statistics and a partial resuscitation of market forces. Both he and Lominadze had supported Stalin against Bukharin in 1929. But both were now probably critical of Stalin and were trying to modify policies which seemed to them to be leading to an economic crisis. In his 1981 article, R. W. Davies found no evidence of an organised group around these leaders and concluded that they had been punished as scapegoats and as a warning to others.

## 8 December

In order to increase the number of women employed in industry and state co-operative organisations, the Council of People's Commissars of the RSFSR decreed various measures including the provision of crèches and children's playgrounds.

## 17–21 December

A joint session of the Central Committee and the Central Control Com-

**1930**

mission decided to expel Rykov from the Politburo where he was succeeded by Ordzhonikidze. Andreev ceased to be a candidate member on appointment as head of the Central Control Commission in succession to Ordzhonikidze. Rykov was also removed from the presidency of the Council of People's Commissars and the presidency of the Council of Labour and Defence (STO), in both of which posts he was succeeded by Molotov. Rykov remained in the Council of People's Commissars as Commissar for Posts and Telegraphs.

The Commissariat of Trade was redivided into foreign and internal components, the latter becoming a Commissariat of Supplies. Supplies were increasingly allocated under a complex system of multiple prices for different categories of purchaser.

## 31 December

For the calendar year 1930 the overall increase in grain production from a good harvest was more than offset by the decline in livestock production brought about by the shortage of fodder and the wholesale slaughter of about 25 per cent of the nation's livestock by peasants under threat of collectivisation. In consequence 1930 showed a slight decline in total gross agricultural production in relation to 1929.

The fiscal year running from October one year to September in the next was abolished. Consequently the third year of the five-year plan (which began on 1 October 1928) opened on 1 January 1931.

During the year, propaganda on the subject of military preparedness was intensified.

# 1931

## January

Prison sentences were introduced for violations of labour discipline. Dallin and Nicolaevsky estimated that the number in 'places of detention' in the USSR rose to 2 million in 1931.

## 1 January

Party membership was given as 1,369,406 with 842,819 candidate members.

## 14 January

A decree, followed by others on 20 March and 23 July, tightened up controls over bank credits.

## 16–26 January

The Ninth Komsomol Congress stressed the role of Komsomol members in collective farms whether as tractor drivers, administrators, recruiters of new members or assistants in rural electrification schemes.

## 23 January

A decree set up 'staff offices' to organise the supply of labour for industry.

## 25 January

A Central Committee resolution expressed dissatisfaction with the rate of progress on the Magnitogorsk metallurgical plant, part of the Urals–Kuznetsk Combine, which was to have an initial capacity of 2.5 million tons of pig-iron. The resolution called for reports on a number of different aspects of the work and demanded improved planning and the introduction of one-man management throughout the project. According to the GSE, the iron ore mine opened on 15 May 1931, the first blast furnace started up on 31 January 1932, the first open-hearth furnace on 8 July 1933, the blooming mill on 28 July 1933, the continuous-billet mill in November 1933 and the heavy-gauge rolling mill in August 1934.

A Central Committee resolution censured the editors of the philosophical journal *Pod znamenem marksisma (Under the banner of Marxism)* largely for overvaluing Plekhanov as a theoretician and neglecting Lenin: this had led them into failure to acknowledge the Central Committee as the theoretical centre of Marxism-Leninism. In other words they did not accept the pretensions of the party to control all forms of thought. The resolution also had implications for RAPP in which the influence of Plekhanov's ideas was significant (see April 1928).

### End January

The First All-Union Conference of Managers of Socialist Industry was held to promote mastery of technique. Serious problems had arisen, notably in the new Stalingrad tractor works, because of the lack of staff capable of handling the new machinery.

### February

A large delegation of German industrialists visited the USSR.

A number of distinguished historians were secretly sentenced to imprisonment. Some were restored to their academic posts after a few years.

### 3 February

A decree subordinated Gosplan directly to the Council of People's Commissars and gave it increased planning powers at the expense of the Supreme Council of National Economy.

### 4 February

Stalin spoke of fulfilling the five-year plan in three years in the main branches of industry. He admitted that the USSR was fifty or a hundred years behind the advanced countries and said that it must make good this disparity in ten years or be crushed. In order to catch up, the Bolsheviks 'must become masters of technique'.

Even more unrealistic economic targets were set and even greater priority was given to heavy industry.

### 1–9 March

A group of fourteen Mensheviks, including the journalist and econom-

ist, Sukhanov, Groman and other Gosplan economists, were tried on charges of counter-revolutionary activities aimed at the restoration of capitalism. (Groman and his group had, up to 1928, made a major contribution to the development of the planning concepts subsequently embodied in the first five-year plan.) The defendants were imprisoned and most of them, including Sukhanov, disappeared. According to Roy Medvedev, Sukhanov was released, re-arrested in 1937 and shot. A defendant who survived gave Medvedev an account of the fraudulent manner in which the trial was conducted.

### 7 March

A five-year Soviet–Turkish protocol on naval armaments was signed in Ankara, under which each party agreed not to increase its naval strength in or near the Black Sea without giving six months' notice to the other.

### 8–17 March

In a speech to the Sixth All-Union Congress of Soviets, Molotov gave a rosy account of conditions in Soviet prison camps. He did not deny that prison labour was being used on road and railway-building, peat extraction, mining, quarrying, construction projects and so on, but rejected the idea that products of prison labour were being exported (as claimed in the West). Foreign correspondents and workers' delegations were invited to visit the camps, some of which (according to subsequent accounts from escaped prisoners) had been carefully cleaned out in advance for the purpose.

Kalinin admitted to the British

consul in Moscow later in the year that forced labour existed but thought that not more than about 400,000 prisoners were engaged in it.

## 16 March

A Soviet–Turkish treaty of commerce and navigation was signed in Moscow.

## 20 March

A Council of People's Commissars decree sought to reintroduce into Soviet industry the principle of economic accounting or *khozraschet* which meant that an enterprise should be run on business lines with minimum production costs and maximum efficiency and productivity so as to make a profit.

## 21 March

A Central Committee resolution on mass party work in factories and brigades stated that a decision of the Sixteenth Congress that every single communist and Komsomol member must engage in socialist competition and the shock-worker movement remained to a considerable extent unfulfilled. The Central Committee ordered local party organisations to correct this failure as a means of ensuring that production targets were met. The resolution also called for the setting-up of factory schools and courses to train workers and for the undeviating implementation of one-man management.

## 25 March

The Central Committee prohibited the diversion of workers for current political campaigns or administrative tasks or their being given time off during the working day for any purpose including education.

## 14 April

A Soviet–German credit agreement was signed in Berlin.

## 27 April

A Soviet–Italian credit agreement was signed in Rome. Despite Mussolini's fascist regime, criticism of Italy in the Soviet press was noticeably absent in the early 1930s. As in the case of Turkey, vigorous action by the government against the local communist party proved to be no barrier to friendly state relations with the USSR.

## 28 April

An agreement was announced between the USSR and the Metropolitan-Vickers Co. Ltd concerning technical assistance in the manufacture of equipment and machinery.

## 6 May

A protocol was signed between the USSR and Lithuania prolonging the non-aggression treaty of 28 September 1926 for five years.

## 11 May

Kuibyshev, the chairman of Gosplan, defined the goal of the second five-year plan covering the years 1933–7 as the construction of a socialist economic system. This entailed the elimination of differences between countryside and city through an improvement in living conditions, the complete industrialisation of agriculture and the elimination of differences between physical and intellectual work through improved technical education. In a speech a few days earlier, Lomov, who was concerned at the time with the electrification programme, said that economic targets must be determined by the slogan of catching up with and overtaking the capitalist economies. Some of the goals set by Kuibyshev 'for working purposes' (not necessarily to be achieved by 1937) included 150 billion kWh of electric power, 390–500 million tons of coal, 130–150 million tons of crude oil and gas, 50–60 million tons of pig-iron, about 400,000 tons of aluminium, 847,000 tons of refined copper, a total sown area of over 200 million hectares and 70–90 million head of cattle, figures broadly comparable with US production at the time. Gosplan was to submit the plan to the government in the autumn of 1932, having consulted all the planning agencies, scientific research institutes and 'social organisations'. The procedure also entailed drawing up annual plans for 1931 and 1932. In fact it was not until November 1934 that the five-year plan was officially confirmed with production targets drastically lower than Kuibyshev's figures. Meanwhile the plan for 1931 had, in Zaleski's words, 'lost all linkage' with the first five-year plan still formally in force.

The inconsistencies between the annual and five-year plans, the constant readjustments to them and the fact that they tended to follow rather than precede performance were among the reasons for Zaleski's conclusion that the principle purpose of the plans was to promote the myth of balanced, rational economic development as an inducement to the population to commit itself to serving the regime's ends despite the austerity they imposed. Other characteristics of the system to which Zaleski drew attention were the chaotic overlap between central and local planning bodies, the delays and bargaining involved in the process of consultation between the centre and the periphery, constant changes in government directives and the low level of competence and the high turnover of planning staff. While Zaleski considered that the planning system in some ways helped the regime to increase its control over the economy, it also provided enterprise managers with opportunities to defeat the planners, for example, by using personal influence or chicanery to obtain extra investment in their plant, by deliberately underestimating their construction costs or by taking on additional unskilled labour to meet their targets, an important factor in the overfulfilment of the plan's goals for overall employment and industrial costs and underfulfilment of the target for industrial productivity. Industrial costs which were planned to fall in 1932/3 to 65 per cent of their 1927/8 level actually rose to 146.1 per cent of that level (Soviet sources). Industrial productivity, which was planned to rise to 210 per cent of its 1927/8 level, fell to 65.1 per cent (Soviet estimate), 41.8 per cent (Jasny's estimate) or 36.3 per cent (Nutter's estimate). Under the first five-year plan, the target for real wages in 1932/3 was 168 per cent of their 1927/8 level. In fact they dropped to 65.4 per cent of that level according to official Soviet estimates or 43.6 per cent according to Zaleski's own estimate.

## 6 June

A decree widened the scope of the Chief Administration for Matters of Literature and Publishing (*Glavlit*) in establishing political, ideological, military and economic control over all types of publishable material. *Glavlit* was empowered to forbid any material which either contained agitation and propaganda against the Soviet power and the dictatorship of the proletariat or which revealed state secrets or stirred up ethnic and religious fanaticism or was of a pornographic nature.

## 10 June

A secret circular from the Central Committee to all party organisations which was found in the Smolensk party archives and was quoted by Bailes ordered Soviet managers 'to enhance the authority of the engineering and technical personnel' especially the young ones, to improve their working conditions and to curb legal actions against them. Managers were instructed to appoint more members of the technical intelligentsia to leading positions.

## 23 June

Speaking to a conference of Soviet economists and industrialists, Stalin made six points on labour discipline:

1. Owing to the improved conditions in the villages resulting from collectivisation, an automatic labour supply for industry could no longer be guaranteed. It was therefore essential to organise the existing labour supply properly and speed up the process of mechanisation.

2. The volatility of labour could no longer be tolerated. (See Schwarz, chapter 3 for a detailed account of the sharp increase in labour turnover from 1929 onwards.) Wage equality had to be abandoned and wages had to be restructured in order to secure a permanent nucleus of trained workers in the various factories: wage differentials should be introduced for skilled or heavy work. Emphasis on piece-rates and bonuses was implied.

3. Irresponsibility would have to be rooted out. Particular groups of workers would have to be kept at particular jobs on particular machines and, if necessary, there would have to be a return to the interrupted six-day week as opposed to the continuous five-day working week (see 24 September 1929).

4. Progress was not possible with the existing technical and engineering resources. The working class should develop its own technical intelligentsia regardless of party membership.

5. Policy towards the old technical intelligentsia should be changed: every consideration should be shown to those bourgeois technical specialists and engineers who were willing to an increasing extent to work loyally with the working class. (The trials of November 1930 and early 1931 had generated a wave of 'specialist-baiting' and the educational system had been heavily biased in favour of those of proletarian origin.)

6. To accumulate capital resources, it would be necessary to draw on heavy industry as well as light industry and agriculture. Waste

had to be eliminated and the principles of business accountancy applied: costs should be lowered and funds accumulated to a greater extent within industry.

Social insurance was also used during this period to boost productivity by favouring workers with good records for production and length of service.

## 24 June

A five-year Soviet–Afghan neutrality and non-aggression treaty was signed in Kabul, replacing the treaty of 31 August 1926. It was extended on 29 March 1936 for a further ten years.

A Soviet–German protocol was signed prolonging until 30 June 1933 the agreements of 24 April 1926 and 25 January 1929. The agreements were subsequently terminable at one year's notice. The protocol was not ratified by the Germans until 5 May 1933, after Hitler's accession to power.

## 30 June

Total grain collections during the agricultural year 1930/1 at 22.1 million tons were over 6 million tons higher than in 1929/30. Heavy pressure on individual producers to deliver a high proportion of their output was used to drive them back into collective farms. Two-thirds of the increase in grain collections was allocated to exports which rose from 1.3 million tons in 1929/30 to 5.8 million tons, nearly 60 per cent of the pre-revolutionary level.

## End of June

The *Basmachi* leader, Ibrahim Bek, who had crossed back into the USSR from Afghanistan with 800 followers in April, was captured by the Red Army in Tadzhikistan and was later executed. Despite his execution, small-scale cross-border *Basmachi* operations continued up to 1950.

## 31 July

The Soviet trading organisation in Buenos Aires, *Iuzhamtorg*, was raided by police who claimed to have obtained evidence that it was acting clandestinely as the diplomatic, political and consular agent of the Soviet government (which Argentina had not recognised) and that the staff included secret service men. The director of *Iuzhamtorg* announced that the Soviets had decided to break off commercial relations with Argentina. Argentina, like the United States and Canada, had accused the USSR of 'dumping'.

## 2 August

Peasant desertion of the collective farms having been reversed in the second half of 1930 by a combination of force and economic pressure, the Central Committee declared that collectivisation was virtually complete in the North Caucasus, some parts of the Ukraine, the Urals and the Lower and Central Volga regions.

A decree announced that the cotton-growing area of Central Asia, Kazakhstan and Transcaucasia and the beet-growing areas of the Ukraine and central black-earth regions were due for collectivisation during 1931. The percentage of households collectivised rose to over 50 per cent in the course of the year.

## 15 August

The Central Committee published a

resolution demanding that imaginative literature should reflect far more fully the heroism of socialist construction and the class struggle. Financial incentives were introduced for authors who responded to this demand.

## 22 August

A decree required peasants to devote six days' labour per year to road-building. Discharge from this obligation could be purchased for a fixed sum.

## 25 August

A Central Committee resolution (published on 5 September) declared that schools were failing to equip candidates for technical and higher educational establishments with the grounding they needed in science, mathematics, native languages, geography and history. Socially productive labour performed by students was to be subordinated to their studies.

In broad terms this marked the end of the post-revolutionary experimental period in education and the beginning of a restoration of traditional teaching methods and discipline which continued into 1935. In the 1920s there had been much purging of teaching staff; the authority of teachers (who were predominantly non-communist) was undermined and in the late 1920s there was talk of the withering-away of the school, a notion specifically condemned by the resolution. After the revolution, experimental teaching methods had been imported from abroad: examinations were abolished and emphasis was laid on collective at the expense of individual studies. 'Pupil power' and 'student power' tended to get out of hand: according to Bailes the reaction against this began in January 1930. In July 1928 it was decided that vocational training should be introduced at the elementary level to meet the needs of the five-year plan. From September 1930 onwards this decision and the other trends mentioned began to be reversed but implementation of the resolution in the provinces varied widely (see Fitzpatrick's *Education and Social Mobility* for details).

## 29 August

A Franco-Soviet non-aggression pact was initialled.

## 18–19 September

An incident between Chinese and Japanese troops in Manchuria was used by the Japanese army to put into effect a well-prepared plan to occupy Mukden, Changchun and Kirin. Thereafter the Japanese extended their influence throughout Manchuria setting up on 9 March 1932 the pseudonymous 'Independent Government of Manchukuo'. Manchurian and, in some cases, Japanese officials displaced the Chinese on the Chinese Eastern railway. The Soviets adopted a 'neutral' attitude amounting almost to appeasement of the Japanese, conduct which gave rise to Chinese suspicions of a secret Soviet–Japanese understanding.

## October

An anti-drought conference was held in Moscow. Molotov said that several million hectares had suffered from the exceptionally dry season.

# 1 October

The Commissar of Transport was sacked as part of the effort to improve the chaotic situation on the railways.

A provisional commercial agreement was signed in Urumchi (Tihwa) between the USSR and the provincial government of Sinkiang. According to Slusser and Triska, the agreement was signed without the knowledge of the Nanking government who repudiated it when it became known to them in 1933.

# 11 October

A price committee attached to the Council of Labour and Defence (STO) was set up to liquidate the remnants of private trade and to fix prices in the state and co-operative sectors. Ostensibly its aim was to reduce price levels but in fact the period was one of steep decline in living standards leading up to the famine of 1933.

# 27 October

A Soviet–Persian commercial convention was signed in Tehran.

# 30 October

In the course of a visit by Litvinov to Turkey, the Soviet–Turkish agreements of 17 December 1925, 17 December 1929 and 7 March 1931 were extended.

# 31 October

According to Dallin the Soviets concluded a secret agreement with the governor of Sinkiang, General Chin Shu-jen, who was facing an uprising by the local Muslim majority backed by the Chinese Muslim Tungans from Kansu province led by General Ma Chung-yin. The agreement covered Soviet military and economic support for Chin in return for trade concessions and other privileges for the Soviets in Sinkiang which, according to Whiting, included the establishment of Soviet trade agencies in Urumchi and seven other centres in Sinkiang. Two Soviet consulates had been established in Sinkiang in 1920 and the number was enlarged to five in 1924.

# 3 November

The Lenin Institute merged with the Marx-Engels Institute to form the Marx-Engels-Lenin Institute. The Lenin Institute had been founded on 31 March 1923 for the study of Lenin's life and works with Kamenev as its director and Tovstukha, Stalin's private secretary, as his assistant. Rosenfeldt surmised that Tovstukha, with his access to the Lenin archive, had much to do with the build-up of Stalin as Lenin's true heir and successor in the ideological field. In 1928 the Commission on the History of the October Revolution and the RKP(B) (*Istpart*) had merged with the Lenin Institute.

# 7 November

On Comintern instructions, a Chinese Soviet Republic was declared in the village of Juichin in the south of Kiangsi province. The republic consisted of six widely separated and shifting regions controlled by scattered communist forces collected together by Chu Teh and Mao Tse-tung after the repressions of 1927. The republic survived until October 1934 when Kuomintang pressure finally compelled the communists to set out on their long march to Shensi in north-west China.

### 21 November

A non-continuous six-day week (five days' work with fixed holidays on the sixth, twelfth, eighteenth, twenty-fourth and thirtieth of the month) was introduced in public services and offices and the continuous five-day working week (see 24 September 1929) was progressively phased out in industry. Three-shift schedules also fell into disfavour. Restrictions on overtime imposed by the labour code (see 31 October 1922) were increasingly ignored as were regulations on the employment of women and children, industrial safety, etc.

### 27 November

A joint order from the Council of People's Commissars and the Central Committee dismissed the chairman of the State Grain Farms' Union and severely punished and expelled from the party many other members of it. Consumption of grain by the farms above the authorised level was made a criminal offence and supervisors were appointed by the Commissariat of Agriculture to watch over state farms.

### December

The Soviet government made an unsuccessful attempt to initiate negotiations for a non-aggression pact with the Japanese.

Stalin's criticisms of egalitarianism led to the introduction of new wage scales in the course of the year with differentials of up to 3.7:1 between skilled and unskilled workers. In 1925/6, employees and engineering-technical personnel in heavy industry earned 188 per cent of an average worker's wage (see Fitzpatrick's *Education and Social Mobility*).

### 24–25 December

The Soviet Central Executive Committee adopted the annual plan for 1932. Since it had been decided that the first five-year plan should be completed in four years, 1932 was considered to be the last year of the plan. Zaleski showed that there were marked differences between the outputs of different commodities and the quantitative relationships between them in the 1932 plan and the original five-year plan. The 1932 plan projected lower growth rates for national income and industrial production than the 1931 plan, transport being the principal bottleneck with fuel and the metal industry severe problem areas.

# 1932

## 1 January

Party membership was given as 1,769,773 with 1,347,477 candidate members.

## 5 January

The Supreme Council of National Economy was wound up and its responsibilities were divided between people's commissariats dealing with different sectors of production, initially, heavy industry, light industry and wood-working.

## 21 January

A three-year Soviet–Finnish non-aggression treaty was signed in Helsinki, the first of four such treaties to be signed on Soviet initiative with states bordering the USSR in the next few months.

## 25 January

A Soviet–Polish non-aggression pact was initialled. Signature was delayed by the Poles in the hope that a similar pact would be signed with Romania. Negotiations on this pact, however, foundered over the question of Bessarabia.

## 30 January–4 February

The resolutions of the party's Seven-teenth Conference listed the following shortcomings in the fulfilment of the annual plan for 1931:

1. the poor work of the transport system;
2. defects in the organisation of labour;
3. poor leadership of enterprises by the industrial corporations;
4. the lack of a proper relationship between wage rises and productivity;
5. inadequate observance of business methods; and
6. failure to check up on the fulfilment of decisions.

Molotov, Kuibyshev and the conference resolutions based on their reports gave the social and political objectives of the second five-year plan as the complete elimination of capitalist elements from the economy and from the mentality of the people, the elimination of classes and the factors underlying their formation and the transformation of the working people into active builders of a classless socialist society. A new variant of the second five-year plan was presented at the conference with production goals markedly less ambitious than Kuibyshev's figures of 11 May 1931.

Ordzhonikidze's report underlined the need to master technology (and hence the need to raise the level of technical education) in order that newly created industrial plant could be used effectively.

The resolutions gave the central economic tasks for 1932 as the abolition of the lag in ferrous metallurgy, the further mechanisation of the coal industry and the development of machine construction. The resolutions also reflected the six points made by Stalin on 23 June 1931.

## 4 February

Rudzutak, on his appointment as chairman of the Central Control Commission, relinquished his membership of the Politburo in which his place was taken by Andreev, his predecessor at the Control Commission.

A decree laid down that the *artel* (see 2 March 1930) should be the standard model of collective farm. Some of the larger collectives and giant state farms were broken up into smaller units.

## 5 February

A three-year Soviet–Latvian non-aggression treaty was signed in Riga.

## 11 February

Despite denunciations of the League of Nations by Radek who described it as an abortion of the World War which existed only to set its seal on any imperialist conspiracy directed against peace, Litvinov addressed the World Disarmament Conference in Geneva. Litvinov said that the Soviet government, although prepared to discuss other proposals, still believed that security could be obtained only through total disarmament. He declared that his government's sole

aim was the building of socialism on the territory of the Soviet Union.

A decree established the 'brigade system' of allotting specific areas of cultivation or specific agricultural tasks to brigades of workers under permanent brigade leaders.

## 20 February

Trotsky was deprived of his Soviet citizenship.

## 23 February

The fourteenth anniversary of the Red Army was used to launch a campaign to alert the workers to the threat of war and to prepare them to defend the Soviet Union. *Osoaviakhim*, said by this time to have had over 10 million members, played a leading part in the campaign, assisted by the Komsomol.

## 4 March

*Izvestiia* published an article on 'Japanese provocations', drawing attention to demands made by Japanese individuals and groups for war with the USSR and occupation by the Japanese of eastern Siberia.

## 9 March

The Japanese puppet 'Manchukuo' regime was set up in Manchuria.

## 7 April

The death penalty was introduced for the pilfering of foodstuffs from collective farms.

## 16 April

The tenth anniversary of the Treaty of Rapallo was celebrated with references to Soviet–German relations as a model of good relations between states with different political systems.

## 23 April

A Central Committee resolution wound up RAPP, VOAPP and other 'proletarian' literary organisations which had increasingly reflected the intolerance and extremism of the young communists of the time. The old organisations were replaced by a single Union of Soviet Writers containing a communist fraction. The Union was to embrace all Soviet writers who accepted the general policy of the Soviet government and supported 'socialist construction', i.e. bourgeois 'fellow-travellers' as well as 'proletarians'. The statute of the Union of Soviet Writers, dated 6 May 1934, required that its members should follow the method of 'socialist realism', a term introduced by Ivan Gronskii, the editor of *Izvestiia* and effectively the party supervisor of literature, at a literary meeting on 20 May 1932. This was followed by a leading article on the subject in *Literaturnaia Gazeta* on 29 May. The objective of socialist realism was later defined as 'the creation of works of high artistic significance, saturated with the heroic struggle of the world proletariat and with the grandeur of the victory of socialism and reflecting the great wisdom and heroism of the communist party'. The artist was expected to combine a truthful and historically concrete depiction of reality with the task of educating and moulding the working people ideologically in the spirit of socialism. The definition of socialist realism was debated at great length. While part of the intention behind its introduction was to raise literary standards

(which 'proletarian' five-year plan literature had debased) and to re-emphasise the role of human beings in the productive process, in practice it demanded of artists an optimistic and edifying portrayal within conventional forms of life under socialism. In rejecting 'bourgeois formalism', it rejected much of earlier Soviet literature and was used to discourage experiment in the theatre (e.g. Meyerhold), modernism in music (Shostakovich's *Lady Macbeth of Mtsensk*) and abstraction in the visual arts. The arts in fact had to conform with what the party and in the last resort Stalin thought acceptable and politically useful in re-educating the masses and 'building socialism'. Writers, as Stalin put it to a group of writers in Gorky's apartment on 26 October, had to become 'engineers of human souls'.

A Literary Institute was set up to train young writers. The 'proletarian' musicians' association (RAPM) was dissolved and replaced by a Union of Soviet Composers.

In the course of the year the Kazan cathedral in Leningrad was converted into a museum of the history of religion and atheism.

## Spring

According to evidence cited by Dalrymple, famine made its appearance in the Ukraine. The situation improved with the harvest but began to deteriorate again before the end of the year.

The creation of the Soviet Far Eastern fleet was announced. It consisted initially of small surface forces and a few submarines.

## 4 May

A three-year Soviet–Estonian non-aggression treaty was signed in Moscow.

## 6 May

A decree allowed free sales of grain by collective farms after the state's procurement plan had been fulfilled. On 10 May this was extended to livestock products. Decrees of 22 August and 2 December provided for sentences of up to ten years' imprisonment for selling grain before the state quotas had been fulfilled.

## 26 June

The Germans agreed to the closing-down of the Lipetsk air-training base in the USSR, the initiative for which seems to have come from the Soviet side and to have been dictated by Soviet anxieties over political developments in Germany. It seems that the base did not actually close until 30 October 1933 (but see 28 September 1933).

## 1 July

The last official breakdown of party membership for nearly thirty years gave percentages of members by social origin as 65.2 per cent workers, 26.9 per cent peasants and 7.9 per cent white-collar workers and others. By current occupation, workers accounted for 43.5 per cent, collective farmers 17.9 per cent, individual peasants 0.4 per cent, white-collar workers 28.4 per cent, students 7.5 per cent, artisans 0.4 per cent and others 1.9 per cent.

## 6–9 July

At the Ukrainian communist party's Third Conference, attended by Molotov and Kaganovich, an unrealistically high target of 6.6 million tons was set for grain collections from the Ukraine.

## 25 July

A three-year Soviet–Polish non-aggression treaty renewable for two years was signed in Moscow. It had been initialled on 25 January and caused some concern to the Germans.

## 28 July

The ice-breaker *Sibiriakov* left Archangel and made the first west-east passage of the Northern Sea Route in one navigation season, entering the Bering Strait on 1 October.

## 2 August

The Egyptian authorities asked the Soviet trade commissioner to leave the country and closed down his offices. The first Soviet trading agency, *Textilimport*, had been established in Alexandria in 1927. Soviet activities had been regarded with suspicion by the Egyptian government from the start on both political and economic grounds.

## 7 August

Under the law on Protection of Property of State Enterprises, Collective Farms and Co-operatives, the death penalty or in the presence of extenuating circumstances, deprivation of liberty for not less than ten years, was introduced for the theft of state property which included cattle, crops, etc. belonging to collective farms. Some of these penalties had been foreshadowed in a decree of 7 April.

## 25 August

A Central Committee resolution re-established classroom lectures by the teacher as the basic Soviet teaching method and sought to involve parents in the restoration of school discipline.

## 27 August

Over 2,000 delegates from twenty-seven countries assembled for an anti-war congress in Amsterdam, inspired largely by Münzenberg. Barbusse delivered the main address.

## 18 September–11 October

Tukhachevskii visited Germany, attended manoeuvres and was shown various factories.

## 19 September

In response to widespread dissatis-faction with the quality of the engin-eers produced by the drive initiated by the Central Committee plenum of 4–12 July 1928, a decree of the Soviet Central Executive Committee ordered a reorganisation of higher technical education. This drastically reduced the time spent on practical production work and restored theor-etical subjects to a central place in the curriculum. Examinations were reintroduced and the secondary school system was revived and expanded at the expense of technical schools attached to industry.

## 28 September–2 October

According to Conquest in *The Great Terror*, a Central Committee plenum expelled the Riutin group as 'traitors to the party . . . who have attempted to restore capitalism and kulakdom in the USSR'. Zinoviev, Kamenev and seventeen others were also expelled. In the late summer, Riutin, a former Bukharin supporter, had circulated a 200-page document, the 'Riutin platform', demanding the removal of Stalin, reduced industrial investment, liberation of the peasan-try from collectivisation and the reinstatement of opposition leaders including Trotsky.

## October

Zaleski quoted a contemporary official Soviet source as admitting that the metallurgical industry was the main bottleneck in the develop-ing economy.

## 10 October

Dneproges, the hydroelectric plant on the river Dnieper, was officially opened. According to the GSE, it reached its design capacity of 560 MW in 1939.

## 17 October

Pursuant to an undertaking on pref-erences given at the Imperial Eco-nomic Conference in Ottawa from 21 July to 4 August, the British govern-ment gave six months' notice of denunciation of the temporary Anglo-Soviet trade agreement of 16 April 1930.

## 8–9 November

Stalin's second wife, Nadezhda Alli-lueva, committed suicide.

## 10 November

The criminal code was amended to

make the conduct of commerce (i.e. the purchase and resale of goods) a criminal offence.

## 15 November

In response to the growing economic crisis, labour discipline was further tightened up. One day's absence from work was deemed to be grounds for instant dismissal plus loss of ration card and living accommodation, regardless of the time of year. In industry, piece-rates continued to replace time-rates and in the countryside, peasants who abandoned collective farms were denied land.

## 23 November

A Soviet–Polish conciliation convention was signed in Moscow.

## 29 November

A two-year Franco-Soviet non-aggression pact and a conciliation convention were signed in Paris. Negotiations had begun in June 1931 and a treaty was initialled on 29 August 1931. The French had insisted that the treaty should not be incompatible with French obligations to Poland, Romania and the League of Nations. At the same time there was French interest in the Red Army as a possible counter-weight to resurgent German militarism.

## 10 December

The Central Committee announced the suspension of admissions to the party and ordered a purge of the membership. This, it said, was necessitated by the remarkable growth in party membership and the low standard of the political education of many members, particularly in the countryside, who were not competent to resist 'the class enemy'.

Lewin (in Fitzpatrick's *Cultural Revolution*) mentioned a 'reduction of personnel' in 1932–3 in which 153,000 government officials were fired.

## 12 December

Sino-Soviet diplomatic relations were restored by an exchange of notes in Geneva. Both sides were given an incentive for this move by continuing Japanese military encroachment in Manchuria and the inauguration of the puppet 'Manchukuo' government there on 9 March.

## 17 December

The Council of People's Commissars decreed the formation of a Central Administration of the Northern Sea Route (*Glavsevmorputi*) to complete development of the Northern Sea Route from the White Sea to the Bering Strait and to take charge of all existing meteorological and radio stations in the Arctic.

## 27 December

An internal passport system, similar to the system which Lenin had condemned in Tsarist days, was introduced. Administration of the system was placed in the hands of the militia (police) over which the OGPU was given control. The system severely restricted the freedom of workers to move from job to job. Peasants, who were not given passports, were effectively tied to their collective or state farms.

## 31 December

The first five-year plan was deemed

to have been completed nine months ahead of schedule. Gregory and Stuart gave the following figures of percentage fulfilment of the targets of the first five-year plan according to official Soviet estimates, the figures in brackets being western estimates based on the work of Jasny, Zaleski and Nove: national income 92 per cent (70 per cent); industrial output 101 per cent (60–70 per cent); producer goods 128 per cent (72 per cent); consumer goods 81 per cent (46 per cent); agricultural production 58 per cent (50–52 per cent); labour productivity 65 per cent (36–42 per cent); retail trade (39 per cent).

About 61 per cent of households were said to have been collectivised at the end of the year, much the same proportion as at its beginning. Although the amount of grain extracted from the peasants in 1932–3 was only about 20 per cent down on the previous year, the position was aggravated by the government's decision to give priority to exports and the supply of the cities. The combination of collectivisation and other government actions induced a severe famine in many rural areas in 1932–3 (see March 1933).

The Japanese occupied Harbin, the headquarters of the Chinese Eastern railway.

During the year, work started on building the Moscow 'metro'.

# 1933

## 1 January

Party membership was given as 2,203,951 with 1,351,387 candidate members.

## 2 January

The Presidium of the All-Union Central Council of Trade Unions (AUCCTU) decided that piece-rates and performance quotas in industry were to be determined by management and that the approval of joint labour–management bodies was no longer required. This marked the final extinction of collective bargaining agreements and a further stage in the use of the trade unions by the regime to keep wage-rates down. In July, Veinberg, secretary of the AUCCTU, said that responsibility for decisions on wage systems and job standards must lie with plant administrators and technical managers. To suggest that unions should have as much say over wages as management was a 'leftist opportunist' distortion which undermined management and must be stopped.

## 7–12 January

The thirteenth and last joint plenary session of the Central Committee and the Central Control Commission heard a report from Stalin who extolled the results of the first five-year plan achieved in four years. He also accepted the third version of the second five-year plan whose growth targets had been scaled down to between 13 per cent and 14 per cent compared with 22 per cent for the first plan. The two following resolutions resulted from the meeting.

## 11 January

A resolution, recognising in effect the weakness of the party's existing organisations in the countryside, established political departments in the Machine Tractor Stations (MTS) as a means of exerting closer party supervision over collective farms to ensure that they met their commitments and to stamp out thieving. The chief of the political department was also the deputy director of the MTS. He was assisted by two deputies, one for party work (normally the OGPU representative) and the other for Komsomol affairs. The set-up gave rise to a series of jurisdictional conflicts: between the director of the MTS, who was supposed to run it on the principle of 'one-man management' and the head of the political department, who was responsible to the party for seeing that the MTS fulfilled its production plans; between the political departments and the local party organisations; and between the heads of political departments and their OGPU deputies to whose intelligence and security activities they were not privy. The system lasted officially only until 28 November 1934.

## 12 January

A joint resolution of the Central Committee and the Central Control Commission announced a party purge whose purpose was 'to ensure iron proletarian discipline . . . and to cleanse the party's ranks of all unreliable, unstable and hanger-on elements'.

A. P. Smirnov, former Commissar for Agriculture of the RSFSR, was charged with forming an anti-party group. He was expelled from the Central Committee and in December 1934 from the party. Smirnov and his group are said to have discussed the replacement of Stalin as General Secretary: a few years later, Smirnov was shot.

## 14 January

Bukharin published a far-reaching recantation stimulated, according to his own account, by the extreme dangers arising from peasant resistance, famine and the rise of Nazism in Germany.

## 24 January

The All-Union Central Committee censured the Ukrainian party for failures in the organisation of grain collection and storage. By the end of 1932 only 4.7 million tons of grain (or 72 per cent of the quota) had been delivered. Thereafter Postyshev was sent from Russia to the Ukraine

as Second Secretary with some 5,000 other officials.

## 30 January

Hitler was appointed German Chancellor.

## 5 February

A decree established that Machine Tractor Stations should receive 20 per cent of the grain harvest in kind in return for undertaking the basic agricultural work on a collective farm. This was used as another means of bringing pressure to bear on the peasantry.

## 12 February

A Central Committee resolution deplored the lack of basic school textbooks and directed that such textbooks should be prepared.

## 25 February

A Soviet–German credit agreement was signed in Berlin.

## 27 February

The Reichstag building in Berlin was set alight by a Dutchman, Van der Lubbe, who had been a communist. The communists were immediately blamed and during the night several hundred were arrested. Communist deputies countered with accusations that the fire was a Nazi provocation for which Göring was personally responsible.

## March onwards

Famine, which had appeared in the Ukraine in the spring of 1932, reached the peak of its severity in the spring and summer of 1933. The worst-affected zones were the grain-producing areas of the Ukraine, the North Caucasus, particularly the Kuban, the Middle and Lower Volga and Kazakhstan. Dalrymple hazarded a guess that famine caused 5 million deaths. Conquest's estimate in *The Harvest of Sorrow* was 5 million in the Ukraine, 1 million in the North Caucasus and 1 million elsewhere. In April 1987 Rosefielde defended an estimate of 4.2 million deaths from famine in 1933–4, his and Conquest's figures having been challenged by Wheatcroft who in his 1985 article suggested a maximum of 3 to 4 million deaths from famine. Famine returned in the autumn of 1933 and continued until the summer of 1934 though less information is available about this last period. Far from seeking external aid with the famine problem as in 1921, the regime took largely successful steps through censorship and travel control to prevent knowledge of the famine from spreading. Dalrymple and others attributed the famine to the regime's grain procurement policies designed to raise foreign exchange (grain was the largest food export), build up emergency supplies in the face of the Japanese threat, feed the urban population and extinguish peasant resistance to the regime.

## 2 March

Hitler publicly blamed the Reichstag fire on the Bolsheviks and launched a violent attack on Soviet domestic policy.

## 9 March

Dimitrov, the head of the Comintern's West European Bureau, and two Bulgarian colleagues were arrested and charged with complicity in the Reichstag fire.

## 11 March

The collegium of the OGPU examined the cases of seventy-five 'conspirators' in the commissariat responsible for agriculture and state farms who were accused of sabotage. It was announced on 12 March that thirty-five were sentenced to be shot, twenty-two to ten years' and eighteen to six years' imprisonment. The sentences had been carried out.

A number of employees of Metropolitan-Vickers Ltd in the USSR, including six British subjects, were arrested on espionage and sabotage charges.

## 12 March

The OGPU's right to order executions was legally established.

## 17 March

A decree laid down that a peasant could not leave a collective farm without a contract from his future employers ratified by the collective farm authorities.

## 27 March

The Japanese notified their intention to withdraw from the League of Nations. The Germans followed their example on 21 October. The withdrawals had a direct bearing on the Soviet decision to join the League in September 1934.

## 28 March

At a stormy meeting with Litvinov, the British ambassador in Moscow, Sir Esmond Ovey, warned him, on instructions from the British government, that if the British Metro-Vickers employees were tried Britain would impose an embargo on trade with the USSR. Ovey was recalled to London for consultations and left Moscow on 30 March.

## 1 and 24 April

The Prussian police raided the premises of the German–Russian Petroleum Company (Derop).

## 8 April

The Japanese-backed 'Manchukuo' authorities interrupted the flow of goods traffic from the Chinese Eastern railway to the Trans-Baikal line at Manchouli evoking a protest from the Soviet government on 16 April. On 31 May 'Manchukuo' imposed a similar ban at Pogranichnyi on the frontier with the Maritime Province and changed the name of the railway to the North Manchurian railway.

## 12 April

A coup unseated Chin Shu-jen, the governor of Sinkiang. Some White Russians whom Chin had engaged took part in the coup. Chin fled to Nanking and was imprisoned there for the concessions he had made to Moscow. General Sheng Shih-ts'ai who, according to his own account, had become a Marxist in 1919, succeeded Chin in effect though not named as governor.

## 12–18 April

At the trial of the Metro-Vickers employees, almost all the Soviet citizens and two British subjects were given prison sentences.

## 19 April

The British government proclaimed an embargo on about 80 per cent of normal imports of Soviet goods from 26 April in protest against the Metro-Vickers trial. On 21 April the Soviets retaliated with a similar embargo on British goods, published on 22 April.

## 29 April

*Izvestiia* named Rudzutak as chairman of a central purging commission appointed by the Central Committee to conduct the purge decreed on 12 January. Ezhov (a member of the Secretariat), Kaganovich and Kirov (both members of the Politburo) were among the seven other members of the purging commission. Rudzutak was head of the Central Control Commission which had conducted previous purges.

## 2 May

Bogomolov presented his credentials as ambassador to China.

Litvinov offered to sell Soviet rights in the Chinese Eastern railway to the Japanese, dismissing Chinese objections that the Soviets had no right to do so.

## 4 May

Budennyi told the newly arrived French military attaché, Colonel Mendras, that at Stalin's behest he had cancelled another engagement which he had accepted on Voroshilov's orders so as to be able to meet Mendras at a reception.

## 5 May

The Germans ratified their agreement of 24 June 1931 with the USSR, prolonging their neutrality pact of 24 April 1926 and conciliation agreement of 25 January 1929.

## 6 May

A Soviet–Italian credit agreement was signed in Rome.

## 8 May

A secret circular signed by Stalin and Molotov and addressed to all party, OGPU and judicial organs ordered an immediate end to the indiscriminate arrests by unauthorised individuals which had accompanied forced collectivisation: arrests were to be carried out only by the procuracy, the OGPU or the militia. The circular, which was found in the Smolensk party archives, ordered a reduction in the number of persons in places of detention other than camps and colonies from 800,000 to 400,000 within two months. The circular envisaged that 'especially dangerous elements' would be transferred to forced-labour camps. A further circular dated 25 May from the Central Control Commission and the Commissariat of Workers' and Peasants' Inspection said that mass arrests were still continuing and were causing intolerable overcrowding in places of imprisonment: the circular referred to a 'number of instances of extremely misdirected legal repression'.

## 8–28 May

The German General von Bockelberg visited the USSR at the invitation of Tukhachevskii. The visit passed off in the usual friendly atmosphere but was closely followed by a demand from the Red Army that the German army should wind up all its installations in the USSR. The Red Army refused to attend further courses at the German war academy. Soviet officials claimed that the Germans had leaked information about the Soviet–German liaison to the French. Although the initiative for termination at this moment may have come from the Soviet side, Carsten stated that Hitler also decreed that co-operation with the Red Army should be terminated.

## 18 May

The Franco-Soviet non-aggression pact was unanimously approved by the French Chamber of Deputies.

## 25 May

Kamenev, who, like Zinoviev, had been brought back from exile, published another confession of error in *Pravda* and called on all oppositionists in the party to cease resistance.

## 1 June

The purge ordered on 12 January officially began. It lasted until 26 December 1935. About 18 per cent of the total party membership, many of them recent recruits, were expelled. A further 15 per cent of the membership had either withdrawn voluntarily from the party or could not be traced. As in 1929 the majority of those expelled were accused of corruption, indiscipline, personal misconduct or passivity rather than opposition to the leadership. Getty quoted evidence of the central leadership's dissatisfaction with the conduct of the purge by local party leaders who appeared to be primarily concerned with protecting their own local interests and influence. The purge highlighted the chaotic state of local party records. The campaign to recruit new members having been wound down during 1932, recruitment ceased altogether until November 1936.

## 4–6 June

An anti-fascist workers' congress, instigated by Münzenberg, was held in the Salle Pleyel in Paris and attracted over 3,000 delegates. It set up a standing committee of anti-fascist workers which merged two months later with the anti-war bureau formed at the Amsterdam conference of 27 August 1932. Together they constituted the 'Amsterdam-Pleyel' movement which was active in 1934 and 1935 and contributed towards the reversion to united front tactics finally endorsed by the Seventh Comintern Congress in July–August 1935.

## 12 June

The World Economic Conference, held under League of Nations auspices, opened in London. Litvinov, who led the Soviet delegation, advocated a pact of 'economic non-aggression' which would do away with tariff wars, currency wars and all forms of trade discrimination or boycott.

## 16 June

Zinoviev, who had been readmitted to the party with Kamenev, published an article in *Pravda* condemning the opposition and praising Stalin.

## 20 June

The office of Procurator-General was established. Vyshinskii, though to begin with only First Deputy Procurator-General, was the leading figure in the office.

## 26 June

Negotiations over the sale of the Chinese Eastern railway opened in Tokyo but were discontinued in October.

## 1 July

The two imprisoned British Metro-Vickers employees were released. The mutual British and Soviet trade embargoes were lifted and negotiations for a new trade agreement were resumed.

## 3 July

Taking advantage of the World Economic Conference and as a follow-up to the Kellogg Pact, the USSR signed in London an eight-power convention on the definition of aggression with Afghanistan, Estonia, Latvia, Persia, Poland, Romania and Turkey. Finland adhered to the convention on 31 January 1934. Separate but similar agreements were signed by the USSR with Czechoslovakia, Romania, Turkey and Yugoslavia on 4 July and with Lithuania on 5 July.

## 7 July

Skrypnik, an Old Bolshevik and Commissar for Education in the Ukraine, committed suicide having come under heavy attack in June from Postyshev and others for displaying excessive Ukrainian national feeling. His death occurred in the course of a purge of leading Ukrainian figures, both party and non-party.

## 26 July

The Red Army having let it be known that none of their officers would be visiting Germany during the summer, the Germans informed the Soviets that their officers would not be attending Red Army exercises.

## 28 July

The USSR established diplomatic relations with Spain but missions were not exchanged, initially because of the death of the Soviet ambassador-designate, Lunacharskii, later because of Spanish objections to Comintern activities in Spain.

## 31 July

At a dinner given by the French ambassador in Moscow, Voroshilov raised the possibility of French help to the Soviet navy.

## 1 August

The Soviet Central Executive Committee and the Council of People's Commissars of the RSFSR approved a decree on the Corrective Labour Code of the RSFSR. It enumerated places of detention as

1. isolators for persons under investigation;
2. deportation prisons;
3. corrective colonies which might be factory or agricultural colonies for inculcating labour discipline, mass labour colonies with a more severe regime for class-hostile elements or penal colonies for persons who had shown systematic insubordination;
4. institutes for psychiatric examination and colonies for tubercular and other patients;
5. institutions for minors.

The decree also covered persons sentenced to exile with corrective labour in, for example, state institutions or on mass projects.

## 2 August

In a conversation with the French military attaché, Colonel Mendras, mainly about artillery, Tukhachevskii tried to enlist his help in negotiations with a French firm, hinting that a restoration of the pre–1914 relationship between the Russian army and French industry might be timely. At the end of October Mendras reported that the Soviets had given it to be understood that the place vacated by the Germans was there for the filling in military and economic terms.

The Baltic–White Sea canal was declared complete. Extensive use was made of forced labour in its construction. Dallin and Nicolaevsky estimated that at its peak the number of working prisoners employed on it reached 300,000.

## 18 August

This date was celebrated for the first time as Aviation Day. The Soviet press emphasised the importance of expanding the air forces of the USSR.

## 2 September

The USSR and Italy signed a five-year treaty of friendship, non-aggression and neutrality in Rome.

## 8 September

A Soviet–Greek trade and clearing agreement was signed in Athens. Similar agreements were signed or extended annually until the end of 1938.

## 12–21 September

Pierre Cot, the French Minister for Aviation, visited Kharkov, Kiev and Moscow and was shown aviation institutes, factories, laboratories, schools and so forth. Tukhachevskii explained to the Germans that the visit was justified by the Soviet command's understandable desire to get its own eyes on the French air force. A return visit was paid by a Soviet air mission which arrived in Paris on 7 August 1934. A French air mission spent six months in the USSR in 1934.

M. Herriot also visited the USSR during the first two weeks of September 1933.

## 21 September–23 December

The trial of those accused in connection with the Reichstag fire ended with a death sentence for Van der Lubbe and an acquittal for Dimitrov. Dimitrov's performance during the trial earned him the status of an international left-wing hero. Deprived of his Bulgarian citizenship, he was granted Soviet nationality and arrived in the USSR on 27 February 1934 to play an increasingly important role in the Comintern, using his influence in favour of a return to united front tactics in opposition to fascism and Nazism.

## 23 September

The Soviet government lodged a strong protest with the Japanese over their alleged instigation of a plot by the 'Manchukuo' authorities to use force to take control of the Chinese Eastern railway. Two days later six Soviet employees of the railway were arrested. This led to a further Soviet protest followed by Soviet publication of relevant Japanese documents whose authenticity was immediately denied by the Japanese authorities. The tougher Soviet line towards the Japanese seems to have owed something to an improvement in US–Soviet relations.

## 28 September

According to German documents the liquidation of German military installations in the USSR was completed.

## 10 October

President Roosevelt invited Kalinin, as the USSR's head of state, to send a representative to the United States to discuss the abnormal situation arising from the absence of diplomatic relations between the two powers.

## 7 November

Litvinov arrived in the United States in response to President Roosevelt's letter of 10 October.

## 16 November

The United States and Soviet governments exchanged notes effecting diplomatic recognition. In addition reciprocal pledges were given on abstention from interference or hostile propaganda activities by either country in the territory of the other. Assurances were given by the Soviet side on the protection and freedom of worship of US citizens in Soviet territory together with an explanation of the Soviet definition of the term 'economic espionage'. Other exchanges dealt with claims and counter-claims arising out of commercial transactions. The Soviets agreed to waive claims arising out of US military intervention in Siberia during the civil war.

## 17 & 19 November

Bullitt was appointed US ambassador in Moscow and Troianovskii was appointed Soviet ambassador in Washington.

## 19 November

Postyshev claimed that 2,000 nationalists, about 300 of them scientists and writers, had been purged from the Ukrainian Commissariat of Education, 200 from other central Ukrainian Soviet institutions and a further 2,000 from the co-operatives and grain reserve systems. The purge continued in the following years.

## 25 November

The GSE claims that the first Soviet rocket with a liquid propellant was launched. The first Soviet liquid-fuel rocket engines had been built by Glushko in 1930–1.

## December

According to Dallin, the Soviets reached a secret agreement with Sheng Shih-ts'ai, the governor of Sinkiang, providing him with Soviet military assistance in return for oil, gold and other mining concessions and the right to build a railway from Urumchi (Tihwa) to the Soviet border to link with the Turksib line. (The text of this agreement is not given in Shapiro or in Slusser and Triska.) The White Russians were purged from the Sinkiang administration, leaving Soviet influence predominant. Whiting stated that in January 1934 Soviet troops crossed the frontier to smash General Ma Chung-yin's rebel forces. By June 1934 the province had been pacified. General Ma Chung-yin, who had been strongly anti-communist, left for the USSR where he was given asylum and was well treated, perhaps with a view to using him in Sinkiang in the event of a further change in the regime.

## 4 December

The USSR and Latvia signed a treaty of commerce and an economic agreement in Moscow.

## 11 December

A decree gave wage increases and relief from compulsory deliveries of grain and other products for ten years to the inhabitants of eastern Siberia with a view to increasing its population and stabilising the area against the threat from the Japanese. In February 1934 similar decrees covered Transbaikalia and the Buriat-Mongolian Republic. (Other less striking privileges and incentives had been granted by a series of decrees from 1923 onwards.)

## 28 & 29 December

Speeches by Molotov and Litvinov to the Soviet Central Executive Committee both referred to the policy of eastward expansion of the Third Reich and connected it with Japanese policy. From a Soviet point of view the threat from Japan in the Far East looked the more immediate; that from Germany potentially more lethal in the longer term.

The 1933 harvest was a good one.

# 1934

## January

As the first move in an attempt to create an Eastern Security Pact, the Soviets persuaded the Poles to make simultaneous approaches with them to the Baltic states with a view to guaranteeing the independence of the latter. The Baltic states in general showed reluctance to accept guarantees from the USSR and Poland alone. In March therefore, Litvinov approached the Germans who showed no interest in the project. (See May below.)

## 1 January

Party membership was given as 1,826,756 with 874,252 candidate members.

## 11 January

A provisional Franco-Soviet trade agreement was signed in Paris: it was modified and prolonged on 6 January 1936. The agreement seems to have been intended to mark closer Franco-Soviet political relations at least as much as to secure an increase in trade.

## 13 January

The system of advanced university degrees, which had been abolished on 1 October 1918, was to some extent restored: several academic ranks and two advanced academic degrees were reintroduced. Up to 1925 'professorial scholarships' and thereafter 'aspirantura' training had provided partial substitutes for the old system of higher degrees.

## 26 January

Hitler concluded a ten-year non-aggression pact with Poland.

## 26 January–10 February

The party's Seventeenth Congress ('The Congress of Victors') was held against the background of the successful harvest of 1933. In his report on the work of the Central Committee, Stalin said that a new imperialist war was coming. It would certainly unleash revolution and place the very existence of capitalism in question in a number of countries as happened during the first imperialist war. He denied that the establishment of the fascist regime in Germany was responsible for the improvement of Soviet relations with France and Poland or that the USSR had become a supporter of the Versailles Treaty. While the Soviets were 'far from enthusiastic' about the fascist regime, fascism itself was not the issue: fascism in Italy had not prevented the USSR from establishing the best of

279

relations with that country. The difficulty in Soviet–German relations arose from the fact that an anti-Russian line was prevailing in Germany over the old line embodied in the Soviet–German treaties.

Stalin said that in the three years since the Sixteenth Congress, the USSR had been transformed from a backward agrarian country into an industrial country; from a land of small individual holdings into a land of large-scale, collectivised, mechanised agriculture; from an illiterate, uncultured society into an increasingly literate and cultured society. At the same time there were defects in Soviet performance. In industry the list of defects was headed by the lag in the iron and steel industries; poor quality, low productivity and lack of consumer goods were among other defects mentioned. Agriculture had developed more slowly than industry and over half the nation's livestock had been lost since the beginning of collectivisation in 1929. Stalin referred to the liquidation of the Trotskyite, right-wing and nationalist opposition groups, most of which had capitulated and recognised that the general line of the party was correct: 'At this congress, there is nothing more to prove and, it seems, no-one to fight.' Industrialisation, collectivisation and the liquidation of the kulaks had proved that it was possible for socialism to achieve victory in one country. However, Stalin warned that traces of the ideologies of the opposition groups were still to be found in the party; in the Ukraine, the nationalist deviation had become the main danger.

Stalin claimed that nine-tenths of the country's defects and failures were due to the lack of a properly organised system for checking on the fulfilment of decisions. He attacked regional party chiefs for their inadequate response to central party directives and their 'bureaucratism' deriving from their refusal to conduct self-criticism or to permit criticism from below. What was needed was a Soviet Control Commission under the USSR Council of People's Commissars whose members would be nominated by the party congress and endorsed by the Council of People's Commissars and the Soviet Central Executive Committee. The party's Central Control Commission had been set up to avert a split in the party. That danger was over. The new requirement was for a Party Control Commission under the Central Committee (i.e. in practice under the Secretariat) whose members would be elected by the congress and which would control the fulfilment of decisions. In Getty's analysis, the struggle of the central party leadership to impose its will on the recalcitrant periphery was a central feature of the next three and a half years.

Stalin claimed that the civil defence and paramilitary organisation *Osoaviakhim* had over 12 million members.

Kuibyshev's report listed the principal economic tasks of the second five-year plan as: the improvement of transport; the improvement of several branches of heavy industry including ferrous and non-ferrous metallurgy, oil, chemicals and coal mechanisation; and the improvement of the well-being of the workers.

The resolution on the reports of Molotov and Kuibyshev said that the principle task of the second five-year plan was the reconstruction of the whole national economy: mastery of technique was the decisive condition for success.

The resolution on organisational questions dissolved the Commissariat of Workers' and Peasants' Inspection (*Rabkrin*) and transferred its apparatus to the new Soviet Control Commission of the Council of People's Commissars. The Central Control Commission became the Party Control Commission. The resolution also tightened up the rules on admission to the party: new members would require more recommendations from existing party members who had to be of longer standing. Groups of 'sympathisers' who submitted to party decisions without being members were to be set up.

Former opposition leaders including Bukharin, Zinoviev, Kamenev, Lominadze, Preobrazhenskii, Piatakov, Radek, Rykov and Tomskii all spoke in praise of Stalin and acknowledged their past errors. But Bukharin took the opposite line to Stalin on fascism, insisting that Hitler's anti-bolshevism and designs on Russian territory, together with the Japanese threat in the Far East, had to be taken seriously.

Piatakov was elected to the Central Committee of seventy-one members; Bukharin, Rykov and Tomskii were among the sixty-eight candidate members elected. Of the 1,966 delegates at the congress, 1,108 were to be shot during the next few years.

The congress adopted the second five-year plan which was supposed to have been in operation since 1 January 1933 and which was published on 17 November 1934. In delivering the main report on the plan, Molotov announced a projected annual rate of industrial growth of 18.9 per cent, despite the decision in January 1933

to go for a rate of between 13 per cent and 14 per cent. Ordzhonikidze challenged Molotov's figure and proposed 16.5 per cent which was accepted by an ad hoc commission in closed session.

According to Nove the three guiding principles of the plan were consolidation (mainly the bringing into use of unfinished projects, especially in the Urals, Siberia and Kazakhstan), the mastering of technique and an effort to improve living standards. In practice the last principle was again sacrificed in the interest of investment in heavy industry, partly to meet the increased needs of defence. High growth rates were achieved in the years 1934–6 as some of the grandiose projects of the first five-year plan, such as the Urals–Kuznetsk Combine, came into production (see 25 January 1931).

The expansion of industry in the Urals and Siberia, begun during the first five-year plan, was also a feature of the second five-year plan, the Caucasus and Central Asia being included as well. Altogether, 25 per cent of proposed capital investment under the second plan was to be devoted to the industrialisation of Asiatic Russia.

The need to improve the political education of party members, roughly half of whom according to Rudzutak did not even read the party press, was a prominent theme of the congress. Kirov claimed that the main task of the party was the propagation of Marxism-Leninism and that most of the problems confronting the party could be solved by better political education of the membership. Getty pointed out that Stalin, Kirov and Zhdanov were associated together in shifting the emphasis towards increased political work for party members at the expense of their direct involvement in economic activity.

At the Central Committee plenum immediately after the congress, Stalin, Molotov, Kaganovich, Voroshilov, Kalinin, Ordzhonikidze, Kuibyshev, Kirov, Andreev and Kosior were elected to the Politburo. Mikoyan, Chubar', Petrovskii, Postyshev and Rudzutak were elected candidate members.

The Secretariat consisted of Stalin, Kaganovich, Kirov and Zhdanov, head of the Nizhny Novgorod (Gorky) party organisation. Kaganovich became head of the Party Control Commission with Ezhov as his deputy.

A 'special section' of the Central Committee was set up under Poskrebyshev, the head of Stalin's private secretariat.

Soviet sources including Roy Medvedev have alleged that a group of party leaders from the regions and non-Russian party committees discussed with Kirov the possibility of his replacing Stalin as General Secretary. Kirov is said to have refused either to help get rid of Stalin or to be elected General Secretary himself. *Moscow News*, the weekly publication of the Union of Soviet Societies for Friendship and Cultural Relations with Foreign Countries and the *Novosti* press agency, stated on 27 November 1988 that Stalin had polled 300 votes fewer than Kirov at the Seventeenth Congress.

*Note*: Argument over the reliability of the evidence of the emergence of serious opposition to Stalin at the Seventeenth Congress is likely to continue.

## 4–6 February

The Soviet and Hungarian governments established diplomatic relations.

## 13 February

The ice-breaker *Cheliuskin* was crushed by ice and sank in the Arctic en route from Leningrad to Vladivostok. Professor Shmidt and his scientific colleagues were saved by a dramatic air rescue operation.

## 16 February

A temporary Anglo-Soviet trade agreement was signed which aimed at a rough balance in trade between the two countries by 1937.

## 21 February

Bukharin was appointed editor of *Izvestiia*.

## 26 February

The Soviets made a new offer on the sale of the Chinese Eastern railway, the Soviet railway employees who had been imprisoned in Manchuria (see 23 September 1933) having been released.

## 15 March

A decree gave military commanders responsibility for both the military and political training of their troops. Political commissars were renamed political leaders or *politruks* and subordinated to the military commanders.

## 4 April

The Soviet–Lithuanian, Soviet–Latvian and Soviet–Estonian non-aggression pacts of 28 September 1926, 5 February and 4 May 1932 were prolonged until the end of 1945.

## 7 April

The Soviet–Finnish non-aggression pact of 21 January 1932 was prolonged until the end of 1945.

## 23 April

A Central Committee resolution condemned the overloading of schoolchildren and Pioneers with social and political tasks.

## May

Litvinov discussed with the French a Franco-Soviet pact which would form part of a wider multilateral pact of consultation, non-aggression and mutual support embracing France, the USSR, Poland, Germany, Czechoslovakia and the Baltic states. France made its agreement conditional on the USSR joining the League of Nations and guaranteeing the Locarno pact.

## 5 May

The Soviet–Polish non-aggression pact of 25 July 1932 was prolonged until the end of 1945. Naval and air visits were exchanged between the two countries during the year but by its end relations had again deteriorated, Poland having veered towards Germany.

## 7 May

The Birobidzhan Jewish National Area became the Jewish Autonomous District within the Far Eastern Region.

## 15 May

The Council of People's Commissars and the Central Committee issued a decree 'On the teaching of civic history in the schools of the USSR'. The decree rejected the approach associated with the leading Marxist historian, Pokrovskii, who had died in 1932. His account of Russian history in terms of economic and sociological processes was considered too abstract, too negative in its portrayal of the Tsarist regime as backward and oppressive and inadequate in its coverage of events and of the role of the individual in history, all of which was inconsistent with Stalin's desire to revive and exploit traditional Russian patriotism. Although Pokrovskii was not denounced by name until 27 January 1936, most of his associates lost their positions, his works were discarded and Shestakov's *History of the USSR* was adopted as the new textbook. A new wave of historical novels extolled Russia's past military heroes and national achievements.

## 2 June

Stalin ordered a tightening of the tax screw on individual peasants in order to ensure the uninterrupted growth of collectivisation, which was said to have covered 70 per cent of peasant households in 1934.

## 8 June

A Soviet Central Executive Committee decree on treason to the fatherland (which covered espionage, desertion and flight abroad carrying the death sentence) provided that the close relatives of a traitor, even if ignorant of his offence, should be liable to punishment by deprivation of voting rights and five years' exile in Siberia.

Romania and Czechoslovakia (which were associated with France in the 'Little Entente') established diplomatic relations with the USSR.

## 20 June

A decree of the Council of People's Commissars set up a new People's Commissariat of Defence in the place of the old Commissariat of the Army and Navy. Voroshilov was made commissar. The Supreme Military Council was reduced in status to a consultative body. During the year it was decided that the armed forces should be expanded to a strength of 940,000 with a greatly increased budget.

## 30 June

On the 'night of the long knives', Hitler launched the 'blood purge' of some of his most ardent former supporters. According to Krivitsky, Stalin insisted that this would strengthen Hitler's regime.

## End of June

The French outlined to the British the discussions they had been having with Litvinov. The British commented that the French and the Soviets should both enter into the same commitments to the Germans as they had made to one another. Barthou, the French Foreign Minister, having accepted this idea, the British undertook to recommend the scheme to the Polish and German governments. In due course both these governments responded negatively to the British approach and by November it

was clear that the idea of a multilateral pact was stillborn.

## 10 July

The OGPU was absorbed into a reorganised People's Commissariat for Internal Affairs (NKVD) with Iagoda at its head. The intelligence and security functions of the OGPU were inherited by the Main Administration of State Security (GUGB) within the NKVD which was also responsible for the militia (police), border and internal NKVD troops, corrective labour camps, register offices, fire guards and, later, other functions such as survey and cartography, forest guards, highways, population transfers, archives, hydrotechnical and railway construction.

*Note*: The security and intelligence service is usually referred to as the 'NKVD' from 1934 to 1941, the obsolete term OGPU also being frequently used. Strictly speaking, GUGB would be more accurate but the more familiar term 'NKVD' will be used below for the years in question.

## 11 July

*Pravda* stressed the importance of the dissolution of the special OGPU tribunal and the establishment of a 'single court system'. This apparent reform was negated by the setting-up at the same time of an NKVD 'Special Board', an 'administrative organ' entitled to pass sentences of imprisonment, corrective labour or exile on persons considered 'socially dangerous'. The NKVD also had the power to detain persons without formally arresting them. The 'Special Board' seems to have dealt with the majority of political cases. In the provinces, 'troikas' of the local party first secretary, an NKVD representative and a prosecutor had the power to pass death sentences.

## 23 July

Soviet–Bulgarian diplomatic relations were established.

## 17 August–1 September

The First Congress of the Union of Soviet Writers, set up by the resolution of 23 April 1932, was held in Moscow. Zhdanov, the chief government spokesman, said that Soviet literature could not be other than tendentious: in the age of class struggle, non-class, non-tendentious, apolitical literature could not exist. Literature should portray Soviet heroes and look to the future. Zhdanov's speech was followed by self-criticism from Vsevolod Ivanov and other 'fellow-travellers'.

Special attention was paid to the need for heroic national defence literature to boost the martial spirit of the Red Army.

Bukharin delivered a long address on Soviet poetry, in which he referred to the danger that the compulsory directives the party had been issuing since 1929 would inhibit artistic development for which freedom and diversity were essential. He praised a number of lyrical poets including Boris Pasternak and said that Soviet poetry should move forward from the propaganda poetry of the post-revolutionary period and reflect the growing complexity of life. Pasternak, who attended the congress, subsequently implied that an effort had been made to win him over to the regime's point of view.

Radek denied that the attempts of bourgeois writers like Proust, Joyce and Dos Passos to find new forms had anything important to offer Soviet authors in comparison with the 'highway of socialist realism'.

The statutes of the union were published in advance and there was no general debate on them. There were substantial communist majorities on all the union's governing bodies. The union's Second Congress was not held until 1954.

## 12 September

A tripartite Baltic Pact on co-operation was signed in Geneva between Estonia, Latvia and Lithuania.

## 17 September

Albania re-established diplomatic relations with the USSR.

## 18 September

The League of Nations adopted a resolution against the votes of Portugal, Holland and Switzerland to admit the USSR to membership. As a great power the USSR was awarded a permanent seat on the League's Council. Membership of the League carried with it membership of the International Labour Organisation (ILO) but Soviet participation in the ILO was minimal.

## 20 September

The ice-breaker *Litke* arrived at Murmansk, completing the first unbroken east–west voyage round the north coast of Siberia: she had left Vladivostok on 28 June. In 1935 four ships made through passages by the Northern Sea Route: in 1936 the number rose to fourteen.

**ber**

...na Goldfields Company
...agreement with the Soviets
...laim for compensation.

# 7 November

One of the party slogans on the anniversary of the revolution was 'let us put an end to egalitarian tendencies in pay'. Wage differentials, together with the privileges of party membership, were already leading to a new class stratification of Soviet society.

# 17 November

The final text of the second five-year plan covering the years 1933 to 1937 was published. Production targets had been further reduced since the plan variant of early 1932, which itself represented a drastic scaling-down of Kuibyshev's targets of 11 May 1931. The corresponding figures were: 38 billion kWh of electric power, 152.5 million tons of coal, 46.8 million tons of crude oil and gas, 16 million tons of pig-iron, 80,000 tons of aluminium, 135,000 tons of refined copper, a total sown area of 139.7 million hectares and 65.5 million head of cattle. The delay in approving the plan, its internal inconsistencies, the lack of correlation between the goals and results of the annual plans and those of the five-year plan itself and the constant modification of the plans were among the factors which persuaded Zaleski that at no time was the second five-year plan 'operational'. Nevertheless, high growth rates were achieved in 1934 after the slow-down in 1931 to 1933. Western estimates quoted by Zaleski of the growth rate for gross industrial production for this year are

not far removed from the Soviet claim of 17.4 per cent.

# 27 November

An oral Soviet–Mongolian 'gentleman's agreement' was reached on mutual aid in the event of an attack on either party.

# 28 November

At a Central Committee plenum, the political departments of the Machine Tractor Stations (see 11 January 1933) were abolished because of friction between them and the party's rural district committees. In some cases the political departments became the district committees of newly established districts: most became subordinate units of existing district committees.

# 1 December

Kirov, the secretary of the Leningrad party committee and a member of the Politburo, was assassinated by Leonid Nikolaev, a young disaffected communist. At the time Nikolaev was described by the regime as a follower of Zinoviev and Kamenev who were accused of 'moral complicity' in the assassination. In 1936 Zinoviev and Kamenev were said to have ordered the killing. In 1938 it was said that these two together with Trotsky had given the order and that Iagoda, the head of the NKVD, had arranged for the assassin to have access to party headquarters in Leningrad where the killing took place. Using later evidence from Khrushchev and other sources, Conquest, in *The Great Terror*, concluded that Stalin, thwarted by the more moderate members of the Politburo in his desire to liquidate Riutin and other opponents in the party, organised the assassination of Kirov in order to provide himself with a pretext for conducting the great purges of the next few years. Roy Medvedev described Stalin's guilt in the assassination as 'logically and politically almost proved'. Getty, on the other hand, challenged the evidence for supposing that there was a 'moderate' group in the Politburo headed by Kirov: given the evidence that Stalin, Kirov and Zhdanov were allies in attacking bureaucratism and improving ideological work, he disputed the idea that Stalin had a motive for disposing of Kirov.

## 2 December

A decree dated 1 December was published establishing special procedures for the investigation and trial of terrorist acts. The investigation was to be concluded within ten days, the indictment was to be handed to the accused twenty-four hours before the trial, the case was to be heard without the participation of the defendant or his counsel, appeals and petitions for mercy were forbidden and the death sentence was to be carried out immediately on the rendering of judgment. The decree was approved by the Politburo on the following day. While Conquest saw the decree as evidence of a pre-planned crescendo of Stalinist terror, Getty saw it as a confused and panicky reaction to the assassination and claimed that the decree was little used in practice. In his view, once the immediate wave of post-assassination killings was over, the period up to 29 July 1936 was characterised, not by a purge of opposition elements but by a campaign for party democracy designed to increase the participation of the party rank and file in political life and to use them against the deeply entrenched local party satraps.

## 5 December

In Leningrad thirty-seven, and in Moscow thirty-three 'White Guards' were sentenced to death for the 'preparation and organisation of terrorist acts against officials of the Soviet regime'.

An agreement was signed in Geneva between Litvinov and the French Foreign Minister, Laval, to the effect that neither party would enter into negotiations with other powers which might prejudice the proposed Eastern Pact without first consulting the other. Czechoslovakia acceded to the agreement on 7 December.

## 13 December

Twenty-eight Ukrainians were sentenced to death in Kiev on the same charge as those sentenced on 5 December. It is believed that thousands of other political suspects throughout the country were arrested without publicity at this time.

## 16 December

Zinoviev and Kamenev were arrested.

Zhdanov succeeded Kirov as head of the Leningrad party committee.

## 29 December

Kirov's assassin, Nikolaev, and thirteen alleged accomplices and members of an oppositionist 'Leningrad Centre' were reported to have been sentenced to death and executed.

# 1935

## 1 January

Party membership was given as 1,659,104 with 699,610 candidates members.

Bread-rationing was abolished but its price was sharply increased.

## 15–16 January

Zinoviev, Kamenev and seventeen other members of the 'Moscow Centre' were tried in Leningrad and sentenced to imprisonment for terms of between five and ten years for their 'moral and political responsibility' for the assassination of Kirov. The Latvian consul-general in Leningrad and the German government were said to have been implicated. A further wave of arrests and deportations from the Leningrad area, 'conservatively estimated' by the British embassy at 30,000, followed the trial and accounted for most of the remaining 'bourgeois elements' in the area. Getty, quoting *Leningradskaia Pravda*, listed over a thousand such cases including former members of the nobility, industrialists and Tsarist officials.

## 16 January

Enukidze, secretary of the Soviet Central Executive Committee and responsible for the administration of the Kremlin, published a self-critical article in *Pravda* on his role in the civil war.

## 18 January

The Central Committee issued a circular (referred to in the top secret circular of 29 July 1936) on the lessons of the Kirov assassination calling for vigilance against hostile elements in the party and for increased political education of the membership in party history as a means of heightening that vigilance.

## 23 January

Twelve leading members of the Leningrad NKVD were tried in connection with the Kirov assassination and received comparatively light sentences.

## 25 January

Kuibyshev, the head of Gosplan, died, allegedly of heart disease.

## 28 January–6 February

Molotov, chairman of the Council of People's Commissars, addressing the Seventh All-Union Congress of Soviets, drew attention to the passages in Hitler's book *Mein Kampf* on the need for Germany to acquire by conquest new territory from Russia and her border states. He described rumours of the Sovietisation of Sinkiang as Japanese-inspired slander.

The congress authorised the drafting of democratic amendments to the constitution providing for direct elections by secret ballot and equal representation for peasants and workers, i.e. for rural and urban districts. Bukharin and Radek were both members of the drafting commission headed by Stalin as were Molotov and Zhdanov. Bukharin claimed to have done most of the drafting.

Tukhachevskii announced that the planned increase in the strength of the Red Army from 562,000 to 940,000 had been achieved. The number of tanks in service is believed to have reached about 7,000 in 1935.

## 31 January

Soviet–US negotiations on pre-revolutionary Russian debts and other financial claims which had begun a year earlier were broken off. Immediately afterwards the staff of the US embassy in Moscow was sharply reduced, the consulate-general being closed and the air and naval attachés and some diplomatic staff being withdrawn.

## 1 February

The Central Committee elected Mikoyan and Chubar' to the Politburo in place of Kirov and Kuibyshev. Zhdanov and Eikhe were elected to candidate membership.

## 11–13 February

The Second All-Union Congress of *Kolkhoz* Shock-workers adopted model regulations for the standard

*artel* type of collective farm. The regulations were confirmed by the Council of People's Commissars and the Central Committee on 17 February. Under them, farms undertook to abide by plans established by the 'worker–peasant government' and, as the first charge on their production, to fulfil their obligations to the state, including paying the Machine Tractor Stations in kind. After all these obligations had been met, the remainder of the product was to be divided between the members of the collective according to the number of 'labour-days' worked, a 'labour-day' being defined, not in hours worked, but in terms of so much land ploughed or grain threshed, etc. Each peasant household was allowed a private plot normally of not more than half a hectare and some livestock. The highest organ of the collective farm was the general meeting which elected the chairman and a board of five to nine members to act for it between general meetings. The collective undertook to hand over to the courts wreckers and thieves of collective property. In the course of 1935 the percentage of farms collectivised was said to have gone up from 75 per cent to 90 per cent.

## 23 February

Ezhov became head of the Party Control Commission as well as being a member of the Secretariat.

## 7 March

A circular ordered the removal from all libraries of all the works of Trotsky, Zinoviev and Kamenev. Preobrazhenskii, Shliapnikov, Lunacharskii and many others were added to the list of forbidden authors later in the year.

## 9 March

*Pravda* announced the appointment of Khrushchev as first secretary of the Moscow party organisation.

## 23 March

Despite a further protest from the Chinese on 11 March, agreements covering transfer of ownership of the Chinese Eastern railway to 'Manchukuo' were signed in Tokyo between 'Manchukuo', Japan and the USSR.

## 25 March

The USSR and Czechoslovakia signed a treaty of commerce and navigation in Prague.

## 27–31 March

Anthony Eden, Lord Privy Seal, visited the USSR and had conversations with Stalin, Molotov and Litvinov. A joint communiqué was issued in favour of collective security in conformity with the principles of the League of Nations: it noted that there was no conflict of interest between the Soviet and British governments on any of the main issues of international policy and looked forward to collaboration in the cause of peace.

## 7 April

Children of 12 and over were made liable to all penalties, including the death penalty. The measure related to the still unsolved problem of homeless and delinquent children which had afflicted Soviet society as a result of war, revolution, civil war

and famine. It was also relevant to show-trials in that the threatening and taking of reprisals against the wives and children of those under interrogation by the NKVD was one important means of extracting confessions.

## 9 April

An agreement was signed for a German credit to the USSR of 200 million marks over five years. Negotiations had been opened on German initiative.

## 2 May

The USSR and France concluded a five-year pact under which they undertook to come to each other's aid in the event of aggression against either of them in contravention of the League of Nations' covenant, even if the League of Nations Council failed to make any recommendation. The protocol of signature made it clear that the pact was seen as part of the intended wider security system for Eastern Europe which was not in the event to be established. The pact was not followed by a military convention as desired by the Soviet side.

## 4 May

Stalin made a speech on 'socialist humanism' introducing the slogan 'cadres decide everything'. The first five-year plan having solved the problem of creating a technical base, the pressing need was to develop adequate human cadres in every sphere of life. The speech stressed the importance of better training, greater incentives to production, personal cleanliness and a rehabilitation of family values. It introduced a slight cultural 'thaw'; for example, landscape-painting and New Year (the equivalent of Christmas) trees were no longer to be considered ideologically objectionable. The speech foreshadowed the Stakhanovite campaign (see 31 August) and marked a further stage in the revival of emphasis on nationalistic, patriotic and pan-Russian themes which was to continue through the pre-war and Second World War periods. Getty saw the speech as a landmark in the party leadership's drive to activate the party rank and file against the 'bureaucratism' of the local party bosses.

## 13 May

The Central Committee ordered a 'verification' of party documents by local party secretaries. Getty dated the decision to conduct the 'verification' back to October 1934 (i.e. before the Kirov assassination) and related it to the continuing chaos in party records and party management which had allowed undesirables of all types to claim party membership. Responsibility for order in party records lay with the Central Committee's Department of Leading Party Organs (ORPO) of which Ezhov was in charge.

## 15 May

The first line of the Moscow 'metro' opened.

## 16 May

The USSR signed a treaty of mutual assistance with Czechoslovakia similar to the one signed with France on 2 May, except that the provisions for mutual assistance would come into force only if France came to the help of the country attacked.

A communiqué on the visit to Moscow from 13 to 15 May of Laval, the French Foreign Minister, recognised the common obligation of states interested in the preservation of peace 'not to allow their means of national defence to weaken in any respect'. Stalin fully approved France's policy of maintaining her armed forces at a level corresponding with the needs of her security. After the Seventh Comintern Congress in July and August, this induced the French communist party to call off its campaign against lengthening the period of military service in France to two years.

## 25 May

The Central Committee decreed the abolition of the Society of Old Bolsheviks which had been allowed a certain latitude in criticising the party line, for example, on death sentences for members of the party opposition.

## May/June

Army Commander Alksnis, who had been in command of all air forces since June 1931, became chief of the Department of the Air Forces, losing operational control to the army commanders of the districts in which the air forces were located.

## 5–7 June

At a Central Committee meeting, Enukidze was expelled from the Central Committee and the party for 'political and personal dissoluteness' and banished to his birthplace, Tiflis. He had been close to Stalin and the real reasons for his expulsion remain uncertain.

### 25 June

The Society of Former Political Prisoners (Political Ex-Convicts and Exiles) was disbanded.

Colombia and the USSR established diplomatic relations.

### 10 July

A Central Committee report on the 'verification' of party documents was highly critical of many local party organisations for carrying out the procedure hastily and superficially. In some districts the procedure was to be repeated a second or even a third time.

### 13 July

Notes on Soviet–US trade constituting a commercial agreement valid for one year were signed and exchanged. Similar exchanges took place annually up to 1941. The US share of the USSR's total imports rose from $15 million (7.7 per cent) in 1934 to $70 million (28.5 per cent) in 1938. US imports from the USSR doubled from $12 million to $24 million in the same period.

Belgium established diplomatic relations with the USSR, followed by Luxemburg on 26 August. A temporary commercial agreement was signed in Paris on 5 September between the USSR and the Belgium-Luxemburg Economic Union.

### 25 July–20 August

The Seventh (and last) Comintern Congress in Moscow was attended by 510 delegates (371 with votes) from seventy-six parties, nineteen of them

sympathising parties which did not qualify for membership. Stalin was present at the opening session and was elected to the Executive Committee. Dimitrov delivered the keynote speech calling for unity of the working class against fascism as the basis of a broad anti-fascist popular front. (The term 'popular front' had been used in France since the previous October and implied collaboration with bourgeois as well as working-class parties.) The resolution on Dimitrov's report set the Comintern's seal of approval on the reversion to united front tactics which the French, Italian and some Latin American communist parties had already anticipated by reaching agreements with their respective socialist parties during the latter part of 1934. The course had also been charted by the 'front organisations' such as the 'Amsterdam-Pleyel' movement (see 4–6 June 1933). Dimitrov was elected Secretary-General of the Comintern, the other secretaries being Manuil'skii, Kuusinen, Togliatti, Pieck, Marty and Gottwald.

The resolution on the Executive Committee's report instructed the Executive Committee to concentrate on providing guidance on the fundamental political and tactical lines of the international movement and to avoid as a general rule intervention in the internal affairs of the communist parties. These were to be helped with advice and training so that they could achieve greater flexibility in finding and adopting the correct responses to their local conditions, avoiding the mechanical application of stereotyped methods.

The British and US ambassadors in Moscow protested against Soviet propaganda activities on 19 and 25 August respectively.

## August

An international conference on physiology was held in Moscow. During 1935 Soviet scientists were permitted to attend international scientific conferences abroad in greater numbers than before.

## 27 August

A new treaty of settlement, commerce and navigation was signed by the USSR and Iran over whose trade the USSR had been making a systematic bid to gain control. In effect the treaty closed the Caspian Sea to vessels or seamen of any nation other than the USSR and Iran.

## 31 August

The Soviet press reported that a coal-hewer in the Donets basin named Aleksei Stakhanov had hewed 102 tons of coal in one shift, overfulfilling his quota by 1,400 per cent. He was heavily decorated and used as a model for socialist emulation by other workers whose exertions were often used as the pretext for setting higher production norms.

## 22 September

The Red Army staff was renamed the General Staff of the Workers–Peasants' Red Army and ranks from lieutenant to marshal, omitting the rank of general, were reintroduced. The ranks below that of marshal were designated as 'army commanders (first and second class), corps commanders and divisional commanders'. The navy continued to use the term 'flagman' instead of 'admiral'. Senior and middle-grade officers were given extra privileges including immunity from arrest by the civil authorities without special dispensation from the Defence Commissar. The first marshals were Voroshilov, Tukhachevskii, Egorov, Budennyi and Bliukher.

## 25 September

The Communist International of Youth held a congress in Moscow.

## 1 October

The rationing of meat, fats, fish, sugar and potatoes was abandoned. Rationing of cotton goods, leather and rubber footwear and cigarettes was abolished at the end of the year.

## 10 October

By fifty votes to one, the League of Nations Assembly agreed to take collective measures against Italy for its actions in Abyssinia. The USSR supported the imposition of sanctions and immediately cut off shipments to Italy of embargoed products such as iron ore, manganese and chromium. However, trade in other commodities was stepped up so that the overall volume of Soviet–Italian trade was little affected.

## 7 November

The Soviet–Turkish friendship and neutrality treaty of 17 December 1925 and the protocols of 17 December 1929, 7 March and 30 October 1931 were extended until 7 November 1945.

## 27 November

An unsuccessful uprising led by the

communist Luiz Carlos Prestes took place in Brazil. Litvinov stoutly denied Soviet involvement but the Brazilian inquiry into the rising's origins had little difficulty in demonstrating that it was the work of the National Liberation Alliance, a creature of the Brazilian communist party and the Comintern.

## 1 December

It was announced that, in pursuance of the decision of 13 May, 81.1 per cent of party members had been screened and 9.1 per cent expelled from the party.

## 8 and 10 December

In articles in *Izvestiia*, Bukharin wrote that 'socialist humanism' meant a concern for all-round development, for a many-sided material and spiritual life: it meant a society in which the criterion was the 'freedom of maximum development of the maximum number of people'. These were two of many articles on the theme of 'socialist humanism' published by Bukharin in the 1934–6 period, drawing attention to the brutalising effect of coercion under fascism. The relevance to Stalinism of his critique of fascism was obvious.

## 25 December

The Central Committee issued a resolution calling for the acceptance and further extension of the Stakhanovite movement and the setting of new production norms making widespread use of Stakhanovite cadres.

Ezhov reported to the Central Committee on the 'verification' of party documents. Although only 81.1 per cent of the membership had passed through the procedure which had taken over six months instead of the two or three intended, Ezhov claimed that party organisational work had improved. Nevertheless, an exchange of party documents was ordered between 1 February and 1 May 1936 to replace worn-out party cards and to review borderline cases for expulsion or reinstatement.

## 28 December

An Uruguayan note broke off diplomatic relations with the USSR in protest at the support given to communist activities in Brazil by the Soviet legation in Montevideo. The Uruguayan note referred to the transmission by the legation of large sums of money by cheque, 'the destination of which could not be determined'. The Soviet government protested against the Uruguayan action to the League of Nations Council on 23 January 1936.

## 29 December

A decree of the Soviet Central Executive Committee and the Council of People's Commissars formally dropped social criteria (i.e. consideration of a child's parentage) in selection for higher education. According to Fitzpatrick, this factor had been of decreasing importance for the two previous years.

# 1936

## 1 January

Party membership was given as 1,489,907 with 586,935 candidate members.

According to Dallin, a further Soviet agreement with Sinkiang included clauses under which the parties agreed to exclude foreign influences. The Soviets undertook to assist Sinkiang politically, economically and militarily if it was attacked and to support it if it should declare its independence. Economic links were strengthened: oil wells were drilled and a refinery was built; trade was reoriented towards the USSR. In 1937 it was agreed that the Soviets should build a road across Sinkiang to Lanchow and Szechwan. This eventually became a military supply route.

In his *Soviet Treaty Series*, Shapiro gave the text of an agreement of this date. Slusser and Triska, following Whiting, listed it as unverified. Whatever the truth about this particular agreement, there is no doubt about the growth of Soviet influence in Sinkiang abetted, by his own account, by Sheng Shih-ts'ai. Sinkiang temporarily entered what Whiting described as the status of a 'voluntary disguised satellite of the Soviet Union'. Whiting mentioned fear of Japanese expansionism as one of the factors behind the Soviets' aggressive extension of their influence in Sinkiang.

## 10 January

In a report to the Soviet Central Executive Committee, Molotov again drew attention to the passages in Hitler's *Mein Kampf* about Germany's designs on 'new lands' in Russia and her border states which he said the German government had made no attempt to disown. Molotov also drew attention to the Soviet–German credit agreement of 9 April 1935.

## 14 January

The Central Committee confirmed the order for an exchange of Party documents between February and April and issued detailed instructions. 'Passive elements' were refused new documents. Documents were still being exchanged in November. Getty commented that the 'verification' and the exchange of documents were continuations of the purges of 1929 and 1933, the new feature being the Central Committee's use of local party activists against local party leaders.

Molotov announced an increase in defence expenditure from 6,500 million rubles in 1935 to 14,800 million in 1936. The strength of the armed forces was to be increased to 1.2 million and the proportion of regular troops sharply increased.

## 15 January

Tukhachevskii reported to the Soviet Central Executive Committee on the modernisation and mechanisation of the Red Army. He was explicit and emphatic on the Nazi-German threat to the USSR.

## 27 January

In an article on 'Teaching History in our Schools', *Pravda* mentioned that Stalin, Zhdanov and Kirov had been working together on a new textbook of party history in the summer of 1934.

Tukhachevskii arrived in London for the funeral of King George V having stopped over briefly in Berlin. After the funeral he spent a week in France as the guest of the French general staff.

An All-Union Committee on Art Affairs, subordinated to the Council of People's Commissars, was set up under the chairmanship of P. M. Kerzhentsev, a party member since 1904 and a former deputy chief of the agitation and propaganda department of the Central Committee. It was to take over from the Commissariat for Education responsibility for the direction and development of all the arts and to take over control of all theatres, cinemas and other places of entertainment and schools and other institutions concerned with music, painting and sculpture.

## 28 January

In an article headed 'Confusion in Place of Music', *Pravda* attacked Shostakovich's opera *Lady Macbeth of Mtsensk*, first produced in Moscow on 22 January 1934, for its discordant sounds and condemned it in different respects as both leftist and bourgeois. Further performances were banned. In February a campaign developed against 'formalism' and 'art for art's sake' in literature and the arts generally. 'Simplicity and popularity, heroism and stateliness, joy and beauty' were demanded as the fundamental qualities for Soviet art.

## February

At a writers' conference in Minsk, Pasternak, according to Hayward's account, dissociated himself from the prevailing view of literature and virtually invited the ostracism to which he was thereafter subjected for the rest of the Stalin period.

## 15 February

A Soviet–Romanian payments agreement was signed in Bucharest.

## 22 February

Drafting began on the third five-year plan for 1938 to 1942. The work was due to be completed by mid–1937. The tempo and nature of the work were both affected early in 1937 by the even higher priority accorded to defence industries. Further restrictions were imposed on the release of information on the planning process.

## 27 February

The French Chamber of Deputies ratified the Franco-Soviet treaty of 2 May 1935, followed by the Senate on 12 March.

## 7 March

Hitler's troops marched into the Rhineland, using the Franco-Soviet treaty as a pretext.

## 12 March

In the face of a build-up in Japanese troop strength along the Mongolian frontier and the frequent occurrence of frontier incidents during the previous year, a ten-year Soviet–Mongolian protocol of mutual assistance, confirming the 'gentleman's agreement' of 27 November 1934, was signed in Ulan Bator. In effect it gave the Soviet military a free hand in Mongolia in the event of an emergency. Red Army troops had returned to Mongolia at the end of 1934 and had been built up to a strength of about 50,000.

The Chinese government protested in a note to the Soviet government on 9 April that the agreement constituted an infringement of Chinese sovereignty.

## 17 March

In a speech before the League of Nations Council, Litvinov condemned the German occupation and remilitarisation of the Rhineland.

## 29 March

The Soviet–Afghan treaty of 24 June 1931 was extended for ten years.

## 10–21 April

At the Tenth Komsomol Congress, greater respect for parents and women was advocated. New rules provided that members should undergo military training of some kind.

Membership of nearly 4 million was claimed.

## 17 April

Muralov, who had held senior appointments in the Red Army under Trotsky, was arrested.

## 29 April

A Soviet–German agreement on trade and payments for 1936 was signed in Berlin. On 24 December it was extended until 31 December 1937.

## May

The Cossacks, who had been regarded since the revolution as a reactionary element, returned to official favour and five new Cossack cavalry regiments were formed in the Caucasus.

## 12 June

The draft of the new 'Stalin' constitution (see 25 November) was published and nationwide discussion was invited.

## 18 June

Gorky died. His death was subsequently ascribed to 'Trotskyites' and 'fascists'. In *The Great Terror*, Conquest argued that Gorky's death was timely from Stalin's point of view since Gorky would have been likely to speak out against the second trial of Zinoviev and Kamenev which was imminent. Conquest concluded that Gorky was probably murdered on Stalin's instructions but not by his doctors as alleged at the Bukharin trial. (See also 19 December 1937 and 2–13 March 1938.)

## 21 June

The All-Union Physical Culture Council was renamed the All-Union Committee on Physical Culture and Sports Affairs and was transferred from the Soviet Central Executive Committee to the Council of People's Commissars. The change of name signified official backing for competitive sport which was compatible in spirit with the socialist emulation of the five-year plan period and was considered useful in improving the population's capacity for labour and military preparedness.

## 22 June–20 July

The Soviet opening bid at the Montreux conference on the Black Sea straits was for rigorous limitation of entry into the Black Sea for all non-Black Sea powers, coupled with complete freedom for the Soviets to send unlimited forces, including warships of up to 25,000 tons, in and out of the Black Sea. This was unacceptable to the Turks among others. A compromise convention, signed at the end of the conference on 20 July, gave the right of egress from the Black Sea to Soviet tankers and warships with only minor limitations while Turkey was at peace, whereas more stringent limitations were imposed on entry into the Black Sea by warships of non-Black Sea powers. The Soviets ratified their signature of the convention on 9 November.

## 23 June

A Council of People's Commissars and Central Committee resolution defined the purpose of higher education as being not merely to provide professional, technical and political education but to produce cultured cadres with all-round education.

## 26 June

*Pravda* ordered local party organisations, especially in Kazakhstan, to speed up the hearings of appeals by those expelled from the party during the 'verification' of party documents on grounds of passivity or concealment of social origin. Getty suggested that this reflected Zhdanov's policy of educating and re-educating the party including its passive members in contrast with Ezhov's policy of ejecting passives from the party.

## 27 June

A decree claiming that Soviet women enjoyed greater equality than any others, said that the abolition of capitalist exploitation and the rise in the level of material, cultural and political well-being made it possible to repeal the decree of 18 November 1920 legalising abortion. Henceforward this would only be allowed where pregnancy represented a severe threat to health or where serious disease might be inherited. The decree provided for improved maternity benefits, generous state aid for large and very large families, sharp increases in the number of maternity homes, crèches and kindergartens and tighter regulations on divorce and paternal contributions to child maintenance.

## 1 July

In a speech to the League of Nations Assembly, Litvinov attributed the failure of the League to take effective action to protect the independence of

Abyssinia from Italian annexation to the performance of individual members of the League, not to the League itself or its Covenant. He argued that the League should be strengthened.

## 15 July

A Soviet air force mission arrived in Prague.

## 17–18 July

Risings in Morocco and Andalucía marked the beginning of the Spanish civil war.

## 20 July

An All-Union People's Commissariat of Justice was set up.

## 29 July

A top secret Central Committee letter, entitled 'On the Terrorist Activities of the Trotskyist–Zinovievist Counter-revolutionary bloc', and probably written by Ezhov shortly after pre-trial confessions had been obtained from Zinoviev and Kamenev, was circulated to district party organisations and was found in the Smolensk party archives. It claimed that, on the basis of new NKVD materials obtained in 1936, Zinoviev and Kamenev had established contact four years earlier with *émigré* Trotskyites. Zinoviev and Kamenev were not only the inspirers of terrorist activity against party and government leaders but were the authors of direct instructions to kill Kirov and to prepare attempts on the lives of other party leaders, especially Stalin. Absence of bolshevik vigilance had enabled members of the counter-revolutionary bloc to escape the party's purge procedures.

Calling for increased vigilance, the letter asserted that the 'inalienable quality of every Bolshevik . . . should be the ability to recognise an enemy of the party no matter how well he may be masked'.

According to documents from the Trotsky archives opened in 1980 and quoted by Getty, Ivan N. Smirnov, a loyal Trotskyite in the USSR, did succeed late in 1932 in communicating to Trotsky a proposal for a united opposition bloc. Trotsky took up this suggestion in clandestine correspondence which may well have leaked to the NKVD.

## 3 August

A levy was announced on wages and salaries throughout the USSR in aid of the Spanish Popular Front in its struggle with the rebel Nationalists in the civil war. The levy was extended to collective farm-workers and was followed by officially organised public demonstrations. On 27 October it was announced that over 47 million rubles had been raised.

## 5 August

The Soviet government, in reply to an approach from the French government with British backing, accepted the principle of non-intervention in the Spanish civil war.

## 11 August

A decree lowered the age for military service from 21 to 19. The effect was to increase the strength of the Red Army from about 1.3 million to about 1.6 million.

## 19 August

The second trial of Zinoviev,

Kamenev and fourteen others opened in Moscow. The indictment said that, at their trial in January 1935, the accused had concealed their direct responsibility for Kirov's death. It was now known that they had formed a bloc with the Trotskyites at the end of 1932 and had been joined by the Lominadze group in organising terrorist gangs on Trotsky's orders to assassinate Stalin, Voroshilov, Kaganovich, Kirov, Ordzhonikidze, Zhdanov, Kosior, Postyshev and others. All but two of the accused pleaded guilty. Kamenev and Zinoviev made their confessions on 20 August, partially incriminating Bukharin, Rykov, Tomskii and others as sympathisers.

## 21 August

In a letter to *Pravda*, the former Trotskyite, Rakovskii, wrote that his ardent sympathy with Stalin impelled him to demand the death sentence for the 'Gestapo agents' on trial.

## 22 August

Vyshinskii, the prosecutor at the trial, announced that an investigation was being launched into the statements made about Tomskii, Rykov, Bukharin, Uglanov, Radek and Piatakov and that legal proceedings would be instituted. On reading the announcement, Tomskii committed suicide.

## 23 August

The Soviet government adhered to an Anglo-French declaration on banning the supply of war material to Spain with the qualification that it would put the declaration into effect as soon as the Italian, German and Portuguese governments had also adhered to it. Krivitsky stated that he received instructions at the beginning of September 'to mobilise all available agents and facilities . . . to purchase and transport arms to Spain'.

## 24 August

All the defendants in the Zinoviev trial were sentenced to death. Stalin's alleged undertakings to Zinoviev and Kamenev to spare their lives and the liberty of their families if they stood trial were not observed. Forty-three persons named as accomplices in the trial, including Uglanov, Shliapnikov and Smil'ga, never appeared in court or confessed publicly, perhaps because their co-operation could not be assured.

## 27 August

Rosenberg arrived in Madrid as Soviet ambassador to Spain, accompanied by General Berzin, formerly head of Soviet military intelligence.

## 6–24 September

Major-General Wavell led a British military delegation to witness Red Army manoeuvres in the Byelorussian military district and thereafter to visit various military and industrial installations.

## 10 September

*Pravda* announced that the investigation of Bukharin and Rykov was being dropped.

## 22 September

Radek was arrested.

## 25 September

Stalin and Zhdanov sent a telegram from Sochi to other members of the Politburo accusing the security service of being four years behind in exposing the Trotskyite–Zinovievite bloc and demanding the appointment of Ezhov as head of the NKVD in place of Iagoda. The change was made the following day. Iagoda replaced Rykov as Commissar for Communications. No new job was announced for Rykov.

Conquest and others pointed out that it was almost exactly four years since the expulsion of the Riutin group: Stalin is alleged to have been prevented by other party leaders from having Riutin executed. Getty suggested that the reference to 'four years behind' is more likely to have related to the formation of the Trotskyite–Zinovievite united opposition bloc (see 29 July). He also suggested that the appointment of Ezhov may have been in part a reaction to a series of explosions in the Kemerovo mines in Siberia on 23 September (see also 29 November).

## 29 September and 21 October

The Central Committee issued circulars calling for an end to unfair expulsions from the party and a stepping-up of fair ones.

## October

Two persons were tried and one was sentenced to death at Ashkhabad for participating in the murder of the twenty-six Baku commissars (see 15 September 1918). No reference was made to the previous claims that the British were responsible for the murders.

## 7 October

Speaking on instructions from his government, the Soviet charge d'affaires in London said that, if violations of the Spanish non-intervention agreement by Portugal, Germany and Italy did not cease immediately, the USSR would consider itself free of any obligations arising from that agreement.

## 11 October

On being awarded the Order of Lenin, Litvinov made a speech in which he argued that other powers besides the USSR were threatened by German attempts to isolate and subjugate them. There were only two courses open to countries thus threatened: collective security (for which Litvinov persistently argued) or a *rapprochement* with the aggressor.

## 14 October

The first group of 500 volunteers to fight in the Spanish civil war in the International Brigades, the majority of them communists or sympathisers, arrived for training at Albacete.

## 15 October

The first Soviet ship carrying war stores arrived in Spain.

## 23 October

Maisky, the Soviet ambassador in London, declared that, in accordance with its statement of 7 October, the Soviet government no longer considered itself bound by the Spanish non-intervention agreement.

## 25 October

Partly to pay for supplies and partly

for safe-keeping, the bulk of Spain's holdings of gold, about 500 tons, was shipped from Cartagena to Odessa.

## 28 October

Maisky stated in effect that until guarantees had been created against the supply of war materials to the Nationalists by the Germans and Italians, his government would continue to send supplies to the legitimate Spanish Republican government. The USSR remained a member of the Anglo-French sponsored Non-Intervention Committee throughout the rest of 1936 and 1937. At the same time Soviet support for the Republican government reached at times a scale comparable with that of the Germans and Italians for Franco's Nationalist forces. Soviet support included the provision of staff officers, military instructors, airmen, artillery officers, aircraft, tanks, artillery, ammunition, petrol and oil, help with civil administration, the supply of food, notably to Valencia and Barcelona, and the procurement of arms from non-Soviet sources. According to documents of the German military attaché in Ankara who apparently had access to Turkish records, 731 armoured vehicles and 242 aircraft passed through the Black Sea straits from the USSR for Spain between September 1936 and March 1938. The level of supplies fell away from the autumn of 1937 onwards. Hugh Thomas estimated that, while the number of Soviet participants in the civil war was under 2,000 in total and not more than 500 at any one time, they occupied relatively important positions on the staff as instructors and as aircraft and tank crews. The total value of Soviet and Comintern aid to the Republicans is estimated at roughly £88 million. It almost certainly included more aircraft and armoured vehicles than the German military attaché in Ankara recorded.

The NKVD was strongly represented in Spain and in addition to supervising Soviet military personnel, exerted considerable, and often murderous, influence in favour of the Spanish communist party at the expense of socialists, anarchists and non-Stalinist communists. Soviet officers who returned to the USSR after service in Spain were particularly heavily purged at the cost of great and lasting bitterness between the Soviet armed forces and the NKVD.

## 29 October

A group of Soviet tanks with Soviet crews under Soviet command went into action south of Madrid to whose defence from November onwards the Soviets and the International Brigades made an important contribution.

## 1 November

The party started recruiting new members again for the first time since 1933 but on a new basis. The aim was to recruit 'the best people' rather than those of proletarian origin. In the period November 1936 to March 1939, 41 per cent of new members were workers, 15.2 per cent peasants and 43.8 per cent white-collar workers and members of the intelligentsia. The comparable figures for 1929 were 81.2 per cent, 17.1 per cent and 1.7 per cent. The proportion of workers among new recruits dropped to 24 per cent in the period 1937 to June

1941 with a corresponding rise in the proportion of qualified people.

## 10–12 November

In a period in which Soviet and German leaders were expressing their determination to defend their countries against any attack by the other, the German press reported that German citizens had been included in a new wave of arrests in the USSR. One was sentenced to death on 21 November but the sentence was commuted to ten years' imprisonment.

The tension in Soviet–German political relations was not reflected in the trade figures. Although Britain had replaced Germany as the USSR's main supplier in 1934, Soviet–German trade actually increased in 1936.

## 19–22 November

A major sabotage trial was held at Novosibirsk at which nine defendants, including a German engineer, were charged with responsibility for industrial accidents including the explosion at Kemerovo on 23 September. The defendants were linked by the prosecution with Muralov and Piatakov and they were also accused of attempting to assassinate Molotov.

## 25 November–5 December

The Eighth (Extraordinary) All-Union Congress of Soviets adopted the new 'Stalin' constitution. Its adoption had been preceded by a press campaign culminating in a speech by Stalin to the congress, in which he maintained that the socialisation of industry under the five-year plans, the collectivisation of agricul- ture and the liquidation of the kulaks had eliminated class antagonism, leaving only workers, peasants and the intelligentsia in harmonious alliance. Hence it was possible to remove undemocratic restrictions on elections. In the new society, only one party, the communist party, could exist, since it represented the interests of the workers and peasants. The new constitution, he said, was of the greatest international significance because it would give moral support to all who were fighting fascism. (Schapiro observed in *The Communist Party of the Soviet Union* that one of the main objects of the constitution was to persuade the world outside the USSR of the democratic nature of the Soviet system at a time when the USSR was trying to win over socialist and liberal opinion in the West to a united front against Hitler.)

The constitution provided for direct elections to Soviets at all levels by secret ballot, equal and universal suffrage (i.e. equal representation for urban and rural areas and the re-enfranchisement of certain categories such as priests and former White Guards) and the right to freedom of the press, of speech, publication, assembly and demonstration provided these rights were exercised in the interests of the working class. It recognised equality of rights between the sexes, races and nationalities together with the right to work, to leisure, to maintenance in sickness and old age, to free, universal, compulsory education for seven years, to domicile, to privacy, to religious belief and to the conduct of anti-religious propaganda and, to some extent, to the ownership of personal property. The duties of Soviet citizens included the maintenance of labour discipline, the safeguarding of state property and universal military service. The employment of any labour whatever in privately owned handicraft enterprises was forbidden. (It had already died out.)

The constitution set up the Supreme Soviet as the 'highest organ of state power in the USSR', its two chambers being the Soviet of the Union (with one deputy for every 300,000 voters) and the Soviet of Nationalities (twenty-five deputies from each of the eleven union-republics, eleven from each autonomous republic, five from each autonomous region and one from each national area). The eleven union-republics were the RSFSR, the Ukraine, Byelorussia, Azerbaijan, Georgia, Armenia and the Turkmen, Uzbek, Tadzhik, Kazakh and Kirghiz republics, the last two being elevated on 5 December from the status of Autonomous SSRs. In 1940 the Karelo-Finnish, Moldavian, Latvian, Lithuanian and Estonian republics were added. The right of republics to secede from the USSR was maintained.

The Supreme Soviet elected its own Presidium whose president fulfilled the functions of head of state. In theory the Supreme Soviet appointed the Council of People's Commissars, the members of the Supreme Court and Special Courts of the USSR and the Procurator-General of the USSR. He in turn appointed the procurators of the republics and regions. The procuracy combined the functions of public prosecutors with supervision over the correct and uniform application of the law throughout the country. In this second capacity the procuracy was considered to be the 'watchdog of legality' for (but not against) the central authorities.

As before, people's commissariats were of three types: all-union, union-republican and republican. Those concerned with heavy industry were largely all-union, those concerned with light industry, agriculture and trade were largely republican.

The right to nominate candidates for election was 'secured to public organisations and societies of the working people' (i.e. in practice the communist party and its ancillary organisations). The communist party was mentioned in the new constitution as the 'leading core of all organisations of the working people, both public and state'.

The chairman of the All-Union Committee of Higher Education became an *ex officio* member of the All-Union Council of People's Commissars.

At the turn of the year 1935–6, barriers to entry to educational institutions for those of non-proletarian origin were removed. The status and salaries of teachers were improved. Over-specialisation was discouraged and the system of intelligence tests which had been in use was 'liquidated'. There was much criticism of and self-criticism by Bubnov and his RSFSR Commissariat of Education. There were complaints of low standards in higher and technical education, especially in the legal and teaching professions. There were even references to a certain 'relapse into illiteracy'.

## 26 November

The anti-Comintern pact was signed between Germany and Japan. The two powers agreed to exchange information on Comintern activities, to collaborate in carrying out preventive measures and to invite other states to join the pact which was to remain in force for five years. In an accompanying secret agreement, the powers agreed not to conclude, without reciprocal concurrence, any sort of treaty with the USSR that was not in keeping with the spirit of the pact. They also agreed that if either of them were to be threatened or attacked by the USSR, the other would take no action „which would 'relieve the position of the USSR' and that they would consult on measures to safeguard their common interests.

## 28 November

It was announced that Soviet strength in military aircraft had increased four times, in submarines seven times and in coastal defence craft three times since 1932–3. 'Flagman' Orlov spoke of the building of a large and efficient Soviet fleet comprising ships of all classes and of the highest technical level.

## 29 November

Vyshinskii ordered a review within a month of all criminal cases involving major conflagrations, accidents and poor-quality output with the aim of exposing counter-revolutionary and sabotage activities and making the guilty parties more heavily liable.

## 14 December

*Izvestiia* declared its opposition to the insurrection in Sian and announced Soviet support for a united popular front with the Nan-

king government of Chiang Kai-shek against Japanese aggression. The insurrection was the work of the Manchurian forces based in Sian who were reluctant to obey orders to take action against the local Chinese Red Army, preferring a united front with them against the Japanese. Chiang Kai-shek, who had flown to Sian to confer with his generals there, was arrested by them on 12 December. Three Chinese communist delegates, including Chou En-lai, were then flown in to Sian and at first lent their support to the insurrection. Moscow having clarified its attitude, Chou negotiated Chiang's release and the latter flew back to Nanking on 25 December.

## 21 December

Stalin, Molotov and Voroshilov addressed a letter to the Spanish Republican Prime Minister, Largo Caballero, urging him to pay particular attention to winning over the peasantry and the petty and middle urban bourgeoisie and to draw the leaders of the Republican party into government 'to prevent the enemies of Spain from regarding it as a communist republic and to forestall their intervention'.

## 30 December

New Provisional Field Service Regulations were issued to the Red Army embodying Soviet theory on offensive and defensive operations conducted in depth. The regulations began by declaring that in any new war only the offensive could bring about the total destruction of the enemy's forces. Heavy emphasis was laid on 'activism' and initiative in offensive tactics and on the necessity for the proper co-ordination between infantry, tanks, artillery and air support. The means by which this co-ordination was to be achieved were spelt out in detail, but in practice communications between the different branches of the forces are often held by western observers to have remained a source of weakness in the Red Army's performance until after the German invasion of June 1941.

# 1937

## 1 January

Party membership was given as 1,453,828 with 527,869 candidate members.

## 6 January

A census of the whole population was carried out but was annulled in September. The census had included a question on religious affiliation. It has been suggested that it was suppressed because it showed either that the population was smaller or that it had more religious affiliations than it suited the authorities to admit or both.

## 9 January

Trotsky arrived in Mexico.

## 13 January

The Central Committee attacked the unsatisfactory leadership of the party in Kiev where Postyshev was First Secretary of the Kiev Provincial Committee. On 16 January Postyshev was replaced in this appointment while retaining his post as Second Secretary of the Ukrainian party.

## 16 January

Bukharin's name appeared for the last time as editor of *Izvestiia*.

## 20 January

Pashukanis, who had been appointed Deputy Commissar of Justice in November 1936, was denounced by *Pravda* as an enemy of the people. Pashukanis had maintained that the law would begin to wither away as socialism was established and as the state itself withered away. He was also the author of a new, relatively liberal, draft criminal code which was not adopted and is said to have excluded the death penalty. His ideas were subsequently attacked by Vyshinskii who succeeded him as director of the law institute of the Academy of Sciences.

## 23–30 January

The trial took place of seventeen members of the 'Anti-Soviet Trotskyite Centre' which was described as a centre for the organisation of terrorism, diversion and espionage seeking to undermine the USSR and hasten its defeat in time of war. The principal defendants were Piatakov, Ordzhonikidze's former Deputy Commissar for Heavy Industry who had been arrested before the end of the previous October, Radek, Muralov, Serebriakov, a former secretary of the Central Committee, and Sokol'nikov, a former candidate member of the Politburo. Vyshinskii led the prosecution. Piatakov and Serebriakov were charged with organising sabotage groups mainly on the railways, in western Siberia and in the chemical industry. These groups allegedly included a number of ex-Trotskyites like Muralov. The defendants were also accused of rejecting industrialisation and collectivisation with support from the German and Japanese governments. They had allegedly organised terrorist groups with the intention of assassinating the leading members of the party. Thirteen of the accused were sentenced to death. Khrushchev and Shvernik were reported to have addressed a demonstration in Red Square demanding that these sentences should be carried out. Sokol'nikov, Radek and two others, against whom the charges were less serious, were given prison sentences. According to the Petrovs, Radek was murdered in a Siberian labour camp in 1938 by a fellow prisoner.

## 28 January

*Pravda* announced that Ezhov had been promoted to the new rank of General Commissar of State Security.

## 29 January

Kandelaki, the Soviet commercial attaché in Berlin and a confidant of Stalin, who had called on Schacht in December, had a second meeting with him to suggest negotiations, either through ambassadors or in secret, on closer trade relations between Germany and the USSR.

## 3 February

The USSR adhered to Part IV of the London Naval Treaty of 1930 relating to the rules of submarine warfare.

## 18 February

Ordhzonikidze died. His death was ascribed to natural causes at the time but in 1956 and 1961 Khrushchev described it as suicide. Conquest has argued that forced suicide or murder on Stalin's instructions are more likely. Kravchenko, who had been a favoured subordinate of Ordzhonikidze, maintained that his death was either suicide or murder: he had been severely shaken by the arrest of his close associate, Piatakov, and had protested vigorously to Stalin over the purging of his subordinates, receiving support from Kosior, Chubar' and Rudzutak. Roy Medvedev considered there was insufficient evidence of murder to dispute the suicide version.

## 23 February

The Chinese communists having, in accordance with the resolutions of the Seventh Comintern Congress of July–August 1935, put out numerous feelers for a new united front with the Kuomintang against the Japanese, Chiang Kai-shek finally accepted a communist declaration containing four pledges:

1. that the communist party would work for the realisation of Sun Yat-sen's principles;
2. that it would abandon its policy of armed uprisings, land seizures and Sovietisation;
3. that it would dissolve its existing Soviet government and practise democracy; and
4. that its armed forces would cease to be called the Red Army and would

be integrated into the National Revolutionary Forces under Nationalist command.

Chiang wrote that he genuinely believed at the time that the communists were sincere in their expressed readiness to join with the rest of the nation against aggression. He later discovered and acknowledged his mistake and quoted Mao Tse-tung as having told his troops at Yenan in the autumn of 1937 that the war with Japan gave the Chinese communist party an excellent opportunity to grow: 70 per cent of their efforts would be devoted to the expansion of the party, 20 per cent to coping with the government and 10 per cent to fighting the Japanese.

## 23 February–5 March

Little was published about the 'February–March plenum' of the Central Committee although it was acknowledged that the 'anti-party activities' of Bukharin and Rykov were discussed. A Central Committee resolution of 27 February published in Pravda on 6 March called on the party to solidify the basis of the dictatorship of the proletariat by democratising its own internal practices in accordance with the spirit of the new constitution. It directed that the practice of co-opting members of party committees should be liquidated and that members of the party's guiding organs should be individually elected by secret ballot as provided in the party rules. Every party member should be afforded an unlimited right to recall candidates and criticise them. Elections for all party organisations up to central committees of national communist parties were to be held by 20 May and thereafter annually in regions, districts and towns and every eighteen months in republics.

The resolution was based on Zhdanov's speech published on 6 March. Zhdanov underlined the need for self-criticism by local party leaders and for criticism of them by the rank and file. (The Smolensk party archives, as quoted by Getty, provide confirmation that in that area at least, the plenum provoked vigorous criticism of the local party leadership.)

According to an edited version of his speech published in the third week of April, Molotov claimed that there was widespread penetration of spies, wreckers and saboteurs of heavy industry (the former bailiwick of Ordzhonikidze and Piatakov), light industry, food production, forestry, communications, agriculture and the State Bank. These wreckers obstructed rapid economic growth. Workers should criticise their leaders who should develop their own self-criticism in order to improve their performance.

In two speeches published on 29 March and 1 April, Stalin referred to widespread wrecking and espionage which party leaders, their vigilance weakened by their economic successes, had failed to prevent. The threat from capitalist encirclement was real and there were about 12,000 party members who were to some extent Trotskyite sympathisers and therefore potential enemies. The real wreckers amongst them had to be 'smashed'. At the same time, wholesale expulsions of former Trotskyites, passive or inadequate party members were to be avoided; local party leaders should consider expulsion cases individually. Democratic elections were necessary to counter local nepotism and patronage. The work of local party leaders needed to be checked from above and from below: courses of up to six months' duration would be organised to retrain them politically and ideologically.

References in the published speeches indicate that Ezhov accused Bukharin of having knowledge of Trotskyite treason. Cohen, quoting Bukharin's widow, gave the date of Bukharin's arrest as 27 February.

## 13 March

*Pravda* published an article by Pospelov denouncing Bukharin, Rykov and Tomskii for their criminal links with the Trotskyites.

## 17 March

The Ukrainian Central Committee removed Postyshev from his post of Second Secretary.

## 18 March

According to Krivitsky, Ezhov denounced Iagoda as a former Tsarist police spy and launched a purge of the NKVD. According to Conquest quoting Alexander Orlov's *The Secret History of Stalin's Crimes*, 1954, some 3,000 NKVD officers were executed in 1937. The Petrovs also gave a figure of about 3,000 high-ranking NKVD officials killed. At the same time a massive purge was carried out among the prosecutors, 90 per cent of those in the provinces being removed. Many of them had apparently attempted to maintain some semblance of legality (Conquest quoting Soviet publications).

## 20 March

The Central Committee issued an order on the forthcoming elections in the party. In the following weeks a number of articles appeared in the party press on criticism, self-criticism, the answerability of party leaders to the rank and file and the need for them to be 'verified'.

## 3 April

*Pravda* reported the arrest of Iagoda. Averbakh, the former leader of the RAPP, was attacked in *Literaturnaia Gazeta* on 20 April. Both Averbakh and his friend, the playwright Kirshon, have been described by different sources as relatives by marriage of Iagoda.

## 14 April

Ponomarev published an article on 'Internal Party Democracy and Bolshevik Discipline', launching a campaign against elements like Postyshev who 'interfered with party democracy'.

## 23 April

*Pravda* published an article on 'Foreign Espionage in the Soviet Far East' claiming that the Japanese secret service was making extensive use as agents of Korean and Chinese immigrants in that area. Kolarz in *The Peoples of the Soviet Far East* connected this article with the wholesale deportations from the Far East by the NKVD for security reasons of Koreans and Chinese (also some Japanese) which took place at this time and which provided for the wartime deportations from Poland, the Baltic states and minority areas of the USSR. Korean immigrants had been welcomed in Tsarist times because of their agricultural skills and their ability to assimilate. Up to 50 per cent of the workers in the coal mines of the Far Eastern territory in the 1920s were said to have been Chinese or other orientals. Up to 1937 the Soviet regime had permitted separate schools and newspapers for these minorities. Relations with the Koreans in particular were seriously impaired by collectivisation. The Koreans were resettled mainly in Uzbekistan. The Chinese appear to have been dispersed elsewhere: many were later reported to be in prison camps. On 20 December *Pravda* expressed the Soviet party's and government's gratitude to the Far Eastern NKVD and railway staff for their 'exemplary and precise fulfilment of a government assignment in the field of transport'.

## April/May

According to evidence from *Pravda* cited by Getty, elections in the party by secret ballot resulted in a turnover of up to 50 per cent in the local party leadership below the regional level. Getty cited evidence from the Smolensk party archives of genuine criticism of the local leadership from below leading to changes even before the elections were held.

## May

Whiting recorded that Soviet troops intervened in Sinkiang to suppress a rebellion against Sheng Shih-ts'ai.

## 1 May

Rudzutak, a member of the Politburo, was missing from the May Day parade. He had been arrested. He was shot at the end of July 1938.

## 4 May

The Soviet government informed the British government that for health reasons, Marshal Tukhachevskii would not attend the coronation of King George VI.

## 7 May

An article in *Pravda* signalled the revival of the anti-religious campaign which had been foreshadowed by an article in *Bol'shevik* in the spring.

## 8 May

The system of 'dual command' in the Red Army, which had been abolished on 15 March 1934 when political commissars were subordinated to the military commanders, was reintroduced with increased powers for the political commissars. The new regulations were amplified and formally decreed on 15 August.

## 10–11 May

Tukhachevskii and Gamarnik were relieved of their posts as Deputy Commissars of Defence and other postings of senior Red Army commanders were announced. Shaposhnikov replaced Tukhachevskii as chief of the general staff.

## 11 May

Army Commander Kork, head of the Frunze Military Academy, and the chief of staff of the Far Eastern army, Lapin, were arrested.

## 17 May

In an article on 'A Trotskyite Agency

in Literature', *Pravda* denounced Averbakh and attacked Pil'niak specifically for his *Tale of the Inextinguishable Moon* which had implied that Frunze had been murdered. Shortly afterwards, Pil'niak was arrested. He was shot in 1938 or 1939. Pasternak was among the other prominent literary figures criticised in the article.

## 21 May

Professor Shmidt informed Moscow by radio that he had established a research station under Papanin's leadership on an ice-floe twenty kilometres from the North Pole. Four aircraft had been used to land the expedition there. Shmidt (or Schmidt) contributed an article to *The Times* of 8 June on the importance of a semi-permanent polar base for meteorological, biological and oceanographic studies, highlighting also its significance for regular trans-polar flights from Europe to North America.

## Late May/Early June

Twenty-five annual regional party conferences were reported in the Soviet press. Four regional party secretaries and their staffs were removed. In five cases (Moscow, Leningrad, Saratov, Orenburg and Uzbekistan), the political line of the regional committee was judged to be correct and its work satisfactory. In four cases (Armenia, the Far East, Yaroslavl and Piatigorsk), the committees' work was unsatisfactory and eight committees (Ukraine, Kalinin, Voronezh, Cheliabinsk, Kirghiz, Kuibyshev, Stalinabad, Engel's and the Western Region centred on Smo-lensk) were accused of serious mistakes.

## 11 June

In an article on 'The Crisis of Foreign Bourgeois Intelligence', *Pravda* announced that the following had been charged with treason: Marshal Tukhachevskii, former Deputy People's Commissar of Defence; Army Commander Iakir, commanding the Kiev military district; Army Commander Uborevich, commanding the Byelorussian military district; Corps Commander Eideman, head of the paramilitary and civil defence organisation, *Osoaviakhim;* Army Commander Kork, head of the Frunze Military Academy; Corps Commander Putna, former military attaché in London; Corps Commander Fel'dman, head of Red Army administration; and Corps Commander Primakov, deputy commander of Leningrad military district. Gamarnik, head of the army's political administration, whose suicide had been announced on 1 June, was described as implicated in the conspiracy. Tukhachevskii had been arrested on 27 May, Iakir on 31 May, Uborevich on 29 May, Eideman on 22 May and Fel'dman a day or two later.

## 12 June

It was announced that the accused Red Army commanders had been tried and executed.

## 15 June

*Pravda* published a report to Voroshilov by the Moscow Proletarian Rifle Red Banner Division on the executed Red Army commanders.

The report associated them with Trotsky and accused them of espionage and of planning the assassination of party and government leaders.

The move against them had evidently been in preparation for many months. Several commanders associated with Iakir had been implicated in the Zinoviev trial in 1936 and arrested. Putna, who had been implicated in the Piatakov trial, had already been arrested by September 1936 and Primakov by November 1936.

After the trial the purge of the Red Army continued for more than a year. There is some variation in the figures given for the number of officers accounted for in the purge. Three out of five marshals were purged, thirteen, fourteen or fifteen out of fifteen or sixteen army commanders, eight or ten of the most senior naval commanders (including Orlov and Muklevich), about two-thirds of the corps commanders, 60 per cent of the 200-odd divisional commanders and half of the 400 brigade commanders. Roy Medvedev quoted even higher figures for the last three categories. The purge is said to have been particularly severe amongst the political commissars, the air force, tank and mechanised units, military intelligence and veterans of the Spanish civil war. Many members of the families of senior commanders were victimised. The aircraft designer, Tupolev, who had done much to build up the bomber force, was imprisoned.

Various explanations have been offered for the attack on the armed forces. Some have argued that there was a genuine military plot directed against Stalin. Others have found the evidence for this unconvincing. Some

authors such as Deutscher in *Stalin: a Political Biography* have suggested that the purge was a pre-emptive strike by Stalin against those leaders and their potential supporters who might have been tempted to exploit war or the threat of war to unseat the regime as others had exploited the First World War to overthrow Tsarism: into the vacuum created by the purge poured a new generation of officers and officials who, inexperienced as they were, owed their rapid advancement to Stalin and when war came proved loyal to him.

Documents forged by the Germans purporting to provide compromising evidence of Tukhachevskii's relations with them were passed to the Soviets through intelligence channels and would have reached Stalin in May. An earlier story to the same effect was passed on to the Soviets by President Benes of Czechoslovakia at the end of 1936. It has been argued that, although these stories may have influenced the timing of the trial and provided a convenient pretext for it, no official use of them as evidence seems to have been made at the trial; they may however have been used in the effort to persuade surviving officers of the guilt of those executed.

Getty's conclusion in 1985 was that, in the absence of relevant primary sources, the trial of Tukhachevskii and others remains a mystery.

## 18–20 June

The Soviet Arctic aviator Chkalov flew from Moscow over the North Pole to the US army air base at Vancouver, Washington. On 12–14 July Gromov followed roughly the same route, landing at San Jacinto, California. In August Levanevskii, who had flown from Los Angeles to Moscow via Alaska in 1936, disappeared without trace near the North Pole, trying to follow Chkalov and Gromov. Nevertheless, the possibility of operating intercontinental flights over the North Pole had been established. Much propaganda use was made of Chkalov's and other record-breaking flights. It has been argued that they were used to distract attention from the purges. Bailes also suggested that concentration on record-breaking may have been in part responsible for weaknesses in the fighting capacity of Soviet aircraft, shown up in the Spanish civil war, at Khalkhin-Gol and in June 1941.

## 19–21 June

Some documentation is available from the Smolensk party archives on an extraordinary meeting of the party committee of the Western Region which was attended by Kaganovich. At or before this meeting, Rumiantsev, the regional party secretary, and all the members of the regional bureau were arrested by the NKVD on the Central Committee's orders and accused of 'wrecking'. They were linked with Army Commander Uborevich who was commander of the western military district when arrested and who was said to have implicated Rumiantsev. The pattern of Kaganovich's purging visit to Smolensk was followed in June by Malenkov in Byelorussia and elsewhere, in July by Beria in Georgia and in August by Molotov, Ezhov and Khrushchev in the Ukraine and by Malenkov and Mikoyan in Armenia.

Getty concluded that the military arrests gave a powerful boost to the great purge or Ezhovshchina (the time of Ezhov) which reached its peak in the second half of 1937. Getty distinguished the Ezhovshchina from earlier party purges and 'verifications'. While earlier purges were aimed primarily at ridding the party rank and file of passive and unsuitable elements and were conducted by the party machinery, the Ezhovshchina was aimed at leading figures both inside the party and outside it in the armed forces, industry, the economy generally, the administration, the intelligentsia and the priesthood. The Ezhovshchina was conducted by the NKVD and, unlike earlier purges, usually resulted in the imprisonment or execution of its victims.

Getty did not give a date for the beginning of the Ezhovshchina. Conquest implied that it began in May 1937, particularly in the Leningrad and Ukrainian party organisations. He mentioned that, of the sixty-five members of the Leningrad party committee elected in May 1937, only two were re-elected on 4 June 1938, five others being transferred to posts outside the city: all seven of the Leningrad members and candidate members of the Central Committee were arrested and so were a number of the leading figures in industry. Other authors have dated the Ezhovshchina from 1936, presumably including within it the Central Committee letter of 29 July and the trial of Zinoviev, Kamenev and others, beginning on 19 August 1936.

The Ezhovshchina took a heavy toll of the staff of the Foreign Affairs Commissariat. Uldricks estimated that a third of those of diplomatic rank were purged, the proportion being higher at the most senior level.

Other commissariats on which information is less accessible may have suffered comparable losses.

Large numbers of priests were arrested on charges of being clerico-fascist counter-revolutionaries, spies and saboteurs. In many cases the churches of those arrested were closed.

The Ezhovshchina also fell heavily on the Comintern and the non-Russian communist parties, particularly those whose leaders were in exile in the USSR. The Latvian, Estonian, Lithuanian, German, Hungarian, Finnish and Romanian parties were all hard hit. Münzenberg, whose work in front organisations has been mentioned, refused to obey a summons to Moscow and was found hanged, perhaps murdered, in France in 1940. The worst-affected parties were the Yugoslavs (Tito was one of few survivors among the leaders), the Koreans and the Poles. The Korean party was dissolved. Almost all Polish communists in the USSR were arrested; all twelve members of the Central Committee in the USSR and several hundred others were executed. The party issued its last official statement on 8 June 1938 and was dissolved by the Executive Committee of the Comintern shortly afterwards. At the party's Eighteenth Congress in March 1939, Manuil'skii, the chief Soviet representative in the Comintern, said that agents of Polish fascism had gained positions of leadership in the Polish party. The GSE states that the accusations brought against the party were later proved to be without foundation: it mentions a statement signed by the Soviet, Polish, Italian, Bulgarian and Finnish communist parties in 1956, declaring that the disbanding of the Polish party in 1938 was unjustified.

While Conquest and others have seen the Ezhovshchina as the climax of a systematic, deliberate and premeditated crescendo of terror imposed on the country by Stalin for his own ends, Getty attributed it to the partly fortuitous convergence of the largely Zhdanov-inspired campaign for the reform of the party through criticism and self-criticism, the tension in the party between the centre and the largely unresponsive periphery and the desire of radicals like Molotov and Ezhov to rid the party of spies, traitors, saboteurs and 'wreckers' who were impeding the progress of industrialisation and the building of socialism generally. While not absolving Stalin of responsibility for the Ezhovshchina, Getty argued that the chaotic manner in which it was conducted suggested that to some extent it ran out of control as many of Stalin's underlings settled old scores and sought to demonstrate their superior vigilance by denouncing others.

Hough and Fainsod quoted estimates of the number of deaths in the Ezhovshchina, varying from Kennan's 'tens of thousands' to Nicolaevsky's half a million communists and no fewer than ten million non-Communists. Hough himself favoured a figure in the low hundreds of thousands. Rosefielde in 1987 was still defending a figure of 3,655,000 (see also End of December 1939).

## 21 June

Soviet troops occupied the Bolshoi and Sennufu Islands in the Amur river, over which the 'Manchukuo' authorities had claimed sovereignty.

In the course of fighting on 30 June, a Soviet patrol ship was sunk. After strong Japanese protests, both sides withdrew their forces from the neighbourhood of the islands by 4 July. The Japanese then occupied Bolshoi Island on 6 July. The incident was rated as a reverse for the Soviets and as an indication to the Japanese that vigorous Soviet action against further Japanese military encroachment in China was unlikely.

## 4 July

Completion was announced of the Moscow–Volga canal which had been under construction since 1932. The Council of People's Commissars expressed its thanks to the NKVD and the builders of the canal and announced the early release of 55,000 prisoners. The canal was officially opened on 15 July.

## 7 July

The Japanese launched a full-scale invasion of China which helped to reduce their pressure on the USSR.

## 9 and 10 July

In an attack on Islam characteristic of the purge period, *Pravda* accused counter-revolutionary bourgeois-nationalist Muslim elements of working for the Japanese intelligence service.

## 17 July

Anglo-Soviet and Anglo-German naval agreements were signed in London setting limits to naval armaments and providing for exchange of information on building programmes. Certain exemptions were granted for the Soviet Far Eastern Fleet in the absence of any agreement on naval construction between the USSR and Japan. The United Kingdom notified suspension of the agreement to the League of Nations on 16 November 1939.

## 1 August

A raid was made on the Soviet consulate-general in Tientsin by 'White Guard bandits'. Tientsin was occupied at the time by the Japanese whom the Soviets held responsible for the raid.

## 10 August

Kaganovich wrote to the NKVD demanding the arrest of ten officials of the Commissariat of Transport. A nationwide purge of railway employees ensued. Most were accused of being Japanese spies. Soviet railwaymen with their families numbering about 40,000 had returned home after Soviet rights in the Chinese Eastern railway were sold (see 23 March 1935). They were automatically suspected of having been recruited by the Japanese in Manchuria and of having recruited their friends on return to the USSR.

## 15 August

A decree made political commissars in the army coequal with the commanders in military as well as political affairs. All orders were to be signed jointly.

## 17–18 August

According to Conquest quoting former prisoners, the number of arrests in the purge was so great that time-consuming methods of NKVD interrogation were replaced by beatings in the gaols in Moscow, Kharkov and elsewhere. Fellow prisoners were unable to sleep because of the noise the victims made (see *The Great Terror*, 1968, p. 307)

## 21 August

China signed a five-year non-aggression treaty with the USSR. The parties undertook that, if either of them was the victim of aggression by one or more third powers, the other would give no assistance of any kind to the power or powers concerned. The treaty specified that rights and obligations arising out of existing treaties signed by the two· parties were not affected. In other words, the Chinese tacitly abandoned their objections to the Soviet sale of the Chinese Eastern railway and accepted the Soviet position in Mongolia and Sinkiang. The treaty was followed by Soviet military assistance to Chiang Kai-shek. This included, according to Whiting, 885 aircraft, almost all of which travelled via Sinkiang. Dallin mentioned 400–500 aircraft together with some Soviet pilots and flying instructors who established air-training schools in Urumchi (Sinkiang) and Chengtu (Szechwan). Other sources have mentioned Soviet supplies of tanks, artillery and fuel. A Soviet military mission was set up in Chiang Kai-shek's capital, then at Hankow, and Soviet officers were attached to many of the Chinese armies. Substantial Soviet credits were made available to China from 1938 onwards.

The revived united front between the Kuomintang and the now legalised Chinese communist party ran smoothly until September 1939 when, in the wake of the Nazi–Soviet pact and Soviet–Japanese *rapprochement*, friction arose between the partners.

Whiting stated that the Chinese Communists established a clandestine line of communication with Moscow via Urumchi in 1937. Sheng Shih-ts'ai applied to join the Chinese communist party but, before his application had been decided on, he was enrolled into the All-Union Communist Party by Stalin personally in the course of his visit to Moscow in August 1938.

## 2 September

*Pravda* announced that a new chairman of the Ukrainian Council of People's Commissars had been elected. His predecessor, Liubchenko, whose date of death is given as 29 August in the GSE, is believed to have committed suicide. The precise course of events in the Ukraine at this time is not known but there is no doubt that a major purge ensued. In the course of the next year, the whole of the local Politburo, Orgburo and Secretariat were arrested. Almost all the people's commissars and provincial party secretaries were swept away. Similar purges of 'nationalists' occurred in Byelorussia and many other republics (see also 30 June 1938).

## 22 September

General Miller, the former commander of the White Russian forces in north Russia and governor-general of Archangel who had succeeded General Kutepov as leader of the Russian Armed Services' Union (ROVS – see 26 January 1930), was kidnapped in Paris and not seen again. There was strong circumstantial evidence of Soviet involvement in his disappearance.

## 8 October

A Soviet–Turkish treaty of commerce and navigation was signed in Ankara together with a trade and clearing agreement.

## 12 October

Ezhov was elected a candidate member of the Politburo. According to Khrushchev, in the course of 1937 and 1938 Ezhov sent Stalin 383 lists of names of prominent individuals whose execution required Stalin's personal approval. According to Roy Medvedev the lists contained 44,000 names, mostly of party and government officials, military and cultural figures.

Jasny regarded the purges as a significant cause of the stagnation in economic growth which affected the USSR from 1937 to 1940: not only were many planners, engineers and technicians liquidated or imprisoned but fear paralysed decision-making in general.

## 14 October

Bauman, a candidate member of the Politburo in 1929–30 and head of the Central Committee's scientific department, was shot along with many of his staff.

## 31 October

Stalin praised the leaders of Soviet industry and said it was wrong to persecute all of them, implying that the Ezhovshchina was getting out of control.

## 6 November

Italy's adherence to the German–Japanese anti-Comintern pact called forth a Soviet protest two days later.

## 23 November

It was announced that the German consulates-general at Leningrad and Tbilisi (Tiflis up to 1936) and the consulates at Kharkov, Vladivostok and Odessa would close by 15 January 1938. Other German consulates in the USSR had been closed from mid-October onwards on a reciprocal basis. The British embassy in Moscow estimated that there were 500 German citizens in custody in the USSR at the end of the year. The Italian consulate-general at Kiev, the consulates at Leningrad and Tbilisi and the vice-consulates at Novorossiisk and Batumi were to close by 20 January 1938.

## December

In conversation with an American journalist, J. T. Whitaker, Litvinov observed that Hitler and his generals remembered Bismarck's warning against war on two fronts. When the Germans were prepared to embark on their new adventures, they would come to Moscow to ask the Soviets for a pact. Litvinov admitted frankly that his collective security policy had collapsed. He acknowledged that Germany would take over Austria and thought this would probably occur in the following March. The next German move would be against Czechoslovakia, not Poland. The Soviets were obliged to go to the aid of the Czechs but only if France also met its obligations to the Czechs and France would not fight.

## 12 December

Elections were held to the two chambers of the Supreme Soviet. Out of an electorate of 94 million, 96.5 per cent voted for 1,143 candidates who were all returned unopposed. Getty described the evidence that in the summer it was proposed to hold these elections more democratically: regulations were published in *Pravda* on 2 July allowing for multiple candidates nominated without restriction. The regulations were apparently revoked by an extraordinary plenum of the Central Committee early in October.

## 19 December

It was announced that Enukidze, Karakhan and six others had been tried on 16 December as spies, bourgeois nationalists and terrorists, had confessed and had been executed. At the later Bukharin trial, Enukidze, who had been responsible for the administration of the Kremlin, was said to have been implicated in the murders of Kirov and Gorky.

## 20–21 December

The twentieth anniversary of the founding of the state security service (known successively as the VCHEKA, GPU, OGPU and NKVD) was celebrated with extensive press publicity and a ceremonial meeting in the Bolshoi Theatre in Moscow attended by Kaganovich, Molotov, Voroshilov, Mikoyan and Khrushchev. Mikoyan delivered the main speech.

## 31 December

A new Naval Commissariat, separate from the Defence Commissariat, was created, reflecting the increased scale of resources devoted to the navy. P. A. Smirnov was appointed commissar (he was succeeded by N. G. Kuznetsov in 1939) but real power lay with the Main Naval Soviet under Zhdanov which supervised the Naval Commissariat.

## End of 1937

The Profintern was dissolved.

# 1938

## 1 January

Party membership was given as 1,405,879 with 514,123 candidate members.

## 11 January

The Soviet government requested the closure of the British consulate-general in Leningrad. Closure was officially notified to the Soviets on 18 March. It was suggested that this and other closures of western consulates were intended by the Soviets to prevent foreign observation of defence preparations, especially in the Leningrad area.

The new Supreme Soviet met for the first time.

## 15 January

The Soviet government suspended commercial payments to Italy on the ground that Soviet organisations had not been paid for goods supplied to Italy for over a year. This led to a virtual rupture in trade relations between the two countries.

## 19 January

Postyshev lost his position as a candidate member of the Politburo and was replaced by Khrushchev. Postyshev was arrested a few weeks later and was subsequently shot.

A Central Committee resolution 'On Errors of Party Organisations in Expelling Communists from the Party . . .' condemned party leaders who had sought to further their careers by unjustified, indiscriminate or 'criminally frivolous' mass expulsions of party members and implied that such leaders might be disguised 'enemies of the people'. The resolution gave credit to the Party Control Commission and the NKVD for the reversal of unjust decisions. The resolution was followed in the next three days by articles in *Pravda* calling for continuing vigilance against 'enemies of the people'. In fact, although some party members were rehabilitated and a recruiting campaign began to bring in new members, the Ezhovshchina continued.

## 29 January

*Pravda* announced Khrushchev's appointment as First Secretary in the Ukraine where the party leadership had been heavily purged. He succeeded Kosior who was appointed vice-chairman of the USSR Council of People's Commissars and president of the Soviet Control Commission.

## Early 1938

Lysenko became head of the Lenin

All-Union Academy of Agricultural Sciences, his two predecessors having been arrested. Huxley described Lysenko as a scientific illiterate whose non-scientific theories on the inheritance of environmentally acquired characteristics owed something to Lamarck and the Russian horticulturist and plant-breeder, Michurin. Joravsky explained how from about 1929 onwards, Lysenko succeeded in persuading party leaders concerned with agriculture that his 'peasant remedies' such as the 'vernalisation' of wheat had more to offer in terms of practical solutions to pressing problems of agricultural production than the academic school of neo-Mendelians concerned with long-term scientific research into the chromosomal and genetic factors in inheritance in, for example, fruit flies.

Active discrimination against neo-Mendelians began in 1932 or 1933. In 1936 the Medico-Genetic Institute was dissolved. The Seventh International Congress on Genetics, due to be held in Moscow in 1937, was cancelled. On 17 May 1938 Stalin bestowed an implicit blessing on Lysenko which was made explicit in a *Pravda* editorial of 21 November 1938. Andreev endorsed Lysenkoism in his report on agriculture to the party's Eighteenth Congress in March 1939. Zhdanov on the other hand, who supervised the cultural, scientific and ideological establishments, maintained public silence on the issue. Forty Soviet geneticists who had submitted papers to the Edinburgh Congress of 1939 were at the last moment refused permission to attend and the internationally respected geneticist Vavilov was obliged to resign as president of the

congress. When Vavilov was arrested in August 1940, Lysenko succeeded him as head of the Institute of Genetics which he converted into a centre of Lysenkoism. By this time he was advocating that neo-Mendelism should be barred from educational curricula. In May 1941 he was made a Hero of the Soviet Union.

## 11 February

*The Times* reported from Delhi that 150 boys from Sinkiang who were being educated in Tashkent were being transferred to the military college there and were expected to be joined shortly by a further 200 boys from Sinkiang.

## 14 February

Stalin published an article in *Pravda* stating that the Soviet Union had solved its internal problem by achieving the 'victory of socialist construction in a single country' but that this was not the end of the story. The second, external, problem, that of capitalist encirclement of the USSR, could be solved only by 'joining the efforts of the international proletariat with the still more serious efforts of the whole Soviet people'. He referred to the Red Army as the champion of the 'workers of the world to free them from the yoke of capitalism' and called for further reinforcement of the Soviet armed forces and the paramilitary and civil defence organisation *Osoaviakhim*. In the event of an attack, political assistance from the working class in the bourgeois countries to the USSR, and vice versa, should be organised.

## 22 February

Voroshilov announced the names of

senior army and navy commanders who had been executed.

## 1 March

A Soviet–German agreement on trade and payments extended the agreement of 24 December 1936 (see under 29 April 1936) until 31 December 1938. The agreement was later extended to 31 December 1939 and then 31 December 1940.

## 2–13 March

Bukharin, Rykov, Krestinskii, Rakovskii, Iagoda and sixteen others, including three doctors, were tried on charges of wrecking in industry, agriculture, trade and finance, undermining Soviet military power, provoking an attack on the USSR and working for its dismemberment, seeking to overthrow the socialist system and restore capitalism, conspiracy with Trotskyites, Zinovievists, rightists, Mensheviks, SRs, military plotters and bourgeois nationalists in many of the non-Russian Soviet republics, espionage for Germany, Britain, Japan and Poland, the assassination of Kirov and the medical murder of Kuibyshev, Menzhinskii, Gorky and his son, Peshkov. Some were accused of having been Tsarists agents in the revolutionary movement. Iagoda was charged with trying to poison Ezhov and Bukharin was accused of having tried to seize power and murder Lenin and Stalin in 1918. Vyshinskii led the prosecution. On the first day of the trial, Krestinskii, unlike the other defendants, pleaded not guilty and withdrew the admissions he had apparently made under interrogation. On the second day, after overnight pressure and perhaps torture,

Krestinskii admitted his guilt. Despite Bukharin's categorical denials of espionage or of complicity in attempts on the lives of Lenin, Stalin or others and his mock acceptance of general responsibility for crimes including many of which he had no knowledge, he was found guilty on all counts in common with all his co-defendants. All were sentenced to death except for three, including Rakovskii, who received prison sentences. Most of them have since been rehabilitated including Bukharin in 1988.

## 6–12 March

At another trial, in Alma-Ata, eighteen leading personalities in Kazakhstan were sentenced to be shot.

## 13 March

The Central Committee decided to set up a Main Military Council (Soviet) under Voroshilov with Mekhlis (confidently identified by Rosenfeldt as a former member of Stalin's secretariat) as head of the Political Administration. Heavy emphasis was laid on improving the work of the political commissars in the Red Army.

The teaching of the Russian language in the schools of the non-Russian peoples of the USSR including those in Central Asia was made compulsory.

## 15 March

Hitler having seized Austria between 11 and 13 March and thereby increased the threat to Czechoslovakia, Litvinov told the press that the USSR stood by its obligations to Czechoslovakia (see 16 May 1935)

provided that France did the same. Given that the USSR had no common frontier with Czechoslovakia and that neither Poland nor Romania was willing to allow Soviet troops to cross their territories, it was not clear how Soviet military help could be rendered except possibly by air.

## 17 March

*Pravda* published an article celebrating the return to Moscow of the polar expedition led by Papanin which had been launched on 21 May 1937.

## 9 April

Ezhov was appointed Commissar for Water Transport while retaining, at least nominally, his responsibility for the NKVD.

## 14 April

The Soviets began to put out feelers for negotiations with the Finns on the fortification and possible leasing to them of various islands in the Gulf of Finland. A second secretary in the Soviet legation in Helsinki, suspected of being an NKVD representative, was used as a channel. Unofficial talks continued sporadically and without result until March 1939, the Finns being wary of compromising their neutrality in any way.

## 21 April

N. A. Voznesenskii was appointed chairman of *Gosplan*. A new draft of the third five-year plan was prepared and was submitted to the Eighteenth Congress of the party in March 1939. The draft should have been completed by mid-1937 but *Gosplan* was heavily purged and its work disrupted in 1937–8. Its earlier output was discredited as the product of Trotskyite and Bukharinist saboteurs. The annual plan for 1938 was poorly fulfilled, necessitating further modifications of the plans for 1939–42.

## 29 April

Eikhe was arrested and Koisior at about the same time. Chubar' disappeared in June. According to Roy Medvedev, all three were shot, Kosior on 26 February 1939 and Eikhe on 4 February 1940.

## 2 May

The poet, Osip Mandel'shtam, who had been arrested in 1934 and exiled for three years, was arrested again and sentenced to five years' forced labour in the Far East where he died in a transit camp at Vladivostok on 27 December.

## End May

Isaac Babel', the leading short-story writer and veteran of the civil war, was arrested. He died on 17 March 1941, according to Roy Medvedev, in confinement.

## May–August

The Far Eastern army, which had got off relatively lightly in 1937, was thoroughly purged, beginning with the local NKVD staff, one of whom, Liushkov, escaped and defected to Japan.

## June

The Polish communist party was dissolved by the Executive Committee of the Comintern (see 19–21 June 1937).

## 6, 12, 24, 26 June

Elections were held to the republican Soviets. A 90 per cent vote was recorded in favour of the candidates presented, none of whom was opposed. Stalin was elected to all thirty-three Soviets.

## 12 June

Of the eighty-six members and candidate members of the new Central Committee elected at the Fourteenth Congress of the Ukrainian party, only three had survived from the previous year. None of the members of the Politburo, Orgburo or Secretariat had served previously. Khrushchev's Politburo of six included Timoshenko, commander of the military district, the NKVD chief and three colleagues from Moscow who had been concerned with the purge. The careers of Brezhnev and Kirilenko took off: by 1939 both were provincial party secretaries in the Ukraine.

## 30 June

In its annual review for 1938, the British embassy in Moscow noted the following disappearances and dismissals in the union-republics in the period January to June 1938 as having been reported in the Moscow and provincial press:

RSFSR president of the republic, deputy head of government, ten people's commissars;
Ukraine president of the republic, head of government, three deputy heads of government, fifteen people's commissars;
Belorussia head of government, deputy head of government, fifteen people's commissars, first and second party secretaries;

Azerbaijan president of the republic, head of government, seven people's commissars, first and second party secretaries;
Georgia head of government, four people's commissars, first and second party secretaries;
Armenia three people's commissars, two party secretaries;
Turkoman five people's commissars, one party secretary;
Uzbek head of government, nine people's commissars;
Tadzhik thirteen people's commissars, two party secretaries;
Kazakh president of the republic, head of government, two deputy heads of government, fifteen people's commissars, four party secretaries;
Kirghiz president of the republic, two successive heads of government, six peoples' commissars, four party secretaries.

## 11 July

Red Army troops occupied Changhufeng Hill near Lake Khasan, about seventy-five miles south-west of Vladivostok near the convergence of the Soviet, Korean and Manchurian ('Manchukuo') frontiers. The hill was in a virtual no man's land near a Soviet submarine base under construction. The Japanese claimed that the summit of the hill was on the Manchurian side of the border and captured it from the Red Army between 29 July and 1 August. Part of the height was reoccupied by Soviet troops after heavy fighting between 7 and 9 August, and on 10 August a truce was signed. A mixed commission on frontier questions was agreed on. According to Soviet sources, about 15,000 Soviet troops were employed in these operations.

## 20 July

Beria was appointed deputy head of the NKVD.

## 27 July

A purge of officers of the Soviet Far Eastern fleet was reported.

## 28–29 July

The Ezhovshchina was continuing but without show trials. A number of prominent individuals were reported to have been shot on these two days including Rudzutak, 'Flagman' Orlov, Vatsetis (a former commander-in-chief of the Red Army) and a leading playwright, Kirshon.

## 7 August

*Pravda* stated that party committees had examined 85,273 out of a total of 154,933 appeals by former party members against their expulsion from the party: 54 per cent of the appellants had been readmitted.

## 16 August

A decree on court organisation stressed the educative functions of the courts. Article 3 said:

> By all their activities, the courts shall educate the citizens of the USSR in the spirit of devotion to the motherland and socialism, observance of Soviet laws, care for socialist property, labour discipline and honesty towards public and social duty.

## 18 August

Bliukher was recalled from his command of the Far Eastern army. He was arrested on 22 October and according to Roy Medvedev, was shot on 9 November.

## 28 August

*The Red Fleet* outlined a new naval programme concentrating on capital ships.

## 11 September

The Soviet legation at Jedda was closed.

## 23 September

Litvinov addressed the League of Nations' Political Committee on the Soviet attitude to the crisis over Czechoslovakia. Litvinov's advocacy of collective security (see 11 October 1936) coupled with the fact that the USSR's obligation to assist Czechoslovakia was contingent upon action by France and that neither the Poles nor the Romanians were willing to accept Soviet troop movements across their territories lying between the USSR and Czechoslovakia, enabled the Soviet government both to claim that, in sharp contrast with the French and British, they had been consistent in their support of Czechoslovakia and at the same time, to avoid any serious risk of involvement in war on her behalf.

## 2 October

The Soviet government issued a statement saying that it had had nothing to do with the Munich agreement of 29 September between Germany, Britain, France and Italy. The agreement was described as a shameless capitulation in the face of an aggressor which would bring war under less favourable conditions for England and France.

## 15 November

The Central Committee issued a resolution directing that party propaganda should be based on the Stalinist *History of the All-Union Communist Party (Bolsheviks): Short Course* which had just been published. Its revised version of Soviet party history provided the basis for ideological instruction during the rest of the Stalin period.

## 23 November

A purge of Komsomol leaders was announced.

## 26 November

A joint Soviet–Polish statement reaffirmed the existing treaties governing relations between the two countries but it was only in the commercial field that relations tangibly improved.

## 8 December

Beria replaced Ezhov as Commissar of the NKVD. Ezhov disappeared in February 1939. According to Roy Medvedev, he was shot in the summer of 1940. Getty observed that the fall of Ezhov was followed by an increase in Zhdanov's influence.

There had been some easing up in the scale of the Ezhovshchina in the second half of the year although five senior NKVD officials in the Moldavian ASSR were tried and shot in Kiev between 29 and 31 December. After Beria took over from Ezhov, mass arrests were wound up. A certain number of prisoners awaiting trial were released. There were, however, very few releases of prisoners already in camps apart from some army officers in 1940. Arrests continued of those against whom there were some grounds for suspicion.

For varying estimates of the number of deaths occasioned by the Ezhovshchina, see 19–21 June 1937.

Conquest estimated in *The Great Terror* that by the end of the year not less than 5 per cent of the population had been arrested, the proportion being higher in the educated classes. He quoted rough figures of 5 million already in prisons or camps in January 1937, 7 million arrested in 1937 and 1938, of whom 1 million were executed and 2 million died in camps in 1937 and 1938 leaving 1 million in prison and 8 million in camps at the end of 1938. These figures were challenged in an article by Wheatcroft who maintained on demographic grounds that four to five million was the maximum size of the labour camp population which could have existed in 1939 (see End December 1939).

## 15 December

A Polish trade delegation arrived in Moscow (see also 19 February 1939).

## 20 December

A decree introduced 'work-books'. These were held by management but accompanied workers from job to job, serving further to restrict the worker's freedom of movement.

## 28 December

A decree lengthened the period of notice required of employees who wished to leave their jobs from a week to a month and increased the penalties for so doing in terms of loss of holidays and social insurance payments. Penalties for bad time-keeping and absenteeism were also stiffened by this and a further decree on 8 January 1939. The privileges of shock-workers were enhanced, especially their access to sanatoria and convalescent homes. Maternity benefits were cut and, in common with other social security benefits, their scale was related to length and nature of employment.

## 1938/9

All major national groups in the USSR which had used Latin alphabets changed over to modified forms of the Russian Cyrillic alphabet. Georgia and Armenia were however allowed to retain their native alphabets. According to Kolarz in *The Peoples of the Soviet Far East*, the change-over to Cyrillic was decreed for the peoples of the Far East and Far North as early as 11 February 1937.

# 1939

## 1 January

Party membership was given as 1,514,181 with 792,792 candidate members.

## 17–23 January

A census gave the total population of the USSR as 170,467,186. On this occasion, in contrast with the suppressed census of 6 January 1937, no question was included on religious affiliation. Lorimer (1946), quoting the census figures, gave literacy among those over 9 years old (i.e. ability to read according to the 1926 definition and ability to read and write according to the 1939 definition) as 51.1 per cent in 1926 and 81.2 per cent in 1939. He commented that the figures showed a marked levelling-up in the Asian republics. The literacy rate for men was 90.8 per cent and for women 72.5 per cent.

## 27 January

Glinka's opera *A Life for the Tsar*, dealing with Russia's heroic struggle against Poles and Germans, was renamed *Ivan Susanin* and revived. The year 1938 had seen the production of Eisenstein's *Aleksandr Nevskii*, described by the GSE as a 'patriotic film about the defeat of the German knights in the thirteenth century'.

## 7 February

A Soviet–Italian clearing agreement was signed. It contained six secret protocols covering, among other things, the delivery at Odessa of a destroyer under construction at Leghorn, the supply of Soviet fuel for the Italian navy and the supply to the USSR of Italian military equipment including artillery, bombers and armoured vehicles.

## 19 February

A Soviet–Polish commercial treaty and other agreements on trade were signed in Moscow.

## 2 March

The USSR severed diplomatic relations with Hungary, the latter having signed the anti-Comintern pact on 24 February. Relations were restored on or about 23 September.

## 3 March

The USSR announced its withdrawal from the Non-Intervention [in Spain] Committee, France and Britain having recognised the Franco government on 27 February.

## 10–21 March

The party's Eighteenth Congress was held. Zhdanov and Khrushchev joined Andreev, Kaganovich, Kalinin, Mikoyan, Molotov, Stalin and Voroshilov as full members of the Politburo. Beria and Shvernik (head of the trade unions) were elected candidate members.

According to Conquest's figures in *The Great Terror*, of the 1,966 delegates to the Seventeenth Congress, 1,108 had been arrested for counter-revolutionary crimes, and of the survivors only fifty-nine attended the Eighteenth Congress as delegates. Fifty-five out of seventy-one members and sixty out of sixty-eight candidate members of the 1934 Central Committee no longer appeared in the new Central Committee. Ninety-eight of them had been shot. Among the members and candidates of the new Central Committee were eight representatives of the NKVD. Petrovskii, who had been a candidate member of the Politburo up to the beginning of 1939 and who had been removed from his chairmanship of the Ukrainian Supreme Soviet in June 1938 but had retained his position in the Presidium of the All-Union Supreme Soviet, was not re-elected to the Central Committee. On 31 May he was relieved of his membership of the Presidium of the Supreme Soviet and in June was appointed Assistant Director of the Museum of the Revolution. He died in 1958.

Stalin's report on the work of the Central Committee said that the abandonment of collective security in favour of appeasement by Britain and France was explained not so much by the weakness of the democ-

racies as by their desire to encourage war between the USSR and the aggressor states, Germany and Japan. Stalin said that the USSR was not going to be drawn into conflicts by 'warmongers who are accustomed to have others pull the chestnuts out of the fire for them'.

He declared that Engels' prognosis on the withering-away of the state was correct but only if there were no encirclement by hostile capitalist states. The state with its armed forces, punitive organs and intelligence service was essential to protect socialism in one country. Internally the main tasks of the state were peaceful economic organisation and cultural education.

Stalin said that the exploiting classes had been eliminated in the USSR which had the most democratic constitution in the world. The country had been strengthened by ridding itself of spies, assassins and wreckers like Trotsky, Zinoviev, Kamenev, Iakir, Tukhachevskii, Rosengolts, Bukharin and other fiends. The purges of 1933 to 1936 had reduced the numbers in the party but had improved their quality. There would be no need for further mass purges.

In the interests of the workers and peasants, he demanded respect for and co-operation with the new socialist intelligentsia. The party's main tasks were: to improve the quality of its membership; to improve leadership through closer contact between leading and lower bodies; to centralise cadre selection and training, adapting the allocation of cadres to the requirements of the party line; and to centralise propaganda and agitation under a Central Committee department.

Molotov's report claimed that the greatest successes of the second five-year plan (which finished at the end of 1937) were in heavy industry but pig-iron, coal and oil production had all fallen short of their targets. The plan for power-station construction had been 55 per cent fulfilled and that for articles of consumption 85 per cent fulfilled. Targets for transport had been overfulfilled although water transport still lagged behind.

*Note:* Gregory and Stuart gave the following official Soviet claims for percentage fulfilment of the second five-year plan, with western estimates in brackets: national income 96 per cent (67 per cent), industrial output 103 per cent (76–93 per cent), producer goods 121 per cent (97 per cent), consumer goods 85 per cent (68 per cent), agricultural production 63–77 per cent (66–78 per cent), labour productivity (86 per cent) and retail trade (54 per cent).

Molotov said that the third five-year plan (which was to have run from 1938 to 1942 but was cut short by the German invasion in June 1941) called for an especially rapid advance in the heavy and defence industries and provided for the accumulation of the necessary stocks and reserves. He said that the average annual rate of increase in industrial output was set at 13.5 per cent, somewhat lower than in the second five-year plan. An accelerated programme of machine-building was bound up with an advance in ferrous and non-ferrous metallurgy. Increased production of coal, oil, chemicals and consumer goods were all high priorities. He claimed that the plan rejected gigantomania in favour of medium and small enterprises. He called for struggles against mismanagement and for higher productivity and the mastery of technique. Further tasks were to achieve universal secondary education in the towns and to complete the introduction of universal seven-year education in the villages and national republics. A full solution of the task of eliminating the distinction between mental and manual labour would require several decades but successful advances were being made. He concluded that the first and second five-year plans had built socialist society in the main: the third five-year plan marked the entry into a new phase of the completion of the building of socialism and the gradual transition from socialism to communism.

In his report on organisation, Zhdanov confirmed that mass purges of the party were to be discontinued. The decision was embodied in a resolution dated 20 March on changes in the party rules. Zhdanov argued that mass purges implied abandonment of the Leninist principle of an individual approach to people and led to unjustified expulsions from the party; they were ineffective against well-disguised hostile elements within the party. He said that the arrests of enemies of the people (i.e. the Ezhovshchina which he contrasted with the earlier purges) had been necessary and had strengthened the country. The party's weaknesses lay in the selection of appropriate cadres and in the verification of the execution of party decisions. These weaknesses had not been overcome. The selection of cadres had been concentrated in the Leading Party Organs section: this was to be reorganised into a Cadres Administration and a Special Organisational Instructional Section. Following the lines of Stalin's report, Zhdanov stressed the primacy of party political work: the Secretariat should devote its attention to supervising the theoretical education of the party membership rather than industrial production.

*Note:* Jonathan Harris saw in Zhdanov's report the origin of a divergence between him and Malenkov who believed that practice and experience rather than theoretical education were the requirements for correct action in industry. Stalin appears to have switched his support from Zhdanov's point of view to Malenkov's when national security was threatened and the interests of industrial production were therefore paramount in the period October 1939 to March 1940 (covering the war with Finland) and from the autumn of 1940 onwards.

The changes in the party rules abolished differential requirements for party membership as between workers, peasants and members of the intelligentsia. A uniform period of candidate membership of one year was established.

The congress adopted the third five-year plan. In the three and a half years the plan was to run, progress was very uneven, the production of consumer goods in particular falling well short of targets. Growth in steel and oil production was notably sluggish. The plan provided for very little increase in personal consumption or real wages.

Manuil'skii reported to the congress as the chief Soviet representative in the Comintern. His report, reflecting changes in the tone of Comintern statements from November 1938 onwards which had reverted to denunciations of social democ-

racy, criticised the application of popular front tactics.

## 15 March

German troops moved forward from the Sudetenland to establish a German protectorate over the whole of Bohemia and Moravia including Prague.

## 18 March

The British ambassador in Moscow received instructions to enquire whether the Soviets would actively help the Romanians to resist German aggression if so asked by the Romanians. This opened a period of Anglo-Soviet and Franco-Soviet negotiations which lasted until August.

Litvinov denounced the Nazi occupation of Prague.

## 31 March

The British having stalled on a Soviet proposal for a conference in Bucharest, attended by representatives from the USSR, Britain, France, Poland, Romania and Turkey, and the Poles having demurred at a British counter-proposal of a declaration by Britain, France, the USSR and Poland that they would consult together on any threat to the political independence of a European state, the British Prime Minister, Chamberlain, declared in Parliament that in the event of any action which clearly threatened Polish independence and which the Polish government considered it vital to resist with their national forces the British government would at once lend all support in their power. He added that the French government took the same position. Maisky, the Soviet ambassador in London, was given a few hours' advance warning of the statement.

## 14–15 April

The British Foreign Secretary instructed the British ambassador in Moscow to suggest to Litvinov that in line with, but independently of, French and British declarations of support for Poland and Romania, the Soviet government should declare that in the event of aggression against any neighbouring European country which was resisted by that country, the assistance of the Soviet government would be available if required. The French government supported the British suggestion and also raised the possibility of a Franco-Soviet pact of mutual assistance against aggressors.

## 17 April

The Soviet ambassador in Berlin hinted at the possibility of improved Soviet–German relations and left for consultations in Moscow shortly afterwards.

## 18 April

The Soviets responded to the French and British proposals of 14–15 April with a suggested pact of mutual assistance (including military assistance) in the event of aggression against any one of the three powers. The pact was to include a guarantee by the three powers that they would render assistance, including military assistance, to East European states bordering on the USSR between the Baltic and the Black Sea in case of aggression against any of them. The pact was to be signed simultaneously with a military convention between the three powers spelling out the extent and form of military assistance which each of the three powers would render. The Soviets suggested that the British government should explain that the assistance it had recently promised Poland concerned exclusively aggression by Germany.

The Soviet proposal ran up against Polish objections to associating themselves with or tying themselves to accept assistance from the USSR which, the Poles said, might well provoke German action against Poland. It also ran up against French and British reluctance to enter into military talks until the complex political questions of precisely who was to guarantee whom against what had been resolved.

Maisky, the Soviet ambassador in London, left for a week's consultation in Moscow.

## 3 May

With great abruptness Molotov succeeded Litvinov as Foreign Commissar. News of the change was published on 4 May.

## 8 May–2 June

Exchanges continued between the Soviets and the British and French with the Soviets sticking to their proposals of 18 April, complaining of the lack of true reciprocity of obligation in the Anglo-French suggestions and raising the questions of military talks and guarantees for the Baltic states. Molotov accused the British and French of seeking to prolong the conversations indefinitely without binding themselves to concrete engagements.

## 11 May

After several incidents from January onwards, fighting broke out in the Nomonhan district on the Mongolian border with 'Manchukuo' when Japanese troops occupied a salient of Mongolian territory to the east of the Khalkhin-Gol river. Zhukov took over command in the area late in July or early in August.

## 20 May

The German ambassador in Moscow asked Molotov about the possibility of renewing Soviet–German commercial negotiations. Molotov replied that the Soviets would only agree if the necessary 'political bases' had first been constructed. He refused to enlarge on this reply.

## 27 May

A joint party–government resolution ordered a survey of private plots of land and prescribed the minimum number of working days to be spent on collective farms by their members. The resolution was designed to counter the widespread and unlawful diversion of land and labour from the collective to the private sector. As a result of the survey, 2.5 million hectares of land were taken away from the peasants and harsher discipline was introduced into collective farms.

According to Karcz in Millar, *The Soviet Rural Community*, private plots in 1937 were producing an estimated 52 per cent of the total output of potatoes and vegetables, 57 per cent of fruit, 71 per cent of milk, 71 per cent of meat, 70 per cent of hides, 43 per cent of wool and less than 1 per cent of grain. According to Gregory and Stuart, however, the share of the socialist sector in gross agricultural production in 1937 was 98.5 per cent.

## 30 May

Weizsäcker, State Secretary in the German Foreign Ministry, told the German ambassador in Moscow by telegram that the Germans had decided, 'contrary to the policy previously planned', to 'undertake definite negotiations with the USSR'.

## 31 May

In a speech on foreign policy to the Supreme Soviet, Molotov underlined Stalin's principle that the USSR should not be drawn into conflicts by warmongers accustomed to having others pull the chestnuts out of the fire for them. Molotov gave a progress report on Soviet negotiations with the French and British. He remarked that, while conducting these negotiations, 'we do not by any means think it necessary to renounce business dealings with countries like Germany and Italy'.

## June

The party decided to reduce the number of party members who were simultaneously members of the Komsomol, one of the party's chief sources of recruits. Office-holders in the Komsomol were nevertheless entitled to remain in the organisation after reaching the statutory age limit and party members over the age limit were eligible for appointment to Komsomol posts which carried with them Komsomol membership. By 1939 over 10 per cent of the relevant age group of the population were Komsomol members.

## 2 June

Molotov gave the British and French ambassadors in Moscow a new draft of the proposed agreement between the three states. This draft named Belgium, Greece, Turkey, Romania, Poland, Latvia, Estonia and Finland as states whom the three powers would agree to defend against aggression.

## 12 June

The British ambassador in Moscow having been prevented by influenza from returning to London for consultations, William Strang, head of the Central Department of the British Foreign Office, was despatched to Moscow to assist him in the negotiations with the Soviets. He arrived in Moscow on 14 June. There followed seven weeks of intensive but fruitless negotiations over the wording of an Anglo-French-Soviet political agreement on mutual assistance. The first major difficulty in the negotiations arose from Soviet insistence on retaining in the agreement the names of the smaller states whom it was proposed to guarantee despite the reluctance of those states to accept such a guarantee which would compromise their neutrality and might provide the USSR with opportunities to interfere in their internal affairs under the pretext of a threat to her own security. Fears on this last score were vigorously expressed by many of the smaller countries concerned. Molotov did not accept the argument that naming the smaller states against their wishes would entail the risk of driving some of them into German arms. A further major difficulty arose over the French and British contention that the independence of Holland and Switzerland was as essential to Franco-British security as was the independence of the Baltic states to Soviet security.

## 14 June

Meyerhold, who had demanded creative freedom for the theatre *in Literaturnaia Gazeta* on 15 March 1936 and whose theatre had been closed as 'alien to Soviet art' on 8 January 1938, allegedly denounced the suppression of art in the USSR. He was arrested shortly afterwards and died in Moscow, presumably in prison, on 2 February 1940.

## 15 June

The Soviet chargé d'affaires in Berlin told the Bulgarian minister there that the Soviets would probably not conclude a treaty with Britain and France if Germany were ready to sign a non-aggression pact with the USSR. The Bulgarian minister reported the conversation to the German Foreign Ministry, speculating at the time that the Soviets had intended that he should do so.

## 16 June

An official Soviet communiqué was issued giving Soviet impressions of a long meeting between Molotov and the French and British ambassadors and Strang on the previous day. It said that fundamental questions of difference of opinion had been discussed and that the results were regarded in the Commissariat of Foreign Affairs as not being entirely favourable.

A Soviet–Chinese trade treaty was signed in Moscow in the course of an expansion of Soviet economic aid to China which is reported to have included a loan of $150 million. An unpublished agreement on Soviet supplies of war material to China may also have been signed.

## 29 June

Zhdanov published an article in *Pravda* stating that the Anglo-French-Soviet negotiations for an effective pact of mutual assistance against aggression had reached an impasse and arguing that the French and British did not want an agreement with the USSR based on the principles of equality and reciprocity.

## 1 July

At a meeting with the French and British ambassadors, Molotov objected to the proposed extension of Soviet obligations to cover the two additional states of Holland and Switzerland. (Luxemburg had also been mentioned by the British and French.) Molotov based his argument in part on the fact that neither Holland nor Switzerland recognised the Soviet government. Molotov raised the question of 'indirect aggression' which had not been mentioned in his draft of 2 June. From then on much of the negotiations revolved round an unsuccessful attempt to find a definition of 'indirect aggression' which would satisfy the Soviets that it covered all the possibilities of the Germans subverting or gaining influence over one or more of the states bordering on the USSR but which would not give, or appear to those states to give, the USSR a licence to interfere in their internal affairs.

## 3 July

The German ambassador in Moscow assured Molotov that the Germans regarded the Soviet–German treaty of 24 April 1926 as still being in force.

## 22 July

The Soviet press announced that negotiations with the Germans on trade and credits had been renewed in Berlin a few days previously.

## 26 July

In conversation with the Soviet chargé d'affaires in Berlin, a senior German Foreign Ministry official argued that an alliance with England would at best offer the Soviet Union participation in a European war and the hostility of Germany. Germany on the other hand could offer the USSR the possibility of neutrality in the event of a European conflict and, if Moscow wished it, a German–Russian understanding which, as in former times, would work to the mutual advantage of the two countries: no German–Russian clash of interest would result over Romania, Poland, Danzig, the Baltic states, Galicia or the Ukraine.

## 27 July

Speaking on instructions from their governments the French and British ambassadors informed Molotov that France and Britain had agreed to the immediate initiation of military talks with the Soviets in Moscow without waiting for final agreement to be reached on the outstanding points in the negotiation of a political agreement between the three powers. French and British military missions were to be despatched as soon as possible.

## 30 July

*Izvestiia* published a strongly anti-fascist article saying that the USSR stood for a peace front capable of halting fascist aggression, based on full reciprocity, equality and repudiation of 'non-intervention'.

## 2 August

The British ambassador in Moscow reported that at a meeting during the afternoon Molotov was a different man from what he had been at the previous meeting on 27 July. The ambassador felt that the Anglo-French negotiations with Molotov had received a severe set-back.

In the evening the German Foreign Minister, Ribbentrop, told the Soviet chargé d'affaires in Berlin that given Moscow's goodwill there was no problem from the Baltic to the Black Sea that could not be solved between the two countries. He hinted at the possibilities of a joint settlement with the Soviets of the fate of Poland and a reconciliation of Soviet differences with Japan.

## 3 August

A similar conversation took place in Moscow between Molotov and the German ambassador. Molotov, however, referred to three reasons for the earlier deterioration in Soviet–German relations: the anti-Comintern pact, German support for Japanese aggressiveness and German refusal to participate in international conferences at which the USSR was represented.

## 4 August

The Foreign Office recalled Strang from Moscow. He left on 7 August.

## 12 August

The British and French military missions, which had arrived in Moscow on 11 August, had their first formal meeting with the Soviets.

## 14 August

A major difficulty arose in the Anglo-French–Soviet military talks over Voroshilov's demand for a precise answer to the question whether, in the event of German aggression against Britain and France or Poland and Romania, Soviet troops would be allowed to pass through Polish and Romanian territory to engage the Germans. Voroshilov further demanded that Britain and France should obtain from the governments of the Baltic states and Finland their permission for the temporary occupation by the French and British fleets of a number of Baltic islands and ports: in the event of a satisfactory outcome, the Soviet Baltic fleet would be based with the British and French fleets in those ports.

Ribbentrop instructed the German ambassador in Moscow to propose that he, Ribbentrop, should visit Moscow for discussions with Molotov and Stalin.

## 15 August

While non-committal on the proposed visit by Ribbentrop, Molotov was unusually cordial with the German ambassador in Moscow and asked whether the German government was seriously interested in a non-aggression pact with the USSR, whether it would use its influence to secure an improvement in Soviet–Japanese relations (fighting was continuing on the Khalkhin-Gol front) and whether it would contemplate a joint guarantee of the Baltic states.

## 16 August

In a telegram to the German ambassador in Moscow, Ribbentrop responded positively on all three of Molotov's points. He said that Hitler was of the opinion that Soviet–German relations should be clarified urgently, given the possibility of serious incidents occurring any day in relation to Poland. Ribbentrop said he was prepared to fly to Moscow at any time from 18 August onwards armed with full powers from Hitler to sign appropriate treaties. (The German attack on Poland was originally planned for 26 August.)

A Central Committee resolution condemned local party officials for neglecting theoretical education and ideological development.

## 17 August

Voroshilov requested an adjournment of the military talks with the British and French, pending a reply to his question on the passage of Soviet troops through Polish and Romanian territory. It was agreed that the talks should be adjourned until 21 August.

The Soviet government's response to Ribbentrop was that the first step towards improved Soviet–German relations should be the conclusion of the trade and credit agreement which had already been discussed, followed by a non-aggression pact or reaffirmation of the neutrality pact of 1926 together with a protocol defining the interests of the two powers in specific areas of foreign policy. In conveying this reply, Molotov added that the Soviets were gratified by Ribbentrop's proposed visit, which they compared favourably with Britain's action in sending a relatively junior official to Moscow in the person of Strang, but they were concerned about publicity and thought the visit needed careful preparation.

## 18 August

Ribbentrop urged the necessity of his paying an immediate visit to Moscow since Polish–German conflict could break out any day. He suggested a twenty-five-year term for the non-aggression treaty and said he would be in a position to sign a protocol setting out spheres of interest in the Baltic etc.

## 19 August

A Soviet–German trade and credit agreement was signed in Berlin, providing for a German credit of 200 million marks over seven years at 5 per cent (reduced by secret protocol to 4.5 per cent). The USSR was to receive machinery and certain types of armament (e.g. armour plate and optical supplies) in return for exports of lumber, cotton, grain, petroleum, phosphates, platinum, etc. to the value of 180 million marks within two years. The agreement was announced in the Soviet press on 21 August.

The Soviets agreed that Ribbentrop should arrive in Moscow on 26 or 27 August and gave the Germans a draft of a five-year renewable non-aggression treaty.

## 20 August

The Polish government told the French and British governments that they refused to agree to the passage of Soviet troops over their territory, making it clear that the principal reason for their objection was their mistrust of Soviet good faith and their belief that once Soviet troops had set foot on their territory it would be impossible to dislodge them.

Zhukov launched a successful offensive against the Japanese on the Khalkhin-Gol front. The fighting involved tanks, artillery and aircraft on a considerable scale. According to Soviet sources, 75,000 Japanese and 112,500 Soviet troops took part. The fighting lasted until 16 September.

## 20–21 August

Hitler telegraphed Stalin accepting the Soviet draft non-aggression treaty and proposing that Ribbentrop should arrive in Moscow on 22 or, at the latest, 23 August to negotiate a protocol to accompany the treaty.

## 21 August

Stalin agreed that Ribbentrop should arrive in Moscow on 23 August.

Voroshilov adjourned indefinitely the military talks with the British and French in view of their failure to secure the required assurance from the Poles on the passage of Soviet troops.

## 22 August

Tass announced that Ribbentrop would visit Moscow in a few days with a view to concluding a non-aggression pact.

The leader of the French military mission saw Voroshilov and informed him that the French government agreed to sign a military convention with the USSR providing for the passage of Soviet troops over defined areas of Polish and, if necessary, Romanian territory once war had broken out between Germany and Poland. Voroshilov refused to reopen the military talks until the attitude of the British, Polish and Romanian governments was clear.

## 23 August

The non-aggression pact between Germany and the USSR (the Nazi–Soviet pact) dated 23 August was signed in the early hours of 24 August and published later the same day. Based on the Soviet–German neutrality pact of 1926, it bound the two signatories not to attack one another either individually or jointly with other powers. If either became the object of warlike action by a third power, the other was bound not to support the third power. The two powers were to confer continuously on matters affecting their joint interests. Neither party would join any grouping of powers directed against the other. Any disputes were to be settled by discussion or if necessary, by arbitration commissions. The pact was to come into effect on signature, to be ratified as soon as possible and to last ten years with provision for a five-year extension.

A secret protocol defined the northern frontier of the German sphere of interest in the Baltic as the northern frontier of Lithuania, both powers recognising Lithuania's interest in Vilna. In Poland the two spheres of interest would be divided by a line following the Narev, Vistula and San rivers. The question of the maintenance of an independent Polish state would be decided between the two powers in the light of events. With regard to south-eastern Europe, the Soviets drew attention to their interest in Bessarabia: the Germans declared their 'complete political disinterestedness in these territories'.

## 25 August

Voroshilov told the leaders of the British and French military missions that in view of the changed political situation there was no sense in continuing their conversations. The missions left Moscow.

The Polish and British governments signed a five-year mutual assistance agreement binding each party to give 'all the support and assistance in its power' if the other became engaged in hostilities with a European power (Germany was identified in a secret protocol) in consequence of aggression by the latter.

## 27 August

Voroshilov hinted that raw materials and supplies would be made available to Poland if it were attacked but the Poles apparently chose not to pursue the offer.

## 31 August

In a speech to a special session of the Supreme Soviet which ratified the Nazi–Soviet pact, Molotov said, 'Only yesterday German fascists were pursuing a foreign policy hostile to us . . . we were enemies in the sphere of foreign relations. Today . . . , we are enemies no longer.' The conclusion of the non-aggression pact had, he said, removed the threat of war between Germany and the USSR.

Nutter's study of Soviet industrial production supported Kravchenko's view that there was a slackening of the Soviet military production effort after signature of the Nazi–Soviet pact. Kravchenko claimed that only after the fall of France was the tempo of military effort stepped up again.

## 1 September

Germany invaded Poland.

A new decree on universal military service in the USSR lowered the age of call-up to 18 or 19 depending on education. The period of service was set at two to five years and new rules were introduced on the deferment of call-up. Over the following months these measures increased the strength of the Soviet armed forces to 4.2 million (Seaton's figure).

## 3 September

Britain and France declared war on Germany.

## 3–4 September

Ribbentrop informed Moscow that the Polish army would be decisively defeated in a few weeks. For military reasons the Germans would have to operate against Polish forces in the area of Poland allotted to the USSR. Ribbentrop recommended that the Soviets should act against these Polish forces and occupy their zone.

## 5 September

Molotov informed the Polish ambassador in Moscow that the entry of Britain and France into the war had created a new situation and that, in view of the strictly neutral position of the USSR as defined in his speech of 31 August, the USSR could neither send nor permit the transit of war supplies to Poland.

The USSR's neutrality in the war, formally notified to all diplomatic missions in Moscow on 17 November, developed by the end of the year into what the British embassy in Moscow described as a 'state of undeclared war' with France and Britain, the Soviet press taking a consistently hostile line and the international communist movement engaging in the full range of propaganda and subversive activities against the western allies.

## 15 September

An armistice was signed in Moscow to end the fighting with the Japanese Manchurian army along the Khalkhin-Gol river on the Mongolian–Manchurian frontier. The armistice provided for hostilities to cease on the following day and set up a mixed boundary commission. It put an end to frontier incidents for the time being. The campaign is widely regarded as having been an overall success for the Red Army forces under Zhukov's command: Nish described its effect on the Japanese army as 'shattering'.

## 17 September

Molotov sent the Polish ambassador a note saying that in view of the capture of a large part of Polish territory by the Germans and the disintegration of the Polish state and government, Soviet troops had been ordered to cross the frontier and take under their protection the life and property of the people of 'Western Ukraine and Western Byelorussia' and to extricate the Polish people from the unfortunate war into which their leaders had dragged them. The German and other missions in Moscow were similarly informed, the Germans at 2 a.m. The Red Army crossed the Polish frontier at 6 a.m.

## 18 September

The Polish government left Poland for Romania.

A joint Soviet–German declaration stated that their troops in Poland were acting in conformity with the Soviet–German nonaggression pact, their aim being to restore peace and order in Poland and 'to help the Polish population to reconstruct the conditions of [Poland's] political existence'.

The USSR recognised Mgr Tiso's German-sponsored government in Slovakia.

## 27 September–6 October

The Polish garrison in Warsaw and the other remaining units of the Polish regular forces surrendered to the Germans.

## 28 September

Ribbentrop, who had arrived in Moscow on the previous day, negotiated a second treaty with the Soviets, dated 28 September and signed early on 29 September. The treaty defined the boundary between the Soviet and German zones of Poland. A confidential protocol provided for co-operation over facilitating the emigration of Germans from the Soviet zone and Byelorussians and Ukrainians from the German zone.

The secret protocol to the pact of 23 August was amended to include most of Lithuania in the Soviet sphere of interest and to move the frontier of the German sphere in Poland further eastwards in the Warsaw and Lublin provinces. A further secret protocol covered Soviet–German co-operation over the suppression of Polish agitation.

A joint Soviet–German declaration stated that it would serve the interests of all people to end the state of war between Germany on one side and England and France on the other. Both governments would work towards that end. This was the opening of a 'peace offensive' maintained by Hitler with Soviet support into November.

Ribbentrop and Molotov exchanged letters on the further extension of trade covering increased supplies of Soviet oil to Germany and German rail communications with Romania, Iran, Afghanistan and the Far East.

In the course of occupying eastern Poland, the Red Army took about 200,000 Polish prisoners of war. Of the officers, about 8,700 were sent to three camps with 6,000 prisoners of other ranks. Only forty-eight were seen again. In April 1943 at Katyn, near one of the camps, the Germans discovered 4,183 Polish bodies, 2,914 of which were identified. There can be no reasonable doubt that they were killed by the Soviets. The fate of the remaining 10,000 Poles in the other two camps is unknown.

After a press campaign, opened on 19 September, accusing Estonia of endangering the security of the USSR by harbouring Polish and other submarines, the Soviets pressed Estonia into signing a pact of mutual assistance. This was followed by similar pacts with Latvia and Lithuania, signed respectively on 5 and 10 October, providing for the leasing of bases and the stationing of Soviet troops in these three Baltic states. Under the last of these pacts, Vilna was ceded to Lithuania.

## 5 October

Molotov informed the German ambassador that Murmansk was not 'isolated enough' to be suitable as a base for the repair of German ships and submarines and suggested an alternative site further to the east.

## 8 October

A German economic mission arrived in Moscow and concluded an agreement on or about 24 October for the supply to Germany of grain, manganese and flax. Railway and air transport agreements were signed on 23 December. The USSR, by becoming for a while Germany's chief source of supply of cereals, oil and raw materials and by facilitating German transit trade with the Middle and Far East, reduced the effectiveness of the allied blockade of Germany.

## 12–14 October

A Finnish delegation which had been invited to Moscow refused to accept a package of Soviet demands for a slice of territory on the Karelian isthmus near Leningrad, certain islands covering the sea approaches to Leningrad, additional territory in the Petsamo area in the extreme north and a thirty-year lease of the Hangö (Hanko) peninsula commanding the entrance to the Gulf of Finland. In return the Soviets were prepared to offer the Finns some territory to the north of Lake Ladoga. Talks between the two sides continued intermittently until 13 November, the sticking-points being the Soviet demand for Hanko or an alternative site at the western end of the gulf and the depth of territory demanded on the Karelian isthmus.

## 17 October

The Turkish Foreign Minister, Sara-coglu, left Moscow after a visit of over two weeks in which he success-fully resisted a Soviet attempt, encouraged by the Germans, to per-suade Turkey to close the straits to the warships of all non-Black Sea powers.

*Pravda* implied that the party should play a more active role in solving immediate production problems.

## 18 October

Soviet troops began to take up pos-itions in the Baltic states.

## 27 October

The Soviets handed Vilna over to the Lithuanians.

## 1–2 November

'Western Byelorussia' and 'Western Ukraine' became part of the USSR and were formally absorbed into the Byelorussian and Ukrainian SSRs on 12 and 14 November respectively.

## 7 November

The manifesto of the Comintern's Executive Committee on the twenty-second anniversary of the revolution declared that there could be neither a

united Workers' Front nor a People's Front with the leaders of the social democratic or other petty bourgeois parties who had crossed over wholly and completely to the service of the imperialists in their support for the war: it was the duty of all prolet-arians to put a stop to the unjust imperialist war.

## 26 November

The Soviets protested that Finnish troops had fired seven shots across the Soviet–Finish frontier causing Soviet casualties. The Soviets demanded that Finnish troops should withdraw fifteen miles from the fron-tier. The Finns maintained that the shots had been fired from the Soviet side of the border and suggested dis-cussions on mutual troop with-drawals from the frontier area.

## 28 November

The Soviets denounced their non-aggression pact with Finland.

## 29 November

The Finns despatched a note agree-ing to withdraw their troops unilater-ally from the frontier area but before it was delivered the USSR broke off diplomatic relations with Finland. A Soviet unit crossed the Finnish fron-tier near Petsamo.

A Politburo decree ordered the restoration of industrial departments in the Central Committees of all republican parties and local party organisations. These departments had been dismantled by the party's Eighteenth Congress. In Harris's view (see 10–21 March), this decision represented a victory for Malenkov.

## 30 November

A full-scale Soviet attack on Finland was launched. Soviet aircraft bombed Helsinki.

Bela Kun, who had led the communist regime in Hungary in 1919 and who had worked for many years in the Comintern was shot for espionage. He had been accused of working for the Romanians. Twelve other commissars of the 1919 Hungarian government were arrested.

## 1 December

The Soviets recognised a Finnish government set up by Otto Kuusinen, former secretary of the Comintern, at Terijoki. This government had been in the process of formation since 13 November or earlier.

## 2 December

The Kuusinen 'government' signed a twenty-five-year treaty of mutual assistance and friendship with the USSR accepting all the Soviet demands which the legitimate Finnish government had rejected. The treaty envisaged the reunification of the Karelian areas of the USSR with the new 'democratic Finland', thus indicating that a communist takeover of the whole of Finland was envisaged, a view supported by the final article of the treaty which stated that it was to be ratified in Helsinki as soon as possible.

## 6 December

The Red Army occupied Petsamo.

## 11 December–9 January 1940

The Finnish army scored notable successes on the central sector of the front, virtually destroying first of all the Soviet Ninth Army's 163rd Division.

## 14 December

The League of Nations Council decided that by its attack on Finland the USSR had placed itself outside the League of Nations and was no longer a member. Soviet membership of the ILO, in which it had not been active for two years, automatically lapsed.

Except in the Petsamo area, the Red Army's advance into Finland had been checked.

## 16–20 December

A major Soviet attack on the Mannerheim Line, the Finnish defences on the Karelian isthmus, was beaten off.

## 21 December

Stalin's sixtieth birthday was celebrated with, among other things, a special issue of *Pravda* and fulsome tributes from all the members of the Politburo with the conspicuous exception of Zhdanov who, according to Harris, was not restored to favour until the end of the war with Finland.

## End December

According to Academician Sakharov (quoted by Conquest), in the period 1936–9 over 1.2 million party members, half the total membership, were arrested. Only 50,000 regained their freedom. Of the others, 600,000 were shot and the rest died in camps. At least 10 to 15 million people perished by torture or execution in camps.

In 1981 Wheatcroft cited evidence

from party statistics indicating a level of membership turnover which, though large, was considerably smaller than that indicated by Sakharov. Wheatcroft also concluded that 4 to 5 million was the maximum figure for the population of camps under GULag management in 1939. Wheatcroft did not quantify the numbers undergoing forced labour without confinement at their normal place of residence or in exile.

The debate between the exponents of low figures for the Soviet prison camp population and 'excess deaths' in the pre-war period (notably Wheatcroft) and the exponents of high figures (Rosefielde and Conquest, for example) continued through the 1980s. Despite Wheatcroft's claim in 1985 that there was no demographic evidence to indicate a population loss of more than 6 million between 1926 and 1939 or more than 3 or 4 million in the famine, Rosefielde in 1987 defended an estimate of 20.5 million 'excess deaths' in the USSR between 1 January 1929 and 1 January 1939. He attributed 4.3 million of these to GULag, 5.8 million to collectivisation between 1929 and 1932, 4.2 million to famine in 1933–4, 3.6 million to terror and 2.6 million 'others'. He claimed that demographic evidence supported the hypothesis that the Soviet authorities falsified the 1939 census and other critical data including their electoral statistics.

*Moscow News* of 27 November 1988 stated baldly that the political trials of the 1930s were staged, that the charges against prominent Bolsheviks were fabricated and that the triumphs of the Stalinist leadership were mythical. In the same issue, Roy Medvedev wrote that 10 million people could safely be said to have been dispossessed during collectivisation of whom at least 2 or 3 million died. His guess at the number of deaths from famine was 6 million. After Kirov's assassination, about 1 million were exiled. By 1937 Stalin had already victimised 17 to 18 million people of whom at least 10 million died. Between 5 and 7 million persons were 'repressed' in 1937 to 1938. Of these, nearly 1 million were party members and 1 million former party members who had been purged from the party between the late 1920s and the mid–1930s: the remaining 3 to 5 million were non-party people from all walks of life. Most of those arrested in 1937–8 were put in corrective labour camps. A realistic figure for the number of top party and government echelons shot would be 1 million. Around 2 million could have been deported from Poland, the Baltic states, Bessarabia and Bukovina.

Apart from humanitarian aspects, the debate on the numbers killed and imprisoned has a bearing on questions such as the economic significance of forced labour in the USSR and the calculation of the overall productivity of Soviet labour.

# 1940

## 1 January

Party membership was given as 1,982,743 with 1,417,232 candidate members.

## 5 January

The USSR signed a treaty of commerce and navigation with Bulgaria.

## 5 and 6 January

According to Upton, Soviet notes were addressed to Norway and Sweden warning them against cooperating with any allied plans for intervention in Scandinavia.

## 7 January

Timoshenko was nominated to command the newly created north-western front covering the war with Finland.

## 9 January

The Soviet Ninth Army suffered a severe reverse near Suomussalmi in the central sector of the Finnish front, its 44th Ukrainian division being destroyed as an organised formation. According to Upton's account, the Finnish successes on the central front were not sufficiently decisive, given the strength of Soviet reserves, to enable the Finns substan-tially to reinforce the Karelian isthmus.

## 10 January

An unofficial Finnish representative left for Stockholm to sound out the Soviet ambassador there, Alexandra Kollontai, about the possibility of peace talks.

## 29 January

The Soviet government accepted the Swedish government's offer to mediate between the Soviets and the Finns. The note indicated that the USSR had no objection in principle to concluding an agreement with the Helsinki government (i.e. they were prepared to abandon the Kuusinen government) but that the terms would be stiffer than those which had been on offer in the previous October. Negotiations were spun out while the Finns explored the possibilities of further help from the Swedes or from the French and British.

## 1 February

After two weeks of artillery barrages, the Red Army went over to the offensive against the Mannerheim Line on the Karelian isthmus and on

13 February achieved a significant penetration of it.

## 10 February

The first of the mass deportations of Polish civilians to the USSR was carried out. Further deportations occurred in April and June 1940 and in June 1941. The categories of people liable to deportation were similar to those in Lithuania (see 28 November 1940) but included also all those of university standing, well-to-do and many poor peasants, soldiers' families, small merchants and traders and refugees from German-occupied Poland. Estimates of the numbers involved range from 440,000 to 1.25 million (Gross). The last deportation included many Poles who had in one way or another assisted the Soviet authorities in carrying out the first three deportations.

## 11 February

A Soviet–German agreement provided for the supply of raw materials by the USSR to a value of 650 million Reichsmarks in the first year. The most important materials were grain, oil, cotton, lumber, phosphates, chrome ore, iron ore, manganese ore, scrap and pig-iron and metals, including platinum, copper, nickel, tin, molybdenum, wolfram and cobalt, intended for use in the manufacture of German deliveries to the USSR of industrial products including war material. The USSR expressed its willingness to act as buyer of metals and raw materials for Germany in third countries.

## 15–17 February

The Finnish army withdrew from the Mannerheim Line to intermediate positions covering Viipuri.

## 26 February

The Finnish Army fell back to a new line running close to Viipuri.

## 6 March

With the resistance of the Finnish army crumbling and hope vanishing of any possible help from the French and British arriving in time, particularly in view of Norwegian and Swedish objections to allowing allied troops to cross their territory, the Finns despatched a peace delegation to Moscow where it arrived on the following day.

## 12 March

The Red Army having entered Viipuri after bitter fighting and having exhausted the heavily outnumbered Finnish army, the Finns accepted Soviet terms and signed a peace treaty in Moscow which entered into force on signature. (The date of the treaty is as given in Slusser and Triska quoting Soviet and Finnish sources.)

Under the treaty, whose declared purposes included safeguarding the security of Leningrad, Murmansk and the Murmansk railway, the Finns ceded to the Soviets a number of islands in the Gulf of Finland, the whole of the Karelian isthmus including the city of Viipuri, an area of high ground in north-central Finland where the Murmansk railway ran close to the Finnish frontier and the Finnish part of the Rybachii peninsula covering the western sea approach to Murmansk. In addition, the Finns granted the Soviets a thirty-year lease of the Hanko peninsula and adjacent islands as a naval base. The treaty included a mutual non-aggression clause: neither power was to enter into alliances directed against the other. A railway was to be built across Finland linking the Murmansk railway with Sweden. The Petsamo area was returned to Finland.

Most of the ceded territory, from which many thousands of Finnish residents fled before it was handed over, was combined with the existing Karelian Autonomous SSR on 30 April to form the new Karelo-Finnish SSR under Kuusinen's leadership. (It reverted to the status of an Autonomous SSR within the RSFSR in 1956.)

According to Soviet sources, the Red Army's losses were 48,000 killed and 158,000 wounded. Finnish estimates were much higher.

Upton and others have argued that the Red Army's poor showing in the difficult conditions of the war with Finland was a factor in the underestimate of its true potential by Hitler and also the allies. The possibility that French and British troops might be sent to Scandinavia, despite the objections of Norway and Sweden, may have been a factor in inducing the Soviets to make peace with Finland when they did.

## 25 March

A trade and navigation agreement was signed between the USSR and Iran.

## 9 April

Hitler occupied Denmark and invaded Norway. The German ambassador in Moscow reported that these actions were followed by an immediate and marked improvement in the Soviet attitude towards Germany: he suspected that the Soviets had feared British and French intervention in Scandinavia and were much relieved that Germany had forestalled it. Shortly afterwards, the Soviets provided the Germans with a naval base on the Murman coast which the Germans had been seeking for some months (see 5 October 1939). On 5 September Berlin notified the German ambassador in Moscow that the German navy was abandoning this base which was no longer needed in view of the bases available in Norway.

## 14 April

The Supreme Military Council was convoked to consider the shortcomings of the Red Army's performance in the war with Finland. Among them were: the failure to equip the infantry with light automatic weapons; obsolete communications equipment and therefore poor co-ordination between units; shortages of engineering equipment to deal with steel and concrete fortifications; inadequate transport; failure to supply proper clothing for the Arctic conditions; lack of training for these conditions and the use of unsuitable troops, e.g. from the southern Ukraine; and lack of intelligence, e.g. on the fortifications of the Mannerheim Line. In an address to the meeting on 17 April, Stalin accused the Red Army leadership of being prisoners of the civil war tradition and demanded that they bring themselves up to date.

## 19 April

The British government informed Maisky, the Soviet ambassador in London, that it was prepared to explore the basis for a new trade agreement with the USSR. The Soviet government, however, showed itself disinclined to accept limitations on Soviet trade with Germany.

## 1 May

The May Day manifesto of the Executive Committee of the Comintern denounced the war and called on the workers to struggle for peace.

## 7 May

Timoshenko, Shaposhnikov, chief of the general staff, and Kulik, chief of the artillery administration, were promoted to the rank of marshal. Timoshenko was appointed Defence Commissar in place of Voroshilov who became deputy chairman of the Council of People's Commissars and chairman of its Defence Committee. A month later Zhukov took the newly revived rank of general. The rank of admiral was also revived. The term 'commander' continued to be used in place of 'officer'. Saluting was reintroduced.

## 10 May

As a preliminary to the invasion of France, Hitler attacked Holland, Belgium and Luxemburg. Molotov reacted to the news with understanding and confidence in German success.

## 11 May

A Soviet–Yugoslav treaty of commerce and navigation was signed in Moscow.

## 16 May

An order listed the shortcomings which had been identified in the Red Army during the Finnish campaign.

## 28 May

A Soviet noted to Lithuania complained about the alleged kidnapping of Soviet soldiers.

## 6 June

Moscow radio issued a warning to the Italian government that the Soviet government would not remain passive in the face of a threat to the Balkans.

## 9 June

The border commission set up after the fighting on the Khalkhin-Gol river in the Nomonhan area on the Mongolian–Manchurian frontier in 1939 finally reached agreement.

## 10 June

Italy entered the war.

## 12 June

Sir Stafford Cripps arrived in Moscow as the new British ambassador.

## 14 June

A Soviet ultimatum to Lithuania demanding the trial of the Minister of Home Affairs, the stationing of Soviet troops in all major centres and the formation of a new government was accepted by the Lithuanians on 15 June. The occupation of the country was carried out by the Red Army on the same day. A particularly severe persecution of the Catholic church (over 80 per cent of the population were Catholic) was immediately put in hand.

## 16 June

Similar Soviet ultimata were issued to Latvia and Estonia and both were taken over by the Red Army on 17 June.

## 17 June

A new Lithuanian government was formed under the supervision of Dekanozov, the Soviet Assistant Commissar for Foreign Affairs and a former state security official.

## 20 June

A new Latvian government was formed under Vyshinskii's supervision.

## 22 June

A new Estonian government was formed under Zhdanov's supervision.

The Franco-German armistice was signed, followed by a Franco-Italian armistice on 24 June and the cessation of hostilities in France early on 25 June.

## 24 June

Soviet–Yugoslav diplomatic relations were established.

## 26 June

Having given advance notice of their intention to the Germans on 23 June, the Soviets issued a twenty-four-hour ultimatum to Romania for the cession of Bessarabia and northern Bukovina. Northern Bukovina had not been mentioned in the Nazi–Soviet pact and its inclusion in the ultimatum caused the Germans some disquiet. Nevertheless, the Germans advised the Romanians to comply and they did so on 27 June, the territories being absorbed into the USSR on 28 June.

In order to boost production for national defence preparedness, the seven-hour day was replaced by the eight-hour day. The working week was lengthened from five days out of six to six days out of seven. Sunday was to be the normal day of rest. This and other measures announced on 2 and 19 October tightened up the direction of labour and the penalties for absenteeism. No one was allowed to leave a job without permission. The penalty for so doing was two to four months' imprisonment. Plant managers who failed to enforce the regulations were liable to prosecution and judges who failed to prosecute were disciplined. Underground work by women, which had been tolerated since 1933 or earlier, was officially sanctioned. Educational reforms emphasised the need for discipline, production and patriotism. Compulsory training schemes for school-leavers were introduced. Direction of labour was imposed on many kinds of specialist.

## 28 June

The USSR and Finland signed a trade agreement.

## 5 July

A Soviet–German agreement provided for the reopening of the German consulate at Leningrad and the opening of new consulates at Vladivostok and elsewhere.

## 10 July

A decree made the production of goods of substandard quality a criminal offence. Senior staff of undertakings in which such offences occurred were liable to prison sentences of five to eight years.

## 14–15 July

The existing parliaments in Lithuania, Latvia and Estonia having been dissolved, new elections were held on the Soviet model. Votes of 90 per cent of the electorate were recorded in favour of the single communist or pro-communist candidates presented.

## 21 July

The newly elected parliaments in Lithuania, Latvia and Estonia petitioned for incorporation into the USSR as SSRs. Lithuania was admitted on 3 August, Latvia on 5 August and Estonia on 6 August. The communist parties of the three former states were incorporated into the All-Union Communist Party (Bolsheviks) in October.

## 27 July

In an effort to improve US–Soviet relations, US Secretary of State Sumner Welles had the first of a series of twenty-seven meetings with the Soviet ambassador in Washington, which continued up to June 1941. Some improvement in trade resulted.

## 29 July

The Presidium of the Supreme Court promulgated a decree on the responsibility of judges for enforcing discipline.

The chief of staff of the German army initiated contingency planning for a campaign against the USSR. Cecil pointed out that Hitler made a number of moves in August indicating that, by then, he was determined to give priority to the attack on the USSR over the invasion of Britain.

## 2 August

The Ukrainian-speaking districts of Bessarabia were incorporated into the Ukrainian SSR and a new Moldavian SSR was created out of the Moldavian Autonomous Republic (formerly part of the Ukrainian SSR) and the Romanian-speaking districts of Bessarabia.

## 10 August

A decree excluded lay assessors, who had hitherto assisted judges in Soviet courts, from sitting in cases of industrial absenteeism or unauthorised job-quitting.

## 12 August

The system of dual command in the Red Army, which had proved unsatisfactory in the war with Finland, was abandoned. Political commissars were replaced by assistant commissars for political affairs.

## 20 August

Trotsky was attacked in Mexico by a Soviet agent known variously as Jacson, Jacques Mornard or Ramón Mercader and died the following day.

## 24 August–12 September

A joint review of Soviet–German

trade revealed that German deliveries to the USSR were well behind schedule and led to Soviet threats of a temporary suspension of supplies to Germany.

## September

A People's Commissariat of State Control was established to bolster 'state discipline' and to supervise the implementation of government decrees.

## 3 September

A Soviet–Hungarian treaty of commerce and navigation was signed in Moscow.

## 7 September

*Pravda* announced that Zhdanov had been freed from his duties as head of the Propaganda Department of the Central Committee.

## 12 September

The Germans signed an agreement with the Finns covering the transit of German troops through Finland to northern Norway and the setting-up of camps and depots on Finnish territory.

## 27 September

The three-power German–Italian–Japanese military assistance pact was signed. Molotov was informed of this on 26 September and told that the pact was aimed at deterring US warmongers and did not affect the relations of any of the powers concerned with the USSR.

## 2 October

A decree set up a State Labour Reserve Administration subordinate to the Council of People's Commissars. Between half a million and 1 million boys were mobilised annually for vocational training courses lasting two years for the younger ones and six months for the older ones, followed by four years' work in government enterprises. Students in secondary and higher education were exempt.

With some exceptions, fees were introduced for the last three years of secondary education, for technical and professional schools and for university courses.

## 12 October

A new and more severe code of military discipline was introduced in the Red Army, demanding unqualified obedience to all orders. (The revolutionary code had exempted troops from obeying anti-Soviet orders.) Commanders were expected to use their weapons if necessary to ensure obedience even in peacetime and were liable to court-martial if they failed to do so.

## 13 October

Ribbentrop wrote to Stalin reviewing the progress of the war and describing German activities in Scandinavia and the Balkans, about which the Soviets had shown some apprehensions. Ribbentrop suggested that Molotov should visit Berlin to discuss the 'historical mission of the Four Powers – the USSR, Italy, Japan and Germany – to adopt a long-range policy . . . and delimit their interests on a world-wide scale'. The letter was delivered on 17 October and the invitation was accepted on 21 October.

## 19 October

A decree gave people's commissariats power to order the transfer of specialists and skilled workers from plant to plant.

## 28 October–21 December

Soviet–German friction was evident at a conference in Bucharest to discuss control of the Danube.

## 12 November

Paragraph 5 of Hitler's Strategic Directive no. 18 read in part:

> Political discussions for the purpose of clarifying Russia's attitude in the immediate future have already begun. Regardless of the outcome of these conversations . . . further directives will follow on this subject as soon as the basic operational plan of the Army has been submitted to me and approved.

## 12–14 November

Molotov visited Berlin. Hitler told him that the war was as good as won. He expanded on his ideas of co-operation between the USSR, Germany, Italy and Japan in defining the developing spheres of interest to the south of these countries, mainly at the expense of the moribund British Empire – the Germans in central Africa, the Italians in north and north-east Africa, Japan in east Asia south of Japan, and the USSR in the direction of the Indian Ocean. While not rejecting these ideas, Molotov showed himself more interested in the area to the south of Batumi and Baku in the direction of the Persian Gulf and in more immediate questions such as the presence of German troops in Finland, the German guarantee of Romania, a possible Soviet guarantee of Bulgaria, revision of the Montreux Convention, possible Soviet bases in the area of the Black Sea straits and the renunciation by Japan of her coal and oil concessions in north Sakhalin. Upton contended that Molotov, who had been applying increasing pressure on the Finns in the preceding months over British interest in the Petsamo nickel mines and other matters, went to Berlin to seek a free hand for the Soviets to solve the Finnish question on the same lines as the Bessarabian problem. Hitler, while acknowledging that Finland remained within the Soviet sphere of influence, made it plain that he was not prepared to countenance any further conflicts in the Baltic area.

A draft ten-year agreement between the USSR and the members of the three-power pact of 27 September was drawn up by the Germans but not signed. The draft covered mutual respect for each member's sphere of influence and undertakings against joining or supporting any combination of powers against any one or more of the signatories. The first secret protocol envisaged territorial revisions in Europe at the end of the war for Germany and Italy but not for the USSR or Japan. A second secret protocol between Germany, Italy and the USSR dealt with the question of winning over Turkey to their side and replacing the Montreux convention so as to give Soviet warships unrestricted rights of passage through the Black Sea straits.

## 20 November

Hungary joined the German–Italian–Japanese pact, followed by Romania on 23 November and Slovakia on 24 November.

## 25 November

Molotov informed the German ambassador in Moscow that the Soviet government was prepared to accept the draft four-power pact provided that

1. German troops were immediately withdrawn from Finland, the USSR undertaking to protect German interests in Finnish lumber and nickel;
2. a mutual assistance pact were to be signed between the USSR and Bulgaria and a Soviet land and naval base established within range of the Black Sea straits;
3. the area south of Batumi and Baku in the direction of the Persian Gulf were to be recognised as the centre of the USSR's aspirations;
4. Japan were to renounce her coal and oil concessions in north Sakhalin.

Molotov requested three additional secret protocols covering his points about Finland, north Sakhalin and Bulgaria.

## 26 November

Sheng Shih-ts'ai, for the government of Sinkiang, signed a fifty-year agreement with the USSR (listed in Slusser and Triska) giving the Soviets exclusive rights to the exploitation of Sinkiang's tin, associated minerals and related communications networks.

## 28 November

Order no. 0054 from the Soviet Lithuanian People's Commissar for the Interior was issued listing the categories of people whom the Soviets considered to be actual or potential opponents of the Soviet regime and ordering the compilation of lists of persons in these categories. The categories included members of political parties other than the communist party, members of the police, gendarmerie and prison staffs, army officers, volunteer soldiers of all armies other than the Red Army, ex-members of the communist party, refugees, political *émigrés* and smugglers, citizens of foreign states, representatives of foreign firms, persons who had travelled abroad or who were in contact with representatives of foreign states, Esperantists, philatelists, Lithuanian government officials, Red Cross staff, clergy and active members of religious communities, aristocrats, landowners, wealthy merchants, bankers, industrialists, hotel and restaurant proprietors. The lists covered about 700,000 out of a total Lithuanian population of 3 million and served as the basis for deportations which were carried out on 6 June 1941.

*Note*: The text of this order is given in *The Dark Side of the Moon* (Anonymous, 1946), but without an explanation of how it came into Polish possession. It has been accepted as authentic by, for example, Vigor.

## 6 December

The USSR signed a treaty of commerce and navigation with Slovakia.

## 18 December

Hitler's Strategic Directive no. 21 on 'Case *Barbarossa*', the plan for the German attack on the USSR, was issued in secret. Preparations for the attack were to be completed by 15 May 1941. The final objective was 'to erect a barrier against Asiatic Russia on the general line Volga–Archangel'. The industrial area in the Urals could then if necessary be eliminated by the air force. Hitler said that the active support of Finland and Romania could be counted on.

## 23 December

Timoshenko called a special military conference to review the results of the reorganisation and retraining programmes which had been introduced into the Red Army since the war with Finland and which had been tested in extensive exercises during the autumn.

# 1941

## 1 January

Party membership was given as 2,490,479 with 1,381,986 candidate members, the total membership of 3,872,465 exceeding for the first time that reached in 1933.

## 10 January

A Soviet–German economic agreement was signed providing for increased deliveries of Soviet oil, wheat and other products in return for German machinery in the second period of the agreement originally signed on 11 February 1940. Agreement was also reached on the renunciation by the Germans of a strip of Lithuanian territory which the Soviets had occupied in breach of the treaty of 28 September 1939. The Soviets agreed to pay the Germans compensation of 31.5 million Reichsmarks in gold and non-ferrous metals.

## 17 January

The Soviets, referring to large-scale German troop movements in Romania, warned the Germans both in Moscow and in Berlin that the appearance of any foreign armed forces in Bulgaria or the area of the Black Sea straits would be considered a violation of the security interests of the USSR. Molotov also said that he was surprised at the lack of a German response to his statement to the German ambassador on 25 November 1940 reiterating the points he had raised during his visit to Berlin earlier in the month. He never received a reply.

## 22 January

The Germans informed the Soviets that their troop movements in the Balkans were exclusively related to their determination to prevent the British from establishing a foothold in Greece.

## End of January

A decision was taken to split off the security and intelligence functions of the Main Administration of State Security (GUGB) from the People's Commissariat of the Interior (NKVD) and form a new People's Commissariat of State Security (NKGB). The German invasion supervened before the change had been effected and the intelligence and security element remained within the NKVD until April 1943.

## 3 February

The German High Command issued

orders for the massive build-up of forces in the east to begin.

## 15–20 February

The party's Eighteenth Conference was very largely concerned with problems of industrial production including party and government control over industry. The main resolution spoke of the need to promote the technically competent and weed out the ineffective and idle regardless of whether or not they were party members. Malenkov's report spoke of increased intervention by the party in industrial matters. He accused local party officials of having ignored production problems. Zhdanov did not address the conference.

## 21 February

N. A. Voznesenskii, the director of Gosplan, Malenkov and Shcherbakov, leader of the Moscow party organisation, were elected candidate members of the Politburo. On 10 March Voznesenskii was promoted to the chairmanship of the Council of People's Commissars' Economic Council, retaining overall control over economic planning.

Molotov's Jewish wife, Polina Zhemchuzhina, was removed from the Central Committee.

## 26 February

A Soviet–Romanian trade and payments agreement was signed in Moscow.

## 1 March

Bulgaria joined the Tripartite Pact, the Soviet government having been warned of this development on the previous evening. German troops entered Bulgaria and Molotov was informed the same day. The German ambassador explained that the move was necessitated by the British presence in Greece. He said that Turkish sovereignty would be respected and that the German troops would be withdrawn when the British threat had been eliminated. The Soviets, who had been making strenuous efforts in the previous three months to prevent this development, protested publicly to the Bulgarian government on 4 March and in private to the German government.

## 12 March

The USSR established diplomatic relations with Thailand.

## 24 March

The Japanese Foreign Minister, Matsuoka, met Stalin and Molotov in Moscow on his way to Berlin.

## 25 March

Yugoslavia joined the Tripartite Pact but the Regency and the government were overthrown during the night of 26–27 March. The new government under King Peter announced its neutrality and sought Soviet support.

A joint declaration by the Soviet and Turkish governments was published to the effect that if one of them became the victim of aggression it could rest assured of the neutrality of the other in accordance with the pact of 17 December 1925.

## 27–29 March

In conversations with the Japanese Foreign Minister, Matsuoka, Ribbentrop said that Soviet adherence to the Tripartite Pact was out of the question: the USSR had imposed unacceptable conditions affecting German interests in Finland and the Balkans. Soviet–German relations were correct but not friendly. Germany had been watching carefully the cultivation of closer ties between the USSR and England since the arrival of Cripps in Moscow (on 12 June 1940). Ribbentrop said he did not think Stalin would take the wrong path but war between Germany and the USSR, though not probable, had to be regarded as a possibility. If the USSR were to attack Japan, Japan could be assured that Germany would immediately strike against the USSR and would crush her within months. Japan could therefore move against Singapore without fear of complications with the Soviets in her rear and should not allow herself to be diverted from this goal. Matsuoka said he had spoken to Stalin about a possible alignment between the Japanese and the Soviets against the Anglo-Saxons. Stalin had promised Matsuoka a reply on his return journey. Ribbentrop said he could see no objection to purely commercial agreements between the Japanese and the Soviets but he cautioned Matsuoka against going deeply into the question of a non-aggression or neutrality pact which would 'probably not altogether fit into the framework of the present situation'. The real Soviet interest was in a protracted war which would tire out the peoples and make them ripe for bolshevik influence. The rapid defeat of France had not suited Stalin. It was possible that the state of affairs would lead rather rapidly to Soviet–German conflict.

## 5–6 April

A Soviet–Yugoslav treaty of friendship and non-aggression, dated 5 April, was negotiated and signed.

## 6 April

The German army invaded Yugoslavia and Greece. The Soviet–Yugoslav pact had no practical effect on the course of events leading to the capitulation of the Yugoslav army on 17 April or the conquest of Greece which, apart from Crete, was completed on 23 April.

## 13 April

A five-year Soviet–Japanese neutrality pact was signed in Moscow by Matsuoka on his return journey to Japan. Each party pledged itself to neutrality should the other 'become the object of hostilities on the part of one or several third powers'. In a joint declaration the two countries also bound themselves to observe the territorial integrity of 'Manchukuo' and the Mongolian People's Republic. Matsuoka undertook to try to persuade the Japanese government to abandon their coal and oil concessions in north Sakhalin. On Matsuoka's departure from Moscow, Stalin and Molotov went out of their way to demonstrate publicly their friendly relations with both the Japanese and the Germans.

## 21 April

The Soviets protested to the Germans over violations of Soviet airspace by German aircraft, eighty cases of which had occurred between 27 March and 18 April. A German aircraft carrying a camera, maps and exposed film had crashed near Rovno on 15 April. To avoid provoking the Germans, no attempt had been made by the Soviets to shoot down German aircraft.

## May

A decree officially restored the diplomatic ranks of ambassador, minister, chargé d'affaires, etc. (see 4 June 1918).

## 6 May

Stalin took over from Molotov as chairman of the Council of People's Commissars. Molotov continued as Foreign Commissar and vice-chairman of the Council of People's Commissars.

## 7, 11, 21 May, 3 June

Four telegrams sent from Moscow to Soviet diplomatic missions in the Far East giving them guidance on foreign policy matters said that the USSR was trying to avert friction with Germany over Turkey and the Near East, that the USSR was sharing out spheres of interest with Germany and Italy, that, while the USSR had no sympathy with German or Italian imperialism, it was using them against British and US imperialism, that relations with the Anglo-Saxon powers were deteriorating and that unrest should be fomented in them. The telegrams were quoted by Cecil from German texts found in an unpublished section of German Foreign Ministry archives.

## 8 May

The Soviets withdrew recognition from the governments-in-exile of Belgium, Norway and Yugoslavia

taking similar action on 3 June in relation to Greece.

## 13–16 May

The Soviets recognised Rashid Ali al-Gailani's government in Iraq (which had brought off an anti-British, pro-Axis coup on 3 April) and established diplomatic relations with it.

## 15 May

In a communication to his Foreign Minister, the German ambassador in Moscow, taking into account the most recent Soviet actions with regard to Belgium, Norway, Yugoslavia and Iraq, interpreted Stalin's assumption of the chairmanship of the Council of People's Commissars as an indication of his determination to preserve the USSR from a conflict with Germany.

A German memorandum indicated German satisfaction with Soviet deliveries to Germany, especially of grain and rubber, the latter being shipped from the Far East via the Trans-Siberian railway. Seventy German engineers and technicians were still engaged on building a cruiser in Leningrad.

## Mid-May

Timoshenko and Zhukov (who had been appointed chief of staff as part of the reorganisation of the Soviet high command decided on in the light of the military conference in December 1940) gave orders for the formation of a front of reserve armies to be deployed behind the existing ten armies defending the USSR's western frontier. The front of reserve armies was intended to act as a unified counter-attack force in the event of a German invasion. To form this front (or army group), massive transfers of troops were ordered, mainly from Siberia and the Urals. Their redeployment was still incomplete when the German attack was launched.

According to Mackintosh's account, the reorganisation and re-equipment of the Red Army, which had been seen to be necessary in December 1940, had been proceeding slowly and with much wrangling and indecision in 1941 owing to the universal belief that the Red Army could not be taken by surprise and Stalin's apparent confidence, despite intelligence warnings from a variety of sources including the western allies, that the Germans were not about to attack the USSR and should not be provoked into doing so. In consequence, the defences of the newly occupied territories in Poland, Finland, the Baltic states and Bessarabia were incomplete. Owing to production problems, the Red Army's armoured formations only began to receive the new generation of tanks in April. The deficiency in automatic infantry weapons noted during the war with Finland had not been corrected; neither had the lack of transport, engineering and signalling equipment. Production problems had also affected the air forces leaving them with a high proportion of obsolete aircraft.

## 6 June

A mass deportation of active or potential opponents of the Soviet regime was carried out in Lithuania. Similar deportations were carried out in Latvia on 14 June and in Estonia. Dallin and Nicolaevsky quoted a

study by the Baltic Humanitarian Association in Sweden in 1946 as concluding that the numbers killed, arrested and deported amounted to 60,973 Estonians, 34,250 Letts and 38,450 Lithuanians. They were sent either to labour camps or into exile, the initial destinations being, for the Lithuanians, stations on the Krasnoiarsk, Karaganda, Tomsk and Moscow–Kiev railways, for the Letts, the Altai region, Kotlas and Starobel'sk and, for the Estonians, stations on the Gorky, Tomsk, Moscow–Donbas and Moscow–Kiev railways.

## 11 June

A new five-year Soviet-Japanese trade agreement was initialled but not signed.

## 13–14 June

A Tass statement, handed to the German ambassador and broadcast on 13 June and published in the press on 14 June, denied rumours of the imminence of war between Germany and the USSR and reaffirmed that the USSR would continue to abide by the Soviet–German non-aggression pact. The statement may well have been intended to elicit indications of the Germans attitude. It was not carried by the Nazi press.

## 17 June

A Soviet–Japanese agreement on the demarcation of the Mongolian–Manchurian frontier was signed.

## 21 June

The Soviet ambassador in Berlin lodged a protest against a further 180 German violations of Soviet airspace.

Molotov summoned the German ambassador in Moscow to a meeting at 9.30 p.m. and asked him the reasons for Germany's apparent dissatisfaction with the Soviet government. The German ambassador replied that he had no pertinent information.

## 22 June

In the early hours the Germans launched their attack on the USSR, catching the Red Army at a moment when its reorganisation, re-equipment and redeployment were all incomplete. At 4 a.m. the German ambassador in Moscow called on Molotov to say that Soviet troop concentrations near the German border were intolerable and that the German government was taking counter-measures. Molotov already knew that German troops had crossed the Soviet border.

# LIST OF SOURCES

Official British documents in the Public Record Office – mainly, in the FO 371 series, the annual reports of the British embassy, Moscow from 1930 to 1941 and FO 371/3979/157024 Report on the British Military Mission, South Russia, 8 October 1919. In the War Office series: WO 32/5707 Report on the Work of the British Military Mission to Siberia 1918–19 dated 10 December 1919 by General Knox; WO 32/5718 Report by Brigadier-General Percy on the Evacuation of Novorossisk on 26 March 1920; WO 33/971 Major General Sir H. C. Holman's Final Report on the British Military Mission, South Russia; WO33/977A Narrative of Events in Siberia 1918–1920.

The Parliamentary Debates: Official Report (*Hansard*), House of Commons, fifth series, vol. 131, 14 July 1920; vol. 133, 18 August 1920; vol. 196, May to 18 June 1926; and vol. 206, 9 to 27 May 1927.

*The Official History of the Great War: the Campaign in Mesopotamia: 1914–1918*, vol. IV, Brig.-General F. J. Moberly, HM Stationery Office, 1927.

*Documents on British Foreign Policy 1919–1939*, first series, vol. I, ed. E. T. Woodward and Rohan Butler, 1947; and vols VIII and XI, ed. Rohan Butler and J. P. T. Bury, 1958 and 1961, HM Stationery Office.

*Documents on British Foreign Policy 1919–1939*, third series, vols IV, V, VI and VII, ed. E. L. Woodward and R. Butler, 1939, HM Stationery Office, 1951, 1952, 1953 and 1954.

*Documents on German Foreign Policy 1918–1945*, series D, vols VI and VII, HM Stationery Office, 1956.

## British Parliamentary Papers

Cmd 9105 (1918) Treaty of Peace signed at Brest-Litovsk between the Central Powers and the Ukrainian People's Republic.

Cmd 8 (1919) A Collection of Reports on Bolshevism in Russia.

Cmd 587 (1920) Agreement between HM government and the Soviet government of Russia for the exchange of prisoners.

Cmd 818 (1920) The evacuation of North Russia, 1919.

Cmd 1041 (1920) Interim report of the Committee to Collect Information on Russia.

Cmd 1869 (1923) Correspondence between HM government and the Soviet government respecting the relations between the two governments.

Cmd 1874 (1923) Reply to the Soviet government to HM government respecting the relations between the two governments.

Cmd 1890 (1923) Further correspondence between HM government and the Soviet government respecting the relations between the two governments.

Cmd 2822 (1927) Note from HM government to the government of the USSR respecting the relations between the two governments and note in reply.

Cmd 2874 (1927) Documents illustrating the hostile activities of the Soviet government and Third International against Great Britain [mainly documents seized in the Arcos raid].

Cmd 2895 (1927) A selection of papers dealing with the relations between HM government and the Soviet government.

Cmd 3418 (1929) Correspondence regarding the resumption of relations with the government of the USSR.

Cmd 3467 (1929) Notes exchanged on the resumption of diplomatic relations with the USSR.

Cmd 3511 (1930) Decree of the All-Russian Central Executive Committee and the Council of People's Commissars respecting Religious Associations, 8 April 1929.

Cmd 3552 (1930) Temporary commercial agreement between HM government in the United Kingdom and the government of the USSR.

Cmd 3641 (1930) Certain legislation respecting religion in force in the USSR.

Cmd 3775 (1931) A selection of documents relative to the labour legislation in force in the USSR.

Cmd 4286 (1933) Correspondence relating to the arrest of employees of the Metropolitan-Vickers Co. at Moscow.

Cmd 4290 (1933) Further correspondence relating to the arrest of employees of the Metropolitan-Vickers Co. at Moscow.

Cmd 5679 (1938) Agreement between HM government in the United Kingdom and the government of the USSR providing for the limitation of naval armament and the exchange of information concerning naval construction.

Cmd 5794 (1938) Protocol modifying the Anglo-Soviet agreement of 17 July 1937 for the limitation of naval armament.

Cmd 6144, Treaty Series no. 58 (1939) Agreement between the Government of the United Kingdom and the Polish Government regarding Mutual Assistance.

Cmd 6616 (Poland no. 1, 1945) Agreement between the Government of the United Kingdom and the Polish Government regarding Mutual Assistance with protocol.

## US Official Publications

Department of State Publication 3023. *Nazi-Soviet Relations 1939–1941: Documents from the Archives of the German Foreign Office*, ed. Raymond J. Sontag and James S. Beddie, 1948.

'Soviet Political Agreements and Results'. Staff Study for the Committee to

Investigate the Administration of the Internal Security Act and other
Internal Security Laws of the Committee on the Judiciary, US Senate,
86th Congress first session, US Government Printing Office, 1959.
Nicholas DeWitt, *Education and Professional Employment in the USSR*,
National Science Foundation, US Government Printing Office, 1961.

## Encylopaedias

*Great Soviet Encyclopedia*, English translation of the third edition of the
*Bol'shaia Sovetskaia Entsiklopedia*, A. M. Prokhorov (editor-in-chief),
Sovetskaia Entsiklopedia Publishing House, Moscow, 1970–9: New York
Macmillan Inc.; London, Collier Macmillan, 1973–82..
*The Cambridge Encyclopedia of Russia and the Soviet Union*, ed. Archie
Brown, John Fennell, Michael Kaser, H. T. Willetts, Cambridge Univer-
sity Press, 1982, article on censorship by Martin Dewhirst.
*The Modern Encyclopaedia of Russia and Soviet History*, ed. Joseph L.
Wiecynski, Academic International Press, 1976–88.

## Newspapers

*The Times, The New York Times, Manchester Guardian, Pravda, Izvestiia,
Petrogradskaia Pravda, Moscow News.*

## Royal Institute of International Affairs, Chatham House (RIIA):

*A History of the Peace Conference of Paris*, ed. H. W. V. Temperley, vols.
II, III and VI, Henry Frowde and Hodder and Stoughton, 1924.
*Survey of International Affairs*, annual volumes from 1920 to 1941, Oxford
University Press.
*Documents on International Affairs* for 1928, 1929 and 1934, ed. J. W.
Wheeler-Bennett and S. Heald, Oxford University Press.
*Soviet Documents on Foreign Policy*, ed. Jane Degras, Oxford University
Press, vol. I, 1917–1924, 1951; vol. II, 1925–1932, 1952; vol. III, 1933–1941,
1953.
*The Communist International 1919–1943: Documents*, ed. Jane Degras, vol.
I 1919–1922, Oxford University Press, 1956; vol. II 1923–1928 and vol. III
1929–1943, Frank Cass, 1971.

## Books

Abraham, Gerald, 'Shostakovich: A study of music and politics', *Horizon*,
vol. VI, no. 33, September 1942.
Acharyya, S. (ed.), *The Third Five-Year Plan: Development of National
Economy in USSR: Report on the Third Five-Year Plan by V. Molotov*,
Calcutta, Book Forum, 1944.
Adams, Arthur E., *Bolsheviks in the Ukraine: The second campaign
1918–1919*, Yale University Press, 1963.

Agabekov, Georges, *OGPU: The Russian Secret Terror*, trans. Henry W. Bunn, Brentano's, 1931.

Agar, Capt. Augustus, *Baltic Episode*, Hodder and Stoughton, 1963.

Alexandrov, G. F., Mintz, I. I., Pospelov, P. N., Yaroslavsky, E., Genkina, E. B., Gorodetsky, E. N., Razgon I. M. and Tovstukha I. P., *The History of the Civil War in the USSR*, vol. 2, *The Great Proletarian Revolution (October–November 1917)*, Foreign Languages Publishing House, Moscow, 1946.

Alliluyeva, Svetlana, *Twenty Letters to a Friend*, trans. Priscilla Johnson, Hutchinson, 1967.

Anonymous, *Forward to the Second Five-Year Plan of Socialist Construction: The resolutions of the XVII Party Conference*, Moscow, Co-operative Publishing Society of Foreign Workers in the USSR, 1932.

____, *Socialism Victorious* (Speeches of Stalin, Molotov, Kaganovich, Voroshilov, Kuibyshev, Ordzhonikidze and Manuilsky to the Seventeenth Congress of the CPSU), Martin Lawrence, ?1934.

Anonymous (but close to Gen. Sikorski), *The Dark Side of the Moon*, Faber and Faber, 1946.

Anweiler, Oskar, *The Soviets: The Russian Workers, Peasants and Soldiers Councils 1905–1921*, trans. Ruth Hein, Pantheon Books, 1974.

Armstrong, John A., *The Politics of Totalitarianism: The Communist Party of the Soviet Union from 1934 to the present*, Random House, 1961.

Avalishvili, ˙Zourab, *The Independence of Georgia in International Politics 1918–1921*, Headley Brothers, ?1940.

Avrich, Paul, *Kronstadt 1921*, Princeton University Press, 1970.

Bailes, Kendall E., *Technology and Society under Lenin and Stalin: Origins of the Soviet technical intelligentsia, 1917–1941*, Princeton University Press, 1978.

Bailey, Lt.-Col. F. M., *Mission to Tashkent*, Jonathan Cape, 1946.

Bailey, Geoffrey, *The Conspirators*, Victor Gollancz, 1961.

Barber, John, *Soviet Historians in Crisis, 1928–1932*, Macmillan, 1981.

Becker, Seymour, *Russia's Protectorates in Central Asia: Bukhara and Khiva, 1865–1924*, Harvard University Press, 1968.

Beloff, Max, *The Foreign Policy of Soviet Russia 1929–1941*, vols I and II, Oxford University Press for the RIIA, 1947.

Bennett, Geoffrey, *Cowan's War: The story of British naval operations in the Baltic 1918–1920*, Collins, 1964.

Berman, Harold J., *Soviet Criminal Law and Procedures: The RSFSR Codes*, Harvard University Press, 1966.

____, *Justice in Russia: An interpretation of Soviet law*, Harvard University Press, 1950.

Biggart, John, 'Bukharin and the origins of the "Proletarian Culture" debate', *Soviet Studies*, vol. XXXIX, no. 2, April 1987.

Borkenau, F., *World Communism: A history of the Communist International*, University of Michigan Press, 1962.

Bradley, J. F. N., *Civil War in Russia 1917–1920*, Batsford, 1975.

____, 'The Allies and Russia in the light of French archives (7 November 1917–15 March 1918)', *Soviet Studies*, vol. XVI, no. 2, October 1964.

Brinkley, George A., *The Volunteer Army and the Allied Intervention in South Russia, 1917–1921*, University of Notre Dame Press, 1966.

Browder, Robert P., and Kerensky, A. F. (eds), *The Russian Provisional Government 1917: Documents*, vols I-III, Hoover Institution Publications, Stanford University Press, 1961.

Brown, Edward J., *The Proletarian Episode in Russian Literature 1928–1932*, Columbia University Press, 1953.

Bullock, Alan, *Hitler: A study in tyranny*, revised edition, Hamlyn, 1973.

Bunyan, James, *Intervention, Civil War and Communism in Russia April–December 1918: Documents and materials*, Johns Hopkins Press, 1936.

Calhoun, Daniel F., *The United Front: The TUC and the Russians 1923–1928*, Cambridge University Press, 1976.

Carley, Michael J., *Revolution and Intervention: The French government and the Russian civil war 1917–1919*, McGill-Queen's University Press, 1983.

Carr, E. H., *The Bolshevik Revolution 1917–1923*, vols I-III, Macmillan, 1950–3.

____, *The Interregnum 1923–1924*, Macmillan, 1954.

____, *Socialism in One Country 1924–1926*, vols I-III, Macmillan, 1958–64.

____, *Foundations of a Planned Economy 1926–1929*, vols I-III, Macmillan, 1969–78.

____, *The Twilight of Comintern 1930–1935*, Macmillan, 1982.

____, *The Comintern and the Spanish Civil War*, ed. Tamara Deutscher, Macmillan, 1984.

Carsten, F. L., 'The Reichswehr and the Red Army 1920–1923', *Survey*, October 1962.

Cecil, Robert, *Hitler's Decision to Invade Russia 1941*, Davis-Poynter, 1975.

Chamberlin, W. H., *The Russian Revolution 1917–1921*, vols I and II, Macmillan, 1935, 1952.

Chiang Kai-shek, *A Summing Up at Seventy: Soviet Russia in China*, Farrar, Strauss and Cudahy Inc., Harrap, 1957.

Churchill, Winston S., *The World Crisis: The aftermath*, Thornton Butterworth, 1929.

____, *The Second World War: The gathering storm*, Cassell, 1948.

Cohen, Stephen F., *Bukharin and the Bolshevik Revolution: A political biography 1888–1938*, Wildwood House, 1971.

Connolly, Violet, *Soviet Trade from the Pacific to the Levant*, Oxford University Press, 1935.

Conquest, Robert, *Religion in the USSR*, The Bodley Head, 1968.

____, *The Harvest of Sorrow: Soviet Collectivisation and the Terror-Famine*, Hutchinson, 1986.

____, *The Great Terror*, Macmillan, 1968.

Corson, W. R., and Crowley, R. T., *The New KGB: Engine of Soviet power*, William Morrow, 1985; Wheatsheaf Books, 1986.

Cumming, C. K., and Pettit, Walter W., *Russian-American Relations March*

*1917-March 1920: Documents and Papers*, Harcourt, Brace and Howe, 1920.

Dallin, David J., *Soviet Russia and the Far East*, Hollis and Carter, 1949.

\_\_\_\_and Nicolaevsky, Boris I. *Forced Labour in Soviet Russia*, Yale University Press, 1947; Hollis and Carter, 1948.

Dalrymple, Dana G., 'The Soviet Famine of 1932–1934', *Soviet Studies*, vol. xv, issue 3, 1963–4.

Davies, Norman, *White Eagle, Red Star: The Polish–Soviet War 1919–1920*, Macdonald, 1972.

Davies, R. W., *The Socialist Offensive: The collectivisation of Soviet agriculture 1929–1930*, Macmillan, 1980.

\_\_\_\_, *The Development of the Soviet Budgetary System*, Cambridge University Press, 1958.

\_\_\_\_, 'The Syrtsov–Lominadze Affair', *Soviet Studies*, vol. xxxiii, no. 1, January 1981.

\_\_\_\_, (ed.), *Soviet Investment for Planned Industrialisation 1929–1937: Policy and Practice*, Berkeley Slavic Specialities, 1984.

\_\_\_\_ and Wheatcroft, S. G. 'Steven Rosefielde's *Kliukva*', *Slavic Review*, vol. 39, no. 4, December 1980.

Denikine, General A., *The White Army*, trans. Catherine Zvegintzov, Jonathan Cape, 1930.

Deutscher, Isaac, *Stalin: A political biography*, second edition, Oxford University Press, 1967.

\_\_\_\_, *The Prophet Unarmed: Trotsky: 1921–1929*, Oxford University Press, 1959.

DeWitt, Nicholas, *Soviet Professional Manpower: Its education, training and supply*, National Science Foundation, Washington DC, 1955.

\_\_\_\_, *The October Revolution and Soviet Education*, reprint no. 43 from *Canadian Slavonic Papers*, vol. x, no. 3, Indiana University, 1968.

Dimitrov, Georgi, *Selected Speeches and Articles*, Lawrence and Wishart, 1951.

Drachkovitch, Milorad M., and Lazitch, Branko, *The Comintern: Historical highlights*, Frederick Praeger for the Hoover Institution on War, Revolution and Peace, 1966.

Dunsterville, Maj.-Gen. L. C., *The Adventures of Dunsterforce*, Edward Arnold, 1920.

Eastman, Max, *Since Lenin Died*, London, The Labour Publishing Co., 1925.

Ellis, C. H., *The Transcaspian Episode 1918–1919*, Hutchinson, 1963.

Erickson, John, *The Soviet High Command*, Macmillan, 1962.

Ermolaev, Herman, *Soviet Literary Theories 1917–1934: The genesis of socialist realism*, University of California Press, 1963.

Eudin, Xenia J., and Fisher H. H. *Soviet Russia and the West 1920–1927: A documentary survey*, Stanford University Press, 1957.

Fainsod, Merle, *How Russia is Ruled*, Harvard University Press, 1956.

\_\_\_\_, *Smolensk under Soviet Rule*, Macmillan, 1959.

Fic, Victor M., *The Bolsheviks and the Czechoslovak Legion: The origin of *their armed conflict March-May 1918*, New Delhi, Abhinav Publications, 1978.

Fischer, Louis, *The Soviets in World Affairs*, Jonathan Cape, 1930.

Fischer, Ruth, *Stalin and German Communism: A study in the origins of the State Party*, Harvard University Press, Oxford University Press, 1948.

Fisher, H. H., *The Famine in Soviet Russia 1919–1923: The operations of the American Relief Administration*, Macmillan, 1927.

Fisher, Ralph T., Jr, *Pattern for Soviet Youth: A study of the congresses of the Komsomol 1918–1954*, Columbia University Press, 1959.

Fitzpatrick, Sheila, *The Commissariat of Enlightenment: Soviet organisation of education and the arts under Lunacharsky between 1917–1921*, Cambridge University Press, 1970.

____, *Education and Social Mobility in the Soviet Union 1921–1934*, Cambridge Univerity Press, 1979.

____, 'Culture and politics under Stalin: a reappraisal', *Slavic Review*, vol. 35, no. 2, June 1976.

____ (ed.), *Cultural Revolution in Russia, 1928–1931*, Indiana University Press, 1978.

Fleming, Peter, *The Fate of Admiral Kolchak*, Rupert Hart-Davis, 1963.

Footman, David, *Civil War in Russia*, Faber and Faber, 1961.

____, *Siberian Partisans in the Civil War*, St Antony's Papers no. 1, Soviet Affairs no. 1, Chatto and Windus, 1956.

____, *Nestor Makhno*, St Antony's Papers no. 6, Soviet Affairs no. 2, Chatto and Windus, 1959.

Francis, David R., *Russia from the American Embassy 1916–1918*, Scribners, reprinted by Arno Press and *The New York Times*, 1970.

Frazer-Tytler, W. K., *Afghanistan: A study of political developments in Central Asia*, Oxford University Press, 1950.

Futrell, Michael, *Northern Underground*, Faber and Faber, 1963.

Garthoff, Raymond L. (ed.), *Sino-Soviet Military Relations*, chapter 2, 'Armed conflict in the Chinese borderlands, 1917–1950' by O. Edmund Clubb; and chapter 3, 'Soviet military aid to Nationalist China, 1923–1941' by James C. Bowden, Frederick A. Praeger, 1966.

Gatske, Hans W., 'Russo-German military collaboration during the Weimar Republic', *The American Historical Review*, vol. LXIII, no. 3, April 1958.

Getty, J. Arch, *The Origins of the Great Purges: The Soviet Communist Party reconsidered, 1933–1938*, Cambridge University Press, 1985.

Getzler, Israel, *Kronstadt 1917–1921: The fate of a Soviet democracy*, Cambridge University Press, 1983.

Gillette, Philip S., 'Armand Hammer, Lenin and the first American concession in Soviet Russia', *Slavic Review*, vol. 40, no. 3, Fall 1981.

Golitsyn, Anatoliy, *New Lies for Old*, Dodd, Mead, 1984; The Bodley Head, 1984; Wheatsheaf Books, 1986.

Gooderham, Peter, 'The *Komsomol* and worker youth: The inculcation of Communist values in Leningrad during NEP', *Soviet Studies*, vol. XXXIV, no. 4, October 1982.

Gorky, M., Molotov, V., Voroshilov, K., Kirov, S., Zhdanov A. and Stalin

J. (eds), *The History of the Civil War in the USSR*, vol I, *The Prelude of the Great Proletarian Revolution*, Lawrence and Wishart, 1937.

Gorodetsky, Gabriel, *The Precarious Truce: Anglo-Soviet relations 1924–27*, Cambridge Univerity Press, 1977.

Graham, Loren R., *The Soviet Academy of Sciences and the Communist Party 1927–1932*, Princeton University Press, 1967.

Grant, Natalie, 'The "Zinoviev Letter" Case', *Soviet Studies*, vol. XIX, no. 2, 1967–8.

Graves, William S., *America's Siberian Adventure 1918–1920*, Harrison Smith, Jonathan Cape, 1931; reprint Arno Press and *The New York Times*, 1971.

Gregory, Paul R., and Stuart, Robert C., *Soviet Economic Structure and Performance*, third edition, Harper and Row, 1986.

Grierson, Philip, *Books on Soviet Russia 1917–1923*, Methuen, 1943.

Gross, Jan T., 'A Note on the Nature of Soviet Totalitarianism', *Soviet Studies*, vol. XXXIV, no. 3, July 1982.

Hammer, Armand, and Lyndon, Neil, *Hammer: Witness to History*, Simon and Schuster, 1987.

Hammond, Thomas T. (ed.), *The Anatomy of Communist Takeovers*, Yale University Press, 1975.

Harris, Jonathan, 'The Origins of Conflict between Malenkov and Zhdanov, 1939–1941', *Slavic Review*, vol. 35, no. 2, June 1976.

Harrison, Mark, *Soviet Planning in Peace and War 1938–1945*, Cambridge University Press, 1985.

Hasegawa, Tsuyoshi, *The February Revolution: Petrograd 1917*, University of Washington Press, 1981.

Hayward, Max, *Writers in Russia 1917–1978*, ed. Patricia Blake, Harvill Press, 1983.

Hazard, John N., *Law and Social Change in the USSR*, Stevens and Sons Ltd, 1953.

Hilger, Gustav, and Meyer, Alfred G., *The Incompatible Allies: A memoir-history of German–Soviet relations 1918–1941*, Macmillan, 1953.

Hoover, Marjorie L., *Meyerhold: The art of conscious theater*, University of Massachusetts Press, 1974.

Hough, Jerry F., and Fainsod, Merle, *How the Soviet Union is Governed*, Harvard University Press, 1979.

Hovanissian, Richard G., *Armenia on the Road to Independence 1918*, University of California Press, Cambridge University Press, 1967.

Huxley, Julian, *Soviet Genetics and World Science: Lysenko and the meaning of heredity*, Chatto and Windus, 1949.

Ironside, Field Marshal Lord, *Archangel 1918–1919*, Constable, 1953.

Isaacs, Harold R., *The Tragedy of the Chinese Revolution*, Stanford University Press, revised edition, 1951.

Jacobs, Dan N., *Borodin: Stalin's man in China*, Harvard University Press, 1981.

Jasny, Naum, *Soviet Industrialisation 1928–1952*, University of Chicago Press, 1961.

Joravsky, David, *The Lysenko Affair*, Harvard University Press, 1970.

Karcz, Jerzy F., 'Thoughts on the Grain Problem', *Soviet Studies*, vol. XVIII, no. 4, April 1967.

Katkov, George, *Russia 1917: The Kornilov Affair: Kerensky and the break-up of the Russian army*, Longman, 1980.

____, *Russia 1917: The February Revolution*, Harper and Row, 1967.

____, *The Kronstadt Rising*, St Antony's Papers no. 6, Soviet Affairs no. 2, Chatto and Windus, 1959.

____, *The Assassination of Count Mirbach*, St Antony's Papers no. 12, Soviet Affairs no. 3, Chatto and Windus, 1962.

Kazemzadeh, Firuz, *The Struggle for Transcaucasia (1917–1921)*, New York Philosophical Library; Oxford, George Ronald, 1951.

Kenez, Peter, *Civil War in South Russia, 1918*, University of California Press, 1971.

____, *Civil War in South Russia, 1919–1920: The defeat of the Whites*, University of California Press, 1977.

Kennan, George F., *Russia Leaves the War*, Princeton University Press, 1956, Faber and Faber.

____, *The Decision to Intervene*, Princeton University Press, 1958, Faber and Faber.

____, *Russia and the West under Lenin and Stalin*, Hutchinson, 1961.

King, Beatrice, *Russia Goes to School: A guide to Soviet education*, Heinemann, 1948.

Kerensky, A. F., *The Kerensky Memoirs: Russia and history's turning point*, Duell, 1965; Cassell, 1966.

Kolarz, Walter, *Religion in the Soviet Union*, Macmillan, 1961.

____, *Russia and her Colonies*, George Philip and Son, 1953.

____, *The Peoples of the Soviet Far East*, George Philip and Son, 1954.

Kravchenko, Victor, *I Chose Freedom: The personal and political life of a Soviet official*, Scribners, 1946.

Krivitsky, W. G., *I was Stalin's Agent*, Hamish Hamilton, 1939.

Lang, D. M., *A Modern History of Georgia*, Weidenfeld and Nicolson, 1962.

Leggett, George, *The Cheka: Lenin's political police*, Oxford University Press, 1981.

Lenin, V. I., *Collected Works*, English translation of the fourth Russian edition, vols 23–44, Lawrence and Wishart, 1960 onwards.

Leontyev, A., *The Seventeenth Conference of the CPSU. Towards a Classless Society: The Second Five-Year Plan explained*, Moscow, Co-operative Publishing Society of Foreign Workers in the USSR, 1932.

Lewin, Moshe, *Russian Peasants and Soviet Power: A study of collectivization*, trans. Irene Nove, George Allen and Unwin, 1968.

Lockhart, R. H. Bruce, *Memoirs of a British Agent*, Putnam, 1932.

____, *The Diaries of Sir Robert Bruce Lockhart 1915–1938*, Macmillan, 1973.

Lorimer, Frank, *The Population of the Soviet Union: History and prospects*, Geneva, League of Nations, 1946.

MacDonell, Ranald, '. . . And Nothing Long', Constable, 1938.

Mackintosh, Malcolm, *Juggernaut: A history of the Soviet armed forces*, Secker and Warburg, 1967.

Maclean, Fitzroy, *To the Back of Beyond: An illustrated companion to Central Asia and Mongolia*, Jonathan Cape, 1974.

McNeal, Robert H. (ed.), *Resolutions and Decisions of the Communist Party of the Soviet Union*, vol. II, *The Early Soviet Period 1917–1929*, ed. Richard Gregor; and vol. III, *The Stalin Years 1929–1953*, University of Toronto Press, 1974.

Male, D. J., *Russian Peasant Organisation before Collectivisation: A study of commune and gathering 1926–1930*, Cambridge University Press, 1971.

Malet, Michael, *Nestor Makhno in the Russian Civil War*, Macmillan and the London School of Economics, 1982.

Matlock, Jack F., Jr, 'The "Governing Organs" of the Union of Soviet Writers', *The American Slavic and East European Review*, vol. XV, 1956.

Matthews, Mervyn, *Soviet Government: A selection of official documents on internal policies*, Jonathan Cape, 1974.

Mawdsley, Evan, *The Russian Civil War*, Allen and Unwin, 1987.

Maynard, Maj.-Gen. Sir C., *The Murmansk Adventure*, Hodder and Stoughton, 1928.

Medvedev, Roy A., *Let History Judge: The origins and consequences of Stalinism*, Alfred A. Knopf, 1971; Macmillan, 1972.

____, *On Stalin and Stalinism*, Oxford University Press, 1979.

Millar, James R. (ed.), *The Soviet Rural Community*, chapter 1, 'Agricultural administration in Russia from the Stolypin land reform to forced collectivization: an interpretive study' by George L. Yaney; and chapter 2, 'From Stalin to Brezhnev: Soviet agricultural policy in historical perspective' by Jerzy F. Karcz, University of Illinois Press, 1971.

____ and Alec Nove, 'A Debate on collectivization: was Stalin really necessary', *Problems of Communism*, July–August, 1976.

Molotov, V. M., *The XVII Conference of the CPSU: The Second Five-Year Plan*, Moscow, Co-operative Publishing Society of Foreign Workers in the USSR, 1932.

Namier, L. B., *Diplomatic Prelude 1938–1939*, Macmillan, 1948.

Nish, Ian, *Japanese Foreign Policy 1869–1942: Kasumigaseki to Miyakezaka*, Routledge and Kegan Paul, 1977.

Norton, Henry K., *The Far Eastern Republic of Siberia*, George Allen and Unwin, 1923.

Nove, Alec, *An Economic History of the USSR*, Allen Lane, the Penguin Press, 1969, 1976.

Nutter, G. Warren, *Growth of Industrial Production in the Soviet Union*, National Bureau of Economic Research, Princeton University Press, 1962.

Olcott, Martha B., 'The *Basmachi* or Freemen's Revolt in Turkestan 1918–1924', *Soviet Studies*, vol. XXXIII, no. 3, July 1981.

Orjonikidze, S., *Report to the Seventeenth Conference of the Communist Party of the Soviet Union: Industrial development in 1931 and the tasks for 1932*, Moscow, Co-operative Publishing Society of Foreign Workers in the USSR, 1932.

Page, Stanley W., *The Formation of the Baltic States*, Harvard University Press, 1959.

Palij, Michael, *The Anarchism of Nestor Makhno 1918–1921: An aspect of the Ukrainian Revolution*, University of Washington Press, Seattle, 1976.

Park, Alexander G., *Bolshevism in Turkestan 1917–1927*, Columbia University Press, 1957.

Petrov, V. and E., *Empire of Fear*, André Deutsch, 1956.

Pipes, Richard, *The Formation of the Soviet Union*, revised edition, Harvard University Press, 1964.

_____ (ed.), *Revolutionary Russia*, Harvard University Press, 1968.

Ponomaryov, B. N., Khvostov, V. M., Kuchkin, A. P., Mints, I. I., Shatagin, N. I., Slepov, L. A., Timofeyevsky, A. A., Volin, M. S., Volkov, I. M. and Zaitsev, V. S. *History of the Communist Party of the Soviet Union*, English trans. ed. Andrew Rothstein, Moscow, Foreign Languages Publishing House, 1960.

Poole, DeWitt C., 'Light on Nazi foreign policy', *Foreign Affairs*, vol. xxv, no. 1, October 1946.

Possony, Stefan T., *Lenin: The compulsive revolutionary*, Henry Regnery, 1964; George Allen and Unwin, 1966.

Rabinowitch, Alexander, *The Bolsheviks Come to Power*, W. W. Norton, 1976.

Rassweiler, Anne D., 'Soviet labor policy in the First Five-Year Plan: the Dneprostroi experience', *Slavic Review*, vol. 42, no. 2, Summer 1983.

Reshetar, John S., Jr, *The Ukrainian Revolution, 1917–1920: A study in nationalism*, Princeton University Press, 1952.

Rigby, T. H., *Communist Party Membership in the USSR 1917–1967*, Princeton University Press, 1968.

_____, *Lenin's Government: Sovnarkom 1917–1922*, Cambridge University Press, 1979.

_____ (ed.), *The Stalin Dictatorship: Khrushchev's secret speech and other documents*, Sydney University Press, 1968.

Riordan, James, *Sport in Soviet Society: Development of sport and physical education in Russia and the USSR*, Cambridge University Press, 1977.

Ritter, William S., 'The final phase in the liquidation of Anti-Soviet resistance in Tadzhikistan: Ibrahim Bek and the *Basmachi* 1924–1931', *Soviet Studies*, vol.xxxvii, no. 4, October 1985.

Rocca, Raymond G., and John J. Dziak, *Bibliography on Soviet Intelligence and Security Services*, Westview Press, 1985.

Rosefielde, Steven, 'An assessment of the sources and uses of GULag forced labour 1929–1956', *Soviet Studies*, vol. xxxiii, no. 1, January 1981.

_____, 'New demographic evidence on collectivisation deaths: a rejoinder to Stephen Wheatcroft', *Slavic Review*, vol. 44, no. 3, Fall 1985.

_____, 'Incriminating evidence: excess deaths and forced labour under Stalin: a final reply to critics', Soviet Studies, vol. xxxix, no. 2, April 1987.

Rosenfeldt, Niels E., *Knowledge and Power: The role of Stalin's secret chancellery in the Soviet system of government*, Copenhagen, Rosenkilde and Bagger, 1978.

Rupen, Robert, *How Mongolia is Really Ruled: A political history of the Mongolian People's Republic 1900–1978*, Hoover Institution Press, Stanford University, 1979.

Schapiro, Leonard B., *The Communist Party of the Soviet Union*, Methuen, 1960, second edition, 1970.

——, *1917: The Russian Revolution and the origins of present day Communism*, Maurice Temple-Smith, 1984.

——, *The Origin of the Communist Autocracy*, second edition, Macmillan, 1977.

——, *Russian Studies*, ed. Ellen Dahrendorf, Collins Harvill, 1986.

Schlesinger, Rudolf, *The Family in the USSR*, Routledge and Kegan Paul, 1949.

Schwarz, Solomon M., *Labor in the Soviet Union*, The Cresset Press, 1953.

Seaton, Albert and Joan, *The Soviet Army: 1918 to the present*, The Bodley Head, 1986.

Senn, Alfred Erich, *The Emergence of Modern Lithuania*, Columbia University Press, 1959.

Serge, Victor, *Memoirs of a Revolutionary 1901–1941*, trans. Peter Sedgwick, Oxford University Press, 1963.

Shapiro, Leonard (ed.), *Soviet Treaty Series: A collection of bilateral treaties, agreements and conventions, etc. concluded between the Soviet Union and foreign powers*, vol. I 1917–1928, vol. II 1929–1939, Georgetown University Press, 1950, 1955.

Shorish, M. Mobin, 'The pedagogical, linguistic and logistical problems of teaching Russian to the local Soviet Central Asians', *Slavic Review*, vol. 35, no. 3, September 1976.

Shub, David, *Lenin: A biography*, Doubleday, 1948; Penguin Books, 1966.

Slusser, Robert M., and Triska, Jan F. (eds), *A Calendar of Soviet Treaties 1917–1957*, Stanford University Press, 1959.

Smith, Clarence Jay, *Finland and the Russian Revolution 1917–1922*, University of Georgia Press, 1958.

Solomon, Peter H., Jr, 'Soviet penal policy 1917–1934: a reinterpretation', *Slavic Review*, vol. 39, no. 2, June 1980.

Sorenson, Jay B., *The Life and Death of Soviet Trade Unionism 1917–1928*, New York, Atherton Press, 1969.

Souvarine, Boris, *Stalin: A critical survey of Bolshevism*, trans. C. L. R. James, Secker and Warburg, ?1939.

Stalin, Joseph, *Selected Writing*, Westport, Connecticut, Greenwood Press, 1970.

——, *Problems of Leninism*, Moscow, Foreign Language Publishing House, 1953.

——, *Political Report of the Central Committee to the Fourteenth Congress of the CPSU(B)*, Moscow, Foreign Languages Publishing House, 1950.

——, *The Tasks of the Working Class in Mastering the Technique of Production*, London, Modern Books, 1931.

——, *Political Report of the Central Committee to the Fifteenth Congress of the CPSU(B), December 3, 1927*, Moscow, Foreign Languages Publishing House, 1950.

____, *Report to the Seventeenth Congress of the CPSU(B) on the Work of the Central Committee*, Moscow, Foreign Languages Publishing House, 1951.

____, *Report on the Work of the Central Committee to the Eighteenth Congress of the Communist Party of the Soviet Union (Bolsheviks)*, London, Modern Books, 1939.

____, *Theory and Practice of Leninism*, Communist Party of Great Britain, second edition, 1926.

____, *Works*, vols I-XIII, Moscow, Foreign Languages Publishing House; London, Lawrence and Wishart, 1952–5.

Stewart, George, *The White Armies of Russia: A chronicle of counter-revolution and allied intervention*, Macmillan, 1933.

Strakhovsky, Leonid, *The Origins of American Intervention in North Russia (1918)*, Princeton University Press, Oxford University Press, 1937.

____, *Intervention at Archangel: The story of allied intervention and Russian counter-revolution in North Russia 1918–1920*, Princeton University Press, Oxford University Press, 1944.

Struve, Gleb, *Russian Literature under Lenin and Stalin 1917–1953*, University of Oklahoma Press, 1971.

Sukhanov, N. N., (Himmer), *The Russian Revolution 1917*, ed., trans. and abr. Joel Carmichael, Oxford University Press, 1955.

Summers, Anthony, and Mangold, Tom, *The File on the Tsar*, Victor Gollancz, 1976.

Suny, Ronald G., *The Baku Commune 1917–1918: Class and nationality in the Russian Revolution*, Princeton University Press, 1972.

____ (ed), *Transcaucasia: Nationalism and social change: essays in the history of Armenia, Azerbaijan and Georgia*, University of Michigan, 1983.

____, *The Making of the Georgian Nation*, London, I. B. Tauris, Indiana University Press, 1989.

Swietochowski, Tadeusz, *Russian Azerbaijan 1905–1920: The shaping of national identity in a Muslim community*, Cambridge University Press, 1985.

Tang, Peter S. H., *Russian and Soviet Policy in Manchuria and Outer Mongolia 1911–1931*, Duke University Press, 1959.

Tanner, Väinö, *The Winter War, Finland against Russia 1939–1940*, Stanford University Press, 1957.

Taracouzio, T. A., *Soviets in the Arctic*, New York, Macmillan, 1938.

____, *War and Peace in Soviet Diplomacy*, Macmillan, 1940.

Thomas, Hugh, *The Spanish Civil War*, Eyre and Spottiswoode, 1961.

Tillett, Lowell R., 'The Soviet role in League sanctions against Italy 1935–1936', *The American Slavic and East European Review*, vol. xv, 1956, p. 11ff.

Timasheff, N. S., *Religion in Soviet Russia 1917–1942*, Sheed and Ward, 1944.

Treadgold, Donald W., *Twentieth Century Russia*, third edition, Rand McNally, 1959, 1964, 1972.

Trevor-Roper, H. R. (ed.), *Hitler's War Directives, 1939–1945*, Pan Books, 1966.

Trotsky, Leon, *History of the Russian Revolution*, trans. Max Eastman, Victor Gollancz, 1934.

____, *My Life*, Thornton Butterworth, 1930.

____, *Stalin: An appraisal of the man and his influence*, ed. and trans. Charles Malamuth, Stein and Day, 1967.

Tucker, Robert C., 'The emergence of Stalin's foreign policy', *Slavic Review*, vol. 36, no. 4, December 1977.

____ (ed.), *Stalinism: Essays in historial interpretation*, W. W. Norton, 1977.

Ulam, Adam B., *The Bolsheviks*, USA, 1965.

____, *Lenin and the Bolsheviks*, Secker and Warburg, 1966.

____, *Stalin: The man and his era*, Allen Lane, 1974.

Uldricks, Teddy J., 'The impact of the great purges on the People's Commissariat of Foreign Affairs', *Slavic Review*, vol. 36, no. 2, June 1977.

Ullman, Richard H., *Anglo-Soviet Relations 1917–1921: Intervention and the war*, Princeton University Press, Oxford University Press, 1961.

____, *Anglo-Soviet Relations 1917–1921: Britain and the Russian Civil War*, Princeton University Press, Oxford University Press, 1968.

____, *Anglo-Soviet Relations 1917–1921: The Anglo-Soviet Accord*, Princeton University Press, Oxford University Press, 1972.

Unterberger, Betty Miller, *America's Siberian Expedition, 1918–1920: A study of national policy*, Duke University Press, 1956.

Upton, Anthony F., *Finland 1939–40*, Davis-Poynter, 1974.

____, *Finland in Crisis 1940–1941*, Faber and Faber, 1964.

____, *The Finnish Revolution 1917–1918*, University of Minnesota Press, 1980.

Varneck, Elena, and Fisher, H. H. *The Testimony of Kolchak and Other Siberian Materials*, Stanford University Press, 1935.

Vigor, P. H., *The Soviet View of War, Peace and Neutrality*, Routledge and Kegan Paul, 1975.

____, *Books on Communism and the Communist Countries*, Ampersand, 1971.

Vihavainen, Timo, 'The Soviet decision for war against Finland, November 1939: a comment', *Soviet Studies*, vol. xxxix, no. 2, April 1987.

Wandycz, Piotr S., *Soviet-Polish Relations 1917–1921*, Harvard University Press, 1969.

Watt, D. C., 'Soviet military aid to the Spanish Republic in the Civil War 1936–1938', *The Slavonic and East European Review*, vol. xxxviii, no. 91, June 1960.

____, 'The initiation of the negotiations leading to the Nazi-Soviet Pact', in *Essays in Honour of E. H. Carr*, ed. Chimen Abramsky, Macmillan, 1974.

Wheatcroft, S. G., 'On assessing the size of forced concentration camp labour in the Soviet Union 1929–1956', *Soviet Studies*, vol. xxxiii, no. 2, April 1981.

____, 'New demographic evidence on excess collectivisation deaths', *Slavic Review*, vol. 44, no. 3, Fall 1985.

Wheeler, Geoffrey, *The Modern History of Soviet Central Asia*, Weidenfeld and Nicolson, 1964.

___, 'The *Basmachis*: the Central Asian resistance movement, 1918–1924', *Central Asian Review*, vol. VII, no. 3, 1959.

Wheeler-Bennett, John W., *Brest-Litovsk: The forgotten peace March 1918*, Macmillan, St Martin's Press, 1963.

___, *Munich: Prelude to tragedy*, Macmillan, 1948.

Whitaker, J. T., *We Cannot Escape History*, Macmillan, New York, 1943.

White, John Albert, *The Siberian Intervention*, Princeton University Press, 1950.

White, Stephen, *The Origins of Detente: The Genoa Conference and Soviet–Western relations, 1921–1922*, Cambridge University Press, 1985.

Whiting, Allen S., and Sheng Shih-t'sai, *Sinkiang: Pawn or pivot?*, Michigan State University Press, 1958.

Wolin, Simon, and Robert M. Slusser (eds), *The Soviet Secret Police*, Methuen, 1957.

Woytinsky, W., 'The Gatchina Campaign', *Soviet Studies*, vol. XXXII, no. 2, April 1980.

Wrangel, Gen. P. N., *The Memoirs of General Wrangel*, trans. Sophie Goulston, Williams and Norgate, 1929.

Young, A. Morgan, *Japan under Taisho Tenno 1912–1926*, George Allen and Unwin, 1928.

Young, C. Walter, *The International Relations of Manchuria*, University of Chicago Press, 1929.

Zaleski, Eugène, *Planning for Economic Growth in the Soviet Union, 1918–1932*, trans. and ed. Marie-Christine MacAndrew and G. Warren Nutter, University of North Carolina Press, 1962; English edition, 1971.

___, *Stalinist Planning for Economic Growth, 1933–1952*, trans. and ed. Marie-Christine MacAndrew and John H. Moore, University of North Carolina Press, 1980.

Zeman, Z. A. B., *Germany and the Revolution in Russia 1915–1918: Documents from the archives of the German Foreign Ministry*, Oxford University Press, 1958.

# Index
# of
# Personal and Geographical Names

[References in the text to authors named in the List of Sources have not been indexed]

Aaland Islands 51, 52
Abdul Aziz Ibn Saud, King 193, 205
Abyssinia (Ethiopia) 293, 299
Afghanistan 51, 96, 131, 133, 137, 145, 154, 186, 197, 218, 227–8, 247, 258, 274, 297, 340
Africa 119, 123, 352
Akhmatova 144
Alaska 314
Albacete 301
Albania 171, 285
Aleksandropol' (Leninakan) 59, 126
Aleksandrovsk (Zaporozh'e) 104
Alekseev, General 11, 15, 22–3, 34, 38, 75
Alexandria 265
Alksnis 291
Allilueva, Nadezhda 266
Alma-Ata 36, 215, 224–5, 322
Altai region 359
Amanullah, Emir later King 133, 218, 228
Amsterdam 118, 142, 184, 266, 274, 292
Amur river, district 8, 73, 115, 217, 315
Anatolia 138, 154
Andalucía 299
Andreev, Andrei Andreevich 196, 214–15, 248, 252, 263, 282, 321, 329
Andreev (Chekist) 66
Angara river 110
Angora (see also Ankara) 132, 138, 147
Ankara (see also Angora) 204, 254, 302, 318
Antonov, Aleksandr Stepanovich 122, 139
Antonov-Ovseenko 28, 30–1, 37, 39, 90, 96–7, 168, 172
Aral Sea 111
Archangel 46, 57–9, 63. 67–73, 87–8, 91, 96–7, 99, 100, 102, 104, 111–12, 265, 317, 354
Arctic Ocean, region 38, 50, 221, 267, 282
Ardahan 50, 132
Argentina 258
Armenia 12, 22, 36, 39, 42, 49, 59, 60, 62, 110, 121, 126–8, 131, 138, 145, 149, 304, 312, 314, 324, 327
Arskii 54
Artvin 132
Ashkhabad 67, 70–1, 73, 76, 101, 301

Asia (see also Central Asia) 42, 48, 119, 123, 328, 352
Astrakhan 8, 69, 70, 144, 215
Athens 276
Atlantic Ocean 39
Australia 240
Austria 90, 146–7, 171, 318, 322
Austria-Hungary 33, 35
Averbakh 200, 218, 310, 312
Avilov 30
Avksentiev 78
Azerbaijan 22, 49, 60, 62, 77, 100, 110, 116, 121, 124, 127, 131, 138, 149, 304, 324
Azov 200
Azov, Sea of 104, 111, 121

Babel' 323
Baikal, Lake 64, 86
Baisun 152
Bakaev 203
Bakhmet'ev 153
Baku 33, 55–6, 61–2, 68–73, 76–7, 79, 113, 116, 123, 139, 192, 301, 352–3
Baldwin 203, 207
Balkans 348, 351, 355, 357
Baltic provinces, states 47, 50, 79, 82, 88, 91, 103–4, 108, 115, 197, 233, 279, 283, 285, 310, 332, 334–6, 338, 341, 344, 352, 359
Baltic Sea, fleet 33, 72, 79, 82, 102, 120, 132–3, 239, 275, 336
Barbusse 144, 227, 266
Barcelona 302
Barnaul 236
Barthou 284
Bashkir Republic 144
Batumi 4, 50, 56, 62, 79, 105, 118, 132, 138, 318, 352–3
Bauman 224, 230, 246, 318
Belaia Tserkov' 77, 81
Belgium 46, 141, 292, 334, 348, 358
Benes, President 313
Berdiansk 104
Berdichev 117
Berens, Admiral 171
Bereza-Kartuska 88
Berezina River 102
Beria 314, 325–6, 329

Bering Strait 265, 267
Berlin 56, 71, 77, 86, 106, 112, 120, 140–1, 144–5, 151, 153, 188, 194, 200, 227, 255, 270, 296–7, 308, 332, 334–7, 347, 351–2, 355–6, 359
Bermondt-Avalov 105
Berne 90
Berzin, General 300
Bessarabia 38–9, 45, 55, 81, 96–7, 99, 125, 172, 227, 262, 339, 344, 349, 350, 359
Bialystok 89, 120, 123
Birobidzhan 217, 283
Bismarck 318
Bizerta 127
Black Sea, Straits, fleet, coast 12, 33, 54, 61, 63, 71–2, 76–7, 81, 113, 127, 138, 154, 158, 166, 171, 254, 298, 302, 332, 336, 352–3, 355
Blagoveshchensk 73
Bliukher (Galen or Galin), General 139, 147, 167, 176, 193–4, 203, 209, 236, 293, 325
Bliumkin 66
Blok 44, 48, 143
Blomberg, General von 221
Bockelberg, General von 273
Bogdanov (Malinovskii), A.A. 127
Bogdo Gegen 131, 142, 179
Bogomolov 272
Bohemia 331
Bokhara see Bukhara
Bolshoi Island 315
Bolshoi Theatre 128, 319
Borchali 131
Borisov 113
Borodin, Mikhail 167, 184, 193–4, 203–4, 209
Bothnia, Gulf of 52
Brazil 294
Brest-Litovsk 34–5, 37–9, 41, 43–7, 49, 50, 52–3, 56, 58, 64–5, 71, 77, 88–9, 120, 122, 132, 180, 229
Brezhnev 324
Britain, Great including England, British Empire 11, 29, 33, 45–6, 48–9, 95, 98, 101, 103, 106, 110, 119, 120, 123, 125, 137, 147, 166–7, 171, 177, 188, 191, 207, 228, 238, 240, 244, 246, 266, 272, 274, 282, 284, 303, 316, 322, 325, 328–9, 331–2, 334–7, 339–41, 350, 352, 357
Brockdorff-Rantzau 157
Brusilov, General 15, 18, 116
Brussels 203
Bubnov 25, 41, 48, 172, 180, 237, 248, 304
Bucharest 296, 331, 352
Budapest 102
Budennyi 76, 106, 117–18, 122–3, 272, 293
Budkiewicz, Mgr 149, 161
Buenos Aires 243, 258
Buguruslan 96
Bukhara 4, 53–4, 123, 131, 134, 145, 151–2, 178

Bukharin 36, 43, 48, 51, 53, 60, 90, 94, 114, 139, 150, 152, 158, 162–3, 169, 172, 174–7, 179, 181, 184–5, 187, 189–92, 195, 197–9, 211, 214, 217–30, 233–4, 236, 238–9, 245, 247–8, 250–1, 266, 270, 281–2, 285, 289, 294, 297, 300, 307, 309, 310, 319, 322, 329
Bukovina 97, 344, 349
Bulgaria 35, 143, 166–7, 184, 285, 345, 352–3, 355–6
Bullitt, William C. 91–2, 277
Buriat-Mongolian ASSR 234, 277
Buzuluk 96
Byelorussia 4, 50, 72, 81, 86, 89, 91, 99, 100, 116, 118, 130, 304, 314, 317, 324, 340, 342

Canada 171, 240, 258
Cannes 148
Canton 166–7, 170, 175–6, 193–4, 198, 205, 214
Cartagena 302
Caspian Sea, fleet 69, 70, 77, 79, 116, 293
Caucasus including North Caucasus 39, 58, 62–3, 68, 70, 74, 79, 91, 95, 99, 105, 111, 174, 186, 242, 258, 271, 281, 297
Central Asia 154, 258, 281, 322
Central Powers 35, 39
Chaikovskii 69, 73–4, 87
Chalainor 238
Chamberlain 331
Chang Tso-lin, Marshal 178, 209
Changchun 155, 259
Changhufeng Hill 324
Chaplin, Captain 69, 73
Cheliabinsk 55, 58–60, 101, 312
Ch'en Tu-hsiu 209
Chengchow 208
Chengtu 317
Cheremisov, General 28
Chernov 17
Chiang Kai-shek 166, 175–6, 193–4, 203–6, 208–9, 305, 308–9, 317
Chiaturi 186
Chicherin 45, 56, 58, 61, 63, 68–9, 94–5, 106, 111, 117, 119, 148, 150, 158, 175, 188, 214, 238, 249
Chin Shu-jen, General 260, 272
China 145, 148, 155, 160, 166–7, 175–6, 178, 183, 186, 194, 203, 205, 208–9, 235–6, 240, 259, 260, 267, 272, 290, 297, 316–17, 334–5
Chinese Soviet Republic 260
Chinkiang 214
Chita 72, 110, 125, 131
Chkalov 313–4
Choibalsan 133
Chou En-lai 176, 305
Christiania (Oslo) 144
Chu Teh 260
Chubar' 196, 214, 248, 282, 289, 308, 323
Churchill. W.S. 92, 243
Cieplak, Archbishop 161

378    INDEX

Clemenceau 98
Colombia 292
Conradi 163
Constantinople (Istanbul from 1930) 12, 33, 36, 66, 121, 147, 166, 225
Copenhagen 107, 112
Cot, Pierre 276
Crete 357
Crimea 39, 57, 63, 82, 95, 100, 113, 117, 126–7
Cripps 348, 357
Cromie, Captain 70, 72
Curzon, Lord 119, 121–2, 163
Czechoslovakia 53–4, 141, 147, 152, 274, 283–4, 287, 290–1, 313, 318, 322–3, 325

Daghestan 139
Danzig (Gdansk) 120, 171, 227, 335
Danube 352
Dekanozov 349
Delhi 321
Denikin, General 34, 56, 60–1, 63, 67–8, 71, 75, 77, 79, 80, 87, 89–91, 94–8, 100–17, 140, 152, 242
Denmark 163, 171, 176, 347
Detroit 243
de Vertement, Colonel 80
Diamandi 42
Dimitrov 184, 271, 276, 292
Diterikhs, General 103–4, 106
Dnieper River 115–16, 125, 266
Dniester River 144
Don River, basin, region 7, 8, 28, 34, 36–8, 44, 46, 56, 59–61, 64, 72, 107, 109, 200, 216
Donets basin 293, 359
Donskoi 68
Dorpat (Tartu) 111, 125, 146
Dos Passos 285
Dukhonin, General 23, 31–5
Duncan, Isadora 191
Dunsterville, General 69, 71, 73
Dushanbe (Stalinabad 1929–61) 131
Dutov 28, 36, 88
Dvina River (north Russia) 111
Dvina River (west Russia) 102
Dvinsk (Dünaburg, Daugavpils) 34–5, 109
DVR see Far Eastern Republic
Dybenko 30
Dzerzhinskii 38, 66, 92, 99, 104, 120, 124, 139, 148, 159, 161, 164, 167, 171–2, 175, 180, 188, 192, 196

Eboli, Prince 49
Eden, Anthony 290
Edinburgh 321
Egorov, General 117, 122, 293
Egypt 265
Eichhorn, General von 59, 68
Eideman, Corps Commander 312
Eikhe 289, 323

Einstein 203
Eisenstein 328
Ekaterinburg (Sverdlovsk) 67–8, 94, 101
Ekaterinodar (Krasnodar) 49, 53, 56, 71, 80, 113, 121
Ekaterinoslav (Dnepropetrovsk) 41, 97, 100, 105, 108
Elizavetgrad (Kirovograd) 97, 102
Engels 130, 329
Engel's region 312
Enisei 8
Enukidze 288, 291, 319
Enver Pasha 145, 151, 154
Enzeli (see also [Bandar] Pahlevi) 116
Erevan 59, 79, 128, 131
Esenin 191
Estonia 34, 51, 72, 77, 81–2, 90, 99, 103, 106, 111, 130, 141, 146–7, 227, 230, 265, 274, 282, 285, 304, 334, 341, 349, 350, 359
Europe 39, 115, 127, 146, 149, 312, 352
Ezhov 272, 282, 289, 291, 294, 298–9, 301, 308, 310, 314–15, 318, 326

Far East 39, 52, 58, 108, 115, 139, 155, 157, 184, 193, 207, 215, 217, 236, 240, 264, 278, 281, 283, 310–12, 323, 327, 341, 358
Far Eastern Republic (DVR) 115–16, 118, 125, 131, 139, 149, 153, 155–8
Fedin, Konstantin 130
Fel'dman, Corps Commander 312
Feng Yu-hsiang, General 208–9
Fili 153
Filimonov 28
Finland 11, 18, 24, 36, 40, 42–4, 50–2, 55, 59, 61, 67–8, 71, 74, 79, 91, 99, 103, 106, 112, 115, 125, 138, 141, 146–7, 166, 262, 274, 283, 323, 331, 334, 336, 341–3, 345–54, 357, 359
Fischer, Ruth 2, 167, 179, 180, 184, 213
Forestier-Walker, General 79
France 11, 29, 33, 46, 63, 77, 95, 98, 110, 121, 125, 141, 144, 166, 179, 188, 191, 211, 259, 267, 272–3, 276, 279, 283–4, 287, 290–2, 296, 318, 323, 325–6, 328–9, 331–2, 334–41, 348–9, 357
France, Anatole 144
Francis, David R. 45, 57, 61, 68
Franco, General 302, 328
Friede, Col. 80
Frunze 96, 125, 172, 175, 183, 188–9, 311–12
Frunze (city) 200
Fukdin 238

Gajda, General 91, 101, 106
Galen or Galin see Bliukher
Galicia 12, 16, 18, 88, 102, 107, 118, 120, 123, 335
Gamarnik 311–12
Gary, Indiana 244
Gatchina 31, 105

Geneva 62, 153, 163, 186, 212, 218, 263, 267, 285, 287
Genoa 148, 150–1, 153
George, Lloyd 92, 98, 106, 117, 119–21, 123
George V, King 296
George VI, King 311
Georgia 22, 39, 49, 59–62, 91, 100, 110, 113, 116–18, 128, 130–2, 138–40, 149, 161–2, 178, 304, 314, 324, 327
Germany 7, 13, 29, 35, 37–9, 46, 49–64, 66–72, 74–5, 77–9, 90, 98, 103, 119, 140–1, 147, 151, 153–4, 159, 167, 176, 184, 186, 188, 191, 194–5, 226, 234–5, 244–5, 254–5, 263, 265–6, 270–3, 275–6, 278–80, 283–4, 288, 290, 295, 297, 301, 303–4, 308, 316, 318, 322, 325, 329, 332–42, 346–60
Germany, East 143
Ghilan 116
Ghulam Nabi 228
Glazkov 110
Glinka 328
Glushko 277
Golitsyn, Prince 8
Gongotta 118
Göring 270
Gorky, Maxim 4, 26, 67, 143, 219, 239, 264, 297, 319, 322
Gorky city (see also Nizhny Novgorod) 282, 359
Gottwald 292
Grandi, Count 250
Graves, General 71, 78, 109, 114
Greece 166, 171, 276, 334, 355–8
Grenard 80
Grigor'ev 89–91, 94–7, 99–102
Groman 249, 254
Gromov 313–4
Gronskii 264
Guchkov 12, 14
Gulai Polye 90
Gumilev 144

Hague, The 150, 153, 186
Hamburg 167
Hammer, Dr Armand 145, 166
Hanko (Hangö) 55, 341–2, 347
Hankow (see also Wuhan) 203, 207, 209, 214, 317
Harbin 90, 122, 233, 235, 268
Harriman 186
Hejaz 171, 193, 205
Helfferich 68
Helsingfors (see also Helsinki) 11, 44, 55–6, 97
Helsinki (see also Helsingfors) 262, 323, 343, 345
Herriot 179, 276
Hitler 151, 235, 258, 270–1, 273, 279, 281, 284, 288, 295, 297, 303, 318, 322, 337–8, 341, 347, 350, 352, 354

Hoffmann, E.T.A. 130
Hoffmann, General 43, 47
Holland 90, 285, 334–5, 348
Honan Province 209
Hoorgin see Khurgin
Hoover, Herbert 92, 95, 143
Hsuchow 209
Hull 178
Humbert–Droz 221, 224
Hungary 58, 94, 96, 102, 141, 143, 178, 282, 328, 343, 351, 353
Hythe 120

Iagoda 196, 220, 284, 286, 301, 310, 322
Iakir, Army Commander 312–13, 329
Iakovlev 239
Iakushev 145
Ibrahim Bek 154, 227, 247, 258
Iceland 195
India 70, 137, 145, 148, 228, 240
Indian Ocean 352
Indonesia 148, 176
Ioffe 34, 56, 77, 155, 160, 212
Iran (see also Persia) 293, 341, 347
Iraq 189, 358
Irish Free State 240
Irkutsk 60, 64, 67, 77, 106, 108–13, 139, 148
Ironside, General 75, 87, 90, 94, 97, 101–2, 104
Italy 11, 33, 77, 95, 98, 110, 125, 141, 147, 166, 171, 176, 218, 249, 250, 255, 273, 275, 279, 293, 301, 318, 320, 325, 328, 333, 348–9, 351–3, 358
Iudenich, General 75, 97, 99, 100–6
Ivanov, General 9, 10
Ivanov, Vsevolod 130, 285

Jacson (Mornard or Mercader) 350
Janin, General 86, 110
Japan 49, 54–6, 73, 78, 90–1, 98, 106, 125, 127, 148, 155–6, 160, 166, 182–3, 215, 259, 261, 271, 276, 278, 290, 304–5, 308–9, 316, 322–3, 329, 336, 351–3, 356–7, 359
Java 198
Jedda 193, 325
Joyce 285
Joynson–Hicks 194
Juichin 260
Junkers 153, 200

Kabul 258
Kaganovich 196, 214–15, 248, 263, 272, 282, 300, 314, 316, 319, 329
Kaiser see Wilhelm II
Kalamatiano 80
Kaledin, General 28, 34, 36–8, 46–7
Kalinin 94, 133, 139, 150, 163, 175, 185, 190, 192, 214, 234, 248, 254, 276, 282, 329
Kalinin region 312
Kalmyk ASSR 234
Kalmykov 78

Kaluga 215
Kama 154, 221
Kamchatka 115
Kamenev, Lev B. 11, 13, 24–6, 28, 30–2, 49,
  94, 120–4, 139, 150, 158, 161, 163, 169,
  174–6, 180, 184, 187, 189, 190, 192, 194,
  196–9, 202, 212–16, 219, 220, 226, 229,
  260, 266, 273–4, 281, 286–9, 297, 299, 300,
  314, 329
Kamenev, General Sergei S. 97, 101
Kandahar 218, 228
Kandelaki 308
Kanegiesser 72
Kansu province 260
Kaplan, Fanny (Dora) 72
Karabakh 116
Karaganda 359
Karakhan 155, 166–7, 172, 175, 182–3, 193,
  197, 319
Karaulov 28
Karelia, East 146
Karelian Isthmus 341–3, 345–6
Karelo–Finnish SSR 304, 347
Kars 50, 56, 126, 138
Katyn 341
Kaunas (Kovno) 86
Kazakh region, republic 36, 123, 221–2, 258,
  271, 281, 298, 304, 322, 324
Kazan 70, 73, 154, 221
Kazan Cathedral 264
Kellogg 222, 227, 236, 239, 274
Kem 62, 64
Kemal Atatürk, Mustapha 117, 145
Kemerovo 301, 303
Kemp, Admiral 52
Kerensky 4, 8, 10, 14, 16, 18–23, 27–9, 31
Kerzhentsev 296
Khabalov, General 8, 9
Khabarovsk 73, 110, 114, 147, 236, 238, 240
Khalkhin-Gol 314, 333, 337–8, 340, 348
Kharkov 39, 41, 55, 86, 97, 99, 100, 102, 107,
  118, 125, 222, 227, 245, 276, 316, 318
Khasan, Lake 324
Kherson 81, 90
Khinchuk 112
Khiva 111, 115, 151
Khorezm 115–16, 178
Khrushchev 158, 161, 286, 290, 308, 314,
  318–20, 324, 329
Khurgin (Hoorgin) 176
Kiakhta 133, 140
Kiangsi province 260
Kiev 16, 28, 34, 37, 45–6, 50, 53, 68, 77, 81,
  88, 97, 102–3, 107, 115–17, 221, 227, 276,
  287, 307, 312, 318, 326, 359
Kirghiz congress, republic 36, 123, 144, 304,
  312, 324
Kirilenko 324
Kirin 259

Kirov 2, 111, 192, 196, 214, 248, 272, 281–2,
  286–9, 291, 296, 299, 300, 319, 322, 344
Kirshon 310, 325
Knox, General 71, 86, 91, 94
Kokand 36, 47
Kokoshkin 37
Kolchak, Admiral 70, 78–9, 82, 86–8, 91, 94,
  96–104, 106, 108–11
Kollontai 126, 128, 130, 149, 345
Kon 120
Koo, Dr Wellington 175
Korea 143, 148
Kork, Army Commander 311–2
Kornilov, General 10, 14, 18–22, 34, 36, 38,
  49, 56
Kosior 214–15, 245, 248, 282, 300, 308, 320,
  323
Kotlas 99, 101, 359
Kotlin Island 132, 138
Kowerda 208
Krasin 112, 116–17, 120, 123, 127, 147, 199,
  200
Krasnaia Gorka 100
Krasnoiarsk 8, 22, 109, 359
Krasnoshchekov 110, 115, 139
Krasnov, General 31, 58–60, 64, 68, 87, 89
Krasnovodsk 70, 73, 95, 112
Kremlin 29, 31, 73, 288, 319
Krestinskii 92, 94, 322
Kronstadt 11, 14, 17, 28, 37, 100, 102, 132–5,
  137–8, 140–1
Kronwerk arsenal 26
Krupps 154
Krupskaia 158, 161, 174, 187, 196–7, 200, 225
Krutitskii see Peter, Metropolitan of
Krylenko 25, 30, 33–5
Krymov, General 19, 21–2
Krzhizhanovskii 112, 132, 193, 225, 251
Kuban region 8, 28, 46, 49, 60, 63, 113, 121,
  271
Kubiak 216
Kuibyshev 150, 183, 196, 198, 214, 222–4,
  248, 255–6, 262, 280, 282, 286, 288–9, 322
Kuibyshev region (see also Samara) 312
Kuitun 111
Kulik 348
Kun, Bela 94, 96, 102, 123, 343
Kurdistan 39
Kursk 104, 106
Kutaisi 138
Kutepov, General 108, 112, 242–3, 317
Kuusinen 292, 343, 345, 347
Kuznetsk 248, 253, 281
Kuznetsov, N. 165, 167
Kuznetsov, N.G 319


Lama Bodo 142
Lamarck 321
Lanchow 295
Lapin 311

Largo Caballero 305
Larin 185
Lashevich 188, 195–6, 213
Latin America 180, 220
Latsis 66
Latvia 33, 41, 79–82, 88, 92, 98–100, 121, 130, 147, 208, 227, 263, 274, 277, 282, 285, 304, 334, 341, 349, 350, 359
Lausanne 158, 163, 166, 171
Laval 287, 291
Leghorn (Livorno) 328
Lena River, goldfields 185, 239, 240, 249, 286
Lenin 7, 12–19, 21–6, 28–34, 36–7, 42–5, 48, 50–3, 58, 64, 66–8, 72, 74–5, 80, 86, 88, 90–4, 97–9, 107–8, 110, 113–14, 117, 119, 126–9, 131, 133–7, 139, 145, 149–52, 156–63, 170–1, 173–5, 180, 183, 188, 197, 211, 220, 225–6, 228–9, 253, 260, 267, 322
Leningrad (see also Petersburg, Petrograd) 153, 170, 185–7, 189, 190, 192, 200, 206, 211–12, 222, 225, 227, 264, 282, 286–8, 312, 314, 318, 320, 341, 346, 349, 358
Levanevskii 313–14
Libau (Libava, Liepaja) 88, 105
Liebknecht 86
Lindley 67
Lipetsk 153, 221, 265
*Litbel* 89
Lithuania 37, 47, 80–2, 86, 89, 92, 96, 99, 118, 130, 147, 197, 207, 227, 255, 274, 282, 285, 304, 338, 341–2, 346, 348–50, 353, 355, 359
Litvinov 45, 49, 74, 107, 112, 143, 163, 203, 212, 239, 249, 250, 260, 263, 271–2, 274, 276–7, 279, 283–4, 287, 290, 294, 297–9, 301, 318, 322, 325, 331–2
Liubchenko 317
Liushkov 323
Livonia 51, 72
Locarno 188, 190, 194, 283
Lockhart 45, 52–3, 61, 70–4, 80
Lominadze 251, 281, 300
Lomov 30, 48, 256
London 33, 49, 71, 74, 117, 120, 124, 137, 147, 171, 173, 176–8, 200, 203, 206–7, 228, 238, 240, 242, 246, 272, 274, 296, 301, 308, 312, 316, 332, 334, 348
Lori 131
Los Angeles 313
Lozovskii 117, 217
Lublin 341
Lucerne 141
Ludendorf 64
Luga 105
Lunacharskii 28, 30, 140, 200, 217, 219, 234, 237, 275, 289
Luxemburg 292, 335, 348
Luxemburg, Rosa 86–7
L'vov, Prince Georgii Evgen'evich 10, 12, 18
L'vov, Vladimir Nikolaevich 20–1

L'vov (city) 122
Lympne 120
Lysenko 320–1

Ma Chung-yin, General 260, 277
Madrid 300, 302
Magnitogorsk 244, 253
Maisky 301–2, 331–2, 348
Makharadze 161
Makhno 90, 98–102, 104–5, 109, 118, 125, 127, 144
Malenkov 314, 331, 342, 356
Malinovskii, A. A. see Bogdanov, A. A.
Malleson, General 70–1, 73, 88, 95
Mamontov, General 102
Manchouli 238, 272
'Manchukuo' 259, 263, 267, 272, 276, 290, 315, 333, 357
Manchuria 69, 115, 125, 155, 178, 235–6, 238–40, 259, 263, 267, 282, 316
Mandel'shtam 323
Mannerheim, General 43, 52, 55, 57
Manuil'skii 292, 315, 331
Mao Tse-tung 209, 216, 260, 309
Marchand 80
Marchlevskii 120
Maring (Sneevliet) 154
Maritime Province 73, 114–15, 117, 155, 272
Mariupol' (Zhdanov) 104, 111
Marmara, Sea of 87
Martens, Ludwig 94, 145
Martov 27
Marty 292
Marx 130
Masaryk, Thomas 54
Matsuoka 356–7
Matveev 74
Mayakovsky 246
Maynard, General 59, 63–4, 89, 90, 97, 104
Mdivani 111, 161
Mediterranean Sea 158
Mekhlis 322
Melgunov, Professor 122
Mendras, Col. 272, 275
Menzhinskii 30, 196, 322
Mercader (Jacson, Mornard) 350
Merv 70, 76, 87, 98
Mexico 167, 171, 180, 243, 307, 350
Meyerhold 264, 334
Miasnikov 150, 163, 165, 167
Michael, Grand Duke 10, 140
Michurin 321
Middle East 184, 341
Mikaszewicze 105
Mikoyan 196, 214–15, 234, 236, 248, 282, 289, 314, 319, 329
Milan 250
Miliukov 10, 12, 14, 15, 64
Miliutin 30, 32

Miller, General Evgenii K. 87, 96, 101–3, 112, 317
Millerand 120
Minsk 48, 81, 102, 118, 122, 296
Mirbach, Count von 2, 56, 61, 63, 66
Mogilev 8–11, 18–22, 34–5, 37, 116, 161
Moldavian republic 304, 326, 350
Mologales 191
Molotov 8, 9, 135, 139, 150, 163, 174–5, 192, 213–14, 224, 229, 234, 238, 248, 252, 254, 259, 262, 265, 273, 277, 280–2, 288–90, 295–6, 303, 305, 309, 314–15, 319, 329, 330, 332–7, 339–41, 348, 351–3, 355–8, 360
Mongolia (and Outer Mongolia) 3, 107, 125–6, 131, 133, 137, 140–3, 145, 148, 155, 175, 179, 183, 209, 286, 297, 317, 333, 357
Montevideo 294
Montreux 298, 352
Moravia 331
Mornard (Jacson, Mercader) 350
Morocco 299
Moscow (selected references) 9, 13, 20, 23, 25, 28–33, 39, 53–4, 56–7, 61, 69, 71, 74, 79, 80, 101, 104, 130, 139, 155, 169, 189, 192, 206, 210–12, 215, 222–3, 225, 227, 246, 268, 287–8, 290–1, 312–14, 316–17, 332, 356
Mosul 189
Mountain Republic of North Caucasus 58, 100
Mozyr 113
Mudros 76
Mukden 259
Muklevich 195, 245, 313
Munich 95, 325
Münzenberg 106, 144, 203, 227, 266, 274, 315
Muralov 168, 172, 212, 297, 303, 307–8
Muranov 11, 124
Murav'ev 37, 46, 67
Murman Coast 58, 347
Murmansk 49, 50, 52, 57, 59, 61–8, 72, 89, 91, 97, 103–5, 112, 285, 341, 346–7
Murom 66
Murphy, J. T. 117
Mussolini 171, 255

Nanchang 203
Nanking 208, 214, 260, 272, 305
Nansen, Dr Fridtjof 95, 144, 153
Narev River 338
Narva 49, 50, 81
Nazarov, General 50
Nehru 203
Nejd 193, 205
Neman River see Niemen
Neva River 27
New York 94, 168, 176
New Zealand 240
Newfoundland 240
Nicholas II, Tsar 8–11, 19, 67–8

Niemen (Nemen) River 124
Nikolaev, Leonid 286–7
Nikolaev (city) 46, 91
Nikolaeva 203
Nikolaevsk 112–13, 117, 156, 183
Nikolai Nikolaevich, Grand Duke 11
Nikol'sk-Ussuriisk 110, 114
Nikopol' 104
Nizhneudinsk 108
Nizhny Novgorod (see also Gorky) 191, 282
Nogin 30, 32, 112, 168
Nomonhan district 333, 348
North America 207, 312
North Pole 312, 314
North Tauride Province 117, 125
Norway 90, 141, 144, 147, 171, 189, 345, 347, 351, 358
Noulens 61
Novgorod province 102
Novocherkassk 34, 38, 50, 56–7, 59, 60, 63
Novonikolaevsk (see also Novosibirsk) 60, 142
Novorossiisk 53, 63, 71, 79, 113, 121, 318
Novosibirsk (see also Novonikolaevsk) 303

Odessa 46, 53, 81, 88, 90–1, 94–5, 103, 111, 225, 227, 302, 318, 328
O'Grady 107, 112
Omsk 55, 57–8, 60–2, 65, 73–4, 77–8, 106, 108
Onega, Lake 97, 104
Onega town 101
Operput (Selianinov) 142
Oranienbaum (Lomonosov) 134
Ordzhonikidze 75–6, 111, 113, 116, 159, 161, 196, 198, 237, 245, 248, 252, 262, 281–2, 300, 307–9
Orel 105
Orenburg (Chkalov 1938–57) 8, 28, 36, 88, 144, 312
Orlando 98
Orlov, 'Flagman' V. M. 245, 305, 313, 325
Osinskii 93, 128, 168, 206
Osipov 87
Ottawa 266
Ottoman Empire 33
Ovey 271–2

Pacific Ocean, coast 73, 157
Pahlevi [Bandar] (see also Enzeli) 211
Palestine 33
Papanin 312, 323
Paris 49, 78, 87, 94–5, 100, 110, 130, 141, 144–5, 155, 168, 189, 200, 211, 222, 243, 267, 274, 276, 279, 317
Pashukanis 307
Pasternak, Boris 285, 296, 312
Pavlov 225
Pavlovsk 106
Pechenga see Petsamo

Peking 126, 155, 166, 172, 175, 178, 182–3, 197, 203–5, 207, 214
Penza 54, 60, 122
Peregonovka 104
Perekop Isthmus 126
Perm' 68, 92, 101
Persia (see also Iran) 33, 36, 42, 51, 69, 70, 73, 100, 116, 132, 147, 186, 210–11, 227, 260, 274
Persian Gulf 352–3
Peshkov 322
Pestkovskii 180
Peter, King 356
Peter and Paul fortress 18, 26
Peter, Metropolitan of Krutitskii 189, 191
Petersburg (see also Petrograd) 8
Petliura 77, 81, 86, 89, 102–3, 107, 115
Petrograd (see also Petersburg, Leningrad) 7–31, 33–5, 39, 42–3, 45, 48–50, 52–4, 59, 62–4, 69–72, 75, 91, 97, 99–106, 130–4, 143–4, 149, 155, 170
Petropavlovsk 106
Petrovskii 72, 192, 214, 248, 282, 329
Petsamo (Pechenga) 50, 59, 61, 63, 341–3, 347, 352
Philippines 176
Piatakov 158, 168, 185, 197, 213, 216, 228, 281, 300, 303, 307–9, 313
Piatigorsk 312
Pieck 292
Pil'niak 131, 189, 239, 312
Pilsudski, General 96, 115, 124–5, 195
Pius XI, Pope 244
Platten 42
Plekhanov 217, 253
Pleyel, Salle 274, 292
Pogranichnyi 272
Pokrovskii 131, 283
Poland 12, 77, 88–9, 99, 111, 113, 115–25, 130, 138, 142, 147, 153, 155, 166, 178, 195, 197, 207–8, 227, 233, 262, 265, 267, 274, 279, 283-4, 310, 318, 322–3, 325–6, 328, 331–2, 334-41, 344, 346, 359
Polkovnikov, Colonel 26, 31
Poltava 97, 102
Ponomarev 310
Poole, General 59, 69, 70, 75
Poole, DeWitt C. 58
Portugal 285, 301
Poskrebyshev 150, 282
Pospelov 310
Postyshev 215, 270, 274, 277, 282, 300, 307, 310, 320
Potemkin 251
Poti 61, 186
Prague 141, 152, 178, 290, 299, 331
Preobrazhenskii 124, 168, 177, 181, 210, 235, 281, 289
Prestes 294
Primakov, Corps Commander 312–3

Prinkipo 87, 91
Pripet marshes 117
Proust 285
Pskov 9, 31, 35, 49, 75, 102–3
Pulkovo Heights 31, 106
Putilov works 131
Putna, Corps Commander 312–13

Radek 90, 111, 123–4, 175–6, 187, 213, 215, 235, 263, 281, 285, 289, 300, 307–8
Rakovskii 97, 200, 211–15, 235–6, 300, 322
Ramzin, Professor 250–1
Rapallo 151, 188, 194, 263
Rashid Ali al-Gailani 358
Red Square 98, 308
Reichstag 184, 270–1, 276
Reilly, Sidney 70, 80
Reinstein 145
Resht 116
Reval (Tallinn) 49, 72, 81, 102, 180
Rheinmetall 244
Rhineland 297
Ribbentrop 336–41, 351, 356–7
Riga 19, 20, 72, 81, 86, 98, 100, 105, 121–2, 124–5, 138, 143, 263
Rio de Janeiro 243
Riutin 266, 287, 301
Robins 45, 51, 54, 58
Rokossovskii 141
Rolland, Romain 144
Romania 38, 42, 45, 55, 97, 125, 143–4, 166, 227, 233, 262, 267, 274, 284, 296, 323, 331–2, 334–8, 340–1, 349, 352–6
Rome 171, 202, 255, 273, 276
Roosevelt, President 276
Root, Senator 15
Rosenberg 300
Rosengolts 329
Rostov 34, 36–7, 49, 57, 72, 109, 112
Rovno (Rowne) 118, 357
Rozanov, General 106
Rozovskii 112
Rudzutak 123, 163, 175, 192, 196, 214, 248, 263, 272, 281–2, 308, 311, 325
Rumiantsev 314
Rybachii Peninsula 346
Rybinsk 66
Rykov 30, 32, 150, 163, 171, 175–6, 192, 196, 214, 217, 220, 223, 225–30, 238–9, 248, 252, 281, 300–1, 309, 310, 322

Sadoul 45
Saionji 98
Sakhalin 115, 117, 155, 157, 160, 183, 352–3, 357
Sakharov 343
Salonika 79
Samara (Kuibyshev) 55, 60, 62–3, 65, 70, 73–4, 154, 208
San River 339
San Jacinto 313

Sana'a 223
Sapronov 93, 213
Saracoglu 342
Saratov 122, 154, 236, 312
Savinkov 20–1, 61, 66, 142, 178
Saxony 167
Scandinavia 167, 345, 347, 351
Scarborough 188
Schacht 308
Schmidt see Shmidt
Selianinov see Operput
Semenov 49, 72, 78, 108, 125
Semipalatinsk 36, 200
Semirech'e 8, 200
Sennufu Island 315
Seraia Loshad' 100
Serapion brothers 130
Serbs, Croats and Slovenes, Kingdom of 166
Serebriakov 307–8
Sergei of Nizhny Novgorod, Metropolitan
   191, 195, 209, 210, 212
Sestroretsk 25
Sevastopol' 57, 79, 81–2, 96
Sèvres 121, 138
Shakhty 216
Shanghai 204–5, 214
Shanin 177
Shantung 204
Shaposhnikov 172, 311, 348
Shatskin 251
Shcherbakov 356
Sheng Shih-t'sai, General 272, 277, 295, 311,
   317, 353
Shenkursk 87
Shensi 261
Shestakov 283
Shevchenko 230
Shingarev 37
Shliapnikov 9, 30, 32, 126, 128, 130, 149, 289,
   300
Shmidt, Professor 282, 312
Sholokhov 217–18
Shostakovich 264, 296
Shvernik 215, 229, 308, 329
Shvirski 153
Sian 305
Siberia 7, 8, 19, 38, 41, 49, 53, 58–9, 64–5,
   69, 71, 73–4, 77–9, 86, 91, 99, 106, 108,
   110, 130, 133, 185, 191, 200, 215, 227, 236,
   239, 263, 277, 281, 284–5, 301, 308, 359
Sikorski, General 121
Simbirsk (Ul'ianovsk) 67, 73
Singapore 357
Sinkiang 214, 260, 272, 277, 289, 295, 311,
   317, 321, 353
Sisson 51
Sivash shallows 126
Skobelev, General 112
Skoropadskii 57, 77, 81, 89
Skrypnik 274

Skvortsov 30
Slovakia 340, 353
Smil'ga 111, 197, 212–13, 235, 300
Smirnov, A. P. 216, 270
Smirnov, Ivan N. 299
Smirnov, P. A. 319
Smolensk 2, 244, 257, 273, 299, 309, 311–12,
   314
Sneevliet (see Maring)
Sochi 301
Sofia 141, 184
Sokol'nikov 25, 175, 187, 197, 240, 307–8
Solomon 235
Sorokin 74, 76, 79
South Africa 240
South America 207
Souvarine 172, 178, 213
Soviet House, London, 206–7
Spain 167, 275, 299–302, 305, 328
Stakhanov 293
Stalin 3, 9, 11, 12, 24, 30, 32, 36, 44, 61–2,
   64, 68, 75–6, 80, 92, 94–5, 97, 101, 119,
   122, 126, 133, 135, 139, 147, 150, 158–63,
   169, 170, 172–6, 179–82, 184, 186–90,
   192–3, 196–9, 206, 209, 211–17, 219–24,
   226, 228–9, 233, 238–40, 243–5, 247–8,
   251, 254, 257, 260–1, 264, 266, 269, 270,
   272–4, 279–84, 286–7, 289–92, 296–7,
   299–301, 303, 305, 308–10, 313, 315,
   317–18, 321–2, 324, 329, 331, 333, 336,
   338, 343–4, 347, 351, 356–9
Stalinabad (see also Dushanbe) 312
Stalingrad (Volgograd) (see also Tsaritsyn)
   64, 205, 251, 254
Starobel'sk 359
Stavropol' 77, 79
Stevens, John F. 15, 90–1, 156
Stockholm 112, 345
Strang 334, 336–7
Strumilin 193
Sudetenland 331
Sukhanov 249, 254
Sukhe-Bator 133, 137, 142
Sumatra 198
Sun Yat-sen, Dr 154, 160, 166–7, 175, 184,
   187, 308
Suomussalmi 345
Sverdlov 19, 55–6, 94, 173, 180, 185
Sverdlovsk (see also Ekaterinburg) 68, 94,
   211
Svinhufvud 57
Sweden 13, 36, 50, 61, 90, 141, 147, 171,
   345–7, 359
Switzerland 13, 163, 205, 285, 334
Sykes-Picot agreement 33
Syrtsov 248, 251
Sytin 76
Szechwan 295, 317

Tadzhikistan, Tadzhik republic 154, 239, 258,
   304, 324

Taganrog 57, 105, 111
Tagantsev, Professor 144
Taiga 108
Taman Peninsula 121
Tambov 63, 102, 122, 139
Tampere 55
Tannu Tuva (Urianghai) (see also Tuvinian People's Republic) 145
Tasca (Serra) 224
Tashkent 36, 47, 53, 57, 67, 70, 76, 87, 104, 125, 321
Tbilisi (see also Tiflis) 318
Tehran 260
Teodorovich 30, 32
Terek Cossacks 8, 28, 50
Terek republic 50
Tereshchenko 15, 18
Terijoki 343
Ternopol' 18
Thailand 356
Thälmann 195
Thomas, Albert 45
Thomson, General 77
Thuringia 167
Tibet 125
Tientsin 316
Tiflis (see also Tbilisi) 33, 49, 59, 79, 82, 116, 121, 131–2, 291, 318
Tikhon, Patriarch 45, 149, 150, 164, 184, 189, 212
Tikhoretskaia (Tikhoretsk) 67
Timoshenko 324, 345, 348, 354, 358
Timoshevskaia 121
Tiso, Mgr 340
Tito 315
Tobol River 104
Tobol'sk 19, 67, 215
Togliatti 292
Tokyo 71, 274, 290
Tolstoy 217
'Tomka' 154, 221
Tomsk 108, 110, 215, 359
Tomskii 55, 87, 117, 126, 150, 163, 173, 175, 178, 188, 192, 214, 217, 220, 223–9, 238–9, 248, 281, 300, 310
Torgovaia 63
Tovstukha 150, 260
Transbaikalia 8, 73, 115, 119, 122, 140, 277
Transcaspia 67, 70, 76, 87–8, 95, 98–9, 112
Transcaucasia 22, 33, 56, 60, 82, 138, 149, 159, 258
Triapitsyn 112, 117
Troianovskii 277
Trotsky 4, 15, 17, 19, 22–7, 30, 32, 35, 41, 43–6, 48, 50–4, 58–60, 62–3, 66, 68, 70, 72–6, 80, 88, 90, 93–4, 97–9, 101, 105, 108–10, 113–14, 119, 120, 122, 126, 128–9, 131, 134, 139, 150, 158, 161–3, 167–70, 172–6, 179–83, 185, 187, 192, 194–7, 199, 204, 206, 209–16, 224–5, 229, 230, 235, 263,

266, 286, 289, 297, 299, 300, 307, 313, 329, 350
Tsar see Nicholas II
Tsaritsyn (see also Stalingrad) 60–1, 64, 68, 75–6, 100, 109, 144
Tsarskoe Selo (Pushkin) 9, 11, 31, 106
Tsiurupa 71, 173
Tukhachevskii 63, 116, 118, 121, 124, 138–9, 172, 266, 273, 275–6, 289, 293, 296, 311–13, 329
Tula 153
Tupolev 313
Turkestan 36, 57, 70, 87, 139, 145, 151, 178–9, 200
Turkey 35, 62, 76, 117, 121, 132–3, 138, 145, 147, 154, 158, 166, 186, 189–90, 194, 204, 227, 240, 254–5, 260, 274, 293, 298, 318, 331, 334, 342, 352, 356, 358
Turkmen SSR 179, 304, 324
Tuvinian People's Republic 234

Uborevich, General 139, 312, 314
Ufa 73–4, 82, 91, 100, 144
Uglanov 189, 192, 214, 220, 222, 230, 248, 300
Ukraine 16, 37, 39, 41, 44, 46, 50–1, 57, 61, 68, 80–1, 87–92, 97, 99, 100, 102–3, 105, 115–16, 121, 127, 129, 138, 144, 146–7, 152, 230–1, 245, 258, 264–5, 270–1, 274–5, 277, 280, 304, 310, 312, 314, 317, 320, 324, 335, 340, 342, 347
Ulan Bator (see also Urga) 297
Ungern-Sternberg 125–6, 131, 140, 142
United States of America 11, 15, 46, 63, 80, 94–5, 98, 127, 141, 145, 153, 155, 157, 166–7, 191, 235, 249, 258, 276–7, 289, 292
Unshlikht 120
Urals 36, 58, 64, 77, 91, 97, 101, 109, 145, 215, 219, 227, 248, 253, 258, 281, 354, 359
Urga (see also Ulan Bator) 125–6, 131, 140, 142, 179
Urianghai (see Tannu Tuva)
Uritskii 48, 72, 152, 180
Uruguay 141, 197, 294
Urumchi (Tihwa) 260, 277, 317
Ussuri 8 •
Uzbekistan, Uzbek republic 179, 204, 304, 311–12, 324

Valencia 302
Van der Lubbe 270, 276
Vancouver, Washington 313
Vandervelde 152
Varga 177
Vatican 161
Vatsetis 62–3, 67, 72, 97, 101, 325
Vavilov 321
Veinberg 269
Veniamin, Metropolitan 155
Verkhneudinsk (Ulan Ude) 71, 110, 115
Versailles 101, 103, 119, 153, 221, 279

Vienna 146, 172
Viipuri (see also Vyborg) 346
Vilna (Vilnius, Wilno) 86, 89, 96, 118, 125, 130, 197, 338, 341–2
Viren, Admiral 11
Vistula River 338
Vladikavkaz (Ordzhonikidze) 50
Vladivostok 15, 38, 41, 50, 53–60, 64, 67, 69, 71–2, 78, 91, 100, 102, 106, 110, 112, 114–15, 127, 139, 156, 282, 285, 318, 323–4, 350
Voikov 207–8, 246
Volga River, area 63–4, 67, 70, 73, 76, 91, 96, 141, 143, 200, 242, 258, 271, 316, 354
Volodarskii 63, 152
Vologda 46, 50, 61, 63, 67–8
Von der Goltz, General 55–6, 88, 98, 100, 105
Voronezh 104, 106, 154, 221, 312
Voroshilov 64, 75, 109, 172, 188, 192, 203, 206, 214, 221, 248, 272, 275, 282, 284, 293, 300, 305, 312, 319, 321–2, 329, 336–9, 348
Vorovskii 163, 205
Voznesenskii, N. A. 323, 356
Vvedenskii, Metropolitan 189
Vyborg (see also Viipuri) 43, 57
Vyshinskii 274, 300, 305, 307, 322, 349

Warsaw 89, 103, 107, 115, 120–2, 142, 177, 188, 207–8, 246, 340–1
Washington D. C. 57–8, 153–4, 277, 350
Wavell, General 300
Weizsäcker 333
Welles, Sumner 350
Western Region 312, 314
Weygand, General 115
Whampoa 175

Whitaker, J. T. 318
White Sea, area 138, 239, 246, 267, 275
Wilhelm II, Kaiser 35, 64, 77
Wilno (see Vilna)
Wilson, President 41, 64, 67, 87, 92, 98
Windau (Vindava, Ventspils) 72
Winter Palace 28
Wrangel, General 107–8, 114, 117–18, 121, 125–7, 242–3
Wuhan (Hankow, Hanyang and Wuchang) 203–4, 206–9

(*For Russian names sometimes spelt with an initial 'Y' see under 'E' or 'I'*)
Yaitskii 8
Yamburg (Kingisepp) 105–6
Yangtze river 204
Yaroslavl 66, 312
Yemen 223
Yenan 309
Yugoslavia 274, 348–9, 356–8

Zalutskii 9, 189, 213
Zamosc 123
Zenzinov 78
Zhdanov 215, 281–2, 285, 287, 289, 296, 298, 300–1, 309, 315, 319, 321, 326, 329–31, 335, 343, 349, 351, 356
Zhemchuzhina 356
Zhitomir 46, 117
Zhukov 333, 338, 340, 348, 358
Zinoviev 2, 24–6, 30–2, 90, 94, 103, 119, 120, 123, 126, 139, 141, 150, 158, 161–3, 169, 172, 174–6, 179–81, 184–5, 187–199, 206, 209–16, 219, 220, 266, 273–4, 281, 286–9, 297, 299, 300, 313–14, 329
Zlatoust 153